STUDIES

IN THE

PSYCHOLOGY OF SEX

BY

HAVELOCK ELLIS

STUDIES IN THE PSYCHOLOGY OF SEX.

(Complete in Six Volumes.)

I. The Evolution of Modesty, the Phenomena of Sexual Periodicity and Auto-erotism. $2.50, net.

II. Sexual Inversion. $2.00, net.

III. Analysis of the Sexual Impulse. $2.50, net.

IV. Sexual Selection in Man. $2.00, net.

V. Erotic Symbolism. The Mechanism of Detumescence. The Psychic State in Pregnancy. $2.00, net.

VI. Sex in Relation to Society. $3.00, net.

Each volume is sold separately, and is complete in itself.

This is the only edition in English published by the author's permission.

STUDIES

IN THE

PSYCHOLOGY OF SEX

VOLUME I

THE EVOLUTION OF MODESTY
THE PHENOMENA OF SEXUAL PERIODICITY
AUTO-EROTISM

BY

HAVELOCK ELLIS

THIRD EDITION, REVISED AND ENLARGED

PHILADELPHIA

F. A. DAVIS COMPANY, PUBLISHERS

1913

Philadelphia, Pa., U. S. A.
Press of F. A. Davis Company
1914-16 Cherry Street

GENERAL PREFACE.

The origin of these *Studies* dates from many years back. As a youth I was faced, as others are, by the problem of sex. Living partly in an Australian city where the ways of life were plainly seen, partly in the solitude of the bush, I was free both to contemplate and to meditate many things. A resolve slowly grew up within me: one main part of my life-work should be to make clear the problems of sex.

That was more than twenty years ago. Since then I can honestly say that in all that I have done that resolve has never been very far from my thoughts. I have always been slowly working up to this central problem; and in a book published some three years ago—*Man and Woman: a Study of Human Secondary Sexual Characters*—I put forward what was, in my own eyes, an introduction to the study of the primary questions of sexual psychology.

Now that I have at length reached the time for beginning to publish my results, these results scarcely seem to me large. As a youth, I had hoped to settle problems for those who came after; now I am quietly content if I do little more than state them. For even that, I now think, is much; it is at least the half of knowledge. In this particular field the evil of ignorance is magnified by our efforts to suppress that which never can be suppressed, though in the effort of suppression it may become perverted. I have at least tried to find out what are the facts, among normal people as well as among abnormal people; for, while it seems to me that the physician's training is necessary in order to ascertain the facts, the physician for the most part only obtains the abnormal facts, which alone bring little light. I have tried to get at the facts, and, having got at the facts, to look them simply and squarely in the face. If I cannot perhaps turn the lock myself, I bring the key which can alone in the end rightly open the door: the key of sincerity. That is my one panacea: sincerity.

I know that many of my friends, people on whose side I, too, am to be found, retort with another word: reticence. It is a mistake, they say, to try to uncover these things; leave the sexual instincts alone, to grow up and develop in the shy solitude they love, and they will be sure to grow up and develop wholesomely. But, as a matter of fact, that is precisely what we can not and will not ever allow them to do. There are very few middle-aged men and women who can clearly recall the facts of their lives and tell you in all honesty that their sexual instincts have developed easily and wholesomely throughout. And it should not be difficult to see why this is so. Let my friends try to transfer their feelings and theories from the reproductive region to, let us say, the nutritive region, the only other which can be compared to it for importance. Suppose that eating and drinking was never spoken of openly, save in veiled or poetic language, and that no one ever ate food publicly, because it was considered immoral and immodest to reveal the mysteries of this natural function. We know what would occur. A considerable proportion of the community, more especially the more youthful members, possessed by an instinctive and legitimate curiosity, would concentrate their thoughts on the subject. They would have so many problems to puzzle over: How often ought I to eat? What ought I to eat? Is it wrong to eat fruit, which I like? Ought I to eat grass, which I don't like? Instinct notwithstanding, we may be quite sure that only a small minority would succeed in eating reasonably and wholesomely. The sexual secrecy of life is even more disastrous than such a nutritive secrecy would be; partly because we expend such a wealth of moral energy in directing or misdirecting it, partly because the sexual impulse normally develops at the same time as the intellectual impulse, not in the early years of life, when wholesome instinctive habits might be formed. And there is always some ignorant and foolish friend who is prepared still further to muddle things: Eat a meal every other day! Eat twelve meals a day! Never eat fruit! Always eat grass! The advice emphatically given in sexual matters is usually not less absurd than this. When, however, the matter is fully open, the problems of food are not indeed wholly solved, but everyone is enabled by the experience of his fellows to reach some sort of situation suited to his own case. And when the rigid secrecy is once swept away a sane and natural reticence becomes for the first time possible.

This secrecy has not always been maintained. When the Catholic Church was at the summit of its power and influence it fully realized the magnitude of sexual problems and took an active and inquiring interest in all the details of normal and abnormal sexuality. Even to the present time there are certain phenomena of the sexual life which have scarcely been accurately described except in ancient theological treatises. As the type of such treatises I will mention the great tome of Sanchez, *De Matrimonio*. Here you will find the whole sexual life of men and women analyzed in its relationships to sin. Everything is set forth, as clearly and as concisely as it can be—without morbid prudery on the one hand, or morbid sentimentality on the other—in the coldest scientific language; the right course of action is pointed out for all the cases that may occur, and we are told what is lawful, what a venial sin, what a mortal sin. Now I do not consider that sexual matters concern the theologian alone, and I deny altogether that he is competent to deal with them. In his hands, also, undoubtedly, they sometimes become prurient, as they can scarcely fail to become on the non-natural and unwholesome basis of asceticism, and as they with difficulty become in the open-air light of science. But we are bound to recognize the thoroughness with which the Catholic theologians dealt with these matters, and, from their own point of view, indeed, the entire reasonableness; we are bound to recognize the admirable spirit in which, successfully or not, they sought to approach them. We need to-day the same spirit and temper applied from a different standpoint. These things concern everyone; the study of these things concerns the physiologist, the psychologist, the moralist. We want to get into possession of the actual facts, and from the investigation of the facts we want to ascertain what is normal and what is abnormal, from the point of view of physiology and of psychology. We want to know what is naturally lawful under the various sexual chances that may befall man, not as the born child of sin, but as a naturally social animal. What is a venial sin against nature, what a mortal sin against nature? The answers are less easy to reach than the theologians' answers generally were, but we can at least put ourselves in the right attitude; we may succeed in asking that question which is sometimes even more than the half of knowledge.

It is perhaps a mistake to show so plainly at the outset that I approach what may seem only a psychological question not without moral fervour. But I do not wish any mistake to be made. I regard sex as the central problem of life. And now that the problem of religion has practically been settled, and that the problem of labor has at least been placed on a practical foundation, the question of sex—with the racial questions that rest on it—stands before the coming generations as the chief problem for solution. Sex lies at the root of life, and we can never learn to reverence life until we know how to understand sex.—So, at least, it seems to me.

Having said so much, I will try to present such results as I have to record in that cold and dry light through which alone the goal of knowledge may truly be seen.

HAVELOCK ELLIS.

July, 1897.

PREFACE TO THE THIRD EDITION.

———

THE first edition of this volume was published in 1899, following "Sexual Inversion," which now forms Volume II. The second edition, issued by the present publishers and substantially identical with the first edition, appeared in the following year. Ten years have elapsed since then and this new edition will be found to reflect the course of that long interval. Not only is the volume greatly enlarged, but nearly every page has been partly rewritten. This is mainly due to three causes: Much new literature required to be taken into account; my own knowledge of the historical and ethnographic aspects of the sexual impulse has increased; many fresh illustrative cases of a valuable and instructive character have accumulated in my hands. It is to these three sources of improvement that the book owes its greatly revised and enlarged condition, and not to the need for modifying any of its essential conclusions. These, far from undergoing any change, have by the new material been greatly strengthened.

It may be added that the General Preface to the whole work, which was originally published in 1898 at the beginning of "Sexual Inversion," now finds its proper place at the outset of the present volume.

HAVELOCK ELLIS.

Carbis Bay,
Cornwall, Eng.

PREFACE TO THE FIRST EDITION.

THE present volume contains three studies which seem to me to be necessary *prolegomena* to that analysis of the sexual instinct which must form the chief part of an investigation into the psychology of sex. The first sketches the main outlines of a complex emotional state which is of fundamental importance in sexual psychology; the second, by bringing together evidence from widely different regions, suggests a tentative explanation of facts that are still imperfectly known; the third attempts to show that even in fields where we assume our knowledge to be adequate a broader view of the phenomena teaches us to suspend judgment and to adopt a more cautious attitude. So far as they go, these studies are complete in themselves; their special use, as an introduction to a more comprehensive analysis of sexual phenomena, is that they bring before us, under varying aspects, a characteristic which, though often ignored, is of the first importance in obtaining a clear understanding of the facts: the tendency of the sexual impulse to appear in a spontaneous and to some extent periodic manner, affecting women differently from men. This is a tendency which, later, I hope to make still more apparent, for it has practical and social, as well as psychological, implications. Here—and more especially in the study of those spontaneous solitary manifestations which I call autoerotic—I have attempted to clear the ground, and to indicate the main lines along which the progress of our knowledge in these fields may best be attained.

It may surprise many medical readers that in the third and longest study I have said little, save incidentally, either of treatment or prevention. The omission of such considerations at this stage is intentional. It may safely be said that in no other field of human activity is so vast an amount of strenuous didactic morality founded on so slender a basis of facts. In most other departments of life we at least make a pretence of learning before we presume to teach; in the field of sex we content ourselves with the smallest and vaguest minimum of information, often ostentatiously second-hand, usually unreliable. I wish to emphasize the fact that before we can safely talk either of curing or preventing these manifestations we must know a great deal more than we know at present regarding their distribution, etiology, and symptomatology; and we must exercise the same coolness and caution as—if our work is to be fruitful—we require in any other field of serious study. We must approach these facts as physicians, it is true, but also as psychologists, primarily concerned to find out the workings of such manifestations in fairly healthy and normal people. If we found a divorce-court judge writing a treatise on marriage we should smile. But it is equally absurd for the physician, so long as his knowledge is confined to disease, to write regarding sex at large; valuable as the facts he brings forward may be, he can never be in a position to generalize concerning them. And to me, at all events, it seems that we have had more than enough pictures of gross sexual perversity, whether furnished by the asylum or the brothel. They are only really instructive when they are seen in their proper perspective as the rare and ultimate extremes of a chain of phenomena which we may more profitably study nearer home.

Yet, although we are, on every hand, surrounded by the normal manifestations of sex, conscious or unconscious, these manifestations are extremely difficult to observe, and, in those cases in which we are best able to observe them, it frequently happens that we are unable to make any use of our knowledge. Moreover, even when we have obtained our data, the difficulties—at all events, for an English investigator—are by no means overcome. He may take for granted that any serious and precise study of the sexual instinct will not meet with general approval; his work will be misunderstood; his motives will be called in question; among those for whom he is chiefly working he will find indifference. Indeed, the pioneer in this field may well count himself happy if he meets with nothing worse than indifference. Hence it is that the present volume will not be published in England, but that, availing myself of the generous sympathy with which my work has been received in America, I have sought the wider medical and scientific audience of the United States. In matters of faith, "liberty of prophesying" was centuries since eloquently vindicated for Englishmen; the liberty of investigating facts is still called in question, under one pretence or another, and to seek out the most vital facts of life is still in England a perilous task.

I desire most heartily to thank the numerous friends and correspondents, some living in remote parts of the world, who have freely assisted me in my work with valuable information and personal histories. To Mr. F. H. Perry-Coste I owe an appendix which is by far the most elaborate attempt yet made to find evidence of periodicity in the spontaneous sexual manifestations of sleep; my debts to various medical and other correspondents are duly stated in the text. To many women friends and correspondents I may here express my gratitude for the manner in which they have furnished me with intimate personal records, and for the cross-examination to which they have allowed me to subject them. I may already say here, what I shall have occasion to say more emphatically in subsequent volumes, that without the assistance I have received from women of fine intelligence and high character my work would be impossible. I regret that I cannot make my thanks more specific.

HAVELOCK ELLIS.

CONTENTS.

II.

III.

AUTO-EROTISM: A STUDY OF THE SPONTANEOUS MANIFESTATIONS OF THE SEXUAL IMPULSE.

I.

II.

III.

APPENDIX A.

APPENDIX B.

APPENDIX C.

THE EVOLUTION OF MODESTY.

I.

The Definition of Modesty—The Significance of Modesty—Difficulties in the Way of Its Analysis—The Varying Phenomena of Modesty Among Different Peoples and in Different Ages.

MODESTY, which may be provisionally defined as an almost instinctive fear prompting to concealment and usually centering around the sexual processes, while common to both sexes is more peculiarly feminine, so that it may almost be regarded as the chief secondary sexual character of women on the psychical side. The woman who is lacking in this kind of fear is lacking, also, in sexual attractiveness to the normal and average man. The apparent exceptions seem to prove the rule, for it will generally be found that the women who are, not immodest (for immodesty is more closely related to modesty than mere negative absence of the sense of modesty), but without that fear which implies the presence of a complex emotional feminine organization to defend, only make a strong sexual appeal to men who are themselves lacking in the complementary masculine qualities. As a psychical secondary sexual character of the first rank, it is necessary, before any psychology of sex can be arranged in order, to obtain a clear view of modesty.

The immense importance of feminine modesty in creating masculine passion must be fairly obvious. I may, however, quote the observations of two writers who have shown evidence of insight and knowledge regarding this matter.

Casanova describes how, when at Berne, he went to the baths, and was, according to custom, attended by a young girl, whom he selected from a group of bath attendants. She undressed him, proceeded to undress herself, and then entered the bath with him, and rubbed him thoroughly all over, the operation being performed in the most serious manner and without a word being spoken. When all was over, however, he perceived that the girl had expected him to make advances, and he proceeds to describe and discuss his own feelings of indifference under such circumstances. "Though without gazing on the girl's figure, I had

1

seen enough to recognize that she had all that a man can desire to find
in a woman: a beautiful face, lively and well-formed eyes, a beautiful
mouth, with good teeth, a healthy complexion, well-developed breasts,
and everything in harmony. It is true that I had felt that her hands
could have been smoother, but I could only attribute this to hard work;
moreover, my Swiss girl was only eighteen, and yet I remained entirely
cold. What was the cause of this? That was the question that I asked
myself."

"It is clear," wrote Stendhal, "that three parts of modesty are
taught. This is, perhaps, the only law born of civilization which produces nothing but happiness. It has been observed that birds of prey
hide themselves to drink, because, being obliged to plunge their heads
in the water, they are at that moment defenceless. After having considered what passes at Otaheite, I can see no other natural foundation
for modesty. Love is the miracle of civilization. Among savage and
very barbarous races we find nothing but physical love of a gross character. It is modesty that gives to love the aid of imagination, and in
so doing imparts life to it. Modesty is very early taught to little girls
by their mothers, and with extreme jealousy, one might say, by *esprit
de corps*. They are watching in advance over the happiness of the
future lover. To a timid and tender woman there ought to be no
greater torture than to allow herself in the presence of a man something which she thinks she ought to blush at. I am convinced that a
proud woman would prefer a thousand deaths. A slight liberty taken
on the tender side by the man she loves gives a woman a moment of
keen pleasure, but if he has the air of blaming her for it, or only of not
enjoying it with transport, an awful doubt must be left in her mind.
For a woman above the vulgar level there is, then, everything to gain
by very reserved manners. The play is not equal. She hazards against
a slight pleasure, or against the advantage of appearing a little amiable,
the danger of biting remorse, and a feeling of shame which must render
even the lover less dear. An evening passed gaily and thoughtlessly,
without thinking of what comes after, is dearly paid at this price. The
sight of a lover with whom one fears that one has had this kind of
wrong must become odious for several days. Can one be surprised at
the force of a habit, the slightest infractions of which are punished with
such atrocious shame? As to the utility of modesty, it is the mother
of love. As to the mechanism of the feeling, nothing is simpler. The
mind is absorbed in feeling shame instead of being occupied with desire.
Desires are forbidden, and desires lead to actions. It is evident that
every tender and proud woman—and these two things, being cause and
effect, naturally go together—must contract habits of coldness which
the people whom she disconcerts call prudery. The power of modesty
is so great that a tender woman betrays herself with her lover rather

by deeds than by words. The evil of modesty is that it constantly leads to falsehood." (Stendhal, *De l'Amour*, Chapter XXIV.)

It thus happens that, as Adler remarks (*Die Mangelhafte Geschlechtsempfindung des Weibes*, p. 133), the sexual impulse in women is fettered by an inhibition which has to be conquered. A thin veil of reticence, shyness, and anxiety is constantly cast anew over a woman's love, and her wooer, in every act of courtship, has the enjoyment of conquering afresh an oft-won woman.

An interesting testimony to the part played by modesty in effecting the union of the sexes is furnished by the fact—to which attention has often been called—that the special modesty of women usually tends to diminish, though not to disappear, with the complete gratification of the sexual impulses. This may be noted among savage as well as among civilized women. The comparatively evanescent character of modesty has led to the argument (Venturi, *Degenerazioni Psico-sessuali*, pp. 92-93) that modesty (*pudore*) is possessed by women alone, men exhibiting, instead, a sense of decency which remains at about the same level of persistency throughout life. Viazzi ("Pudore nell 'uomo e nella donna," *Rivista Mensile di Psichiatria Forense*, 1898), on the contrary, following Sergi, argues that men are, throughout, more modest than women; but the points he brings forward, though often just, scarcely justify his conclusion. While the young virgin, however, is more modest and shy than the young man of the same age, the experienced married woman is usually less so than her husband, and in a woman who is a mother the shy reticences of virginal modesty would be rightly felt to be ridiculous. ("Les petites pudeurs n'existent pas pour les mères," remarks Goncourt, *Journal des Goncourt*, vol. iii, p. 5.) She has put off a sexual livery that has no longer any important part to play in life, and would, indeed, be inconvenient and harmful, just as a bird loses its sexual plumage when the pairing season is over.

Madame Celine Renooz, in an elaborate study of the psychological sexual differences between men and women (*Psychologie Comparée de l'Homme et de la Femme*, 1898, pp. 85-87), also believes that modesty is not really a feminine characteristic. "Modesty," she argues, "is masculine shame attributed to women for two reasons: first, because man believes that woman is subject to the same laws as himself; secondly, because the course of human evolution has reversed the psychology of the sexes, attributing to women the psychological results of masculine sexuality. This is the origin of the conventional lies which by a sort of social suggestion have intimidated women. They have, in appearance at least, accepted the rule of shame imposed on them by men, but only custom inspires the modesty for which they are praised; it is really an outrage to their sex. This reversal of psychological laws has, however, only been accepted by women with a struggle. Primitive woman, proud of her womanhood, for a long time defended her nakedness which ancient art has always represented. And in the actual life of the young girl to-day there is a moment when, by a secret atavism, she feels the pride of her sex, the intuition of her moral superiority, and cannot understand why she must hide its cause. At this moment, wavering between the laws of Nature and social conventions, she scarcely knows if nakedness should or should not affright her. A sort of confused atavistic memory recalls to her a period before clothing was known, and reveals to her as a paradisiacal ideal the customs of that human epoch."

In support of this view the authoress proceeds to point out that the *décolleté* constantly reappears in feminine clothing, never in male; that missionaries experience great difficulty in persuading women to cover themselves; that, while women accept with facility an examination by male doctors, men cannot force themselves to accept examination by a woman doctor, etc. (These and similar points had already been independently brought forward by Sergi, *Archivio di Psichiatria*, vol. xiii, 1892.)

It cannot be said that Madame Renooz's arguments will all bear examination, if only on the ground that nakedness by no means involves absence of modesty, but the point of view which she expresses is one which usually fails to gain recognition, though it probably contains an important element of truth. It is quite true, as Stendhal said, that modesty is very largely taught; from the earliest years, a girl child is trained to show a modesty which she quickly begins really to feel. This fact cannot fail to strike any one who reads the histories of pseudo-hermaphroditic persons, really males, who have from infancy been brought up in the belief that they are girls, and who show, and feel, all the shrinking reticence and blushing modesty of their supposed sex. But when the error is discovered, and they are restored to their proper sex, this is quickly changed, and they exhibit all the boldness of masculinity. (See *e.g.*, Neugebauer, "Beobachtungen aus dem Gebiete des Scheinzwittertumes, *Jahrbuch für Sexuelle Zwischenstufen*, Jahrgang iv, 1902, esp. p. 92.) At the same time this is only one thread in the tangled skein with which we are here concerned. The mass of facts which meets us when we turn to the study of modesty in women cannot be dismissed as a group of artifically-imposed customs. They gain rather than lose in importance if we have to realize that the organic sexual demands of women, calling for coyness in courtship, lead to the temporary suppression of another feminine instinct of opposite, though doubtless allied, nature.

But these somewhat conflicting, though not really contradictory, statements serve to bring out the fact that a woman's modesty is often an incalculable element. The woman who, under some circumstances and at some times, is extreme in her reticences, under other circumstances or at other times, may be extreme in her abandonment. Not that her modesty is an artificial garment, which she throws off or on at will. It is organic, but like the snail's shell, it sometimes forms an impenetrable covering, and sometimes glides off almost altogether. A man's modesty is more rigid, with little tendency to deviate toward either extreme. Thus it is, that, when uninstructed, a man is apt to be impatient with a woman's reticences, and yet shocked at her abandonments.

The significance of our inquiry becomes greater when we reflect that to the reticences of sexual modesty, in their progression, expansion, and complication, we largely owe, not only the refinement and development of the sexual emotions,—"*la pudeur,*" as Guyau remarked, "*a civilisé l'amour,*"—but the subtle and pervading part which the sexual instinct has played in the evolution of all human culture.

"It is certain that very much of what is best in religion, art, and life," remark Stanley Hall and Allin, "owes its charm to the progressively-widening irradiation of sexual feeling. Perhaps the reluctance of the female first long-circuited the exquisite sensations connected with sexual organs and acts to the antics of animal and human courtship, while restraint had the physiological function of developing the colors, plumes, excessive activity, and exuberant life of the pairing season. To keep certain parts of the body covered, irradiated the sense of beauty to eyes, hair, face, complexion, dress, form, etc., while many savage dances, costumes and postures are irradiations of the sexual act. Thus reticence, concealment, and restraint are among the prime conditions of religion and human culture." (Stanley Hall and Allin, "The Psychology of Tickling," *American Journal of Psychology,* 1897, p. 31.)

Groos attributes the deepening of the conjugal relation among birds to the circumstance that the male seeks to overcome the reticence of the female by the display of his charms and abilities. "And in the human world," he continues, "it is the same; without the modest reserve of the woman that must, in most cases, be overcome by lovable qualities, the sexual relationship would with difficulty find a singer who would extol in love the highest movements of the human soul." (Groos, *Spiele der Menschen,* p. 341.)

I have not, however, been able to find that the subject of modesty has been treated in any comprehensive way by psychologists. Though valuable facts and suggestions bearing on the sexual emotions, on disgust, the origins of tatooing, on ornament and clothing, have been brought forward by physiologists, psy-

chologists, and ethnographists, few or no attempts appear to
have been made to reach a general synthetic statement of these
facts and suggestions. It is true that a great many unreliable,
slight, or fragmentary efforts have been made to ascertain the
constitution or basis of this emotion.[1] Many psychologists
have regarded modesty simply as the result of clothing. This
view is overturned by the well-ascertained fact that many races
which go absolutely naked possess a highly-developed sense of
modesty. These writers have not realized that physiological
modesty is earlier in appearance, and more fundamental, than
anatomical modesty. A partial contribution to the analysis of
modesty has been made by Professor James, who, with his usual
insight and lucidity, has set forth certain of its characteristics,
especially the element due to "the application to ourselves of
judgments primarily passed upon our mates." Guyau, in a very
brief discussion of modesty, realized its great significance and
touched on most of its chief elements.[2] Westermarck, again,
followed by Grosse, has very ably and convincingly set forth
certain factors in the origin of ornament and clothing, a
subject which many writers imagine to cover the whole field of
modesty. More recently Ribot, in his work on the emotions, has
vaguely outlined most of the factors of modesty, but has not
developed a coherent view of their origins and relationships.

Since the present *Study* first appeared, Hohenemser, who considers
that my analysis of modesty is unsatisfactory, has made a notable attempt to define the psychological mechanism of shame. ("Versuch einer
Analyse der Scham," *Archiv für die Gesamte Psychologie*, Bd. II, Heft
2-3, 1903.) He regards shame as a general psycho-physical phenomenon,
"a definite tension of the whole soul," with an emotion superadded.
"The state of shame consists in a certain psychic lameness or inhibition,"
sometimes accompanied by physical phenomena of paralysis, such as
sinking of the head and inability to meet the eye. It is a special case
of Lipps's psychic stasis or damming up (*psychische Stauung*), always

[1] The earliest theory I have met with is that of St. Augustine, who
states (*De Civitate Dei*, Bk. XIV, Ch. XVII) that erections of the penis
never occurred until after the Fall of Man. It was the occurrence of
this "shameless novelty" which made nakedness indecent. This theory
fails to account for modesty in women.
[2] Guyau, *L'Irreligion de l'Avenir*, Ch. VII.

produced when the psychic activities are at the same time drawn in two or more different directions. In shame there is always something present in consciousness which conflicts with the rest of the personality, and cannot be brought into harmony with it, which cannot be brought, that is, into moral (not logical) relationship with it. A young man in love with a girl is ashamed when told that he is in love, because his reverence for one whom he regards as a higher being cannot be brought into relationship with his own lower personality. A child in the same way feels shame in approaching a big, grown-up person, who seems a higher sort of being. Sometimes, likewise, we feel shame in approaching a stranger, for a new person tends to seem higher and more interesting than ourselves. It is not so in approaching a new natural phenomenon, because we do not compare it with ourselves. Another kind of shame is seen when this mental contest is lower than our personality, and on this account in conflict with it, as when we are ashamed of sexual thoughts. Sexual ideas tend to evoke shame, Hohenemser remarks, because they so easily tend to pass into sexual feelings; when they do not so pass (as in scientific discussions) they do not evoke shame.

It will be seen that this discussion of modesty is highly generalized and abstracted; it deals simply with the formal mechanism of the process. Hohenemser admits that fear is a form of psychic stasis, and I have sought to show that modesty is a complexus of fears. We may very well accept the conception of psychic stasis at the outset. The analysis of modesty has still to be carried very much further.

The discussion of modesty is complicated by the difficulty, and even impossibility, of excluding closely-allied emotions— shame, shyness, bashfulness, timidity, etc.—all of which, indeed, however defined, adjoin or overlap modesty.[1] It is not, however, impossible to isolate the main body of the emotion of modesty, on account of its special connection, on the whole, with

---

[1] Timidity, as understood by Dugas, in his interesting essay on that subject, is probably most remote. Dr. H. Campbell's "morbid shyness" (*British Medical Journal*, September 26, 1896) is, in part, identical with timidity, in part, with modesty. The matter is further complicated by the fact that modesty itself has in English (like virtue) two distinct meanings. In its original form it has no special connection with sex or women, but may rather be considered as a masculine virtue. Cicero regards "modestia" as the equivalent of the Greek σωφροσύνη. This is the "modesty" which Mary Wollstonecraft eulogized in the last century, the outcome of knowledge and reflection, "soberness of mind," "the graceful calm virtue of maturity." In French, it is possible to avoid the confusion, and *modestie* is entirely distinct from *pudeur*. It is, of course, mainly with *pudeur* that I am here concerned.

the consciousness of sex. I here attempt, however imperfectly, to sketch out a fairly-complete analysis of its constitution and to trace its development.

In entering upon this investigation a few facts with regard to the various manifestations of modesty may be helpful to us. I have selected these from scattered original sources, and have sought to bring out the variety and complexity of the problems with which we are here concerned.

The New Georgians of the Solomon Islands, so low a race that they are ignorant both of pottery and weaving, and wear only a loin cloth, "have the same ideas of what is decent with regard to certain acts and exposures that we ourselves have;" so that it is difficult to observe whether they practice circumcision. (Somerville, *Journal of the Anthropological Institute*, 1897, p. 394.)

In the New Hebrides "the closest secrecy is adopted with regard to the penis, not at all from a sense of decency, but to avoid Narak, the *sight* even of that of another man being considered most dangerous. The natives of this savage island, accordingly, wrap the penis around with many yards of calico, and other like materials, winding and folding them until a preposterous bundle 18 inches, or 2 feet long, and 2 inches or more in diameter is formed, which is then supported upward by means of a belt, in the extremity decorated with flowering grasses, etc. The testicles are left naked." There is no other body covering. (Somerville, *Journal of the Anthropological Institute*, 1894, p. 368.)

In the Pelew Islands, says Kubary, as quoted by Bastian, it is said that when the God Irakaderugel and his wife were creating man and woman (he forming man and she forming woman), and were at work on the sexual organs, the god wished to see his consort's handiwork. She, however, was cross, and persisted in concealing what she had made. Ever since then women wear an apron of pandanus-leaves and men go naked. (A. Bastian, *Inselgruppen in Oceanien*, p. 112.)

In the Pelew Islands, Semper tells us that when approaching a large water-hole he was surprised to hear an affrighted, long-drawn cry from his native friends. "A girl's voice answered out of the bushes, and my people held us back, for there were women bathing there who would not allow us to pass. When I remarked that they were only women, of whom they need not be afraid, they replied that it was not so, that women had an unbounded right to punish men who passed them when bathing without their permission, and could inflict fines or even death. On this account, the women's bathing place is a safe and favorite spot for a secret rendezvous. Fortunately a lady's toilet lasts but a short time in this island." (Carl Semper, *Die Palau-Inseln*, 1873, p. 68.)

Among the Western Tribes of Torres Strait, Haddon states, "the men were formerly nude, and the women wore only a leaf petticoat, but I gather that they were a decent people; now both sexes are prudish. A man would never go nude before me. The women would never voluntarily expose their breasts to white men's gaze; this applies to quite young girls, less so to old women. Amongst themselves they are, of course, much less particular, but I believe they are becoming more so. . . . Formerly, I imagine, there was no restraint in speech; now there is a great deal of prudery; for instance, the men were always much ashamed when I asked for the name of the sexual parts of a woman." (A. C. Haddon, "Ethnography of the Western Tribes of Torres Straits," *Journal of the Anthropological Institute*, 1890, p. 336.) After a subsequent expedition to the same region, the author reiterates his observations as to the "ridiculously prudish manner" of the men, attributable to missionary influence during the past thirty years, and notes that even the children are affected by it. "At Mabuiag, some small children were paddling in the water, and a boy of about ten years of age reprimanded a little girl of five or six years because she held up her dress too high." (*Reports of the Cambridge Anthropological Expedition to Torres Straits*, vol. v, p. 272.)

"Although the women of New Guinea," Vahness says, "are very slightly clothed, they are by no means lacking in a well-developed sense of decorum. If they notice, for instance, that any one is paying special attention to their nakedness, they become ashamed and turn round." When a woman had to climb the fence to enter the wild-pig enclosure, she would never do it in Vahness's presence. (*Zeitschrift für Ethnologie*, Verhdlgen., 1900, Heft 5, p. 415.)

In Australia "the feeling of decency is decidedly less prevalent among males than females;" the clothed females retire out of sight to bathe. (Curr, *Australian Race*.)

"Except for waist-bands, forehead-bands, necklets, and armlets, and a conventional pubic tassel, shell, or, in the case of the women, a small apron, the Central Australian native is naked. The pubic tassel is a diminutive structure, about the size of a five-shilling piece, made of a few short strands of fur-strings flattened out into a fan-shape and attached to the pubic hair. As the string, especially at *corrobboree* times, is covered with white kaolin or gypsum, it serves as a decoration rather than a covering. Among the Arunta and Luritcha the women usually wear nothing, but further north, a small apron is made and worn." (Baldwin Spencer and Gillen, *Native Tribes of Central Australia*, p. 572.)

Of the Central Australians Stirling says: "No sense of shame of exposure was exhibited by the men on removal of the diminutive articles worn as conventional coverings; they were taken off *coram populo*,

and bartered without hesitation. On the other hand, some little persuasion was necessary to allow inspection of the effect of [urethral]
sub-incision, assent being given only after dismissal to a distance of
the women and young children. As to the women, it was nearly always
observed that when in camp without clothing they, especially the
younger ones, exhibited by their attitude a keen sense of modesty, if,
indeed, a consciousness of their nakedness can be thus considered.
When we desired to take a photograph of a group of young women,
they were very coy at the proposal to remove their scanty garments,
and retired behind a wall to do so; but once in a state of nudity they
made no objection to exposure to the camera." (*Report of the Horn
Scientific Expedition*, 1896, vol. iv, p. 37.)

In Northern Queensland "phallocrypts," or "penis-concealers," only
used by the males at *corrobborees* and other public rejoicings, are either
formed of pearl-shell or opossum-string. The *koom-pa-ra*, or opossum-
string form of phallocrypt, forms a kind of tassel, and is colored red;
it is hung from the waist-belt in the middle line. In both sexes the
privates are only covered on special public occasions, or when in close
proximity to white settlements. (W. Roth, *Ethnological Studies among
the Northwest-Central-Queensland Aboriginies*, 1897, pp. 114-115.)

"The principle of chastity," said Forster, of his experiences in
the South Sea Islands in their unspoilt state, "we found in many
families exceedingly well understood. I have seen many fine women
who, with a modesty mixed with politeness, refuse the greatest and
most tempting offers made them by our forward youths; often they
excuse themselves with a simple *tirra-tane*, 'I am married,' and at
other times they smiled and declined it with *epia*, 'no.' . . .
Virtuous women hear a joke without emotion, which, amongst us,
might put some men to the blush. Neither austerity and anger, nor
joy and ecstasy is the consequence, but sometimes a modest, dignified,
serene smile spreads itself over their face, and seems gently to rebuke
the uncouth jester." (J. R. Forster, *Observations made During a Voyage Round the World*, 1728, p. 392.)

Captain Cook, at Tahiti, in 1769, after performing Divine service on Sunday, witnessed "Vespers of a very different kind. A young
man, near six feet high, performed the rites of Venus with a little girl
about eleven or twelve years of age, before several of our people and
a great number of the natives, without the least sense of its being indecent or improper, but, as it appeared, in perfect conformity to the custom of the place. Among the spectators were several women of superior
rank, who may properly be said to have assisted at the ceremony; for
they gave instructions to the girl how to perform her part, which, young
as she was, she did not seem much to stand in need of." (J. Hawkesworth, *Account of the Voyages*, etc., 1775, vol. i, p. 469.)

At Tahiti, according to Cook, it was customary to "gratify every appetite and passion before witnesses," and it is added, "in the conversation of these people, that which is the principal source of their pleasure is always the principal topic; everything is mentioned without any restraint or emotion, and in the most direct terms, by both sexes." (Hawkesworth, *op. cit.*, vol ii, p. 45.)

"I have observed," Captain Cook wrote, "that our friends in the South Seas have not even the idea of indecency, with respect to any object or any action, but this was by no means the case with the inhabitants of New Zealand, in whose carriage and conversation there was as much modest reserve and decorum with respect to actions, which yet in their opinion were not criminal, as are to be found among the politest people in Europe. The women were not impregnable; but the terms and manner of compliance were as decent as those in marriage among us, and according to their notions, the agreement was as innocent. When any of our people made an overture to any of their young women, he was given to understand that the consent of her friends was necessary, and by the influence of a proper present it was generally obtained; but when these preliminaries were settled, it was also necessary to treat the wife for a night with the same delicacy that is here required by the wife for life, and the lover who presumed to take any liberties by which this was violated, was sure to be disappointed." (Hawkesworth, *op. cit.*, vol. ii, p. 254.)

Cook found that the people of New Zealand "bring the prepuce over the gland, and to prevent it from being drawn back by contraction of the part, they tie the string which hangs from the girdle round the end of it. The glans, indeed, seemed to be the only part of their body which they were solicitous to conceal, for they frequently threw off all their dress but the belt and string, with the most careless indifference, but showed manifest signs of confusion when, to gratify our curiosity, they were requested to untie the string, and never consented but with the utmost reluctance and shame. . . . The women's lower garment was always bound fast round them, except when they went into the water to catch lobsters, and then they took great care not to be seen by the men. We surprised several of them at this employment, and the chaste Diana, with her nymphs, could not have discovered more confusion and distress at the sight of Actæon, than these women expressed upon our approach. Some of them hid themselves among the rocks, and the rest crouched down in the sea till they had made themselves a girdle and apron of such weeds as they could find, and when they came out, even with this veil, we could see that their modesty suffered much pain by our presence." (Hawkesworth, *op. cit.*, vol. ii, pp. 257-258.)

In Rotuma, in Polynesia, where the women enjoy much freedom, but where, at all events in old days, married people were, as a rule, faithful to each other, "the language is not chaste according to our ideas, and there is a great deal of freedom in speaking of immoral vices. In this connection a man and his wife will speak freely to one another before their friends. I am informed, though, by European traders well conversant with the language, that there are grades of language, and that certain coarse phrases would never be used to any decent woman; so that probably, in their way, they have much modesty, only we cannot appreciate it." (J. Stanley Gardiner, "The Natives of Rotuma," *Journal of the Anthropological Institute*, May, 1898, p. 481.)

The men of Rotuma, says the same writer, are very clean, the women also, bathing twice a day in the sea; but "bathing in public without the *kukuluga*, or *sulu* [loin-cloth, which is the ordinary dress], around the waist is absolutely unheard of, and would be much looked down upon." (*Journal of the Anthropological Institute*, 1898, p. 410.)

In ancient Samoa the only necessary garment for either man or woman was an apron of leaves, but they possessed so "delicate a sense of propriety" that even "while bathing they have a girdle of leaves or some other covering around the waist." (Turner, *Samoa a Hundred Years Ago*, p. 121.)

After babyhood the Indians of Guiana are never seen naked. When they change their single garment they retire. The women wear a little apron, now generally made of European beads, but the Warraus still make it of the inner bark of a tree, and some of seeds. (Everard im Thurn, *Among the Indians of Guiana*, 1883.)

The Mandurucu women of Brazil, according to Tocantins (quoted by Mantegazza), are completely naked, but they are careful to avoid any postures which might be considered indecorous, and they do this so skilfully that it is impossible to tell when they have their menstrual periods. (Mantegazza, *Fisiologia della Donna*, cap 9.)

The Indians of Central Brazil have no "private parts." In men the little girdle, or string, surrounding the lower part of the abdomen, hides nothing; it is worn after puberty, the penis being often raised and placed beneath it to lengthen the prepuce. The women also use a little strip of bast that goes down the groin and passes between the thighs. Among some tribes (Karibs, Tupis, Nu-Arwaks) a little, triangular, coquettishly-made piece of bark-bast comes just below the mons veneris; it is only a few centimetres in width, and is called the *uluri*. *In both sexes concealment of the sexual mucous membrane is attained.* These articles cannot be called clothing. "The red thread of the Trumai, the elegant *uluri*, and the variegated flag of the Bororó attract attention, like ornaments, instead of drawing attention away." Von den Steinen thinks this proceeding a necessary protection against the attacks of insects, which are often serious in Brazil. He does think, however, that there is more than this, and that the people are ashamed to show the glans penis. (Karl von den Steinen, *Unter den Naturvölkern Zentral-Brasiliens*, 1894, pp. 190 *et seq.*)

Other travelers mention that on the Amazon among some tribes the women are clothed and the men naked; among others the women naked, and the men clothed. Thus, among the Guaycurus the men are quite naked, while the women wear a short petticoat; among the Uaupás the men always wear a loin-cloth, while the women are quite naked.

"The feeling of modesty is very developed among the Fuegians, who are accustomed to live naked. They manifest it in their bearing and in the ease with which they show themselves in a state of nudity, compared with the awkwardness, blushing, and shame which both men and women exhibit if one gazes at certain parts of their bodies. Among themselves this is never done even between husband and wife. There is no Fuegian word for modesty, perhaps because the feeling is universal among them." The women wear a minute triangular garment of skin suspended between the thighs and never removed, being merely raised during conjugal relations. (Hyades and Deniker, *Mission Scientifique du Cap Horn*, vol. vii, pp. 239, 307, and 347.)

Among the Crow Indians of Montana, writes Dr. Holder, who has lived with them for several years, "a sense of modesty forbids the attendance upon the female in labor of any male, white man or Indian, physician or layman. This antipathy to receiving assistance at the hands of the physician is overcome as the tribes progress toward civilization, and it is especially noticeable that half-breeds almost constantly seek the physician's aid." Dr. Holder mentions the case of a young woman who, although brought near the verge of death in a very difficult first confinement, repeatedly refused to allow him to examine her; at last she consented; "her modest preparation was to take bits of quilt and cover thighs and lips of vulva, leaving only the aperture exposed. . . . Their modesty would not be so striking were it not that, almost to a woman, the females of this tribe are prostitutes, and for a consideration will admit the connection of any man." (A. B. Holder, *American Journal of Obstetrics*, vol. xxv, No. 6, 1892.)

"In every North American tribe, from the most northern to the most southern, the skirt of the woman is longer than that of the men. In Esquimau land the *parka* of deerskin and sealskin reaches to the knees. Throughout Central North America the buckskin dress of the women reached quite to the ankles. The West-Coast women, from Oregon to the Gulf of California, wore a petticoat of shredded bark, of plaited grass, or of strings, upon which were strung hundreds of seeds. Even in the most tropical areas the rule was universal, as anyone can see from the codices or in pictures of the natives." (Otis T. Mason, *Woman's Share in Primitive Culture*, p. 237.)

Describing the loin-cloth worn by Nicobarese men, Man says: "From the clumsy mode in which this garment is worn by the Shom Pen—necessitating frequent readjustment of the folds—one is led to infer that its use is not *de rigueur*, but reserved for special occasions, as when receiving or visiting strangers." (E. H. Man, *Journal of the Anthropological Institute*, 1886, p. 442.)

The semi-nude natives of the island of Nias in the Indian Ocean are "modest by nature," paying no attention to their own nudity or that of others, and much scandalized by any attempt to go beyond the limits ordained by custom. When they pass near places where women are bathing they raise their voices in order to warn them of their presence, and even although any bold youth addressed the women, and the latter replied, no attempt would be made to approach them; any such attempt would be severely punished by the head man of the village. (Modigliani, *Un Viaggio a Nias*, p. 460.)

Man says that the Andamanese in modesty and self-respect compare favorably with many classes among civilized peoples. "Women are so modest that they will not renew their leaf-aprons in the presence of one another, but retire to a secluded spot for this purpose; even when parting with one of their *bod* appendages [tails of leaves suspended from back of girdle] to a female friend, the delicacy they manifest for the feelings of the bystanders in their mode of removing it amounts to prudishness; yet they wear no clothing in the ordinary sense." (*Journal of the Anthropological Institute*, 1883, pp. 94 and 331.)

Of the Garo women of Bengal Dalton says: "Their sole garment is a piece of cloth less than a foot in width that just meets around the loins, and in order that it may not restrain the limbs it is only fastened where it meets under the hip at the upper corners. The girls are thus greatly restricted in the positions they may modestly assume, but decorum is, in their opinion, sufficiently preserved if they only keep their legs well together when they sit or kneel." (E. T. Dalton, *Ethnology of Bengal*, 1872, p. 66.)

Of the Naga women of Assam it is said: "Of clothing there was not much to see; but in spite of this I doubt whether we could excel them in true decency and modesty. Ibn Muhammed Wali had already remarked in his history of the conquest of Assam (1662-63), that the Naga women only cover their breasts. They declare that it is absurd to cover those parts of the body which everyone has been able to see from their births, but that it is different with the breasts, which appeared later, and are, therefore, to be covered. Dalton (*Journal of the Asiatic Society*, Bengal, 41, 1, 84) adds that in the presence of strangers Naga women simply cross their arms over their breasts, without caring much what other charms they may reveal to the observer. As regards some clans of the naked Nagas, to whom the Banpara belong, this may still hold good." (K. Klemm, "Peal's Ausflug nach Banpara," *Zeitschrift für Ethnologie*, 1898, Heft 5, p. 334.)

"In Ceylon, a woman always bathes in public streams, but she never removes all her clothes. She washes under the cloth, bit by bit, and then slips on the dry, new cloth, and pulls out the wet one from underneath (much in the same sliding way as servant girls and young women in England). This is the common custom in India and the Malay States. The breasts are always bare in their own houses, but in the public roads are covered whenever a European passes. The vulva is never exposed. They say that a devil, imagined as a white and hairy being, might have intercourse with them." (Private communication.)

In Borneo, "the *sirat*, called *chawal* by the Malays, is a strip of cloth a yard wide, worn round the loins and in between the thighs, so as to cover the pudenda and perinæum; it is generally six yards or so in length, but the younger men of the present generation use as much as twelve or fourteen yards (sometimes even more), which they twist and coil with great precision round and round their body, until the waist and stomach are fully enveloped in its folds." (H. Ling Roth, "Low's Natives of Borneo," *Journal of the Anthropological Institute*, 1892, p. 36.)

"In their own houses in the depths of the forest the Dwarfs are said to neglect coverings for decency in the men as in the women, but certainly when they emerge from the forest into the villages of the agricultural Negroes, they are always observed to be wearing some small piece of bark-cloth or skin, or a bunch of leaves over the pudenda. Elsewhere in all the regions of Africa visited by the writer, or described by other observers, a neglect of decency in the male has only been recorded among the Efik people of Old Calabar. The nudity of women is another question. In parts of West Africa, between the Niger and the Gaboon (especially on the Cameroon River, at Old Calabar, and in the Niger Delta), it is, or was, customary for young women to go about completely nude before they were married. In Swaziland, until quite recently, unmarried women and very often matrons went stark naked. Even amongst the prudish Baganda, who made it a punishable offense for a man to expose any part of his leg above the knee, the wives of the King would attend at his Court perfectly naked. Among the Kavirondo, all unmarried girls are completely nude, and although women who have become mothers are supposed to wear a tiny covering before and behind, they very often completely neglect to do so when in their own villages. Yet, as a general rule, among the Nile Negroes, and still more markedly among the Hamites and people of Masai stock, the women are particular about concealing the pudenda, whereas the men are ostentatiously naked. The Baganda hold nudity in the male to be such an abhorrent thing that for centuries they have referred with scorn and disgust to the Nile Negroes as the 'naked people.' Male nudity extends northwest to within some 200 miles of Khartum, or, in fact, wherever the Nile Negroes of the Dinka-Acholi stock inhabit the country." (Sir H. H. Johnston, *Uganda Protectorate*, vol. ii, pp. 669-672.)

Among the Nilotic Ja-luo, Johnston states that "unmarried men go naked. Married men who have children wear a small piece of goat skin, which, though quite inadequate for purposes of decency, is, nevertheless, a very important thing in etiquette, for a married man with a child must on no account call on his mother-in-law without wearing this piece of goat's skin. To call on her in a state of absolute nudity would be regarded as a serious insult, only to be atoned for by the payment of goats. Even if under the new dispensation he wears European trousers, he must have a piece of goat's skin underneath. Married women wear a tail of strings behind." It is very bad manners for a woman to serve food to her husband without putting on this tail. (Sir H. H. Johnston, *Uganda Protectorate*, vol. ii, p. 781.)

Mrs. French-Sheldon remarks that the Masai and other East African tribes, with regard to menstruation, "observe the greatest delicacy, and are more than modest." (*Journal of the Anthropological Institute*, 1894, p. 383.)

At the same time the Masai, among whom the penis is of enormous size, consider it disreputable to conceal that member, and in the highest degree reputable to display it, even ostentatiously. (Sir H. H. Johnston, *Kilima-njaro Expedition*, p. 413.)

Among the African Dinka, who are scrupulously clean and delicate (smearing themselves with burnt cows' dung, and washing themselves daily with cows' urine), and are exquisite cooks, reaching in many respects a higher stage of civilization, in Schweinfurth's opinion, than is elsewhere attained in Africa, only the women wear aprons. The neighboring tribes of the red soil—Bongo, Mittoo, Niam-Niam, etc.—are called "women" by the Dinka, because among these tribes the men wear an apron, while the women obstinately refuse to wear any clothes whatsoever of skin or stuff, going into the woods every day, however, to get a supple bough for a girdle, with, perhaps, a bundle of fine grass. (Schweinfurth, *Heart of Africa*, vol. i, pp. 152, etc.)

Lombroso and Carrara, examining some Dinka negroes brought from the White Nile, remark: "As to their psychology, what struck us first was the exaggeration of their modesty; not in a single case would the men allow us to examine their genital organs or the women their breasts; we examined the tattoo-marks on the chest of one of the women, and she remained sad and irritable for two days afterward." They add that in sexual and all other respects these people are highly moral. (Lombroso and Carrara, *Archivio di Psichiatria*, 1896, vol. xvii, fasc. 4.)

"The negro is very rarely knowingly indecent or addicted to lubricity," says Sir H. H. Johnston. "In this land of nudity, which I have known for seven years, I do not remember once having seen an indecent gesture on the part of either man or woman, and only very rarely (and that not among unspoiled savages) in the case of that most shameless member of the community—the little boy." He adds that the native dances are only an apparent exception, being serious in character, though indecent to our eyes, almost constituting a religious ceremony. The only really indecent dance indigenous to Central Africa "is one which originally represented the act of coition, but it is so altered to a stereotyped formula that its exact purport is not obvious until explained somewhat shyly by the natives. . . . It may safely be asserted that the negro race in Central Africa is much more truly modest, is much more free from real vice, than are most European nations. Neither boys nor girls wear clothing (unless they are the children of chiefs) until nearing the age of puberty. Among the Wankonda, practically no covering is worn by the men except a ring of brass wire around the stomach. The Wankonda women are likewise almost entirely naked, but generally cover the pudenda with a tiny bead-work apron, often a piece of very beautiful workmanship, and exactly resembling the same article worn by Kaffir women. A like degree of nudity prevails among many of the Awemba, among the A-lungu, the Batumbuka, and the Angoni. Most of the Angoni men, however, adopt the Zulu fashion of covering the glans penis with a small wooden case or the outer shell of a fruit. The Wa-Yao have a strong sense of decency in matters of this kind, which is the more curious since they are more given to obscenity in their rites, ceremonies, and dances than any other tribe. Not only is it extremely rare to see any Yao uncovered, but both men and women have the strongest dislike to exposing their persons even to the inspection of a doctor. The Atonga and many of the A-nyanga people, and all the tribes west of Nyassa (with the exception possibly of the A-lunda) have not the Yao regard for decency, and, although they can seldom or ever be accused of a deliberate intention to expose themselves, the men are relatively indifferent as to whether their nakedness is or is not concealed, though the women are modest and careful in this respect." (H. H. Johnston, *British Central Africa*, 1897, pp. 408-419.)

In Azimba land, Central Africa, H. Crawford Angus, who has spent many years in this part of Africa, writes: "It has been my experience that the more naked the people, and the more to us obscene and shameless their manners and customs, the more moral and strict they are in the matter of sexual intercourse." He proceeds to give a description of the *chensamwali*, or initiation ceremony of girls at puberty, a season of rejoicing when the girl is initiated into all the secrets of marriage, amid songs and dances referring to the act of coition. "The whole matter is looked upon as a matter of course, and not as a thing to be ashamed of or to hide, and, being thus openly treated of and no secrecy made about it, you find in this tribe that the women are very virtuous. They know from the first all that is to be known, and cannot see any reason for secrecy concerning natural laws or the powers and senses that have been given them from birth." (*Zeitschrift für Ethnologie*, 1898, Heft 6, p. 479.)

Of the Monbuttu of Central Africa, another observer says: "It is surprising how a Monbuttu woman of birth can, without the aid of dress, impress others with her dignity and modesty." (*British Medical Journal*, June 14, 1890.)

"The women at Upoto wear no clothes whatever, and came up to us in the most unreserved manner. An interesting gradation in the arrangement of the female costume has been observed by us: as we ascended the Congo, the higher up the river we found ourselves, the higher the dress reached, till it has now, at last, culminated in absolute nudity." (T. H. Parke, *My Personal Experiences in Equatorial Africa*, 1891, p. 61.)

"There exists throughout the Congo population a marked appreciation of the sentiment of decency and shame as applied to private actions," says Mr. Herbert Ward. In explanation of the nudity of the women at Upoto, a chief remarked to Ward that "concealment is food for the inquisitive." (*Journal of the Anthropological Institute*, 1895, p. 293.)

In the Gold Coast and surrounding countries complete nudity is extremely rare, except when circumstances make it desirable; on occasion clothing is abandoned with unconcern. "I have on several occasions," says Dr. Freeman, "seen women at Accra walk from the beach, where they have been bathing, across the road to their houses, where they would proceed to dry themselves, and resume their garments; and women may not infrequently be seen bathing in pools by the wayside, conversing quite unconstrainedly with their male acquaintances, who are seated on the bank. The mere unclothed body conveys to their minds no idea of indecency. Immodesty and indelicacy of manner are practically unknown." He adds that the excessive zeal of missionaries in urging their converts to adopt European dress—which they are only too ready to do—is much to be regretted, since the close-fitting, thin garments are really less modest than the loose clothes they replace, besides being much less cleanly. (R. A. Freeman, *Travels and Life in Ashanti and Jaman*, 1898, p. 379.)

At Loango, says Pechuel-Loesche, "the well-bred negress likes to cover her bosom, and is sensitive to critical male eyes; if she meets a European when without her overgarment, she instinctively, though not without coquetry, takes the attitude of the Medicean Venus." Men and women bathe separately, and hide themselves from each other when naked. The women also exhibit shame when discovered suckling their babies. (*Zeitschrift für Ethnologie,* 1878, pp. 27-31.)

The Koran (Sura XXIV) forbids showing the pudenda, as well as the face. yet a veiled Mohammedan woman, Stern remarks, even in the streets of Constantinople, will stand still and pull up her clothes to scratch her private parts, and in Beyrout, he saw Turkish prostitutes, still veiled, place themselves in the position for coitus. (B. Stern, *Medizin, etc., in der Türkei,* vol. ii, p. 162.)

"An Englishman surprised a woman while bathing in the Euphrates; she held her hands over her face, without troubling as to what else the stranger might see. In Egypt, I have myself seen quite naked young peasant girls, who hastened to see us, after covering their faces. (C. Niebuhr, *Reisebeschreibung nach Arabien,* 1774, vol. i, p. 165.)

When Helfer was taken to visit the ladies in the palace of the Imam of Muskat, at Buscheir, he found that their faces were covered with black masks, though the rest of the body might be clothed in a transparent sort of crape; to look at a naked face was very painful to the ladies themselves; even a mother never lifts the mask from the face of her daughter after the age of twelve; that is reserved for her lord and husband. "I observed that the ladies looked at me with a certain confusion, and after they had glanced into my face, lowered their eyes, ashamed. On making inquiries, I found that my uncovered face was indecent, as a naked person would be to us. They begged me to assume a mask, and when a waiting-woman had bound a splendidly decorated one round my head, they all exclaimed: 'Tahip! tahip!'— beautiful, beautiful." (J. W. Helfer, *Reisen in Vorderasian und Indien,* vol. ii, p. 12.)

In Algeria—in the provinces of Constantine, in Biskra, even Aures, —"among the women especially, not one is restrained by any modesty in unfastening her girdle to any comer" (when a search was being made for tattoo-marks on the lower extremities). "In spite of the great licentiousness of the manners," the same writer continues, "the Arab and the Kabyle possess great personal modesty, and with difficulty are persuaded to exhibit the body nude; is it the result of real modesty, or of their inveterate habits of active pederasty? Whatever the cause, they always hide the sexual organs with their hands or their handkerchiefs, and are disagreeably affected even by the slightest touch of the doctor." (Batut, *Archives d'Anthropologie Criminelle,* January 15, 1893.)

"Moslem modesty," remarks Wellhausen, "was carried to great lengths, insufficient clothing being forbidden. It was marked even among the heathen Arabs, as among Semites and old civilizations generally; we must not be deceived by the occasional examples of immodesty in individual cases. The Sunna prescribes that a man shall not uncover himself even to himself, and shall not wash naked—from fear of God and of spirits; Job did so, and atoned for it heavily. When in Arab antiquity grown-up persons showed themselves naked, it was only under extraordinary circumstances, and to attain unusual ends. . . . Women when mourning uncovered not only the face and bosom, but also tore all their garments. The messenger who brought bad news tore his garments. A mother desiring to bring pressure to bear on her son took off her clothes. A man to whom vengeance is forbidden showed his despair and disapproval by uncovering his posterior and strewing earth on his head, or by raising his garment behind and covering his head with it. This was done also in fulfilling natural necessities." (Wellhausen, *Reste Arabischen Heidentums*, 1897, pp. 173, 195-196.)

Mantegazza mentions that a Lapland woman refused even for the sum of 150 francs to allow him to photograph her naked, though the men placed themselves before the camera in the costume of Adam for a much smaller sum. In the same book Mantegazza remarks that in the eighteenth century, travelers found it extremely difficult to persuade Samoyed women to show themselves naked. Among the same people, he says, the newly-married wife must conceal her face from her husband for two months after marriage, and only then yield to his embraces. (Mantegazza, *La Donna*, cap. IV.)

"The beauty of a Chinese woman," says Dr. Matignon, "resides largely in her foot. 'A foot which is not deformed is a dishonor,' says a poet. For the husband the foot is more interesting than the face. Only the husband may see his wife's foot naked. A Chinese woman is as reticent in showing her feet to a man as a European woman her breasts. I have often had to treat Chinese women with ridiculously small feet for wounds and excoriations, the result of tight-bandaging. They exhibited the prudishness of school-girls, blushed, turned their backs to unfasten the bandages, and then concealed the foot in a cloth, leaving only the affected part uncovered. Modesty is a question of convention; Chinese have it for their feet." (J. Matignon, "A propos d'un Pied de Chinoise," *Archives d'Anthropologie Criminelle*, 1898, p. 445.)

Among the Yakuts of Northeast Siberia, "there was a well-known custom according to which a bride should avoid showing herself or her uncovered body to her father-in-law. In ancient times, they say, a bride concealed herself for seven years from her father-in-law, and from the brothers and other masculine relations of her husband. . . . The men also tried not to meet her, saying, 'The poor child will be ashamed.' If a meeting could not be avoided the young woman put a mask on her face. . . . Nowadays, the young wives only avoid showing to their male relatives-in-law the uncovered body. Amongst the rich they avoid going about in the presence of these in the chemise alone. In some places, they lay especial emphasis on the fact that it is a shame for young wives to show their uncovered hair and feet to the male relatives of their husbands. On the other side, the male relatives of the husband ought to avoid showing to the young wife the body uncovered above the elbow or the sole of the foot, and they ought to avoid indecent expressions and vulgar vituperations in her presence. . . . That these observances are not the result of a specially delicate modesty, is proved by the fact that even young girls constantly twist thread upon the naked thigh, unembarrassed by the presence of men who do not belong to the household; nor do they show any embarrassment if a strange man comes upon them when uncovered to the waist. The one thing which they do not like, and at which they show anger, is that such persons look carefully at their uncovered feet. . . . The former simplicity, with lack of shame in uncovering the body, is disappearing." (Sieroshevski, "The Yakuts," *Journal of the Anthropological Institute,* Jan.-June, 1901, p. 93.)

"In Japan (Captain ——— tells me), the bathing-place of the women was perfectly open (the shampooing, indeed, was done by a man), and Englishmen were offered no obstacle, nor excited the least repugnance; indeed, girls after their bath would freely pass, sometimes as if holding out their hair for innocent admiration, and this continued until countrymen of ours, by vile laughter and jests, made them guard themselves from insult by secrecy. So corruption spreads, and heathenism is blacker by our contact." (Private communication.)

"Speaking once with a Japanese gentleman, I observed that we considered it an act of indecency for men and women to wash together. He shrugged his shoulders as he answered: 'But these Westerns have such prurient minds!'" (Mitford, *Tales of Old Japan,* 1871.)

Dr. Carl Davidsohn, who remarks that he had ample opportunity of noting the great beauty of the Japanese women in a national dance, performed naked, points out that the Japanese have no æsthetic sense for the nude. "This was shown at the Jubilee Exposition at Kyoto. Here, among many rooms full of art objects, one was devoted to oil pictures in the European manner. Among these only one represented a nude figure, a Psyche, or Truth. It was the first time such a picture had been seen. Men and women crowded around it. After they had gazed at it for a time, most began to giggle and laugh; some by their air and gestures clearly showed their disgust; all found that it was not æsthetic to paint a naked woman, though in Nature, nakedness was in no way offensive to them. In the middle of the same city, at a fountain reputed to possess special virtues, men and women will stand together naked and let the water run over them." (Carl Davidsohn, "Das Nackte bei den Japanern," *Globus*, 1896, No. 16.)

"It is very difficult to investigate the hairiness of Ainu women," Baelz remarks, "for they possess a really incredible degree of modesty. Even when in summer they bathe—which happens but seldom—they keep their clothes on." He records that he was once asked to examine a girl at the Mission School, in order to advise as regards the treatment of a diseased spine; although she had been at the school for seven years, she declared that "she would rather die than show her back to a man, even though a doctor." (Baelz, "Die Aino," *Zeitschrift für Ethnologie*, 1901, Heft 2, p. 178.)

The Greeks, Etruscans, and Romans, appear to have been accustomed to cover the foreskin with the *kynodesme* (a band), or the *fibula* (a ring), for custom and modesty demanded that the glans should be concealed. Such covering is represented in persons who were compelled to be naked, and is referred to by Celsus as "decori causâ." (L. Stieda, "Anatomisch-archäologische Studien," *Anatomische Hefte*, Bd. XIX, Heft 2, 1902.)

"Among the Lydians, and, indeed, among the barbarians generally, it is considered a deep disgrace, even for a man, to be seen naked." (Herodotus, Book I, Chapter X.)

"The simple dress which is now common was first worn in Sparta, and there, more than anywhere else, the life of the rich was assimilated to that of the people. The Lacedæmonians, too, were the first who, in their athletic exercises, stripped naked and rubbed themselves over with oil. This was not the ancient custom; athletes formerly, even when they were contending at Olympia, wore girdles about their loins [earlier still, the Mycenæans had always worn a loin-cloth], a practice which lasted until quite lately, and still persists among barbarians, especially those of Asia, where the combatants at boxing and wrestling matches wear girdles." (Thucydides, *History*, Book I, Chapter VI.)

"The notion of the women exercising naked in the schools with the men . . . at the present day would appear truly ridiculous. . . . Not long since it was thought discreditable and ridiculous among the Greeks, as it is now among most barbarous nations, for men to be seen naked. And when the Cretans first, and after them the Lacedæmonians, began the practice of gymnastic exercises, the wits of the time had it in their power to make sport of those novelties. . . . As for the man who laughs at the idea of undressed women going through gymnastic exercises, as a means of revealing what is most perfect, his ridicule is but 'unripe fruit plucked from the tree of wisdom.'" (Plato, *Republic*, Book V.)

According to Plutarch, however, among the Spartans, at all events, nakedness in women was not ridiculous, since the institutes of Lycurgus ordained that at solemn feasts and sacrifices the young women should dance naked and sing, the young men standing around in a circle to see and hear them. Aristotle says that in his time Spartan girls only wore a very slight garment. As described by Pausanias, and as shown by a statue in the Vatican, the ordinary tunic, which was the sole garment worn by women when running, left bare the right shoulder and breast, and only reached to the upper third of the thighs. (M. M. Evans, *Chapters on Greek Dress*, p. 34.)

Among the Greeks who were inclined to accept the doctrines of Cynicism, it was held that, while shame is not unreasonable, what is good may be done and discussed before all men. There are a number of authorities who say that Crates and Hipparchia consummated their marriage in the presence of many spectators. Lactantius (*Inst.* iii, 15) says that the practice was common, but this Zeller is inclined to doubt. (Zeller, *Socrates and the Socratic Schools*, translated from the Third German Edition, 1897.)

"Among the Tyrrhenians, who carry their luxury to an extraordinary pitch, Timæus, in his first book, relates that the female servants wait on the men in a state of nudity. And Theopompus, in the forty-third book of his *History*, states that it is a law among the Tyrrhenians that all their women should be in common; and that the women pay the greatest attention to their persons, and often practice gymnastic exercises, naked, among the men, and sometimes with one another; for that it is not accounted shameful for them to be seen naked. . . . Nor is it reckoned among the Tyrrhenians at all disgraceful either to do or suffer anything in the open air, or to be seen while it is going on; for it is quite the custom of their country, and they are so far from thinking it disgraceful that they even say, when the master of the house is indulging his appetite, and anyone asks for him, that he is doing so and so, using the coarsest possible words. . . . And they are very beautiful, as is natural for people to be who live delicately, and who take care of their persons." (Athenæus, *Deipnosophists*, Yonge's translation, vol. iii, p. 829.)

Dennis throws doubt on the foregoing statement of Athenæus regarding the Tyrrhenians or Etruscans, and points out that the representations of women in Etruscan tombs shows them as clothed, even the breast being rarely uncovered. Nudity, he remarks, was a Greek, not an Etruscan, characteristic. "To the nudity of the Spartan women I need but refer; the Thessalian women are described by Persæus dancing at banquets naked, or with a very scanty covering (*apud* Athenæus, xiii, c. 86). The maidens of Chios wrestled naked with the youths in the gymnasium, which Athenæus (xiii, 20) pronounces to be 'a beautiful sight.' And at the marriage feast of Caranus, the Macedonian women tumblers performed naked before the guests (Athenæus, iv, 3)." (G. Dennis, *Cities and Cemeteries of Etruria*, 1883, vol. i, p. 321.)

In Rome, "when there was at first much less freedom in this matter than in Greece, the bath became common to both sexes, and though each had its basin and hot room apart, they could see each other, meet, speak, form intrigues, arrange meetings, and multiply adulteries. At first, the baths were so dark that men and women could wash side by side, without recognizing each other except by the voice; but soon the light of day was allowed to enter from every side. 'In the bath of Scipio,' said Seneca, 'there were narrow ventholes, rather than windows, hardly admitting enough light to outrage modesty; but nowadays, baths are called caves if they do not receive the sun's rays through large windows.' . . . Hadrian severely prohibited this mingling of men and women, and ordained separate lavacra for the sexes. Marcus Aurelius and Alexander Severus renewed this edict, but in the interval, Heliogabalus had authorized the sexes to meet in the baths." (Dufour, *Histoire de la Prostitution*, vol. ii, Ch. XVIII; *cf.* Smith's *Dictionary of Greek and Roman Antiquities*, Art. Balneæ.)

In Rome, according to ancient custom, actors were compelled to wear drawers (*subligaculum*) on the stage, in order to safeguard the modesty of Roman matrons. Respectable women, it seems, also always wore some sort of *subligaculum*, even sometimes when bathing. The name was also applied to a leathern girdle laced behind, which they were occasionally made to wear as a girdle of chastity. (Dufour, *op. cit.*, vol. ii, p. 150.) Greek women also wore a cloth round the loins when taking the bath, as did the men who bathed there; and a woman is represented bathing and wearing a sort of thin combinations reaching to the middle of the thigh. (Smith's *Dictionary, loc. cit.*) At a later period, St. Augustine refers to the *compestria*, the drawers or apron worn by young men who stripped for exercise in the *campus*. (*De Civitate Dei*, Bk. XIV, Ch. XVII.)

Lecky (*History of Morals*, vol. ii, p. 318), brings together instances of women, in both Pagan and early Christian times, who showed their modesty by drawing their garments around them, even at the moment that they were being brutally killed. Plutarch, in his essay on the "Virtues of Women,"—moralizing on the well-known story of the young women of Milesia, among whom an epidemic of suicide was only brought to an end by the decree that in future women who hanged themselves should be carried naked through the market-places,—observes: "They, who had no dread of the most terrible things in the world, death and pain, could not abide the imagination of dishonor, and exposure to shame, even after death."

In the second century the physician Aretæus, writing at Rome, remarks: "In many cases, owing to involuntary restraint from modesty at assemblies, and at banquets, the bladder becomes distended, and from the consequent loss of its contractile power, it no longer evacuates the urine." (*On the Causes and Symptoms of Acute Diseases*, Book II, Chapter X.)

Apuleius, writing in the second century, says: "Most women, in order to exhibit their native gracefulness and allurements, divest themselves of all their garments, and long to show their naked beauty, being conscious that they shall please more by the rosy redness of their skin than by the golden splendor of their robes." (Thomas Taylor's translation of *Metamorphosis*, p. 28.)

Christianity seems to have profoundly affected habits of thought and feeling by uniting together the merely natural emotion of sexual reserve with, on the one hand, the masculine virtue of modesty—*modestia* —and, on the other, the prescription of sexual abstinence. Tertullian admirably illustrates this confusion, and his treatises *De Pudicitia* and *De Cultu Feminarum* are instructive from the present point of view. In the latter he remarks (Book II, Chapter I): "Salvation—and not of women only, but likewise of men—consists in the exhibition, principally, of modesty. Since we are all the temple of God, modesty is the sacristan and priestess of that temple, who is to suffer nothing unclean or profane to enter it, for fear that the God who inhabits it should be offended. . . . Most women, either from simple ignorance or from dissimulation, have the hardihood so to walk as if modesty consisted only in the integrity of the flesh, and in turning away from fornication, and there were no need for anything else,—in dress and ornament, the studied graces of form,—wearing in their gait the self-same appearance as the women of the nations from whom the sense of *true* modesty is absent."

The earliest Christian ideal of modesty, not long maintained, is well shown in an epistle which, there is some reason to suppose, was written by Clement of Rome. "And if we see it to be requisite to stand and pray for the sake of the woman, and to speak words of exhortation and edification, we call the brethren and all the holy sisters and maidens, likewise all the other women who are there, with all modesty and becoming behavior, to come and feast on the truth. And those among us who are skilled in speaking, speak to them, and exhort them in those words which God has given us. And then we pray, and salute one another, the men the men. But the women and the maidens will wrap their hands in their garments; we also, with circumspection and with all purity, our eyes looking upward, shall wrap our right hand in our garments; and then they will come and give us the salutation on our right hand, wrapped in our garments. Then we go where God permits us." (*Two Epistles Concerning Virginity;*" Second Epistle, Chapter III, vol. xiv. Ante-Nicene Christian Library, p. 384.)

"Women will scarce strip naked before their own husbands, affecting a plausible pretense of modesty," writes Clement of Alexandria,
about the end of the second century, "but any others who wish may
see them at home, shut up in their own baths, for they are not ashamed
to strip before spectators, as if exposing their persons for sale. The
baths are opened promiscuously to men and women; and there they
strip for licentious indulgence (for, from looking, men get to loving),
as if their modesty had been washed away in the bath. Those who
have not become utterly destitute of modesty shut out strangers, but
bathe with their own servants, and strip naked before their slaves, and
are rubbed by them, giving to the crouching menial liberty to lust, by
permitting fearless handling, for those who are introduced before their
naked mistresses while in the bath, study to strip themselves in order to
show audacity in lust, casting off fear in consequence of the wicked
custom. The ancient athletes, ashamed to exhibit a man naked, preserved their modesty by going through the contest in drawers; but
these women, divesting themselves of their modesty along with their
chemise, wish to appear beautiful, but, contrary to their wish, are simply
proved to be wicked." (Clement of Alexandria, *Pædagogus*, Book III,
Chapter V. For elucidations of this passage, see Migne's *Patrologiæ
Cursus Completus*, vol. vii.) Promiscuous bathing was forbidden by the
early Apostolical Constitutions, but Cyprian, Bishop of Carthage, found
it necessary, in the third century, to upbraid even virgins vowed to
chastity for continuing the custom. "What of those," he asks, "who
frequent baths, who prostitute to eyes that are curious to lust, bodies
that are dedicated to chastity and modesty? They who disgracefully
behold naked men, and are seen naked by men? Do they not themselves afford enticement to vice? Do they not solicit and invite the
desires of those present to their own corruption and wrong? 'Let every
one,' say you, 'look to the disposition with which he comes thither:
my care is only that of refreshing and washing my poor body.' That
kind of defence does not clear you, nor does it excuse the crime of
lasciviousness and wantonness. Such a washing defiles; it does not
purify nor cleanse the limbs, but stains them. You behold no one
immodestly, but you, yourself, are gazed upon immodestly; you do
not pollute your eyes with disgraceful delight, but in delighting others
you yourself are polluted; you make a show of the bathing-place; the
places where you assemble are fouler than a theatre. There all modesty
is put off; together with the clothing of garments, the honor and
modesty of the body is laid aside, virginity is exposed, to be pointed
at and to be handled. . . . Let your baths be performed with women,
whose behavior is modest towards you." (Cyprian, *De Habitu Vir-
ginum*, cap. 19, 21.) The Church carried the same spirit among the
barbarians of northern Europe, and several centuries later the pro-

miscuous bathing of men and women was prohibited in some of the Penitentials. (The custom was, however, preserved here and there in Northern Europe, even to the end of the eighteenth century, or later. In Rudeck's *Geschichte der öffentlichen Sittlichkeit in Deutschland*, an interesting chapter, with contemporary illustrations, is devoted to this custom; also, Max Bauer, *Das Geschlechtsleben in der Deutschen Vergangenheit*, pp. 216-265.)

"Women," says Clement again, "should not seek to be graceful by avoiding broad drinking vessels that oblige them to stretch their mouths, in order to drink from narrow alabastra that cause them indecently to throw back the head, revealing to men their necks and breasts. The mere thought of what she is ought to inspire a woman with modesty. . . . On no account must a woman be permitted to show to a man any portion of her body naked, for fear lest both fall: the one by gazing eagerly, the other by delighting to attract those eager glances." (*Pædagogus*, Book II, Chapter V.)

James, Bishop of Nisibis, in the fourth century, was a man of great holiness. We are told by Thedoret that once, when James had newly come into Persia, it was vouchsafed to him to perform a miracle under the following circumstances: He chanced to pass by a fountain where young women were washing their linen, and, his modesty being profoundly shocked by the exposure involved in this occupation, he cursed the fountain, which instantly dried up, and he changed the hair of the girls from black to a sandy color. (Jortin, *Remarks on Ecclesiastical History*, vol. iii, p. 4.)

Procopius, writing in the sixth century after Christ, and narrating how the Empress Theodora, in early life, would often appear almost naked before the public in the theatre, adds that she would willingly have appeared altogether nude, but that "no woman is allowed to expose herself altogether, unless she wears at least short drawers over the lower part of the abdomen." Chrysostom mentions, at the end of the fourth century, that Arcadius attempted to put down the August festival (Majuma), during which women appeared naked in the theatres, or swimming in large baths.

In mediæval days, "ladies, at all events, as represented by the poets, were not, on the whole, very prudish. Meleranz surprised a lady who was taking a bath under a lime tree; the bath was covered with samite, and by it was a magnificent ivory bed, surrounded by tapestries representing the history of Paris and Helen, the destruction of Troy, the adventures of Æneas, etc. As Meleranz rides by, the lady's waiting-maids run away; she herself, however, with quick decision, raises the samite which covers the tub, and orders him to wait on her in place of the maids. He brings her shift and mantle, and shoes, and then stands aside till she is dressed; when she has placed herself on the bed,

she calls him back and commands him to drive away the flies while
she sleeps. Strange to say, the men are represented as more modest
than the women. When two maidens prepared a bath for Parzival,
and proposed to bathe him, according to custom, the inexperienced
young knight was shy, and would not enter the bath until they had
gone; on another occasion, he jumped quickly into bed when the maidens
entered the room. When Wolfdieterich was about to undress, he had to
ask the ladies who pressed around him to leave him alone for a short
time, as he was ashamed they should see him naked. When Amphons
of Spain, bewitched by his step-mother into a were-wolf, was at last
restored, and stood suddenly naked before her, he was greatly ashamed.
The maiden who healed Iwein was tender of his modesty. In his love-
madness, the hero wanders for a time naked through the wood; three
women find him asleep, and send a waiting-maid to annoint him with
salve; when he came to himself, the maiden hid herself. On the whole,
however, the ladies were not so delicate; they had no hesitation in
bathing with gentlemen, and on these occasions would put their finest
ornaments on their heads. I know no pictures of the twelfth and thir-
teenth centuries representing such a scene, but such baths in common
are clearly represented in miniatures of the fifteenth century." (A.
Schultz, *Das höfische Leben zur Zeit der Minnesänger*, vol. i, p. 225.)

"In the years 1450-70, the use of the cod-piece was introduced,
whereby the attributes of manhood were accentuated in the most
shameless manner. It was, in fact, the avowed aim at that period to
attract attention to these parts. The cod-piece was sometimes colored
differently from the rest of the garments, often stuffed out to enlarge
it artificially, and decorated with ribbons." (Rudeck, *Geschichte der
öffentlichen Sittlichkeit in Deutschland*, pp. 45-48; Dufour, *Histoire de
la Prostitution*, vol. vi, pp. 21-23. Groos refers to the significance of
this fashion, *Spiele der Menschen*, p. 337.)

"The first shirt began to be worn [in Germany] in the sixteenth
century. From this fact, as well as from the custom of public bathing,
we reach the remarkable result, that for the German people, the sight
of complete nakedness was the daily rule up to the sixteenth century.
Everyone undressed completely before going to bed, and, in the vapor-
baths, no covering was used. Again, the dances, both of the peasants
and the townspeople, were characterized by very high leaps into the
air. It was the chief delight of the dancers for the male to raise his
partner as high as possible in the air, so that her dress flew up. That
feminine modesty was in this respect very indifferent, we know from
countless references made in the fifteenth and sixteenth centuries. It
must not be forgotten that throughout the middle ages women wore
no underclothes, and even in the seventeenth century, the wearing of
drawers by Italian women was regarded as singular. That with the dis-

appearance of the baths, and the use of body-linen, a powerful influence was exerted on the creation of modesty, there can be little doubt." (Rudeck, *op. cit.*, pp. 57, 399, etc.)

In 1461, when Louis XI entered Paris, three very beautiful maidens, quite naked, represented the Syrens, and declaimed poems before him; they were greatly admired by the public. In 1468, when Charles the Bold entered Lille, he was specially pleased, among the various festivities, with a representation of the Judgment of Paris, in which the three goddesses were nude. When Charles the Fifth entered Antwerp, the most beautiful maidens of the city danced before him, in nothing but gauze, and were closely contemplated by Dürer, as he told his friend, Melancthon. (B. Ritter, "Nuditäten im Mittelalter," *Jahrbücher für Wissenschaft und Kunst*, 1855, p. 227; this writer shows how luxury, fashion, poverty, and certain festivals, all combined to make nudity familiar; *cf.* Fahne, *Der Carneval*, p. 249. Dulaure quotes many old writers concerning the important part played by nude persons in ancient festivals, *Des Divinités Génératrices*, Chapter XIV.)

Passek, a Polish officer who wrote an account of his campaigns, admired the ladies of Denmark in 1658, but considered their customs immodest. "Everyone sleeps naked as at birth, and none consider it shameful to dress or undress before others. No notice, even, is taken of the guest, and in the light one garment is taken off after another, even the chemise is hung on the hook. Then the door is bolted, the light blown out, and one goes to bed. As we blamed their ways, saying that among us a woman would not act so, even in the presence of her husband alone, they replied that they knew nothing of such shame, and that there was no need to be ashamed of limbs which God had created. Moreover, to sleep without a shift was good, because, like the other garments, it sufficiently served the body during the day. Also, why take fleas and other insects to bed with one? Although our men teased them in various ways, they would not change their habits." (Passek, *Denkwürdigkeiten*, German translation, p. 14.)

Until late in the seventeenth century, women in England, as well as France, suffered much in childbirth from the ignorance and superstition of incompetent midwives, owing to the prevailing conceptions of modesty, which rendered it impossible (as it is still, to some extent, in some semi-civilized lands) for male physicians to attend them. Dr. Willoughby, of Derby, tells how, in 1658, he had to creep into the chamber of a lying-in woman on his hands and knees, in order to examine her unperceived. In France, Clement was employed secretly to attend the mistresses of Louis XIV in their confinements; to the first he was conducted blindfold, while the King was concealed among the bed-curtains, and the face of the lady was enveloped in a network of lace.

(E. Malins, "Midwifery and Midwives," *British Medical Journal*, June 22, 1901; Witkowski, *Histoire des Accouchements*, 1887, pp. 689 *et seq.*) Even until the Revolution, the examination of women in France in cases of rape or attempted outrage was left to a jury of matrons. In old English manuals of midwifery, even in the early nineteenth century, we still find much insistence on the demands of modesty. Thus, Dr. John Burns, of Glasgow, in his *Principles of Midwifery*, states that "some women, from motives of false delicacy, are averse from examination until the pains become severe." He adds that "it is usual for the room to be darkened, and the bed-curtains drawn close, during an examination." Many old pictures show the accoucheur groping in the dark, beneath the bed-clothes, to perform operations on women in childbirth. (A. Kind, "Das Weib als Gebärerin in der Kunst," *Geschlecht und Gesellschaft*, Bd. II, Heft 5, p. 203.)

In Iceland, Winkler stated in 1861 that he sometimes slept in the same room as a whole family; "it is often the custom for ten or more persons to use the same room for living in and sleeping, young and old, master and servant, male and female, and from motives of economy, all the clothes, without exception, are removed." (G. Winkler, *Island; seine Bewohner*, etc., pp. 107, 110.)

"At Cork," saye Fynes Moryson, in 1617, "I have seen with these eyes young maids stark naked grinding corn with certain stones to make cakes thereof." (Moryson, *Itinerary*, Part 3, Book III, Chapter V.)

"In the more remote parts of Ireland," Moryson elsewhere says, where the English laws and manners are unknown, "the very chief of the Irish, men as well as women, go naked in very winter-time, only having their privy parts covered with a rag of linen, and their bodies with a loose mantle. This I speak of my own experience." He goes on to tell of a Bohemian baron, just come from the North of Ireland, who "told me in great earnestness that he, coming to the house of Ocane, a great lord among them, was met at the door with sixteen women, all naked, excepting their loose mantles; whereof eight or ten were very fair, and two seemed very nymphs, with which strange sight, his eyes being dazzled, they led him into the house, and then sitting down by the fire with crossed legs, like tailors, and so low as could not but offend chaste eyes, desired him to sit down with them. Soon after, Ocane, the lord of the country, came in, all naked excepting a loose mantle, and shoes, which he put off as soon as he came in, and entertaining the baron after his best manner in the Latin tongue, desired him to put off his apparel, which he thought to be a burthen to him, and to sit naked by the fire with this naked company. But the baron . . . for shame, durst not put off his apparel." (*Ib.* Part 3, Book IV, Chapter II.)

Coryat, when traveling in Italy in the early part of the seventeenth century, found that in Lombardy many of the women and children wore only smocks, or shirts, in the hot weather. At Venice and Padua, he found that wives, widows, and maids, walk with naked breasts, many with backs also naked, almost to the middle. (Coryat, *Crudities*, 1611. The fashion of *décolleté* garments, it may be remarked, only began in the fourteenth century; previously, the women of Europe generally covered themselves up to the neck.)

In Northern Italy, some years ago, a fire occurred at night in a house in which two girls were sleeping, naked, according to the custom. One threw herself out and was saved, the other returned for a garment, and was burnt to death. The narrator of the incident [a man] expressed strong approval of the more modest girl's action. (Private communication.) It may be added that the custom of sleeping naked is still preserved, also (according to Lippert and Stratz), in Jutland, in Iceland, in some parts of Norway, and sometimes even in Berlin.

Lady Mary Wortley Montague writes in 1717, of the Turkish ladies at the baths at Sophia: "The first sofas were covered with cushions and rich carpets, on which sat the ladies, and on the second, their slaves behind them, but without any distinction of rank in their dress, all being in a state of Nature; that is, in plain English, stark naked, without any beauty or defect concealed. Yet there was not the least wanton smile or immodest gesture among them. They walked and moved with the same majestic grace which Milton describes of our general mother. I am here convinced of the truth of a reflection I had often made, that if it was the fashion to go naked, the face would be hardly observed." (*Letters and Works*, 1866, vol. i, p. 285.)

At St. Petersburg, in 1774, Sir Nicholas Wraxall observed "the promiscuous bathing of not less than two hundred persons, of both sexes. There are several of these public bagnios," he adds, "in Petersburg, and every one pays a few copecks for admittance. There are, indeed, separate spaces for the men and women, but they seem quite regardless of this distinction, and sit or bathe in a state of absolute nudity among each other." (Sir N. Wraxall, *A Tour Through Some of the Northern Parts of Europe*, 3d ed., 1776, p. 248.) It is still usual for women in the country parts of Russia to bathe naked in the streams.

In 1790, Wedgwood wrote to Flaxman: "The nude is so general in the work of the ancients, that it will be very difficult to avoid the introduction of naked figures. On the other hand, it is absolutely necessary to do so, or to keep the pieces for our own use; for none, either male or female, of the present generation will take or apply them as furniture if the figures are naked." (Meteyard, *Life of Wedgwood*, vol. ii, p. 589.)

Mary Wollstonecraft quotes (for reprobation and not for approval) the following remarks: "The lady who asked the question whether women may be instructed in the modern system of botany, was accused of ridiculous prudery; nevertheless, if she had proposed the question to me, I should certainly have answered: 'They cannot!'" She further quotes from an educational book: "It would be needless to caution you against putting your hand, by chance, under your neck-handkerchief; for a modest woman never did so." (Mary Wollstone-craft, *The Rights of Woman*, 1792, pp. 277, 289.)

At the present time a knowledge of the physiology of plants is not usually considered inconsistent with modesty, but a knowledge of animal physiology is still so considered by many. Dr. H. R. Hopkins, of New York, wrote in 1895, regarding the teaching of physiology: "How can we teach growing girls the functions of the various parts of the human body, and still leave them their modesty? That is the practical question that has puzzled me for years."

In England, the use of drawers was almost unknown among women half a century ago, and was considered immodest and unfeminine. Tilt, a distinguished gynecologist of that period, advocated such garments, made of fine calico, and not to descend below the knee, on hygienic grounds. "Thus understood," he added, "the adoption of drawers will doubtless become more general in this country, as, being worn without the knowledge of the general observer, they will be robbed of the prejudice usually attached to an appendage deemed masculine." (Tilt, *Elements of Health*, 1852, p. 193.) Drawers came into general use among women during the third quarter of the nineteenth century.

Drawers are an Oriental garment, and seem to have reached Europe through Venice, the great channel of communication with the East. Like many other refinements of decency and cleanliness, they were at first chiefly cultivated by prostitutes, and, on this account, there was long a prejudice against them. Even at the present day, it is said that in France, a young peasant girl will exclaim, if asked whether she wears drawers: "I wear drawers, Madame? A respectable girl!" Drawers, however, quickly became acclimatized in France, and Dufour (*op. cit.*, vol. vi, p. 28) even regards them as essentially a French garment. They were introduced at the Court towards the end of the fourteenth century, and in the sixteenth century were rendered almost necessary by the new fashion of the *vertugale*, or farthingale. In 1615, a lady's *caleçons* are referred to as apparently an ordinary garment. It is noteworthy that in London, in the middle of the same century, young Mrs. Pepys, who was the daughter of French parents, usually wore drawers, which were seemingly of the closed kind. (*Diary of S. Pepys*, ed. Wheatley, May 15, 1663, vol. iii.) They were probably not worn by Englishwomen, and even in France, with the decay of the farthingale, they seem to have dropped out of use during the seventeenth century. In a technical and very complete book, *L'Art de la Lingerie*, published in 1771, women's drawers are not even mentioned, and Mercier (*Tableau de Paris*, 1783, vol. vii, p. 54) says that, except actresses, Parisian women do not wear drawers. Even by ballet dancers and actresses on the stage, they were not invariably worn. Camargo, the famous dancer, who first shortened the skirt in dancing, early in the eighteenth century, always observed great decorum, never showing the leg above the knee; when appealed to as to whether she wore drawers, she replied that she could not possibly appear without such a "precaution." But they were not necessarily worn by dancers, and in 1727 a young *ballerina*, having had her skirt accidentally torn away by a piece of stage machinery, the police issued an order that in future no actress or dancer should appear on the stage without drawers; this regulation does not appear, however, to have been long strictly maintained, though Schulz (*Ueber Paris und die Pariser*, p. 145) refers to it as in force in 1791. (The obscure origin and history of feminine drawers have been discussed from time to time in the *Intermédiaire des Chercheurs et Curieux*, especially vols. xxv, lii, and liii.)

Prof. Irving Rosse, of Washington, refers to "New England prudishness," and "the colossal modesty of some New York policemen, who in certain cases want to give written, rather than oral testimony." He adds: "I have known this sentiment carried to such an extent in a Massachusetts small town, that a shop-keeper was obliged to drape a small, but innocent, statuette displayed in his window." (Irving Rosse, *Virginia Medical Monthly*, October, 1892.) I am told that popular feeling in South Africa would not permit the exhibition of the nude in the Art Collections of Cape Town. Even in Italy, nude statues are disfigured by the addition of tin fig-leaves, and sporadic manifestations of horror at the presence of nude statues, even when of most classic type, are liable to occur in all parts of Europe, including France and Germany. (Examples of this are recorded from time to time in *Sexualreform*, published as an appendix to *Geschlecht und Gesellschaft*.)

Some years ago, (1898), it was stated that the Philadelphia *Ladies' Home Journal* had decided to avoid, in future, all reference to ladies' under-linen, because "the treatment of this subject in print calls for *minutiæ* of detail which is extremely and pardonably offensive to refined and sensitive women."

"A man, married twenty years, told me that he had never seen his wife entirely nude. Such concealment of the external reproductive organs, by married people, appears to be common. Judging from my own inquiry, very few women care to look upon male nakedness, and many women, though not wanting in esthetic feeling, find no beauty in man's form. Some are positively repelled by the sight of nakedness, even that of a husband or lover. On the contrary, most men delight in gazing upon the uncovered figure of women. It seems that only highly-cultivated and imaginative women enjoy the spectacle of a finely-shaped nude man (especially after attending art classes, and drawing from the nude, as I am told by a lady artist). Or else the majority of women dissemble their curiosity or admiration. A woman of seventy, mother of several children, said to a young wife with whom I am acquainted: 'I have never seen a naked man in my life.' This old lady's sister confessed that she had never looked at *her own* nakedness in the whole course of her life. She said that it 'frightened' her. She was the mother of three sons. A maiden woman of the same family told her niece that women were 'disgusting, because they have monthly discharges.' The niece suggested that women have no choice in the matter, to which the aunt replied: 'I know that; but it doesn't make them less disgusting.' I have heard of a girl who died from hæmorrhage of the womb, refusing, through shame, to make the ailment known to her family. The misery suffered by some women at the anticipation of a medical examination, appears to be very acute. Husbands have told me of brides who sob and tremble with fright on the wedding-night, the hysteria being sometimes alarming. E, aged 25, refused her husband for six weeks after marriage, exhibiting the greatest fear of his approach. Ignorance of the nature of the sexual connection is often the cause of exaggerated alarm. In Jersey, I used to hear of a bride who ran to the window and screamed 'murder,' on the wedding-night." (Private communication.)

At the present day it is not regarded as incompatible with modesty to exhibit the lower part of the thigh when in swimming costume, but it is immodest to exhibit the upper part of the thigh. In swimming competitions, a minimum of clothing must be combined with the demands of modesty. In England, the regulations of the Swimming Clubs affiliated to the Amateur Swimming Association, require that the male swimmer's costume shall extend not less than eight inches from the bifurcation downward, and that the female swimmer's costume shall extend to within not more than three inches from the knee. (A prolonged discussion, we are told, arose as to whether the costume should come to one, two, or three inches from the knee, and the proposal of the youngest lady swimmer present, that the costume ought to be very scanty, met with little approval.) The modesty of women is thus seen to be greater than that of men by, roughly speaking, about two inches. The same difference may be seen in the sleeves; the male sleeve must extend for two inches, the female sleeve four inches, down the arm. (Daily Papers, September 26, 1898.)

"At ———, bathing in a state of Nature was *de rigueur* for the *élite* of the bathers, while our Sunday visitors from the slums frequently made a great point of wearing bathing costumes; it was frequently noticed that those who were most anxious to avoid exposing their persons were distinguished by the foulness of their language. My impression was that their foul-mindedness deprived them of the consciousness of safety from coarse jests. If I were bathing alone among blackguards, I should probably feel uncomfortable myself, if without costume." (Private communication.)

A lady in a little city of the south of Italy, told Paola Lombroso that young middle-class girls there are not allowed to go out except to Mass, and cannot even show themselves at the window except under their mother's eye; yet they do not think it necessary to have a cabin when sea-bathing, and even dispense with a bathing costume without consciousness of immodesty. (P. Lombroso, *Archivio di Psichiatria*, 1901, p. 306.)

"A woman mentioned to me that a man came to her and told her in confidence his distress of mind: he feared he had *corrupted* his wife because she got into a bath in his presence, with her baby, and enjoyed his looking at her splashing about. He was deeply distressed, thinking he must have done her harm, and destroyed her modesty. The woman to whom this was said felt naturally indignant, but also it gave her the feeling as if every man may secretly despise a woman for the very things he teaches her, and only meets her confiding delight with regret or dislike." (Private communication.)

"Women will occasionally be found to hide diseases and symptoms from a bashfulness and modesty so great and perverse as to be hardly credible," writes Dr. W. Wynn Westcott, an experienced coroner. "I have known several cases of female deaths, reported as sudden, and of cause unknown, when the medical man called in during the latter hours of life has been quite unaware that his lady patient was dying of gangrene of a strangulated femoral hernia, or was bleeding to death from the bowel, or from ruptured varices of the vulva." (*British Medical Journal*, Feb. 29, 1908.)

The foregoing selection of facts might, of course, be indefinitely enlarged, since I have not generally quoted from any previous collection of facts bearing on the question of modesty. Such collections may be found in Ploss and Max Bartels *Das Weib*, a work that is constantly appearing in new and enlarged editions; Herbert Spencer, *Descriptive Sociology* (especially under such headings as "Clothing," "Moral Sentiments," and "Æsthetic Products"); W. G. Sumner, *Folkways*, Ch. XI; Mantegazza, *Amori degli Uomini*, Chapter II; Westermarck, *Marriage*, Chapter IX; Letourneau, *L'Evolution de la Morale*, pp. 126 *et seq.;* G. Mortimer, *Chapters on Human Love*, Chapter IV; and in the general anthropological works of Waitz-Gerland, Peschel, Ratzel and others.

II.

Modesty an Agglomeration of Fears—Children in Relation to Modesty—Modesty in Animals—The Attitude of the Medicean Venus—The Sexual Factor of Modesty Based on Sexual Periodicity and on the Primitive Phenomena of Courtship—The Necessity of Seclusion in Primitive Sexual Intercourse—The Meaning of Coquetry—The Sexual Charm of Modesty—Modesty as an Expression of Feminine Erotic Impulse—The Fear of Causing Disgust as a Factor of Modesty—The Modesty of Savages in Regard to Eating in the Presence of Others—The Sacro-Pubic Region as a Focus of Disgust—The Idea of Ceremonial Uncleanliness—The Custom of Veiling the Face—Ornaments and Clothing—Modesty Becomes Concentrated in the Garment—The Economic Factor in Modesty—The Contribution of Civilization to Modesty—The Elaboration of Social Ritual.

THAT modesty—like all the closely-allied emotions—is based on fear, one of the most primitive of the emotions, seems to be fairly evident.[1] The association of modesty and fear is even a very ancient observation, and is found in the fragments of Epicharmus, while according to one of the most recent definitions, "modesty is the timidity of the body." Modesty is, indeed, an agglomeration of fears, especially, as I hope to show, of two important and distinct fears: one of much earlier than human origin, and supplied solely by the female; the other of more distinctly human character, and of social, rather than sexual, origin.

A child left to itself, though very bashful, is wholly devoid of modesty.[2] Everyone is familiar with the shocking *inconven-*

---

[1] Fliess (*Die Beziehungen zwischen Nase und weiblichen Geschlechts-Organen*, p. 194) remarks on the fact that, in the Bible narrative of Eden, shame and fear are represented as being brought into the world together: Adam feared God because he was naked. Melinaud ("Psychologie de la Pudeur," *La Revue*, Nov. 15, 1901) remarks that shame differs from modesty in being, not a fear, but a kind of grief; this position seems untenable.

[2] Bashfulness in children has been dealt with by Professor Baldwin; see especially his *Mental Development in the Child and the Race*, Chapter VI, pp. 146 *et seq.*, and *Social Interpretations in Mental Development*, Chapter VI.

ances of children in speech and act, with the charming ways in which they innocently disregard the conventions of modesty their elders thrust upon them, or, even when anxious to carry them out, wholly miss the point at issue: as when a child thinks that to put a little garment round the neck satisfies the demands of modesty. Julius Moses states that modesty in the uncovering of the sexual parts begins about the age of four. But in cases when this occurs it is difficult to exclude teaching and example. Under civilized conditions the convention of modesty long precedes its real development. Bell has found that in love affairs before the age of nine the girl is more aggressive than the boy and that at that age she begins to be modest.[1] It may fairly be said that complete development of modesty only takes place at the advent of puberty.[2] We may admit, with Perez, one of the very few writers who touch on the evolution of this emotion, that modesty may appear at a very early age if sexual desire appears early.[3] We should not, however, be justified in asserting that on this account modesty is a purely sexual phenomenon. The social impulses also develop about puberty, and to that coincidence the compound nature of the emotion of modesty may well be largely due.

The sexual factor is, however, the simplest and most primitive element of modesty, and may, therefore, be mentioned first. Anyone who watches a bitch, not in heat, when approached by a dog with tail wagging gallantly, may see the beginnings of modesty. When the dog's attentions become a little too marked, the bitch squats firmly down on the front legs and hind quarters though when the period of œstrus comes her modesty may be flung to the air and she eagerly turns her hind quarters to her admirer's nose and elevates her tail high in the air. Her attitude of refusal is equivalent, that is to say, to that which in the human race is typified by the classical example of womanly

---

1 Bell, "A Preliminary Study of the Emotion of Love Between the Sexes," *American Journal Psychology*, July, 1902.

2 Professor Starbuck (*Psychology of Religion*, Chapter XXX) refers to unpublished investigations showing that recognition of the rights of others also exhibits a sudden increment at the age of puberty.

3 Perez, *L'Enfant de Trois à Sept Ans*, 1886, pp. 267-277.

modesty in the Medicean Venus, who withdraws the pelvis, at
the same time holding one hand to guard the pubes, the other to
guard the breasts.[1] The essential expression in each case is that
of defence of the sexual centers against the undesired advances of
the male.[2]

Stratz, who criticizes the above statement, argues (with photographs of nude women in illustration) that the normal type of
European surprised modesty is shown by an attitude in which the
arms are crossed over the breast, the most sexually attractive region,
while the thighs are pressed together, one being placed before the other,
the shoulder raised and the back slightly curved; occasionally, he adds,
the hands may be used to cover the face, and then the crossed arms conceal the breasts. The Medicean Venus, he remarks, is only a pretty
woman coquetting with her body. Canova's Venus in the Pitti (who has
drapery in front of her, and presses her arms across her breast) being
a more accurate rendering of the attitude of modesty. But Stratz admits that when a surprised woman is gazed at for some time, she turns
her head away, sinks or closes her eyes, and covers her pubes (or any
other part she thinks is being gazed at) with one hand, while with
the other she hides her breast or face. This he terms the secondary
expression of modesty. (Stratz, *Die Frauenkleidung*, third ed., p. 23.)

It is certainly true that the Medicean Venus merely represents
an artistic convention, a generalized tradition, not founded on exact
and precise observation of the gestures of modesty, and it is equally
true that all the instinctive movements noted by Stratz are commonly
resorted to by a woman whose nakedness is surprised. But in the
absence of any series of carefully recorded observations, one may doubt

---

[1] It must be remembered that the Medicean Venus is merely a comparatively recent and familiar embodiment of a natural attitude which
is very ancient, and had impressed sculptors at a far earlier period.
Reinach, indeed, believes ("La Sculpture en Europe," *L'Anthropologie*,
No. 5, 1895) that the hand was first brought to the breast to press out
the milk, and expresses the idea of exuberance, and that the attitude
of the Venus of Medici as a symbol of modesty came later; he remarks that, as regards both hands, this attitude may be found in a
figurine of Cyprus, 2,000 years before Christ. This is, no doubt, correct, and I may add that Babylonian figurines of Ishtar, the goddess
of fertility, represent her as clasping her hands to her breasts or
her womb.

[2] When there is no sexual fear the impulse of modesty may be
entirely inhibited. French ladies under the old Régime (as A. Franklin
points out in his *Vie Privée d'Autrefois*) sometimes showed no modesty
towards their valets, not admitting the possibility of any sexual advance, and a lady would, for example, stand up in her bath while a
valet added hot water by pouring it between her separated feet.

whether the distinction drawn by Stratz between the primary and the secondary expression of modesty can be upheld as the general rule, while it is most certainly not true for every case. When a young women is surprised in a state of nakedness by a person of the opposite, or even of the same, sex, it is her instinct to conceal the primary centers of sexual function and attractiveness, in the first place, the pubes, in the second place the breasts. The exact attitude and the particular gestures of the hands in achieving the desired end vary with the individual, and with the circumstances. The hand may not be used at all as a veil, and, indeed, the instinct of modesty itself may inhibit the use of the hand for the protection of modesty (to turn the back towards the beholder is often the chief impulse of blushing modesty, even when clothed), but the application of the hand to this end is primitive and natural. The lowly Fuegian woman, depicted by Hyades and Deniker, who holds her hand to her pubes while being photographed, is one at this point with the Roman Venus described by Ovid (*Ars Amatoria*, Book II) :—

> Ipsa Venus pubem, quoties velamnia ponit,
> Protegitur læva semireducta manus."

It may be added that young men of the lower social classes, at all events in England, when bathing at the seaside in complete nudity, commonly grasp the sexual organs with one hand, for concealment, as they walk up from the sea.

The sexual modesty of the female animal is rooted in the sexual periodicity of the female, and is an involuntary expression of the organic fact that the time for love is not now. Inasmuch as this fact is true of the greater part of the lives of all female animals below man, the expression itself becomes so habitual that it even intrudes at those moments when it has ceased to be in place. We may see this again illustrated in the bitch, who, when in heat, herself runs after the male, and again turns to flee, perhaps only submitting with much persuasion to his embrace. Thus, modesty becomes something more than a mere refusal of the male; it becomes an invitation to the male, and is mixed up with his ideas of what is sexually desirable in the female. This would alone serve to account for the existence of modesty as a psychical secondary sexual character. In this sense, and in this sense only, we may say, with Colin Scott, that "the feeling of shame is made to be overcome," and is thus correlated with its physical representative, the hymen, in the rupture of which, as Groos remarks, there is, in some degree, a disruption also of modesty. The sexual modesty of the female is thus an inevitable by-product of the naturally aggressive attitude of the male in sexual relationships, and the naturally defensive attitude of the female, this again being founded on the fact that, while—in man and the species allied to him—the sexual function in the female is periodic, and during most of life a function to be guarded from the opposite sex, in the male it rarely or never needs to be so guarded.[1]

Both male and female, however, need to guard themselves during the exercise of their sexual activities from jealous rivals, as well as from enemies who might take advantage of their position to attack them. It is highly probable that this is one important sexual factor in the constitution of modesty, and it helps to explain how the male, not less than the female, cultivates modesty, and shuns publicity, in the exercise of sexual functions. Northcote has especially emphasized this element in modesty, as originating in the fear of rivals. "That from this seeking after secrecy from motives of fear should arise an instinctive feeling that the sexual act must always be hidden, is a natural enough sequence. And since it is not a long step between thinking of an act as needing concealment and thinking of it as wrong, it is easily conceivable that sexual intercourse comes to be regarded as a stolen and therefore, in some degree, a sinful pleasure."[2]

Animals in a state of nature usually appear to seek seclusion for sexual intercourse, although this instinct is lost under domestication. Even the lowest savages, also, if uncorrupted by civilized influences, seek the solitude of the forest or the pro-

---

[1] I do not hereby mean to deny a certain degree of normal periodicity even to the human male; but such periodicity scarcely involves any element of sexual fear or attitude of sexual defence, in man because it is too slight to involve complete latency of the sexual functions, in other species because latency of sexual function in the male is always accompanied by corresponding latency in the female.

[2] H. Northcote, *Christianity and the Sex Problem*, p. 8. Crawley had previously argued (*The Mystic Rose*, pp. 134, 180) that this same necessity for solitude during the performance of nutritive, sexual, and excretory functions, is a factor in investing such functions with a potential sacredness, so that the concealment of them became a religious duty.

tection of their huts for the same purpose; the rare cases in which coitus is public seem usually to involve a ceremonial or social observance, rather than mere personal gratification. At Loango, for instance, it would be highly improper to have intercourse in an exposed spot; it must only be performed inside the hut, with closed doors, at night, when no one is present.[1]

It is on the sexual factor of modesty, existing in a well-marked form even among animals, that coquetry is founded. I am glad to find myself on this point in agreement with Professor Groos, who, in his elaborate study of the play-instinct, has reached the same conclusion. So far from being the mere heartless play by which a woman shows her power over a man, Groos points out that coquetry possesses "high biological and psychological significance," being rooted in the antagonism between the sexual instinct and inborn modesty. He refers to the roe, who runs away from the stag—but in a circle. (Groos, *Die Spiele der Menschen*, 1899, p. 339; also the same author's *Die Spiele der Thiere*, pp. 288 *et seq.*) Another example of coquetry is furnished by the female kingfisher (*Alcedo ispida*), which will spend all the morning in teasing and flying away from the male, but is careful constantly to look back, and never to let him out of her sight. (Many examples are given by Büchner, in *Liebe und Liebesleben in der Tierwelt*.) Robert Müller (*Sexualbiologie*, p. 302) emphasizes the importance of coquetry as a lure to the male.

"It is quite true," a lady writes to me in a private letter, "that 'coquetry is a poor thing,' and that every milkmaid can assume it, but a woman uses it principally in self-defence, while she is finding out what the man himself is like." This is in accordance with the remark of Marro, that modesty enables a woman "to put lovers to the test, in order to select him who is best able to serve the natural ends of love." It is doubtless the necessity for this probationary period, as a test of masculine qualities, which usually leads a woman to repel instinctively a too hasty and impatient suitor, for, as Arthur Macdonald remarks, "It seems to be instinctive in young women to reject the impetuous lover, without the least consideration of his character, ability, and fitness."

This essential element in courtship, this fundamental attitude of pursuer and pursued, is clearly to be seen even in animals and savages; it is equally pronounced in the most civilized men and women, manifesting itself in crude and subtle ways alike.

---

[1] *Zeitschrift für Ethnologie*, 1878, p. 26.

Shakespeare's Angelo, whose virtue had always resisted the temptations of vice, discovered at last that

"modesty may more betray our sense
Than woman's lightness."

"What," asked the wise Montaigne, "is the object of that virginal shame, that sedate coldness, that severe countenance, that pretence of not knowing things which they understand better than we who teach them, except to increase in us the desire to conquer and curb, to trample under our appetite, all that ceremony and those obstacles? For there is not only matter for pleasure, but for pride also, in ruffling and debauching that soft sweetness and infantine modesty."[1] The masculine attitude in the face of feminine coyness may easily pass into a kind of sadism, but is nevertheless in its origin an innocent and instinctive impulse. Restif de la Bretonne, describing his own shame and timidity as a pretty boy whom the girls would run after and kiss, adds: "It is surprising that at the same time I would imagine the pleasure I should have in embracing a girl who resisted, in inspiring her with timidity, in making her flee and in pursuing her; that was a part which I burned to play.[2] It is the instinct of the sophisticated and the unsophisticated alike. The Arabs have developed an erotic ideal of sensuality, but they emphasize the importance of feminine modesty, and declare that the best woman is "she who sees not men and whom they see not."[3] This deep-rooted modesty of women towards men in courtship is intimately interwoven with the marriage customs and magic rites of even the most primitive peoples, and has survived in many civilized practices to-day.[4] The prostitute must be able to simulate the modesty she may often be far from feeling, and the immense erotic advantage of the innocent over the vicious woman lies largely in the fact that in her the exquisite reactions of

---

[1] *Essais*, livre ii, Ch. XV.

[2] *Monsieur Nicolas*, vol. i, p. 89.

[3] Lane, *Arabian Society*, p. 228. The Arab insistence on the value of virginal modesty is well brought out in one of the most charming stories of the *Arabian Nights*, "The History of the Mirror of Virginity."

[4] This has especially been emphasized by Crawley, *The Mystic Rose*, pp. 181, 324 *et seq.*, 353.

modesty are fresh and vigorous. "I cannot imagine anything that is more sexually exciting," remarks Hans Menjago, "than to observe a person of the opposite sex, who, by some external or internal force, is compelled to fight against her physical modesty. The more modest she is the more sexually exciting is the picture she presents."[1] It is notable that even in abnormal, as well as in normal, erotic passion the desire is for innocent and not for vicious women, and, in association with this, the desired favor to be keenly relished must often be gained by sudden surprise and not by mutual agreement. A foot fetichist writes to me: "It is the *stolen* glimpse of a pretty foot or ankle which produces the greatest effect on me." A urolagnic symbolist was chiefly excited by the act of urination when he caught a young woman unawares in the act. A fetichistic admirer of the nates only desired to see this region in innocent girls, not in prostitutes. The exhibitionist, almost invariably, only exposes himself to apparently respectable girls.

A Russian correspondent, who feels this charm of women in a particularly strong degree, is inclined to think that there is an element of perversity in it. "In the erotic action of the idea of feminine enjoyment," he writes, "I think there are traces of a certain perversity. In fact, owing to the impressions of early youth, woman (even if we feel contempt for her in theory) is placed above us, on a certain pedestal, as an almost sacred being, and the more so because mysterious. Now sensuality and sexual desire are considered as rather vulgar, and a little dirty, even ridiculous and degrading, not to say bestial. The woman who enjoys it, is, therefore, rather like a profaned altar, or, at least, like a divinity who has descended on to the earth. To give enjoyment to a woman is, therefore, like perpetrating a sacrilege, or at least like taking a liberty with a god. The feelings bequeathed to us by a long social civilization maintain themselves in spite of our rational and deliberate opinions. Reason tells us that there is nothing evil in sexual enjoyment, whether in man or woman, but an unconscious feeling directs our emotions, and this feeling (having a germ that was placed in modern men by Christianity, and perhaps by still older religions) says that woman *ought* to be an absolutely pure being, with ethereal sensations, and that in her sexual enjoyment is out of place, improper, scandalous. To arouse sexual emotions in a woman, if not to profane a sacred host, is, at all events, the staining of an immacu-

---

[1] *Geschlecht und Gesellschaft*, Bd. II, Heft 8, p. 358.

late peplos; if not sacrilege, it is, at least, irreverence or impertinence. For all men, the chaster a woman is, the more agreeable it is to bring her to the orgasm. That is felt as a triumph of the body over the soul, of sin over virtue, of earth over heaven. There is something diabolic in such pleasure, especially when it is felt by a man intoxicated with love, and full of religious respect for the virgin of his election. This feeling is, from a rational point of view, absurd, and in its tendencies, immoral; but it is delicious in its sacredly voluptuous subtelty. Defloration thus has its powerful fascination in the respect consciously or unconsciously felt for woman's chastity. In marriage, the feeling is yet more complicated: in deflowering his bride, the Christian (that is, any man brought up in a Christian civilization) has the feeling of committing a sort of sin (for the "flesh" is, for him, always connected with sin) which, by a special privilege, has for him become legitimate. He has received a special permit to corrupt innocence. Hence, the peculiar prestige for civilized Christians, of the wedding night, sung by Shelley, in ecstatic verses:—

> 'Oh, joy! Oh, fear! What will be done
> In the absence of the sun!'"

This feeling has, however, its normal range, and is not, *per se*, a perversity, though it may doubtless become so when unduly heightened by Christian sentiment, and especially if it leads, as to some extent it has led in my Russian correspondent, to an abnormal feeling of the sexual attraction of girls who have only or scarcely reached the age of puberty. The sexual charm of this period of girlhood is well illustrated in many of the poems of Thomas Ashe, and it is worthy of note, as perhaps supporting the contention that this attraction is based on Christian feeling, that Ashe had been a clergyman. An attentiveness to the woman's pleasure remains, in itself, very far from a perversion, but increases, as Colin Scott has pointed out, with civilization, while its absence—the indifference to the partner's pleasure—is a perversion of the most degraded kind.

There is no such instinctive demand on the woman's part for innocence in the man.[1] In the nature of things that could

---

[1] This, however, is not always or altogether true of experienced women. Thus, the Russian correspondent already referred to, who as a youth was accustomed, partly out of shyness, to feign complete ignorance of sexual matters, informs me that it repeatedly happened to him at this time that young married women took pleasure in imposing on themselves, not without shyness but with evident pleasure, the task of initiating him, though they always hastened to tell him that it was for his good, to preserve him from bad women and masturbation. Prostitutes, also, often take pleasure in innocent men, and Hans Ostwald

not be. Such emotion is required for properly playing the part of the pursued; it is by no means an added attraction on the part of the pursuer. There is, however, an allied and corresponding desire which is very often clearly or latently present in the woman: a longing for pleasure that is stolen or forbidden. It is a mistake to suppose that this is an indication of viciousness or perversity. It appears to be an impulse that occurs quite naturally in altogether innocent women. The exciting charm of the risky and dangerous naturally arises on a background of feminine shyness and timidity. We may trace its recognition at a very early stage of history in the story of Eve and the forbidden fruit that has so often been the symbol of the masculine organs of sex. It is on this ground that many have argued the folly of laying external restrictions on women in matters of love. Thus in quoting the great Italian writer who afterwards became Pope Pius II, Robert Burton remarked: "I am of Æneas Sylvius' mind, 'Those jealous Italians do very ill to lock up their wives; for women are of such a disposition they will mostly covet that which is denied most, and offend least when they have free liberty to trespass.' "[1]

It is the spontaneous and natural instinct of the lover to desire modesty in his mistress, and by no means any calculated opinion on his part that modesty is the sign of sexual emotion. It remains true, however, that modesty is an expression of feminine erotic impulse. We have here one of the instances, of which there are so many, of that curious and instinctive harmony by which Nature has sought the more effectively to bring about the ends of courtship. As to the fact itself there can be little doubt. It constantly forces itself on the notice of careful observers, and has long been decided in the affirmative by those who have discussed the matter. Venette, one

tells (*Sexual-Probleme*, June, 1908, p. 357) of a prostitute who fell violently in love with a youth who had never known a woman before; she had never met an innocent man before, and it excited her greatly. And I have been told of an Italian prostitute who spoke of the exciting pleasure which an unspoilt youth gave her by his freshness, *tutta questa freschezza.*

[1] *Anatomy of Melancholy*, Part III, Sect. III. Mem. IV. Subs. I.

of the earliest writers on the psychology of sex, after discussing the question at length, decided that the timid woman is a more ardent lover than the bold woman.[1]   "It is the most pudent girl," remarked Restif de la Bretonne whose experience of women was so extensive, "the girl who blushes most, who is most disposed to the pleasures of love;" he adds that, in girls and boys alike, shyness is a premature consciousness of sex.[2]   This observation has even become embodied in popular proverbs.   "Do as the lasses do —say no, but take it," is a Scotch saying, to which corresponds the Welsh saying, "The more prudish the more unchaste."[3]

It is not, at first, quite clear why an excessively shy and modest woman should be the most apt for intimate relationships with a man, and in such a case the woman is often charged with hypocrisy. There is, however, no hypocrisy in the matter. The shy and reserved woman holds herself aloof from intimacy in ordinary friendship, because she is acutely sensitive to the judgments of others, and fears that any seemingly immodest action may make an unfavorable opinion. With a lover, however, in whose eyes she feels assured that her actions can not be viewed unfavorably, these barriers of modesty fall down, and the resulting intimacy becomes all the more fascinating to the woman because of its contrast with the extreme reserve she is impelled to maintain in other relationships. It thus happens that many modest women who, in non-sexual relationships with their own sex, are not able to act with the physical unreserve not uncommon with women among themselves, yet feel no such reserve with a man, when they are once confident of his good opinion. Much the same is true of modest and sensitive men in their relations with women.

This fundamental animal factor of modesty, rooted in the natural facts of the sexual life of the higher mammals, and especially man, obviously will not explain all the phenomena of modesty. We must turn to the other great primary element of modesty, the social factor.

We cannot doubt that one of the most primitive and universal of the social characteristics of man is an aptitude for disgust, founded, as it is, on a yet more primitive and animal aptitude for disgust, which has little or no social significance.

---

[1] N. Venette, *La Génération de l'Homme*, Part II, Ch. X.
[2] *Monsieur Nicolas*, vol. i, p. 94.
[3] Κρυπτάδια, vol. ii, p. 26, 31. *Ib.* vol. iii, p. 162.

In nearly all races, even the most savage, we seem to find distinct traces of this aptitude for disgust in the presence of certain actions of others, an emotion naturally reflected in the individual's own actions, and hence a guide to conduct. Notwithstanding our gastric community of disgust with lower animals, it is only in man that this disgust seems to become transformed and developed, to possess a distinctly social character, and to serve as a guide to social conduct.[1] The objects of disgust vary infinitely according to the circumstances and habits of particular races, but the reaction of disgust is fundamental throughout.

The best study of the phenomena of disgust known to me is, without doubt, Professor Richet's.[2] Richet concludes that it is the *dangerous* and the *useless* which evoke disgust. The digestive and sexual excretions and secretions, being either useless or, in accordance with wide-spread primitive ideas, highly dangerous, the genito-anal region became a concentrated focus of digust.[3] It is largely for this reason, no doubt, that savage men exhibit modesty, not only toward women, but toward their own sex, and that so many of the lowest savages take great precautions in obtaining seclusion for the fulfillment of natural functions. The statement, now so often made, that the primary object of clothes is to accentuate, rather than to conceal, has in it—as I shall point out later—a large element of truth, but it is by no means a complete account of the matter. It seems difficult not to admit that, alongside the impulse to accentuate sexual differences, there is also in both men and women a genuine impulse to concealment among the most primitive peoples, and the invincible repugnance often felt by savages to remove the girdle or

---

[1] "Modesty is, at first," said Renouvier, "a fear which we have of displeasing others, and of blushing at our own natural imperfections." (Renouvier and Prat, *La Nouvelle Monadologie*, p. 221.)

[2] C. Richet, "Les Causes du Dégoût," *L'Homme et l'Intelligence*, 1884. This eminent physiologist's elaborate study of disgust was not written as a contribution to the psychology of modesty, but it forms an admirable introduction to the investigation of the social factor of modesty.

[3] It is interesting to note that where, as among the Eskimo, urine, for instance, is preserved as a highly-valuable commodity, the act of urination, even at table, is not regarded as in the slightest degree disgusting or immodest (Bourke, *Scatologic Rites*, p. 202).

apron, is scarcely accounted for by the theory that it is solely a sexual lure.

In this connection it seems to me instructive to consider a special form of modesty very strongly marked among savages in some parts of the world. I refer to the feeling of immodesty in eating. Where this feeling exists, modesty is offended when one eats in public; the modest man retires to eat. Indecency, said Cook, was utterly unknown among the Tahitians; but they would not eat together; even brothers and sisters had their separate baskets of provisions, and generally sat some yards apart, with their backs to each other, when they ate.[1] The Warrua of Central Africa, Cameron found, when offered a drink, put up a cloth before their faces while they swallowed it, and would not allow anyone to see them eat or drink; so that every man or woman must have his own fire and cook for himself.[2] Karl von den Steinen remarks, in his interesting book on Brazil, that though the Bakairi of Central Brazil have no feeling of shame about nakedness, they are ashamed to eat in public; they retire to eat, and hung their heads in shame-faced confusion when they saw him innocently eat in public. Hrolf Vaughan Stevens found that, when he gave an Orang-Laut (Malay) woman anything to eat, she not only would not eat it if her husband were present, but if any man were present she would go outside before eating or giving her children to eat.[3] Thus among these peoples the act of eating in public produces the same feelings as among ourselves the indecent exposure of the body in public.[4]

---

[1] Hawkesworth, *An Account of the Voyages*, etc., 1775, vol. ii, p. 52.
[2] *Journal of the Anthropological Institute*, vol. vi, p. 173.
[3] Stevens, "Mittheilungen aus dem Frauenleben der Orang Belendas," *Zeitschrift für Ethnologie*, Heft 4, p. 167, 1896. Crawley, (*Mystic Rose*, Ch. VIII, p. 439) gives numerous other instances, even in Europe, with, however, special reference to sexual taboo. I may remark that English people of lower class, especially women, are often modest about eating in the presence of people of higher class. This feeling is, no doubt, due, in part, to the consciousness of defective etiquette, but that very consciousness is, in part, a development of the fear of causing disgust, which is a component of modesty.
[4] Shame in regard to eating, it may be added, occasionally appears as a neurasthenic obsession in civilization, and has been studied as a form of psychasthenia by Janet. See *e.g.*, (Raymond and Janet, *Les Obsessions et la Psychasthénie*, vol. ii, p. 386) the case of a young girl

It is quite easy to understand how this arises. Whenever there is any pressure on the means of subsistence, as among savages at some time or another there nearly always is, it must necessarily arouse a profound and mixed emotion of desire and disgust to see another person putting into his stomach what one might just as well have put into one's own.[1] The special secrecy sometimes observed by women is probably due to the fact that women would be less able to resist the emotions that the act of eating would arouse in onlookers. As social feeling develops, a man desires not only to eat in safety, but also to avoid being an object of disgust, and to spare his friends all unpleasant emotions. Hence it becomes a requirement of ordinary decency to eat in private. A man who eats in public becomes—like the man who in our cities exposes his person in public—an object of disgust and contempt.

Long ago, when a hospital student on midwifery duty in London slums, I had occasion to observe that among the women of the poor, and more especially in those who had lost the first bloom of youth, modesty consisted chiefly in the fear of being disgusting. There was an almost pathetic anxiety, in the face of pain and discomfort, not to be disgusting in the doctor's eyes. This anxiety expressed itself in the ordinary symptoms of modesty. But, as soon as the woman realized that I found nothing disgusting in whatever was proper and necessary to be done under the circumstances, it almost invariably happened that every sign of modesty at once disappeared.[2] In the special

of 24, who, from the age of 12 or 13 (the epoch of puberty) had been ashamed to eat in public, thinking it nasty and ugly to do so, and arguing that it ought only to be done in private, like urination.

[1] "Desire and disgust are curiously blended," remarks Crawley (*The Mystic Rose*, p. 139), "when, with one's own desire unsatisfied, one sees the satisfaction of another; and here we may see the altruistic stage beginning; this has two sides, the fear of causing desire in others, and the fear of causing disgust; in each case, personal isolation is the psychological result."

[2] Hohenemser argues that the fear of causing disgust cannot be a part of shame. But he also argues that shame is simply psychic stasis, and it is quite easy to see, as in the above case, that the fear of causing disgust is simply a manifestation of psychic stasis. There is a conflict in the woman's mind between the idea of herself which she has already given, and the more degraded idea of herself which she

and elementary conditions of parturition, modesty is reduced to this one fear of causing disgust; so that, when that is negated, the emotion is non-existent, and the subject becomes, without effort, as direct and natural as a little child. A fellow-student on similar duty, who also discovered for himself the same character of modesty—that if he was careful to guard her modesty the woman was careful also, and that if he was not the woman was not—remarked on it to me with sadness; it seemed to him derogatory to womanhood that what he had been accustomed to consider its supreme grace should be so superficial that he could at will set limits to it.[1] I thought then, as I think still, that that was rather a perversion of the matter, and that nothing becomes degrading because we happen to have learned something about its operations. But I am more convinced than ever that the fear of causing disgust—a fear quite distinct from that of losing a sexual lure or breaking a rule of social etiquette—

---

fears she is likely to give, and this conflict is settled when she is made to feel that the first idea may still be maintained under the new circumstances.

[1] We neither of us knew that we had merely made afresh a very ancient discovery. Casanova, more than a century ago, quoted the remark of a friend of his, that the easiest way to overcome the modesty of a woman is to suppose it non-existent; and he adds a saying, which he attributes to Clement of Alexandria, that modesty, which seems so deeply rooted in women, only resides in the linen that covers them, and vanishes when it vanishes. The passage to which Casanova referred occurs in the *Pædagogus*, and has already been quoted. The observation seems to have appealed strongly to the Fathers, always glad to make a point against women, and I have met with it in Cyprian's *De Habitu Feminarum*. It also occurs in Jerome's treatise against Jovinian. Jerome, with more scholarly instinct, rightly presents the remark as a quotation: *"Scribit Herodotus quod mulier cum veste deponat et verecundiam."* In Herodotus the saying is attributed to Gyges (Book I, Chapter VIII). We may thus trace very far back into antiquity an observation which in English has received its classical expression from Chaucer, who, in his "Wife of Bath's Prologue," has:—

> "He sayde, a woman cast hir shame away,
> When she cast of hir smok."

I need not point out that the analysis of modesty offered above robs this venerable saying of any sting it may have possessed as a slur upon women. In such a case, modesty is largely a doubt as to the spectator's attitude, and necessarily disappears when that doubt is satisfactorily resolved. As we have seen, the Central Australian maidens were very modest with regard to the removal of their single garment, but when that removal was accomplished and accepted, they were fearless.

plays a very large part in the modesty of the more modest sex, and in modesty generally. Our Venuses, as Lucretius long since remarked and Montaigne after him, are careful to conceal from their lovers the *vitæ postscenia,* and that fantastic fate which placed so near together the supreme foci of physical attraction and physical repugnance, has immensely contributed to build up all the subtlest coquetries of courtship. Whatever stimulates self-confidence and lulls the fear of evoking disgust—whether it is the presence of a beloved person in whose good opinion complete confidence is felt, or whether it is merely the grosser narcotizing influence of a slight degree of intoxication—always automatically lulls the emotion of modesty.[1] Together with the animal factor of sexual refusal, this social fear of evoking disgust seems to me the most fundamental element in modesty.

It is, of course, impossible to argue that the fact of the sacro-pubic region of the body being the chief focus of concealment proves the importance of this factor of modesty. But it may fairly be argued that it owes this position not merely to being the sexual centre, but also as being the excretory centre. Even among many lower mammals, as well as among birds and insects, there is a well-marked horror of dirt, somewhat disguised by the varying ways in which an animal may be said to define "dirt." Many animals spend more time and energy in the duties of cleanliness than human beings, and they often show well-marked anxiety to remove their own excrement, or to keep away from it.[2] Thus this element of modesty also may be said to have an animal basis.

It is on this animal basis that the human and social fear of arousing disgust has developed. Its probably wide extension is indicated not only by the strong feeling attached to the constant presence of clothing on this part of the body,—such constant presence being quite uncalled for if the garment or ornament

---

[1] The same result occurs more markedly under the deadening influence of insanity. Grimaldi (*Il Manicomio Moderno,* 1888) found that modesty is lacking in 50 per cent. of the insane.

[2] For some facts bearing on this point, see Houssay, *Industries of Animals,* Chapter VII. "The Defence and Sanitation of Dwellings;" also P. Ballion, *De l'Instinct de Propreté chez les Animaux.*

is merely a sort of sexual war-paint,—but by the repugnance felt by many savages very low down in the scale to the public satisfaction of natural needs, and to their more than civilized cleanliness in this connection;[1] it is further of interest to note that in some parts of the world the covering is not in front, but behind; though of this fact there are probably other explanations. Among civilized people, also, it may be added, the final and invincible seat of modesty is sometimes not around the pubes, but the anus; that is to say, that in such cases the fear of arousing disgust is the ultimate and most fundamental element of modesty.[2]

The concentration of modesty around the anus is sometimes very marked. Many women feel so high a degree of shame and reserve with regard to this region, that they are comparatively indifferent to an anterior examination of the sexual organs. A similar feeling is not seldom found in men. "I would permit of an examination of my genitals by a medical man, without any feeling of discomfort," a correspondent writes, "but I think I would rather die than submit to any rectal examination." Even physicians have been known to endure painful rectal disorders for years, rather than undergo examination.

"Among ordinary English girls," a medical correspondent writes, "I have often noticed that the dislike and shame of allowing a man to have sexual intercourse with them, when newly married, is simply due to the fact that the sexual aperture is so closely apposed to the anus and bladder. If the vulva and vagina were situated between a woman's shoulder blades, and a man had a separate instrument for coitus, not used for any excretory purpose, I do not think women would feel about intercourse as they sometimes do. Again, in their ignorance of anatomy, women often look upon the vagina and womb as part of the bowel and its exit of discharge, and sometimes say, for

---

[1] Thus, Stevens mentions (*Zeitschrift für Ethnologie*, p. 182, 1897) that the Dyaks of Malacca always wash the sexual organs, even after urination, and are careful to use the left hand in doing so. The left hand is also reserved for such uses among the Jekris of the Niger coast (*Journal of the Anthropological Institute*, p. 122, 1898).

[2] Lombroso and Ferrero—who adopt the derivation of *pudor* from *putere; i.e.,* from the repugnance caused by the decomposition of the vaginal secretions—consider that the fear of causing disgust to men is the sole origin of modesty among savage women, as also it remains the sole form of modesty among some prostitutes to-day. (*La Donna Delinquente,* p. 540.) Important as this factor is in the constitution of the emotion of modesty, I need scarcely add that I regard so exclusive a theory as altogether untenable.

instance, 'inflammation of the *bowel*, when they mean *womb*. Again, many, perhaps most, women believe that they pass water through the vagina, and are ignorant of the existence of the separate urethral orifice. Again, women associate the vulva with the anus, and so feel ashamed of it; even when speaking to their husbands, or to a doctor, or among themselves; they have absolutely no name for the vulva (I mean among the upper classes, and people of gentle birth), but speak of it as 'down below,' 'low down,' etc."

Even though this feeling is largely based on wrong and ignorant ideas, it must still be recognized that it is to some extent natural and inevitable. "How much is risked," exclaims Dugas, "in the privacies of love! The results may be disillusion, disgust, the consciousness of physical imperfection, of brutality or coldness, of æsthetic disenchantment, of a sentimental shock, seen or divined. To be without modesty, that is to say, to have no fear of the ordeals of love, one must be sure of one's self, of one's grace, of one's physical emotions, of one's feelings, and be sure, moreover, of the effect of all these on the nerves, the imagination, and the heart of another person. Let us suppose modesty reduced to æsthetic discomfort, to a woman's fear of displeasing, or of not seeming beautiful enough. Even thus defined, how can modesty avoid being always awake and restless? What woman could repeat, without risk, the tranquil action of Phryne? And even in that action, who knows how much may not have been due to mere professional insolence!" (Dugas, "La Pudeur," *Revue Philosophique*, November, 1903.) "Men and Women," Schurtz points out (*Altersklassen und Männerbünde*, pp. 41-51), have certainly the capacity mutually to supplement and enrich each other; but when this completion fails, or is not sought, the difference may easily become a strong antipathy;" and he proceeds to develop the wide-reaching significance of this psychic fact.

I have emphasized the proximity of the excretory centres to the sexual focus in discussing this important factor of modesty, because, in analyzing so complex and elusive an emotion as modesty it is desirable to keep as near as possible to the essential and fundamental facts on which it is based. It is scarcely necessary to point out that, in ordinary civilized society, these fundamental facts are not usually present at the surface of consciousness and may even be absent altogether; on the foundation of them may arise all sorts of idealized fears, of delicate reserves, of æsthetic refinements, as the emotions of love become more complex and more subtle, and the crude simplicity of the basis on which they finally rest becomes inevitably concealed.

Another factor of modesty, which reaches a high development in savagery, is the ritual element, especially the idea of ceremonial uncleanness, based on a dread of the supernatural influences which the sexual organs and functions are supposed to exert. It may be to some extent rooted in the elements already referred to, and it leads us into a much wider field than that of modesty, so that it is only necessary to touch slightly on it here; it has been exhaustively studied by Frazer and by Crawley. Offences against the ritual rendered necessary by this mysterious dread, though more serious than offences against sexual reticence or the fear of causing disgust, are so obviously allied that they all reinforce one another and cannot easily be disentangled.

Nearly everywhere all over the world at a primitive stage of thought, and even to some extent in the highest civilization, the sight of the sexual organs or of the sexual act, the image or even the names of the sexual parts of either man or woman, are believed to have a curiously potent influence, sometimes beneficent, but quite as often maleficent. The two kinds of influence may even be combined, and Riedel, quoted by Ploss and Bartels,[1] states that the Ambon islanders carve a schematic representation of the vulva on their fruit trees, in part to promote the productiveness of the trees, and in part to scare any unauthorized person who might be tempted to steal the fruit. The precautions prescribed as regards coitus at Loango[2] are evidently associated with religious fears. In Ceylon, again (as a medical correspondent there informs me), where the penis is worshipped and held sacred, a native never allows it to be seen, except under compulsion, by a doctor, and even a wife must neither see it nor touch it nor ask for coitus, though she must grant as much as the husband desires. All savage and barbarous peoples who have attained any high degree of ceremonialism have included the functions not only of sex, but also of excretion, more or less stringently within the bounds of that ceremonialism.[3] It is only necessary to refer to the Jewish ritual books of the Old Testa-

---

[1] *Das Weib*, Ch. VI.

[2] For references as to a similar feeling among other savages, see Westermarck, *History of Human Marriage*, p. 152.

[3] See *e.g.*, Bourke, *Scatologic Rites*, pp. 141, 145, etc.

ment, to Hesiod, and to the customs prevalent among Mohammedan peoples. Modesty in eating, also, has its roots by no means
only in the fear of causing disgust, but very largely in this kind
of ritual, and Crawley has shown how numerous and frequent
among primitive peoples are the religious implications of eating
and drinking.[1] So profound is this dread of the sacred mystery
of sex, and so widespread is the ritual based upon it, that some
have imagined that here alone we may find the complete explanation of modesty, and Salomon Reinach declares that "at the
origin of the emotion of modesty lies a taboo."[2]

Durkheim ("La Prohibition de l'Inceste," *L'Année Sociologique*,
1898, p. 50), arguing that whatever sense of repugnance women may
inspire must necessarily reach the highest point around the womb, which
is hence subjected to the most stringent taboo, incidentally suggests that
here is an origin of modesty. "The sexual organs must be veiled at an
early period, to prevent the dangerous effluvia which they give off from
reaching the environment. The veil is often a method of intercepting
magic action. Once constituted, the practice would be maintained and
transformed."

It was doubtless as a secondary and derived significance that the
veil became, as Reinach ("Le Voile de l'Oblation," *op. cit.*, pp. 299-311)
shows it was, alike among the Romans and in the Catholic Church, the
sign of consecration to the gods.

At an early stage of culture, again, menstruation is regarded as a process of purification, a dangerous expulsion of
vitiated humors. Hence the term *katharsis* applied to it by
the Greeks. Hence also the mediæval view of women: "*Mulier
speciosa templum ædificatum super cloacam,*" said Boethius. The
sacro-pubic region in women, because it includes the source of
menstruation, thus becomes a specially heightened seat of taboo.
According to the Mosiac law (Leviticus, Chapter XX, v. 18), if
a man uncovered a menstruating woman, both were to be cut off.

It is probable that the Mohammedan custom of veiling the
face and head really has its source solely in another aspect of this
ritual factor of modesty. It must be remembered that this custom is not Mohammedan in its origin, since it existed long pre-

---

[1] Crawley, *op. cit.*, Ch. VII.
[2] S. Reinach, *Cultes, Mythes et Religions*, p. 172.

viously among the Arabians, and is described by Tertullian.[1] In
early Arabia very handsome men also veiled their faces, in order
to preserve themselves from the evil eye, and it has been conjec-
tured with much probability that the origin of the custom of
women veiling their faces may be traced to this magico-religious
precaution.[2] Among the Jews of the same period, according to
Büchler,[3] the women had their heads covered and never cut their
hair; to appear in the streets without such covering would be
like a prostitute and was adequate ground for divorce; adulterous
women were punished by uncovering their heads and cutting their
hair. It is possible, though not certain, that St. Paul's obscure
injunction to women to cover their heads "because of the angels,"
may really be based on the ancient reason, that when uncovered
they would be exposed to the wanton assaults of spirits (1 Cor-
inthians, Ch. XI, vv. 5-6),[4] exactly as Singhalese women believe
that they must keep the vulva covered lest demons should have
intercourse with them. Even at the present day St. Paul's
injunction is still observed by Christendom, which is, however,
far from accepting, or even perhaps understanding, the folk-lore
ground on which are based such injunctions.

Crawley thus summarizes some of the evidence concerning the
significance of the veil:—

"Sexual shyness, not only in woman, but in man, is intensified
at marriage, and forms a chief feature of the dangerous sexual properties mutually feared. When fully ceremonial, the idea takes on the
meaning that satisfaction of these feelings will lead to their neu-
tralization, as, in fact, it does. The bridegroom in ancient Sparta
supped on the wedding night at the men's mess, and then visited his
bride, leaving her before daybreak. This practice was continued, and
sometimes children were born before the pair had ever seen each other's
faces by day. At weddings in the Babar Islands, the bridegroom has

<hr/>

[1] Tertullian, *De Virginibus Velandis*, cap. 17. Hottentot women,
also (Fritsch, *Eingeborene Südafrika's*, p. 311), cover their head with
a cloth, and will not be persuaded to remove it.

[2] Wellhausen, *Reste Arabischen Heidentums*, p. 196. The same
custom is found among Tuareg men though it is not imperative for the
women (Duveyrier, *Les Touaregs du Nord*, p. 291).

[3] Quoted in *Zentralblatt für Anthropologie*, 1906, Heft 1, p. 21.

[4] Or rather, perhaps, because the sight of their nakedness might
lead the angels into sin. See W. G. Sumner, *Folkways*, p. 431.

to hunt for his bride in a darkened room. This lasts a good while if she is shy. In South Africa, the bridegroom may not see his bride till the whole of the marriage ceremonies have been performed. In Persia, a husband never sees his wife till he has consummated the marriage. At marriages in South Arabia, the bride and bridegroom have to sit immovable in the same position from noon till midnight, fasting, in separate rooms. The bride is attended by ladies, and the groom by men. They may not see each other till the night of the fourth day. In Egypt, the groom cannot see the face of his bride, even by a surreptitious glance, till she is in his absolute possession. Then comes the ceremony, which he performs, of uncovering her face. In Egypt, of course, this has been accentuated by the seclusion and veiling of women. In Morocco, at the feast before the marriage, the bride and groom sit together on a sort of throne; all the time, the poor bride's eyes are firmly closed, and she sits amidst the revelry as immovable as a statue. On the next day is the marriage. She is conducted after dark to her future home, accompanied by a crowd with lanterns and candles. She is led with closed eyes along the street by two relatives, each holding one of her hands. The bride's head is held in its proper position by a female relative, who walks behind her. She wears a veil, and is not allowed to open her eyes until she is set on the bridal bed, with a girl friend beside her. Amongst the Zulus, the bridal party proceeds to the house of the groom, having the bride hidden amongst them. They stand facing the groom, while the bride sings a song. Her companions then suddenly break away, and she is discovered standing in the middle, with a fringe of beads covering her .face. Amongst the people of Kumaun, the husband sees his wife first after the joining of hands. Amongst the Bedui of North East Africa, the bride is brought on the evening of the wedding-day by her girl friends, to the groom's house. She is closely muffled up. Amongst the Jews of Jerusalem, the bride, at the marriage ceremony, stands under the nuptial canopy, her eyes being closed, that she may not behold the face of her future husband before she reaches the bridal chamber. In Melanesia, the bride is carried to her new home on some one's back, wrapped in many mats, with palm-fans held about her face, because she is supposed to be modest and shy. Among the Damaras, the groom cannot see his bride for four days after marriage. When a Damara woman is asked in marriage, she covers her face for a time with the flap of a headdress made for this purpose. At the Thlinkeet marriage ceremony, the bride must look down, and keep her head bowed all the time; during the wedding-day, she remains hiding in a corner of the house, and the groom is forbidden to enter. At a Yezedee marriage, the bride is covered from head to foot with a thick veil, and when arrived at her new home, she retires behind a curtain in the corner of a darkened room, where she remains for three days before her husband is permitted to see her. In Corea, the bride has to cover her face with her long sleeves, when meeting the bridegroom at the wedding. The Manchurian bride uncovers her face for the first time when she descends from the nuptial couch. It is dangerous even to see dangerous persons. Sight is a method of contagion in primitive science, and the idea coincides with the psychological aversion to see dangerous things, and with sexual shyness and timidity. In the customs noticed, we can distinguish the feeling that it is dangerous to the bride for her husband's eyes to be upon her, and the feeling of bashfulness in her which induces her neither to see him nor to be seen by him. These ideas explain the origin of the bridal veil and similar concealments. The bridal veil is used, to take a few instances, in China, Burmah, Corea, Russia, Bulgaria, Manchuria, and Persia, and in all these cases it conceals the face entirely." (E. Crawley, *The Mystic Rose*, pp. 328 *et seq.*)

Alexander Walker, writing in 1846, remarks: "Among old-fashioned people, of whom a good example may be found in old country people of the middle class in England, it is indecent to be seen with the head unclothed; such a woman is terrified at the chance of being seen in that condition, and if intruded on at that time, she shrieks with terror, and flies to conceal herself." (A. Walker, *Beauty*, p. 15.) This fear of being seen with the head uncovered exists still, M. Van Gennep informs me, in some regions of France, as in Brittany.

So far it has only been necessary to refer incidentally to the connection of modesty with clothing. I have sought to emphasize the unquestionable, but often forgotten, fact that modesty is in its origin independent of clothing, that physiological modesty takes precedence of anatomical modesty, and that the primary factors of modesty were certainly developed long before the discovery of either ornament or garments. The rise of clothing probably had its first psychical basis on an emotion of modesty already compositely formed of the elements we have traced. Both the main elementary factors, it must be noted, must naturally tend to develop and unite in a more complex, though—it may well be—much less intense, emotion. The impulse which leads the female animal, as it leads some African women when found without their girdles, to squat firmly down on the earth, becomes a more refined and extended play of gesture and ornament and garment. A very notable advance, I may remark, is made when this primary attitude of defence against the action of the male becomes a defence against his eyes. We may thus explain the spread of modesty to various parts of the body, even when we exclude the more special influence of the evil eye. The breasts very early become a focus of modesty in women; this may be observed among many naked, or nearly naked, negro races; the tendency of the nates to become the chief seat of modesty in many parts of Africa may probably be, in large part, thus explained, since the full development of the gluteal regions is often the greatest attraction an African woman can possess.[1] The same cause contributes, doubtless, to the face becoming, in some races, the centre of modesty. We see the influence of this defence against strange eyes in the special precautions in gesture or clothing taken by the women in various parts of the world, against the more offensive eyes of civilized Europeans.

But in thus becoming directed only against sight, and not against action, the gestures of modesty are at once free to become merely those of coquetry. When there is no real danger of offensive action, there is no need for more than playful defence, and no serious anxiety should that defence be taken as a disguised invitation. Thus the road is at once fully open toward the most civilized manifestations of the comedy of courtship.

In the same way the social fear of arousing disgust combines easily and perfectly with any new development in the invention of ornament or clothing as sexual lures. Even among the most civilized races it has often been noted that the fashion of feminine garments (as also sometimes the use of scents) has the double object of concealing and attracting. It is so with the little apron of the young savage belle. The heightening of the attraction is, indeed, a logical outcome of the fear of evoking disgust.

---

[1] In Moruland, Emin Bey remarked that women are mostly naked, but some wear a girdle, with a few leaves hanging behind. The women of some negro tribes, who thus cover themselves behind, if deprived of this sole covering, immediately throw themselves on the ground on their backs, in order to hide their nakedness.

It is possible, as some ethnographists have observed,[1] that intercrural cords and other primitive garments have a physical ground, inasmuch as they protect the most sensitive and unprotected part of the body, especially in women. We may note in this connection the significant remarks of K. von den Steinen, who argues that among Brazilian tribes the object of the *uluri*, etc., is to obtain a maximum of protection for the mucous membrane with a minimum of concealment. Among the Eskimo, as Nansen noted, the corresponding intercrural cord is so thin as to be often practically invisible; this may be noted, I may add, in the excellent photographs of Eskimo women given by Holm.

But it is evident that, in the beginning, protection is to little or no extent the motive for attaching foreign substances to the body. Thus the tribes of Central Australia wear no clothes, although they often suffer from the cold. But, in addition to armlets, neck-bands and head-bands, they have string or hair girdles, with, for the women, a very small apron and, for the men, a pubic tassel. The latter does not conceal the organs, being no larger than a coin, and often brilliantly coated with white pipe-clay, especially during the progress of *corobborrees,* when a large number of men and women meet together; it serves the purpose of drawing attention to the organs.[2] When Forster visited the unspoilt islanders of the Pacific early in the eighteenth century, he tells us that, though they wore no clothes, they found it necessary to cover themselves with various ornaments, especially on the sexual parts. "But though their males," he remarks, "were to all appearances equally anxious in this respect with their females, this part of their dress served only to make that more conspicuous which it intended to hide."[3] He adds the significant remark that "these ideas of decency and modesty are only observed at the age of sexual maturity," just as in Central Australia women may only wear aprons after the initiation of puberty.

---

[1] *E.g.,* Letourneau, *L'Evolution de la Morale,* p. 146.

[2] Speneer and Gillen, *Northern Tribes of Central Australia,* p. 683.

[3] J. R. Forster, *Observations Made During a Voyage Round the World,* 1728, p. 395.

"There are certain things," said Montaigne, "which are hidden in order to be shown;" and there can be no doubt that the contention of Westermarck and others, that ornament and clothing were, in the first place, intended, not to conceal or even to protect the body, but, in large part, to render it sexually attractive, is fully proved.[1] We cannot, in the light of all that has gone before, regard ornaments and clothing as the sole cause of modesty, but the feelings that are thus gathered around the garment constitute a highly important factor of modesty.

Among some Australian tribes it is said that the sexual organs are only covered during their erotic dances; and it is further said that in some parts of the world only prostitutes are clothed. "The scanty covering," as Westermarck observes, "was found to act as the most powerful obtainable sexual stimulus." It is undoubtedly true that this statement may be made not merely of the savage, but of the most civilized world. All observers agree that the complete nudity of savages, unlike the civilized *décolleté* or *détroussé*, has no suggestion of sexual allurement. (Westmarck quotes numerous testimonies on this point, *op. cit.*, pp. 192 *et seq.*) Dr. R. W. Felkin remarks concerning Central Africa, that he has never met more indecency than in Uganda, where the penalty of death is inflicted on an adult found naked in the street. (*Edinburgh Medical Journal*, April, 1884.) A study of pictures or statuary will alone serve to demonstrate that nakedness is always chaster in its effects than partial clothing. As a well-known artist, Du Maurier, has remarked (in *Trilby*), it is "a fact well known to all painters and sculptors who have used the nude model (except a few shady pretenders, whose purity, not being of the right sort, has gone rank from too much watching) that nothing is so chaste as nudity. Venus herself, as she drops her garments and steps on to the model-throne, leaves behind her on the floor every weapon in her armory by which she can pierce to the grosser passions of men." Burton, in the *Anatomy of Melancholy* (Part III, Sect. II, Subsect. 3), deals at length with the "Allurements of Love," and concludes that "the greatest provocations of lust are from our apparel." The artist's model, as one informs me, is much less exposed to liberties from men when nude

---

[1] Westermarck (*History of Human Marriage*, Ch. IX) ably sets forth this argument, with his usual wealth of illustration. Crawley (*Mystic Rose*, p. 135) seeks to qualify this conclusion by arguing that tattooing, etc., of the sex organs is not for ornament but for the purpose of magically insulating the organs, and is practically a permanent amulet or charm.

than when she is partially clothed, and it may be noted that in Paris studios the model who poses naked undresses behind a screen.

An admirable poetic rendering of this element in the philosophy of clothing has been given by Herrick, that master of erotic psychology, in "A Lily in Crystal," where he argues that a lily in crystal, and amber in a stream, and strawberries in cream, gain an added delight from semi-concealment; and so, he concludes, we obtain

"A rule, how far, to teach,
    Your nakedness must reach."

In this connection, also, it is worth noting that Stanley Hall, in a report based on returns from nearly a thousand persons, mostly teachers ("The Early Sense of Self," *American Journal of Psychology*, 1898, p. 366), finds that of the three functions of clothes—protection, ornament, and Lotzean "self-feeling"—the second is by far the most conspicuous in childhood. The attitude of children is testimony to the primitive attitude toward clothing.

It cannot, however, be said that the use of clothing for the sake of showing the natural forms of the body has everywhere been developed. In Japan, where nakedness is accepted without shame, clothes are worn to cover and conceal, and not to reveal, the body. It is so, also, in China. A distinguished Chinese gentleman, who had long resided in Europe, once told Baelz that he had gradually learnt to grasp the European point of view, but that it would be impossible to persuade his fellow-countrymen that a woman who used her clothes to show off her figure could possibly possess the least trace of modesty. (Baelz, *Zeitschrift für Ethnologie*, 1901, Heft 2, p. 179.)

The great artistic elaboration often displayed by articles of ornament or clothing, even when very small, and the fact—as shown by Karl von den Steinen regarding the Brazilian *uluri* —that they may serve as common motives in general decoration, sufficiently prove that such objects attract rather than avoid attention. And while there is an invincible repugnance among some peoples to remove these articles, such repugnance being often strongest when the adornment is most minute, others have no such repugnance or are quite indifferent whether or not their aprons are accurately adjusted. The mere presence or possession of the article gives the required sense of self-respect, of human dignity, of sexual desirability. Thus it is that to unclothe a person is to humiliate him; this was so even in Homeric times, for we may recall the threat of Ulysses to strip Thyestes.[1]

When clothing is once established, another element, this time a social-economic element, often comes in to emphasize its importance and increase the anatomical modesty of women. I mean the growth of the conception of women as property. Waitz, followed by Schurtz and Letourneau, has insisted that the jealousy of husbands is the primary origin of clothing, and, indirectly, of modesty. Diderot in the eighteenth century had already given clear expression to the same view. It is undoubtedly true that only married women are among some peoples clothed, the unmarried women, though full grown, remaining naked. In many parts of the world, also, as Mantegazza and others have shown, where the men are naked and the women covered, clothing is regarded as a sort of disgrace, and men can only with difficulty be persuaded to adopt it. Before marriage a woman was often free, and not bound to chastity, and at the same time was often naked; after marriage she was clothed, and no longer free. To the husband's mind, the garment appears— illogically, though naturally—a moral and physical protection against any attack on his property.[2] Thus a new motive was furnished, this time somewhat artificially, for making nakedness, in women at all events, disgraceful. As the conception of property also extended to the father's right over his daughters, and the appreciation of female chastity developed, this motive spread to unmarried as well as married women. A woman on the west coast of Africa must always be chaste because she is first the property of her parents and afterwards of her husband,[3] and even in the seventeenth century of Christendom so able a thinker as Bishop Burnet furnished precisely the same reason

---

[1] *Iliad*, II, 262. Waitz gives instances (*Anthropology*, p. 301) showing that nakedness is sometimes a mark of submission.

[2] The Celtic races, in their days of developed barbarism, seem to have been relatively free from the idea of proprietorship in women, and it was probably among the Irish (as we learn from the seventeenth century *Itinerary* of Fynes Moryson) that the habit of nakedness was longest preserved among the upper social class women of Western Europe.

[3] A. B. Ellis, *Tshi-Speaking Peoples*, p. 286.

for feminine chastity.[1] This conception probably constituted
the chief and most persistent element furnished to the complex emotion of modesty by the barbarous stages of human
civilization.

This economic factor necessarily involved the introduction
of a new moral element into modesty. If a woman's chastity is
the property of another person, it is essential that she shall be
modest in order that men may not be tempted to incur the penalties involved by the infringement of property rights. Thus
modesty is strictly inculcated on women in order that men may be
safeguarded from temptation. The fact was overlooked that
modesty is itself a temptation. Immodesty being, on this ground,
disapproved by men, a new motive for modesty is furnished to
women. In the book which the Knight of the Tower, Landry,
wrote in the fourteenth century, for the instruction of his
daughters, this factor of modesty is naïvely revealed. He tells
his daughters of the trouble that David got into through the
thoughtlessness of Bathsheba, and warns them that "every
woman ought religiously to conceal herself when dressing and
washing, and neither out of vanity nor yet to attract attention
show either her hair, or her neck, or her breast, or any part which
ought to be covered." Hinton went so far as to regard what he
termed "body modesty," as entirely a custom imposed upon
women by men with the object of preserving their own virtue.
While this motive is far from being the sole source of modesty,
it must certainly be borne in mind as an inevitable outcome of
the economic factor of modesty.

In Europe it seems probable that the generally accepted
conceptions of mediæval chivalry were not without influence in
constituting the forms in which modesty shows itself among us.
In the early middle ages there seems to have been a much greater
degree of physical familiarity between the sexes than is commonly found among barbarians elsewhere. There was certainly
considerable promiscuity in bathing and indifference to nakedness. It seems probable, as Durkheim points out,[2] that this

---

1 Burnet, *Life and Death of Rochester*, p. 110.
2 *L'Année Sociologique*, seventh year, 1904, p. 439.

state of things was modified in part by the growing force of the dictates of Christian morality, which regarded all intimate approaches between the sexes as sinful, and in part by the influence of chivalry with its æsthetic and moral ideals of women, as the representative of all the delicacies and elegancies of civilization. This ideal was regarded as incompatible with the familiarities of the existing social relationships between the sexes, and thus a separation, which at first existed only in art and literature, began by a curious reaction to exert an influence on real life.

The chief new feature—it is scarcely a new element—added to modesty when an advanced civilization slowly emerges from barbarism is the elaboration of its social ritual.[1] Civilization expands the range of modesty, and renders it, at the same time, more changeable. The French seventeenth century, and the English eighteenth, represent early stages of modern European civilization, and they both devoted special attention to the elaboration of the minute details of modesty. The frequenters of the Hotel Rambouillet, the *précieuses* satirized by Molière, were not only engaged in refining the language; they were refining feelings and ideas and enlarging the boundaries of modesty.[2] In England such famous and popular authors as Swift and Sterne bear witness to a new ardor of modesty in the sudden reticences, the dashes, and the asterisks, which are found throughout their works. The altogether new quality of literary prurience, of which Sterne is still the classical example, could only have arisen on the basis of the new modesty which was then overspreading society and literature. Idle people,

---

[1] Tallemont des Réaux, who began to write his *Historiettes* in 1657, says of the Marquise de Rambouillet: "Elle est un peu trop délicate . . . on n'oscrait prononcer le mot de *cul*. Cela va dans l'excès." Half a century later, in England, Mandeville, in the Remarks appended to his *Fable of the Bees*, refers to the almost prudish modesty inculcated on children from their earliest years.

[2] In one of its civilized developments, this ritualized modesty becomes prudery, which is defined by Forel (*Die Sexuelle Frage*, Fifth ed., p. 125) as "codified sexual morality." Prudery is fossilized modesty, and no longer reacts vitally. True modesty, in an intelligent civilized person, is instinctively affected by motives and circumstances, responding sensitively to its relationships.

5

mostly, no doubt, the women in *salons* and drawing-rooms, people more familiar with books than with the realities of life, now laid down the rules of modesty, and were ever enlarging it, ever inventing new subtleties of gesture and speech, which it would be immodest to neglect, and which are ever being rendered vulgar by use and ever changing.

It was at this time, probably, that the custom of inventing an arbitrary private vocabulary of words and phrases for the purpose of disguising references to functions and parts of the body regarded as immodest and indecent, first began to become common. Such private slang, growing up independently in families, and especially among women, as well as between lovers, is now almost universal. It is not confined to any European country, and has been studied in Italy by Niceforo (*Il Gergo*, 1897, cap. 1 and 2), who regards it as a weapon of social defence against an inquisitive or hostile environment, since it enables things to be said with a meaning which is unintelligible to all but the initiated person. While it is quite true that the custom is supported by the consciousness of its practical advantages, it has another source in a desire to avoid what is felt to be the vulgar immodesty of direct speech. This is sufficiently shown by the fact that such slang is mostly concerned with the sacro-pubic sphere. It is one of the chief contributions to the phenomena of modesty furnished by civilization. The claims of modesty having effected the clothing of the body, the impulse of modesty finds a further sphere of activity—half-playful, yet wholly imperative—in the clothing of language.

Modesty of speech has, however, a deep and primitive basis, although in modern Europe it only became conspicuous at the beginning of the eighteenth century. "All over the world," as Dufour put it, "to do is good, to say is bad." Reticences of speech are not adequately accounted for by the statement that modesty tends to irradiate from the action to the words describing the action, for there is a tendency for modesty to be more deeply rooted in the words than in the actions. "Modest women," as Kleinpaul truly remarks, " have a much greater horror of saying immodest things than of doing them; they believe that fig-leaves were especially made for the mouth." (Kleinpaul, *Sprache ohne Worte*," p. 309.) It is a tendency which is linked on to the religious and ritual feeling which we have already found to be a factor of modesty, and which, even when applied to language, appears to have an almost or quite instinctive basis, for it is found among the most primitive savages, who very frequently regard a name as too sacred or dangerous to utter. Among the tribes of Central Australia, in addition to his ordinary name, each individual has his sacred or secret name, only known to the older and fully initiated members of his own totemic group; among the Warramunga, it is not permitted to women to utter even a man's ordinary name, though she knows it. (Spencer and Gillen, *Northern Tribes of Central Australia*, p. 581.) In the mysterious region of sex, this feeling easily takes root. In many parts of the world, men use among themselves, and women use among themselves, words and even languages which they may not use without impropriety in speaking to persons of the opposite sex, and it has been shown that exogamy, or the fact that the wife belongs to a different tribe, will not always account for this phenomenon. (Crawley, *The Mystic Rose*, p. 46.) A special vocabulary for the generative organs and functions is very widespread. Thus, in northwest Central Queensland, there is both a decent and an indecent vocabulary for the sexual parts; in Mitakoodi language, for instance, *me-nc* may be used for the vulva in the best aboriginal society, but *koon-ja* and *pukkil*, which are names for the same parts, are the most blackguardly words known to the natives. (W. Roth, *Ethnological Studies Among the Queensland Aborigines*, p. 184.) Among the Malays, *puki* is also a name for the vulva which it is very indecent to utter, and it is only used in public by people under the influence of an obsessive nervous disorder. (W. Gilman Ellis, "Latah," *Journal of Mental Science*, Jan., 1897.) The Swahili women of Africa have a private metaphorical language of their own, referring to sexual matters (Zache, *Zeitschrift für Ethnologie*, 1899, Heft 2-3, pp. 70 *et seq.*), and in Samoa, again, young girls have a euphemistic name for the penis, *aualuma*, which is not that in common use (*Zeitschrift für Ethnologie*, 1899, Heft 1, p. 31); exactly the same thing is found in Europe, to-day, and is sometimes more marked among young peasant women than among those of better social class, who often avoid, under all circumstances, the necessity for using any definite name.

Singular as it may seem, the Romans, who in their literature impress us by their vigorous and naked grip of the most private facts of life, showed in familiar intercourse a dread of obscene language—a dread untimately founded, it is evident, on religious grounds—far exceeding that which prevails among ourselves to-day in civilization. "It is remarkable," Dufour observes, "that the prostitutes of ancient Rome would have blushed to say an indecent word in public. The little tender words used between lovers and their mistresses were not less correct and innocent when the mistress was a courtesan and the lover an erotic poet. He called her his rose, his queen, his goddess, his dove, his light, his star, and she replied by calling him her jewel, her honey, her bird, her ambrosia, the apple of her eye, and never with any licentious interjection, but only 'I will love!' (*Amabo*), a frequent exclamation, summing up a whole life and vocation. When inti-

mate relations began, they treated each other as 'brother' and 'sister.'
These appellations were common among the humblest and the proudest
courtesans alike." (Dufour, *Histoire de la Prostitution*, vol. ii, p. 78.)
So excessive was the Roman horror of obscenity that even physicians
were compelled to use a euphemism for *urina*, and though the *urinal* or
vas urinarium was openly used at the dining-table (following a custom
introduced by the Sybarites, according to Athenæus, Book XII, cap. 17),
the decorous guest could not ask for it by name, but only by a snap
of the fingers (Dufour, *op. cit.*, vol. ii, p. 174).

In modern Europe, as seems fairly evident from the early realistic
dramatic literature of various countries, no special horror of speaking plainly regarding the sacro-pubic regions and their functions existed among the general population until the seventeenth century.
There is, however, one marked exception. Such a feeling clearly
existed as regards menstruation. It is not difficult to see why it should
have begun at this function. We have here not only a function confined
to one sex and, therefore, easily lending itself to a vocabulary confined
to one sex; but, what is even of more importance, the belief which
existed among the Romans, as elsewhere throughout the world, concerning the specially dangerous and mysterious properties of menstruation, survived throughout mediæval times. (See *e.g.*, Ploss and Bartels, *Das Weib*, Bd. I, XIV; also Havelock Ellis, *Man and Woman*,
fourth ed. Ch. XI.) The very name, *menses* ("monthlies"), is a
euphemism, and most of the old scientific names for this function are
similarly vague. As regards popular feminine terminology previous
to the eighteenth century, Schurig gives us fairly ample information
(*Parthenologia*, 1729, pp. 27 *et saq.*). He remarks that both in Latin
and Germanic countries, menstruation was commonly designated by
some term equivalent to "flowers," because, he says, it is a blossoming
that indicates the possibility of fruit. German peasant women, he tells
us, called it the rose-wreath (Rosenkrantz). Among the other current
feminine names for menstruation which he gives, some are purely fanci-
ful; thus, the Italian women dignified the function with the title of
"marchese magnifico;" German ladies, again, would use the locution,
"I have had a letter," or would say that their cousin or aunt had
arrived. These are closely similar to the euphemisms still used by
women.

It should be added that euphemisms for menstruation are not
confined to Europe, and are found among savages. According to Hill
Tout (*Journal of the Anthropological Institute*, 1904, p. 320; and 1905,
p. 137), one of these euphemisms was "putting on the moccasin," and
in another branch of the same people, "putting the knees together,"
"going outside" (in allusion to the customary seclusion at this period
in a solitary hut), and so on.

It would, however, be a mistake to suppose that this process is an intensification of modesty. It is, on the contrary, an attenuation of it. The observances of modesty become merely a part of a vast body of rules of social etiquette, though a somewhat stringent part on account of the vague sense still persisting of a deep-lying natural basis. It is a significant coincidence that the eighteenth century, which was marked by this new extension of the social ritual of modesty, also saw the first appearance of a new philosophic impulse not merely to analyze, but to dissolve the conception of modesty. This took place more especially in France.

The swift rise to supremacy, during the seventeenth century, of logical and rational methods of thinking, in conjunction with the new development of geometrical and mathematical science, led in the eighteenth century to a widespread belief in France that human customs and human society ought to be founded on a strictly logical and rational basis. It was a belief which ignored those legitimate claims of the emotional nature which the nineteenth century afterwards investigated and developed, but it was of immense service to mankind in clearing away useless prejudices and superstitions, and it culminated in the reforms of the great Revolution which most other nations have since been painfully struggling to attain. Modesty offered a tempting field for the eighteenth century philosophic spirit to explore.

The manner in which the most distinguished and adventurous minds of the century approached it, can scarcely be better illustrated than by a conversation, reported by Madame d'Epinay, which took place in 1750 at the table of Mlle. Quinault, the eminent actress. "A fine virtue," Duclos remarked, "which one fastens on in the morning with pins!" He proceeded to argue that "a moral law must hold good always and everywhere, which modesty does not." Saint-Lambert, the poet, observed that "it must be acknowledged that one can say nothing good about innocence without being a little corrupted," and Duclos added "or of modesty without being impudent." Saint-Lambert finally held forth with much poetic enthusiasm con-

cerning the desirability of consummating marriages in public.[1]
This view of modesty, combined with the introduction of Greek
fashions, gained ground to such an extent that towards the end of
the century women, to the detriment of their health, were sometimes content to dress in transparent gauze, and even to walk
abroad in the Champs Elysées without any clothing; that, however, was too much for the public.[2] The final outcome of the
eighteenth century spirit in this direction was, as we know, by
no means the dissolution of modesty. But it led to a clearer
realization of what is permanent in its organic foundations and
what is merely temporary in its shifting manifestations. That
is a realization which is no mean task to achieve, and is difficult
for many, even yet. So intelligent a traveler as Mrs. Bishop
(Miss Bird), on her first visit to Japan came to the conclusion
that Japanese women had no modesty, because they had no
objection to being seen naked when bathing. Twenty years
later she admitted to Dr. Baelz that she had made a mistake, and
that "a woman may be naked and yet behave like a lady."[3] In
civilized countries the observances of modesty differ in different
regions, and in different social classes, but, however various the
forms may be, the impulse itself remains persistent.[4]

Modesty has thus come to have the force of a tradition,
a vague but massive force, bearing with special power on those
who cannot reason, and yet having its root in the instincts of all
people of all classes.[5] It has become mainly transformed into

[1] *Memoires de Madame d'Epinay*, Part I, Ch. V. Thirty years
earlier, Mandeville had written, in England, that "the modesty of
women is the result of custom and education."

[2] Goncourt, *Histoire de la Société Française pendant le Directoire*,
p. 422. Clothes became so gauze-like, and receded to such an extent
from the limbs, that for a time the chemise was discarded as an
awkward and antiquated garment.

[3] *Zeitschrift für Ethnologie*, 1901, Heft 2, p. 179.

[4] In the rural districts of Hanover, Pastor Grashoff states, "even
when natural necessities are performed with the greatest possible freedom, there is no offence to modesty, in rural opinion." But he makes
a statement which is both contradictory and false, when he adds that
"modesty is, to the country man in general, a foreign idea."
(*Geschlechtlich-Sittliche Verhältnisse im Deutsche Reiche*, vol. ii, p. 45.)

[5] It is frequently stated that prostitutes are devoid of modesty,
but this is incorrect; they possess a partial and diminished modesty which,
for a considerable period, still remains genuine (see *e.g.*, Reuss, *La Prosti-*

the allied emotion of decency, which has been described as "modesty fossilized into social customs." The emotion yields more readily than in its primitive state to any sufficiently-strong motive. Even fashion in the more civilized countries can easily inhibit anatomical modesty, and rapidly exhibit or accentuate, in turn, almost any part of the body, while the savage Indian woman of America, the barbarous woman of some Mohammedan countries, can scarcely sacrifice her modesty in the pangs of childbirth. Even when, among uncivilized races, the focus of modesty may be said to be eccentric and arbitrary, it still remains very rigid. In such savage and barbarous countries modesty possesses the strength of a genuine and irresistible instinct. In civilized countries, however, anyone who places considerations of modesty before the claims of some real human need excites ridicule and contempt.

---

tution, p. 58). Lombroso and Ferrero (*La Donna*, p. 540) refer to the objection of prostitutes to be examined during the monthly periods as often greater than that of respectable women. Again, Càllari states ("Prostituzione in Sicilia," *Archivio di Psichiatria*, 1903, p. 205), that Sicilian prostitutes can only with difficulty be persuaded to expose themselves naked in the practice of their profession. Aretino long since remarked (in *La Pippa*) that no women so detest gratuitous *décolletage* as prostitutes. When prostitutes do not possess modesty, they frequently simulate it, and Ferriani remarks (in his *Delinquenti Minorenni*) that of ninety-seven minors (mostly females) accused of offences against public decency, seventy-five simulated a modesty which, in his opinion, they were entirely without.

III.

The Blush the Sanction of Modesty—The Phenomena of Blushing—
Influences Which Modify the Aptitude to Blush—Darkness, Concealment
of the Face, Etc.

IT is impossible to contemplate this series of phenomena,
so radically persistent whatever its changes of form, and so
constant throughout every stage of civilization, without feeling
that, although modesty cannot properly be called an instinct,
there must be some physiological basis to support it. Undoubtedly such a basis is formed by that vasomotor mechanism of
which the most obvious outward sign is, in human beings, the
blush. All the allied emotional forms of fear—shame, bashfulness, timidity—are to some extent upheld by this mechanism,
but such is especially the case with the emotion we are now
concerned with.[1] The blush is the sanction of modesty.

The blush is, indeed, only a part, almost, perhaps, an accidental
part, of the organic turmoil with which it is associated. Partridge, who has
studied the phenomena of blushing in one hundred and twenty cases
(*Pedagogical Seminary*, April, 1897), finds that the following are the
general symptoms: tremors near the waist, weakness in the limbs,
pressure, trembling, warmth, weight or beating in the chest, warm
wave from feet upward, quivering of heart, stoppage and then rapid
beating of heart, coldness all over followed by heat, dizziness, tingling
of toes and fingers, numbness, something rising in throat, smarting
of eyes, singing in ears, prickling sensations of face, and pressure
inside head. Partridge considers that the disturbance is primarily central, a change in the cerebral circulation, and that the actual redness of
the surface comes late in the nerve storm, and is really but a small part
of it.

---

[1] Melinaud ("Pourquoi Rougit-on?" *Revue des Deux Mondes*, 1 Oc-
tobre, 1893) points out that blushing is always associated with fear, and
indicates, in the various conditions under which it may arise,—modesty,
timidity, confusion,—that we have something to conceal which we fear
may be discovered. "All the evidence," Partridge states, "seems to point
to the conclusion that the mental state underlying blushing belongs to
the fear family. The presence of the feeling of dread, the palpitation of
the heart, the impulse to escape, to hide, the shock, all confirms this
view."

(72)

There has been some discussion as to why, and indeed how far, blushing is confined to the face. Henle (*Ueber das Erröthen*) thought that we blush in the face because all nervous phenomena produced by mental states appear first in the face, owing to the anatomical arrangement of the nerves of the body. Darwin (*Expression of the Emotions*) argued that attention to a part tends to produce capillary activity in the part, and that the face has been the chief object of attention. It has also been argued, on the other hand, that the blush is the vestigial remains of a general erethism of sex, in which shame originated; that the blush was thus once more widely diffused, and is so still among the women of some lower races, its limitation to the face being due to sexual selection and the enhanced beauty thus achieved. Féré once had occasion to examine, when completely nude, a boy of thirteen whose sexual organs were deformed; when accused of masturbation he became covered by a blush which spread uniformly over his face, neck, body and limbs, before and behind, except only the hands and feet. Féré asks whether such a universal blush is more common than we imagine, or whether the state of nudity favors its manifestation. (*Comptes Rendus, Société de Biologie*, April 1, 1905.) It may be added that Partridge mentions one case in which the hands blushed.

The sexual relationships of blushing are unquestionable. It occurs chiefly in women; it attains its chief intensity at puberty and during adolescence; its most common occasion is some more or less sexual suggestion; among one hundred and sixty-two occasions of blushing enumerated by Partridge, by far the most frequent cause was teasing, usually about the other sex. "An erection," it has been said, "is a blushing of the penis." Stanley Hall seems to suggest that the sexual blush is a vicarious genital flushing of blood, diverted from the genital sphere by an inhibition of fear, just as, in girls, giggling is also very frequently a vicarious outlet of shame; the sexual blush would thus be the outcome of an ancestral sex-fear; it is as an irradiation of sexual erethism that the blush may contain an element of pleasure.[1]

Bloch remarks that the blush is sexual, because reddening of the face, as well as of the genitals, is an accompaniment of sexual emotion (*Beiträge zur Ätiologie der Psychopathia Sexualis*, Teil II, p. 39).

---

[1] G. Stanley Hall, "A Study of Fears," *American Journal Psychology*, 1897.

"Do you not think," a correspondent writes, "that the sexual blush, at least, really represents a vaso-relaxor effect quite the same as erection? The embarrassment which arises is due to a perception of this fact under circumstances which are felt to be unsuited for such a condition. There may arise the fear of awakening disgust by the exhibition of a state which is out of place. I have noticed that such a blush is produced when a sufficiently young and susceptible woman is pumped full of compliments. This blush seems accompanied by pleasure which does not always change to fear or disgust, but is felt to be attractive. When discomfort arises, most women say that they feel this because 'it looks as if they had no control over themselves.' When they feel that there is no need for control, they no longer feel fear, and the relaxor effect has a wider field of operation, producing a general rosiness, erection of spinal sexual organs, etc. Such a blush would thus be a partial sexual equivalent, and allow of the inhibition of other sexual effects, through the warning it gives, and the fear aroused, as well as being in itself a slight outlet of relaxor energy. When the relationships of the persons concerned allow freedom to the special sexual stimuli, as in marriage, blushing does not occur so often, and when it does it has not so often the consequent of fear."

There can be no doubt that the blush is sexually attractive. The blush is the expression of an impulse to concealment and flight, which tends automatically to arouse in the beholder the corresponding impulse of pursuit, so that the central situation of courtship is at once presented. Women are more or less conscious of this, as well as men, and this recognition is an added source of embarrassment when it cannot become a source of pleasure. The ancient use of rouge testifies to the beauty of the blush, and Darwin stated that, in Turkish slave-markets, the girls who readily blushed fetched the highest prices. To evoke a blush, even by producing embarrassment, is very commonly a cause of masculine gratification.

Savages, both men and women, blush even beneath a dusky skin (for the phenomenon of blushing among different races, see Waitz, *Anthropologie der Naturvölker*, Bd. I, pp. 149-150), and it is possible that natural selection, as well as sexual selection, has been favorable to the development of the blush. It is scarcely an accident that, as has been often observed, criminals, or the antisocial element of the community—whether by the habits of their lives or by congenital abnormality—blush less easily than normal persons. Kroner (*Das körperliche Gefühl*, 1887, p. 130) remarks: "The origin of a specific connection between shame and blushing is the work of a *social selection*. It is certainly an immediate advantage for a man not to blush; indirectly, however, it is a disadvantage, because in other ways he will be known as shameless, and on that account, as a rule, he will be shut out from propagation. This social selection will be specially exercised on the female sex, and on this account, women blush to a greater extent, and more readily, than men."

The importance of the blush, and the emotional confusion behind it, as the sanction of modesty is shown by the significant fact that, by lulling emotional confusion, it is possible to inhibit the sense of modesty. In other words, we are here in the presence of a fear—to a large extent a sex-fear—impelling to concealment, and dreading self-attention; this fear naturally disappears, even though its ostensible cause remains, when it becomes apparent that there is no reason for fear.

That is the reason why nakedness in itself has nothing to do with modesty or immodesty; it is the conditions under which the nakedness occurs which determine whether or not modesty will be roused. If none of the factors of modesty are violated, if no embarrassing self-attention is excited, if there is a consciousness of perfect propriety alike in the subject and in the spectator, nakedness is entirely compatible with the most scrupulous modesty. A. Duval, a pupil of Ingres, tells that a female model was once quietly posing, completely nude, at the École des Beaux Arts. Suddenly she screamed and ran to cover herself with her garments. She had seen a workman on the roof gazing inquisitively at her through a skylight.[1] And Paola Lombroso describes how a lady, a diplomatist's wife, who went to a gathering where she found herself the only woman in evening dress, felt, to her own surprise, such sudden shame that she could not keep back her tears.

It thus comes about that the emotion of modesty necessarily

[1] Men are also very sensitive to any such inquisitiveness on the part of the opposite sex. To this cause, perhaps, and possibly, also, to the fear of causing disgust, may be ascribed the objection of men to undress before women artists and women doctors. I am told there is often difficulty in getting men to pose nude to women artists. Sir Jonathan Hutchinson was compelled, some years ago, to exclude lady members of the medical profession from the instructive demonstrations at his museum, "on account of the unwillingness of male patients to undress before them." A similar unwillingness is not found among women patients, but it must be remembered that, while women are accustomed to men as doctors, men (in England) are not yet accustomed to women as doctors.

depends on the feelings of the people around. The absence of
the emotion by no means signifies immodesty, provided that the
reactions of modesty are at once set in motion under the stress
of a spectator's eye that is seen to be lustful, inquisitive, or
reproachful. This is proved to be the case among primitive
peoples everywhere. The Japanese woman, naked as in daily
life she sometimes is, remains unconcerned because she excites
no disagreeable attention, but the inquisitive and unmannerly
European's eye at once causes her to feel confusion. Stratz, a
physician, and one, moreover, who had long lived among the
Javanese who frequently go naked, found that naked Japanese
women felt no embarrassment in his presence.

It is doubtless as a cloak to the blush that we must explain
the curious influence of darkness in restraining the manifestations of modesty, as many lovers have discovered, and as we may
notice in our cities after dark. This influence of darkness in
inhibiting modesty is a very ancient observation. Burton, in the
Anatomy of Melancholy, quotes from Dandinus the saying *"Nox
facit impudentes,"* directly associating this with blushing, and
Bargagli, the Siennese novelist, wrote in the sixteenth century
that, "it is commonly said of women, that they will do in the dark
what they would not do in the light." It is true that the
immodesty of a large city at night is to some extent explained
by the irruption of prostitutes at that time; prostitutes, being
habitually nearer to the threshold of immodesty, are more
markedly affected by this influence. But it is an influence to
which the most modest women are, at all events in some degree,
susceptible. It has, indeed, been said that a woman is always
more her real self in the dark than in the glare of daylight; this
is part of what Chamberlain calls her night-inspiration.

"Traces of the night-inspiration, of the influence of the primitive
fire-group, abound in woman. Indeed, it may be said (the life of
Southern Europe and of American society of to-day illustrates this
point abundantly) that she is, in a sense, a night-being, for the activity,
physical and moral, of modern women (revealed *e.g.* in the dance and
the nocturnal intellectualities of society) in this direction is remarkable.
Perhaps we may style a good deal of her ordinary day-labor as rest, or
the commonplaces and banalities of her existence, her evening and night

life being the true side of her activities" (A. F. Chamberlain, "Work and Rest," *Popular Science Monthly*, March, 1902). Giessler, who has studied the general influence of darkness on human psychic life, reaches conclusions which harmonize with these (C. M. Giessler, "Der Einfluss der Dunkelheit auf das Seelenleben des Menschen," *Vierteljahrsschrift für wissenschaftliche Philosophie*, 1904, pp. 255-279). I have not been able to see Giessler's paper, but, according to a summary of it, he comes to the result that in the dark the soul's activities are nearer to its motor pole than to its sensitive pole, and that there is a tendency for phenomena belonging to the early period of development to be prominent, motor memory functioning more than representative memory, attention more than apperception, imagination more than logical thinking, egoistic more than altruistic morals.

It is curious to note that short-sightedness, naturally, though illogically, tends to exert the same influence as darkness in this respect; I am assured by short-sighted persons of both sexes that they are much more liable to the emotions of shyness and modesty with their glasses than without them; such persons with difficulty realize that they are not so dim to others as others are to them. To be in the company of a blind person seems also to be a protection against shyness.[1] It is interesting to learn that congenitally blind children are as sensitive to appearances as normal children, and blush as readily.[2] This would seem to be due to the fact that the habitually blind have permanently adjusted their mental focus to that of normal persons, and react in the same manner as normal persons; blindness is not for them, as it is for the short-sighted without their glasses, a temporary and relative, almost unconscious refuge from clear vision.

It is, of course, not as the mere cloak of a possible blush that darkness gives courage; it is because it lulls detailed self-realization, such conscious self-realization being always a source

[1] "I am acquainted with the case of a shy man," writes Dr. Harry Campbell, in his interesting study of "Morbid Shyness" (*British Medical Journal*, September 26, 1896), "who will make himself quite at home in the house of a blind person, and help himself to wine with the utmost confidence, whereas if a member of the family, who can see, comes into the room, all his old shyness returns, and he wishes himself far away."

[2] Stanley Hall ("Showing Off and Bashfulness," *Pedagogical Seminary*, June, 1903), quotes Dr. Anagnos, of the Perkins Institute for the Blind, to this effect.

of fears, and the blush their definite symbol and visible climax. It is to the blush that we must attribute a curious complementary relationship between the face and the sacro-pubic region as centres of anatomical modesty. The women of some African tribes who go naked, Emin Bey remarked, cover the face with the hand under the influence of modesty. Martial long since observed (Lib. iii, LXVIII) that when an innocent girl looks at the penis she gazes through her fingers. Where, as among many Mohammedan peoples, the face is the chief focus of modesty, the exposure of the rest of the body, including sometimes even the sacro-pubic region, and certainly the legs and thighs, often becomes a matter of indifference.[1]

This concealment of the face is more than a convention; it has a psychological basis. We may observe among ourselves the well-marked feminine tendency to hide the face in order to cloak a possible blush, and to hide the eyes as a method of lulling self-consciousness, a method fabulously attributed to the ostrich with the same end of concealment.[2] A woman who is shy with

---

[1] Thus, Sonnini, in the eighteenth century, noted that the country women in Egypt only wore a single garment, open from the armpits to the knees on each side, so that it revealed the body at every movement; "but this troubles the women little, provided the face is not exposed." (*Voyage dans la Haute et Basse Egypte*, 1779, vol. i, p. 289.) When Casanova was at Constantinople, the Comte de Bonneval, a convert to Islam, assured him that he was mistaken in trying to see a woman's face when he might easily obtain greater favors from her. "The most reserved of Turkish women," the Comte assured him, "only carries her modesty in her face, and as soon as her veil is on she is sure that she will never blush at anything." (*Mémoires*, vol. i, p. 429.)

[2] It is worth noting that this impulse is rooted in the natural instinctive acts and ideas of childhood. Stanley Hall, dealing with the "Early Sense of Self," in the report already mentioned, refers to the eyes as perhaps even more than the hands, feet, and mouth, "the centres of that kind of self-consciousness which is always mindful of how the self appears to others," and proceeds to mention "the very common impression of young children that if the eyes are covered or closed they cannot be seen. Some think the entire body thus vanishes from sight of others; some, that the head also ceases to be visible; and a still higher form of this curious psychosis is that, when they are closed, the soul cannot be seen." (*American Journal of Psychology*, vol. ix, No. 3, 1898.) The instinctive and unreasoned character of this act is further shown by its occurrence in idiots. Näcke mentions that he once had occasion to examine the abdomen of an idiot, who, thereupon, attempted to draw down his shirt with the left hand, while with the right he covered his eyes.

her lover will sometimes experience little or no difficulty in showing any part of her person provided she may cover her face. When, in gynæcological practice, examination of the sexual organs is necessary, women frequently find evident satisfaction in concealing the face with the hands, although not the slightest attention is being directed toward the face, and when an unsophisticated woman is betrayed into a confession which affects her modesty she is apt to turn her back to her interlocutor. "When the face of woman is covered," it has been said, "her heart is bared," and the Catholic Church has recognized this psychological truth by arranging that in the confessional the penitent's face shall not be visible. The gay and innocent freedom of southern women during Carnival is due not entirely to the permitted license of the season or the concealment of identity, but to the mask that hides the face. In England, during Queen Elizabeth's reign and at the Restoration, it was possible for respectable women to be present at the theatre, even during the performance of the most free-spoken plays, because they wore masks. The fan has often subserved a similar end.[1]

All such facts serve to show that, though the forms of modesty may change, it is yet a very radical constituent of human nature in all stages of civilization, and that it is, to a large extent, maintained by the mechanism of blushing.

---

[1] *Cf.* Stanley Hall and T. Smith, "Showing Off and Bashfulness," *American Journal of Psychology*, June, 1903.

IV.

Summary of the Factors of Modesty—The Future of Modesty—
Modesty an Essential Element of Love.

WE have seen that the factors of modesty are numerous. To
attempt to explain modesty by dismissing it as merely an example of psychic paralysis, of *Stauung,* is to elude the problem
by the statement of what is little more than a truism. Modesty
is a complexus of emotions with their concomitant ideas which
we must unravel to comprehend.

We have found among the factors of modesty: (1) the
primitive animal gesture of sexual refusal on the part of the
female, when she is not at that moment of her generative life
at which she desires the male's advances; (2) the fear of
arousing disgust, a fear primarily due to the close proximity of
the sexual centre to the points of exit of those excretions which
are useless and unpleasant, even in many cases to animals; (3)
the fear of the magic influence of sexual phenomena, and the
ceremonial and ritual practices primarily based on this fear, and
ultimately passing into simple rules of decorum which are signs
and guardians of modesty; (4) the development of ornament and
clothing, concomitantly fostering alike the modesty which re-
presses male sexual desire and the coquetry which seeks to allure
it; (5) the conception of women as property, imparting a new
and powerful sanction to an emotion already based on more
natural and primitive facts.

It must always be remembered that these factors do not
usually occur separately. Very often they are all of them implied
in a single impulse of modesty. We unravel the cord in order to
investigate its construction, but in real life the strands are more
or less indistinguishably twisted together.

It may still be asked finally whether, on the whole, modesty
really becomes a more prominent emotion as civilization advances.
I do not think this position can be maintained. It is a great
mistake, as we have seen, to suppose that in becoming extended

(80)

modesty also becomes intensified. On the contrary, this very extension is a sign of weakness. Among savages, modesty is far more radical and invincible than among the civilized. Of the Araucanian women of Chile, Treutler has remarked that they are distinctly more modest than the Christian white population, and such observations might be indefinitely extended. It is, as we have already noted, in a new and crude civilization, eager to mark its separation from a barbarism it has yet scarcely escaped, that we find an extravagant and fantastic anxiety to extend the limits of modesty in life, and art, and literature. In older and more mature civilizations—in classical antiquity, in old Japan, in France—modesty, while still a very real influence, becomes a much less predominant and all-pervading influence. In life it becomes subservient to human use, in art to beauty, in literature to expression.

Among ourselves we may note that modesty is a much more invincible motive among the lower social classes than among the more cultivated classes. This is so even when we should expect the influence of occupation to induce familiarity. Thus I have been told of a ballet-girl who thinks it immodest to bathe in the fashion customary at the sea-side, and cannot make up her mind to do so, but she appears on the stage every night in tights as a matter of course; while Fanny Kemble, in her *Reminiscences,* tells of an actress, accustomed to appear in tights, who died a martyr to modesty rather than allow a surgeon to see her inflamed knee. Modesty is, indeed, a part of self-respect, but in the fully-developed human being self-respect itself holds in check any excessive modesty.[1]

We must remember, moreover, that there are more definite grounds for the subordination of modesty with the development

---

[1] Freud remarks that one may often hear, concerning elderly ladies, that in their youth in the country, they suffered, almost to collapse, from hæmorrhages from the genital passage, because they were too modest to seek medical advice and examination; he adds that it is extremely rare to find such an attitude among our young women to-day. (S. Freud, *Zur Neurosenlehre,* 1906, p. 182.) It would be easy to find evidence of the disappearance of misplaced signs of modesty formerly prevalent, although this mark of increasing civilization has not always penetrated to our laws and regulations.

of civilization. We have seen that the factors of modesty are many, and that most of them are based on emotions which make little urgent appeal save to races in a savage or barbarous condition. Thus, disgust, as Richet has truly pointed out, necessarily decreases as knowledge increases.[1] As we analyze and understand our experiences better, so they cause us less disgust. A rotten egg is disgusting, but the chemist feels no disgust toward sulphuretted hydrogen; while a solution of propylamin does not produce the disgusting impression of that human physical uncleanliness of which it is an odorous constituent. As disgust becomes analyzed, and as self-respect tends to increased physical purity, so the factor of disgust in modesty is minimized. The factor of ceremonial uncleanness, again, which plays so urgent a part in modesty at certain stages of culture, is to-day without influence except in so far as it survives in etiquette. In the same way the social-economic factor of modesty, based on the conception of women as property, belongs to a stage of human development which is wholly alien to an advanced civilization. Even the most fundamental impulse of all, the gesture of sexual refusal, is normally only imperative among animals and savages. Thus civilization tends to subordinate, if not to minimize, modesty, to render it a grace of life rather than a fundamental social law of life. But an essential grace of life it still remains, and whatever delicate variations it may assume we can scarcely conceive of its disappearance.

In the art of love, however, it is more than a grace; it must always be fundamental. Modesty is not indeed the last word of love, but it is the necessary foundation for all love's most exquisite audacities, the foundation which alone gives worth and sweetness to what Senancour calls its "delicious impudence."[2] Without modesty we could not have, nor rightly value at its true worth, that bold and pure candor which is at once the final revelation of love and the seal of its sincerity.

---

[1] "Disgust," he remarks, "is a sort of synthesis which attaches to the total form of objects, and which must diminish and disappear as scientific analysis separates into parts what, as a whole, is so repugnant."

[2] Senancour, *De l'Amour*, 1834, vol. i, p. 316. He remarks that a useless and false reserve is due to stupidity rather than to modesty.

Even Hohenemser—who argues that for the perfect man there could be no shame, because shame rests on an inner conflict in one's own personality, and "the perfect man knows no inner conflict"—believes that, since humanity is imperfect, modesty possesses a high and, indeed, symptomatic value, for "its presence shows that according to the measure of a man's ideal personality, his valuations are established."

Dugas goes further, and asserts that the ideals of modesty develop with human development, and forever take on new and finer forms. "There is," he declares, "a very close relationship between naturalness, or sincerity, and modesty, for in love, naturalness is the ideal attained, and modesty is only the fear of coming short of that ideal. Naturalness is the sign and the test of perfect love. It is the sign of it, for, when love can show itself natural and true, one may conclude that it is purified of its unavowable imperfections or defects, of its alloy of wretched and petty passions, its grossness, its chimerical notions, that it has become strong and healthy and vigorous. It is the ordeal of it, for to show itself natural, to be always true, without shrinking, it must have all the lovable qualities, and have them without seeking, as a second nature. What we call 'natural,' is indeed really acquired; it is the gift of a physical and moral evolution which it is precisely the object of modesty to keep. Modesty is the feeling of the true, that is to say, of the healthy, in love; it long exists as a vision, not yet attained; vague, yet sufficiently clear for all that deviates from it to be repelled as offensive and painful. At first, a remote and seemingly inaccessible ideal, as it comes nearer it grows human and individual, and emerges from the region of dream, ceasing not to be loved as ideal, even when it is possessed as real.

"At first sight, it seems paradoxical to define modesty as an aspiration towards truth in love; it seems, on the contrary, to be an altogether factitious feeling. But to simplify the problem, we have to suppose modesty reduced to its normal functions, disengaged from its superstitions, its variegated customs and prejudices, the true modesty of simple and healthy natures, as far removed from prudery as from immodesty. And what we term the natural, or the true in love, is the singular mingling of two forms of imaginations, wrongly supposed to be incompatible: ideal aspiration and the sense for the realities of life. Thus defined, modesty not only repudiates that cold and dissolving criticism which deprives love of all poetry, and prepares the way for a brutal realism; it also excludes that light and detached imagination which floats above love, the mere idealism of heroic sentiments, which cherishes poetic illusions, and passes, without seeing it, the love that is real and alive. True modesty implies a love not addressed to the heroes of vain romances, but to living people, with their feet on the earth. But on the other hand, modesty is the respect of love; if it is not shocked by its physical necessities, if it accepts physiological and psychological conditions, it also maintains the ideal of those moral proprieties outside of which, for all of us, love cannot be enjoyed. When love is really felt, and not vainly imagined, modesty is the requirement of an ideal of dignity, conceived as the very condition of that love. Separate modesty from love, that is, from love which is not floating in the air, but crystallized around a real person, and its psychological reality, its poignant and tragic character, disappears." (Dugas, "La Pudeur," *Revue Philosophique*, Nov., 1903.) So conceived, modesty becomes a virtue, almost identical with the Roman *modestia*.

THE PHENOMENA OF SEXUAL PERIODICITY.

I.

The Various Physiological and Psychological Rhythms—Menstruation—The Alleged Influence of the Moon—Frequent Suppression of Menstruation among Primitive Races—Mittelschmerz—Possible Tendency to a Future Intermenstrual Cycle—Menstruation among Animals—Menstruating Monkeys and Apes—What is Menstruation—Its Primary Cause Still Obscure—The Relation of Menstruation to Ovulation—The Occasional Absence of Menstruation in Health—The Relation of Menstruation to "Heat"—The Prohibition of Intercourse during Menstruation—The Predominance of Sexual Excitement at and around the Menstrual Period—Its Absence during the Period Frequently Apparent only.

THROUGHOUT the vegetable and animal worlds the sexual functions are periodic. From the usually annual period of flowering in plants, with its play of sperm-cell and germ-cell and consequent seed-production, through the varying sexual energies of animals, up to the monthly effervescence of the generative organism in woman, seeking not without the shedding of blood for the gratification of its reproductive function, from first to last we find unfailing evidence of the periodicity of sex. At first the sun, and then, as some have thought, the moon, have marked throughout a rhythmic impress on the phenomena of sex. To understand these phenomena we have not only to recognize the bare existence of that periodic fact, but to realize its implications.

Rhythm, it is scarcely necessary to remark, is far from characterizing sexual activity alone. It is the character of all biological activity, alike on the physical and the psychic sides. All the organs of the body appear to be in a perpetual process of rhythmic contraction and expansion. The heart is rhythmic, so is the respiration. The spleen is rhythmic, so also the bladder. The uterus constantly undergoes regular rhythmic contractions at brief intervals. The vascular system, down to the smallest capillaries, is acted on by three series of vibrations, and every

(85)

separate fragment of muscular tissue possesses rhythmic contractility. Growth itself is rhythmic, and, as Malling-Hansen and subsequent observers have found, follows a regular annual course as well as a larger cycle. On the psychic sides attention is rhythmic. We are always irresistibly compelled to impart a rhythm to every succession of sounds, however uniform and monotonous. A familiar example of this is the rhythm we can seldom refrain from hearing in the puffing of an engine. A series of experiments, by Bolton, on thirty subjects showed that the clicks of an electric telephone connected in an induction-apparatus nearly always fell into rhythmic groups, usually of two or four, rarely of three or five, the rhythmic perception being accompanied by a strong impulse to make corresponding muscular movements.[1]

It is, however, with the influence—to some extent real, to some extent, perhaps, only apparent—of cosmic rhythm that we are here concerned. The general tendency, physical and psychic, of nervous action to fall into rhythm is merely interesting from the present point of view as showing a biological predisposition to accept any periodicity that is habitually imposed upon the organism.[2] Menstruation has always been associated with the lunar revolutions.[3] Darwin, without specifically mentioning menstruation, has suggested that the explanation of the allied cycle of gestation in mammals, as well as incubation in birds, may be found in the condition under which ascidians live at high and low water in consequence of the phenomena of tidal change.[4] It must, however, be remembered that the ascidian

1 Thaddeus L. Bolton, "Rhythm," *American Journal of Psychology*, January, 1894.

2 It is scarcely necessary to warn the reader that this statement does not prejudge the question of the inheritance of acquired characters, although it fits in with Semon's Mnemic theory. We can, however, very well suppose that the organism became adjusted to the rhythms of its environment by a series of congenital variations. Or it might be held, on the basis of Weismann's doctrine, that the germ-plasm has been directly modified by the environment.

3 Thus, the Papuans, in some districts, believe that the first menstruation is due to an actual connection, during sleep, with the moon in the shape of a man, the girl dreaming that a real man is embracing her. (*Reports Cambridge Expedition to Torres Straits*, vol. v, p. 206.)

4 Darwin, *Descent of Man*, p. 164.

origin of the vertebrates has since been contested from many sides, and, even if we admit that at all events some such allied conditions in the early history of vertebrates and their ancestors tended to impress a lunar cycle on the race, it must still be remembered that the monthly periodicity of menstruation only becomes well marked in the human species.[1] Bearing in mind the influence exerted on both the habits and the emotions even of animals by the brightness of moonlight nights, it is perhaps not extravagant to suppose that, on organisms already ancestrally predisposed to the influence of rhythm in general and of cosmic rhythm in particular, the periodically recurring full moon, not merely by its stimulation of the nervous system, but possibly by the special opportunities which it gave for the exercise of the sexual functions, served to implant a lunar rhythm on menstruation. How important such a factor may be we have evidence in the fact that the daily life of even the most civilized peoples is still regulated by a weekly cycle which is apparently a segment of the cosmic lunar cycle.

Mantegazza has suggested that the sexual period became established with relation to the lunar period because moonlight nights were favorable to courting,[2] and Nelson remarks that in his experience young and robust persons are subject to recurrent periods of wakefulness at night which they attribute to the action of the full moon. One may perhaps refer also to the tendency of bright moonlight to stir the emotions of the young,

---

[1] While in the majority of women the menstrual cycle is regular for the individual, and corresponds to the lunar month of 28 days, it must be added that in a considerable minority it is rather longer, or, more usually, shorter than this, and in many individuals is not constant. Osterloh found a regular type of menstruation in 68 per cent. healthy women, four weeks being the most usual length of the cycle; in 21 per cent. the cycle was always irregular. See Näcke, "Die Menstruation und ihr Einfluss bei chronischen Psychosen," *Archiv für Psychiatrie*, 1896, Bd. 28, Heft 1.

[2] Among the Duala and allied negro peoples of Bantu stock dances of markedly erotic character take place at full moon. Gason describes the dances and sexual festivals of the South Australian blacks, generally followed by promiscuous intercourse, as taking place at full moon. (*Journal of the Anthropological Institute*, November, 1894, p. 174.) In all parts of the world, indeed, including Christendom, festivals are frequently regulated by the phases of the moon.

especially at puberty, a tendency which in neurotic persons may become almost morbid.[1]

It is interesting to point out that, the farther back we are able to trace the beginnings of culture, the more important we find the part played by the moon. Next to the alteration of day and night, the moon's changes are the most conspicuous and startling phenomena of Nature; they first suggest a basis for reckoning time; they are of the greatest use in primitive agriculture; and everywhere the moon is held to have vast influence on the whole of organic life. Hahn has suggested that the reason why mythological systems do not usually present the moon in the supreme position which we should expect, is that its immense importance is so ancient a fact that it tends, with mythological development, to become overlaid by other elements.[2] According to Seler, Quetzalcouatl and Tezcatlipoca, the two most considerable figures in the Mexican pantheon, are to be regarded mainly as complementary forms of the moon divinity, and the moon was the chief Mexican measurer of time.[3] Even in Babylonia, where the sun was most specially revered, at the earliest period the moon ranked higher, being gradually superseded by the worship of the sun.[4] Although such considerations as these will by no means take us as far back as the earliest appearance of menstruation, they may serve to indicate that the phases of the moon probably played a large part in the earliest evolution of man. With that statement we must at present rest content.

It is possible that the monthly character of menstruation, while representing a general tendency of the human race, always and everywhere prevalent, may be modified in the future. It is

---

[1] It has often been held that the course of insanity is influenced by the moon. Of comparatively recent years, this thesis has been maintained by Koster (*Ueber die Gesetze des periodischen Irreseins und verwandter Nervenzustände*, Bonn, 1882), who argues in detail that periodic insanity tends to fall into periods of seven days or multiples of seven.

[2] Ed. Hahn, *Demeter und Baubo*, p. 23.

[3] E. Seler, *Zeitschrift für Ethnologie*, 1907, Heft 1, p. 39. And as regards the primitive importance of the moon, see also Frazer, *Adonis, Attis, Osiris*, Ch. VIII.

[4] Jastrow, *Religion of Babylonia*, 1898, pp. 68, 75-79, 461.

a noteworthy fact that among many primitive races menstruation only occurs at long intervals. Thus among Eskimo women menstruation follows the peculiar cosmic conditions to which the people are subjected; Cook, the ethnologist of the Peary North Greenland expedition, found that menstruation only began after the age of nineteen, and that it was usually suppressed during the winter months, when there is no sun, only about one in ten women continuing to menstruate during this period.[1] It was stated by Velpeau that Lapland and Greenland women usually only menstruate every three months, or even only two or three times during the year. On the Faroe Islands it is said that menstruation is frequently absent. Among the Samoyeds, Mantegazza mentions that menstruation is so slight that some travelers have denied its existence. Azara noted among the Guaranis of Paraguay that menstruation was not only slight in amount, but the periods were separated by long intervals. Among the Indians in North America, again, menstruation appears to be scanty. Thus, Holder, speaking of his experience with the Crow Indians of Montana, says: "I am quite sure that full-blood Indians in this latitude do not menstruate so freely as white women, not usually exceeding three days."[2] Among the naked women of Tierra del Fuego, it is said that there is often no physical sign of the menses for six months at a time. These observations are noteworthy, though they clearly indicate, on the whole, that primitiveness in race is a very powerless factor without a cold climate. On the other hand, again, there is some reason to suppose that in Europe there is a latent tendency in some women for the menstrual cycle to split up further into two cycles, by the appearance of a latent minor climax in the middle of the monthly interval. I allude to the phenomenon usually called *Mittelschmerz,* middle period, or intermenstrual pain.

---

[1] Even in England, Barnes has known women of feeble sexual constitution who menstruated only in summer (R. Barnes, *Diseases of Women,* 1878, p. 192).

[2] A. B. Holder, "Gynecic Notes among American Indians," *American Journal of Obstetrics,* No. 6, 1892.

Since the investigations of Goodman, Stephenson, Van Ott, Reinl, Jacobi, and others, it has been generally recognized that menstruation is a continuous process, the flow being merely the climax of a menstrual cycle, a physiological wave which is in constant flux or reflux. This cycle manifests itself in all a woman's activities, in metabolism, respiration, temperature, etc., as well as on the nervous and psychic side. The healthier the woman is, the less conscious is the cyclic return of her life, but the cycle may be traced (as Hegar has found) even before puberty takes place, while Salerni has found that even in amenorrhœa the menstrual cycle still manifests itself in the temperature and respiration. (*Rivista Sperimentale di Freniatria*, XXX, fasc. 2-3.)

For a summary of the phenomena of the menstrual cycle, see Havelock Ellis, *Man and Woman*, fourth ed., revised and enlarged, Ch. XI; "The Functional Periodicity of Women." *Cf.* Keller, *Archives Générales de Médecine*, May, 1897; Hegar, *Allgemeine Zeitschrift für Psychiatrie*, 1901, Heft 2 and 3; Helen MacMurchy, *Lancet*, Oct. 5. 1901; A. E. Giles, *Transactions Obstetrical Society London*, vol. xxxix, p. 115, etc.

Mittelschmerz is a condition of pain occurring about the middle of the intermenstrual period, either alone or accompanied by a slight sanguineous discharge, or, more frequently, a non-sanguineous discharge. (In a case described by Van Voornveld, the manifestation was confined to a regularly occurring rise of temperature.) The phenomenon varies, but seems usually to occur about the fourteenth day, and to last two or three days. Laycock, in 1840 (*Nervous Diseases of Women*, p. 46), gave instances of women with an intermenstrual period. Depaul and Guéniot (*Dictionnaire Encyclopédique des Sciences Médicales*, Art., "Menstruation," p. 694) speak of intermenstrual symptoms, and even actual flow, as occurring in women who are in a perfect state of health, and constituting genuine "*règles surnuméraries.*" The condition is, however, said to have been first fully described by Valleix; then, in 1872, by Sir William Priestley; and subsequently by Fehling, Fasbender, Sorel, Halliday Croom, Findley, Addinsell, and others. (See, for instance, "Mittelschmerz," by J. Halliday Croom, *Transactions of Edinburgh Obstetrical Society*, vol. xxi, 1896. Also, Krieger, *Menstruation*, pp. 68-69.) Fliess (*Die Beziehungen zwischen Nase und weiblichen Geschlechts-Organen*, p. 118) goes so far as to assert that an intermenstrual period of menstrual symptoms—which he terms *Nebenmenstruation*—is "a phenomenon well known to most healthy women." Observations are at present too few to allow any definite conclusions, and in some of the cases so far recorded a pathological condition of the sexual organs has been found to exist. Rosner, of Cracow, however, found that only in one case out of twelve was there any disease present (*La Gynécologie*, June, 1905), and Storer, who has met with twenty cases, insists on the remarkable and definite regularity of the manifestations, wholly unlike those of neuralgia (*Boston Medical and Surgical Journal*, April 19, 1900). There is no agreement as to the cause of *Mittelschmerz* Addinsell attributed it to disease of the Fallopian tubes. This, however, is denied by such competent authorities as Cullingworth and Bland Sutton. Others, like Priestley, and subsequently Marsh (*American Journal of Obstetrics*, July, 1897), have sought to find the explanation in the occurrence of ovulation. This theory is, however, unsupported by facts, and eventually rests on the exploded belief that ovulation is the cause of menstruation. Rosner, following Richelet, vaguely attributes it to the diffused hyperæmia which is generally present. Van de Velde also attributes it to an abnormal fall of vascular tone, causing passive congestion of the pelvic viscera. Others again, like Armand Routh and MacLean, in the course of an interesting discussion on *Mittelschmerz* at the Obstetric Society of London, on the second day of March, 1898, believe that we may trace here a double menstruation, and would explain the phenomenon by assuming that in certain cases there is an intermenstrual as well as a menstrual cycle. The question is not yet ripe for settlement, though it is fully evident that, looking broadly at the phenomena of rut and menstruation, the main basis of their increasing frequency as we rise toward civilized man is increase of nutrition, heat and sunlight being factors of nutrition. When dealing with civilized man, however, we are probably concerned not merely with general nutrition, but with the nervous direction of that nutrition.

At this stage it is natural to inquire what the corresponding phenomena are among animals. Unfortunately, imperfect as is our comprehension of the human phenomena, our knowledge of the corresponding phenomena among animals is much more fragmentary and incomplete. Among most animals menstruation does not exist, being replaced by what is known as heat, or œstrus, which usually occurs once or twice a year, in spring and in autumn, sometimes affecting the male as well as the female.[1] There is, however, a great deal of progression in the upward march of the phenomena, as we approach our own and

---

[1] In the male, the phenomenon is termed rut, and is most familiar in the stag. I quote from Marshall and Jolly some remarks on the infrequency of rut: " 'The male wild Cat,' Mr. Cocks informs us, (like the stag), 'has a rutting season, calls loudly, almost day and night, making far more noise than the female.' This information is of interest, inasmuch as the males of most carnivores, although they undoubtedly show signs of increased sexual activity at some times more than at others, are not known to have anything of the nature of a

allied zoölogical series. Heat in domesticated cows usually
occurs every three weeks. The female hippopotamus in the
Zoölogical Gardens has been observed to exhibit monthly sexual
excitement, with swelling and secretion from the vulva. Progression is not only toward greater frequency with higher evolution or with increased domestication, but there is also a change in
the character of the flow. As Wiltshire,[1] in his remarkable
lectures on the "Comparative Physiology of Menstruation,"
asserted as a law, the more highly evolved the animal, the more
sanguineous the catamenial flow.

It is not until we reach the monkeys that this character of
the flow becomes well marked. Monthly sanguineous discharges
have been observed among many monkeys. In the seventeenth
century various observers in many parts of the world—Bohnius,
Peyer, Helbigius, Van der Wiel, and others—noted menstruation in monkeys.[2] Buffon observed it among various monkeys
as well as in the orang-utan. J. G. St. Hilaire and Cuvier,
many years ago, declared that menstruation exists among a
variety of monkeys and lower apes. Rengger described a vaginal discharge in a species of cebus in Paraguay, while Raciborski
observed in the Jardin des Plantes that the menstrual hæmorrhage in guenons was so abundant that the floor of the cage
was covered by it to a considerable extent; the same variety of
monkey was observed at Surinam, by Hill, a surgeon in the
Dutch army, who noted an abundant sanguineous flow occurring at every new moon, and lasting about three days, the animal
at this time also showing signs of sexual excitement.[3]

_____

regularly recurrent rutting season. Nothing of the kind is known in
the Dog, nor, so far as we are aware, in the males of the domestic Cat,
or the Ferret, all of which seem to be capable of copulation at any time
of the year. On the other hand, the males of Seals appear to have a rutting season at the same time as the sexual season of the female."
(Marshall and Jolly, "Contributions to the Physiology of Mammalian
Reproduction," _Philosophical Transactions_, 1905, B. 198.)

[1] A. Wiltshire, _British Medical Journal_, March, 1883. The best
account of heat known to me is contained in Ellenberger's _Vergleichende
Physiologie der Haussäugethiere_, 1892, Band 4, Theil 2, pp. 276-284.

[2] Schurig (_Parthenologia_, 1729, p. 125), gives numerous references and quotations.

[3] Quoted by Icard, _La Femme_, etc., p. 63.

The macaque and the baboon appear to be the non-human animals, in which menstruation has been most carefully observed. In the former, besides the flow, Bland Sutton remarks that "all the naked or pale-colored parts of the body, such as the face, neck, and ischial regions, assume a lively pink color; in some cases, it is a vivid red."[1] The flow is slight, but the coloring lasts several days, and in warm weather the labia are much swollen.

Heape[2] has most fully and carefully described menstruation in monkeys. He found at Calcutta that the *Macacus cynomolgus* menstruated regularly on the 20th of December, 20th of January, and about the 20th of February. The *Cynocephalus porcaria* and the *Semnopithecus entellus* both menstruated each month for about four days. In the *Macaci rhesus* and *cynomolgus* at menstruation "the nipples and vulva become swollen and deeply congested, and the skin of the buttocks swollen, tense, and of a brilliant-red or even purple color. The abdominal wall also, for a short space upward, and the inside of the thighs, sometimes as far down as the heel, and the under surface of the tail for half its length or more, are all colored a vivid red, while the skin of the face, especially about the eyes, is flushed or blotched with red." In late gestation the coloring is still more vivid. Something similar is to be seen in the males also.

Distant, who kept a female baboon for some time, has recorded the dates of menstruation during a year. He found that nine periods occurred during the year. The average length between the periods was nearly six weeks, but they occurred more frequently in the late autumn and the winter than in the summer.[3]

It is an interesting fact, Heape noted, that, notwithstanding menstruation, the seasonal influence, or rut, still persisted in the monkeys he investigated.

---

[1] Bland Sutton, *Surgical Diseases of the Ovaries*, and *British Gynecological Journal*, vol. ii.

[2] W. Heape, "The Menstruation of *Semnopithecus Entellus*," *Philosophical Transactions*, 1894; "Menstruation and Ovulation of *Macacus Rhesus*," *Philosophical Transactions*, 1897.

[3] W. L. Distant, "Notes on the Chacma Baboon," *Zoologist*, January, 1897, p. 29.

In the anthropoid apes, Hartmann remarks that several observers have recorded periodic menstruation in the chimpanzee, with flushing and enlargement of the external parts, and protrusion of the external lips, which are not usually visible, while there is often excessive enlargement and reddening of these parts and of the posterior callosities during sexual excitement. Very little, however, appears to be definitely known regarding any form of menstruation in the higher apes. M. Deniker, who has made a special study of the anthropoid apes, informs me that he has so far been unable to make definite observations regarding the existence of menstruation. Moll remarks that he received information regarding such a phenomenon in the orang-utan. A pair of orang-utans was kept in the Berlin Zoölogical Gardens some years ago, and the female was stated to have at intervals a menstrual flow resembling that of women, and during this period to refrain from sexual congress, which was otherwise usually exercised at regular intervals, at least every two or three days; Moll adds, however, that, while his informant is a reliable man, the length of time that has elapsed may have led him to make mistakes in details. Keith, in a paper read before the Zoölogical Society of London, has described menstruation in a chimpanzee; it occurred every twenty-third or twenty-fourth day, and lasted for three days; the discharge was profuse, and first appeared in about the ninth or tenth year.[1]

What is menstruation? It is easy to describe it, by its obvious symptoms, as a monthly discharge of blood from the uterus, but nearly as much as that was known in the infancy of the world. When we seek to probe more intimately into the nature of menstruation we are still baffled, not merely as regards its cause, but even as regards its precise mechanism. "The primary cause of menstruation remains unexplained"; "the cause of menstruation remains as obscure as ever"; so conclude two of the most thorough and cautious investigators into this subject.[2] It is, however, widely accepted that the main cause of

---

[1] *Nature*, March 23, 1899.

[2] W. Heape, "The Menstruation of *Semnopithecus Entellus*," *Philosophical Transactions*, 1894, p. 483; Bland Sutton, *Surgical Diseases of the Ovaries*, 1896.

menstruation is a rhythmic contraction of the uterus,—the result of a disappointed preparation for impregnation,—a kind of miniature childbirth. This seems to be the most reasonable view of menstruation; *i.e.,* as an abortion of a decidua. Burdach (according to Beard) was the first who described menstruation as an abortive parturition. "The hypothesis," Marshall and Jolly conclude, "that the entire pro-œstrous process is of the nature of a preparation for the lodgment of the ovum is in accordance with the facts."[1] Fortunately, since we are here primarily concerned with its psychological aspects, the precise biological cause and physiological nature of menstruation do not greatly concern us.

There is, however, one point which of late years has been definitely determined, and which should not be passed without mention: the relation of menstruation to ovulation. It was once supposed that the maturation of an ovule in the ovaries was the necessary accompaniment, and even cause, of menstruation. We now know that ovulation proceeds throughout the whole of life, even before birth, and during gestation,[2] and that removal of the ovaries by no means necessarily involves a cessation of menstruation. It has been shown that regular and even excessive menstruation may take place in the congenital absence of a trace of ovaries or Fallopian tubes.[3] On the other hand, a rudimentary state of the uterus, and a complete absence of menstruation, may exist with well-developed ovaries and

---

[1] T. Bryce and J. Teacher (*Contributions to the Study of the Early Development of the Human Ovum*, 1908), putting the matter somewhat differently, regard menstruation as a cyclical process, providing for the maintenance of the endometrium in a suitable condition of immaturity for the production of the decidua of pregnancy, which they believe may take place at any time of the month, though most favorably shortly before or after a menstrual period which has been accompanied by ovulation.

[2] Robinson, *American Gynecological and Obstetrical Journal,* August, 1905.

[3] Bossi, *Annali di Ostetrica e Ginecologia,* September, 1896; summarized in the *British Medical Journal,* October 31, 1896. As regards the more normal influence of the ovaries over the uterus, see *e.g.* Carmichael and F. H. A. Marshall, "Correlation of the Ovarian and Uterine Functions," *Proceedings Royal Society,* vol. 79, Series B, 1907.

normal ovulation.[1]   We must regard the uterus as to some extent an independent organ, and menstruation as a process which arose, no doubt, with the object, teleologically speaking, of co-operating more effectively with ovulation, but has become largely independent.[2]

It is sometimes stated that menstruation may be entirely absent in perfect health. Few cases of this condition have, however, been recorded with the detail necessary to prove the assertion. One such case was investigated by Dr. H. W. Mitchell, and described in a paper read to the New York County Medical Society, February 22, 1892 (to be found in *Medical Reprints*, June, 1892). The subject was a young, unmarried woman, 24 years of age. She was born in Ireland, and, until her emigration, lived quietly at home with her parents. Being then twenty years of age, she left home and came to New York. Up to that time no signs of menstruation had appeared, and she had never heard that such a function existed. Soon after her arrival in New York, she obtained a situation as a waiting-maid, and it was noticed, after a time, that she was not unwell at each month. Friends filled her ears with wild stories about the dreadful effects likely to follow the absence of menstruation. This worried her greatly, and as a consequence she became pale and anæmic, with loss of flesh, appetite, and sleep, and a long train of imaginary nervous symptoms. She presented herself for treatment, and insisted upon a uterine examination. This revealed no

---

[1] Beuttner, *Centralblatt für Gynäkologie*, No. 49, 1893; summarized in *British Medical Journal*, December, 1893. Many cases show that pregnancy may occur in the absence of menstruation. See, *e.g.*, *Nouvelles Archives d'Obstétrique et de Gynécologie*, 25 Janvier, 1894, supplement, p. 9.

[2] It is still possible, and even probable, that the primordial cause of both phenomena is the same. Heape (*Transactions Obstetrical Society of London*, 1898, vol. xl, p. 161) argues that both menstruation and ovulation are closely connected with and influenced by congestion, and that in the primitive condition they are largely due to the same cause. This primary cause he is inclined to regard as a ferment, due to a change in the constitution of the blood brought about by climatic influences and food, which he proposes to call gonadin. (W. Heape, *Proceedings of Royal Society*, 1905, vol. B. 76, p. 266.) Marshall, who has found that in the ferret and other animals, ovulation may be dependent upon copulation, also considers that ovulation and menstruation, though connected and able to react on each other, may both be dependent upon a common cause; he finds that in bitches and rats heat can be produced by injection of extract from ovaries in the œstrous state (F. H. A. Marshall, *Philosophical Transactions*, 1903, vol. B. 196; also Marshall and Jolly, *id.*, 1905, B. 198). *Cf.* C. J. Bond, "An Inquiry Into Some Points in Uterine and Ovarian Physiology and Pathology in Rabbits," *British Medical Journal*, July 21, 1906.

pathological condition of her uterus. She was assured that she would not die, or become insane, nor a chronic invalid. In consequence she soon forgot that she differed in any way from other girls. A course of chalybeate tonics, generous diet, and proper care of her general health, soon restored her to her normal condition. After close observation for several years, she submitted to a thorough examination, although entirely free from any abnormal symptoms. The examination revealed the following physical condition: Weight, 105 pounds (her weight before leaving Ireland was 130); girth of chest, twenty-nine and a half inches; girth of abdomen, twenty-five inches; girth of pelvis, thirty-four and a half inches; girth of thigh, upper third, twenty inches; heart healthy, sounds and rhythm perfectly normal; pulse, 76; lungs healthy; respiratory murmur clear and distinct over every part; respiration, easy and twenty per minute; the mammæ are well developed, firm, and round; nipples, small, no areola; her skin is soft, smooth, and healthy; figure erect, plump, and symmetrical; her bowels are regular; kidneys, healthy. She has a good appetite, sleeps well, and in no particular shows any sign of ill health. The uterine examination reveals a short vagina, and a small, round cervix uteri, rather less in size than the average, and projecting very slightly into the vaginal canal. Depth of uterus from os to fundus, two and a quarter inches, is very nearly normal. No external sign of abnormal ovaries. She is a well-developed, healthy young woman, performing all her physiological functions naturally and regularly, except the single function of menstruation. No vicarious menstruation takes the place of the natural function, though she has been watched very closely during the past two years, nor the least periodical excitement. It is added that, though the clitoris is normal, the mons veneris is almost destitute of hair, and the labia rather undeveloped, while, "as far as is known," sexual instincts and desire are entirely absent. These latter facts, I may add, would seem to suggest that, in spite of the health of the subject, there is yet some concealed lack of development of the sexual system, of congenital character. In a case recorded by Plant (*Centralblatt für Gynäkologie*, No. 9, 1896, summarized in the *British Medical Journal*, April 4, 1896), in which the internal sexual organs were almost wholly undeveloped, and menstruation absent, the labia were similarly undeveloped, and the pubic hair scanty, while the axillary hair was wholly absent, though that of the head was long and strong.

We may now regard as purely academic the discussion formerly carried on as to whether menstruation is to be regarded as analogous to heat in female animals. For many centuries at least the resemblance has been sufficiently obvious. Raciborski and Pouchet, who first established the regular periodicity of ovulation in mammals, identified heat and menstruation.[1] During the past century there was, notwithstanding, an occasional tendency to deny any real connection. No satisfactory grounds for this denial have, however, been brought forward. Lawson Tait, indeed, and more recently Beard, have stated that menstruation cannot be the period of heat, because women have a disinclination to the approach of the male at that time.[2] But, as we shall see later, this statement is unfounded. An argument which might, indeed, be brought forward is the very remarkable fact that, while in animals the period of heat is the only period for sexual intercourse, among all human races, from the very lowest, the period of menstruation is the one period during which sexual intercourse is strictly prohibited, sometimes under severe penalties, even life itself. This, however, is a social, not a physiological, fact.

Ploss and Bartels call attention to the curious contrast, in this respect, between heat and menstruation. The same authors also mention that in the Middle Ages, however, preachers found it necessary to warn their hearers against the sin of intercourse during the menstrual period. It may be added that Aquinas and many other early theologians held, not only that such intercourse was a deadly sin, but that it engendered leprous and monstrous children. Some later theologians, however, like Sanchez, argued that the Mosaic enactments (such as Leviticus, Ch. XX, v. 18) no longer hold good. Modern theologians— in part influenced by the tolerant traditions of Liguori, and, in part, like Debreyne (*Moechialogie, pp.* 275 *et seq.*) informed by medical science—no longer prohibit intercourse during menstruation, or regard it as only a venial sin.

We have here a remarkable, but not an isolated, example of the tendency of the human mind in its development to rebel against the claims of primitive nature. The whole of religion is a similar remolding of nature, a repression of natural impulses,

---

[1] Pouchet, *Théorie de l'Ovulation Spontanée.* 1847. As Blair Bell and Pontland Hick remark ("Menstruation," *British Medical Journal,* March 6, 1909), the repeated œstrus of unimpregnated animals (once a fortnight in rabbits) is surely comparable to menstruation.

[2] Tait, *Prorincial Medical Journal,* May, 1891; J. Beard, *The Span of Gestation,* 1897, p. 69. Lawson Tait is reduced to the assertion that ovulation and menstruation are identical.

an effort to turn them into new channels. Prohibition of intercourse during menstruation is a fundamental element of savage ritual, an element which is universal merely because the conditions which caused it are universal, and because—as is now beginning to be generally recognized—the causes of human psychic evolution are everywhere the same. A strictly analogous phenomenon, in the sexual sphere itself, is the opposed attitude in barbarism and civilization toward the sexual organs. Under barbaric conditions and among savages, when no magico-religious ideas intervene, the sexual organs are beautiful and pleasurable objects. Under modern conditions this is not so. This difference of attitude is reflected in sculpture. In savage and barbaric carvings of human beings, the sexual organs of both sexes are often enormously exaggerated. This is true of the archaic European figures on which Salomon Reinach has thrown so much light, but in modern sculpture, from the time when it reached its perfection in Greece onward, the sexual regions in both men and women are systematically minimized.[1]

With advancing culture—as again we shall see later—there is a conflict of claims, and certain considerations are regarded as "higher" and more potent than merely "natural" claims. Nakedness is more natural than clothing, and on many grounds more desirable under the average circumstances of life, yet, everywhere, under the stress of what are regarded as higher considerations, there is a tendency for all races to add more and more to the burden of clothes. In the same way it happens that the tendency of the female to sexual intercourse during menstruation[2] has everywhere been overlaid by the ideas of a cult-

---

[1] As Moll points out, even the secondary sexual characters have undergone a somewhat similar change. The beard was once an important sexual attraction, but men can now afford to dispense with it without fear of loss in attractiveness. (*Libido Sexualis*, Band I, p. 387.) These points are discussed at greater length in the fourth volume of these *Studies*, "Sexual Selection in Man."

[2] It is not absolutely established that in menstruating animals the period of menstruation is always a period of sexual congress; probably not, the influence of menstruation being diminished by the more fundamental influence of breeding seasons, which affect the male also; monkeys have a breeding season, though they menstruate regularly all the year round.

ure which has insisted on regarding menstruation as a supernatural phenomenon which, for the protection of everybody, must be strictly tabooed.[1] This tendency is reinforced, and in high civilization replaced, by the claims of an æsthetic regard for concealment and reserve during this period. Such facts are significant for the early history of culture, but they must not blind us to the real analogy between heat and menstruation, an analogy or even identity which may be said to be accepted now by most careful investigators.[2]

If it is, perhaps, somewhat excessive to declare, with Johnstone, that "woman is the only animal in which rut is omnipresent," we must admit that the two groups of phenomena merge into or replace each other, that their object is identical, that they involve similar psychic conditions. Here, also, we see a striking example of the way in which women preserve a primitive phenomenon which earlier in the zoölogical series was common to both sexes, but which man has now lost. Heat and menstruation, with whatever difference of detail, are practically the same phenomenon. We cannot understand menstruation unless we bear this in mind.

On the psychic side the chief normal and primitive characteristic of the menstrual state is the more predominant presence of the sexual impulse. There are other mental and emotional signs of irritability and instability which tend to slightly impair complete mental integrity, and to render, in some unbalanced individuals explosions of anger or depression, in rarer cases crime, more common;[3] but the heightening of the sexual impulse, languor, shyness, and caprice are the more human manifestations of an emotional state which in some of the lower female animals during heat may produce a state of fury.

The actual period of the menstrual flow, at all events the first two or three days, does not, among European women, usually appear to show any heightening of sexual emotion.[4] This height-

---

[1] See Appendix A.
[2] Bland Sutton, *loc. cit.*, p. 896.
[3] See H. Ellis, *Man and Woman*, Chapter XI.
[4] This is by no means true of European women only. Thus, we read in an Arabic book, *The Perfumed Garden*, that women have an aver-

ening occurs usually a few days before, and especially during, the latter part of the flow, and immediately after it ceases.[1] I have, however, convinced myself by inquiry that this absence of sexual feeling during the height of the flow is, in large part, apparent only.   No doubt, the onset of the flow, often producing a general depression of vitality, may tend directly to depress the emotions, which are heightened by the general emotional state and local congestion of the days immediately preceding; but among some women, at all events, who are normal and in good health, I find that the period of menstruation itself is covered by the period of the climax of sexual feeling.   Thus, a married lady writes: "My feelings are always very strong, not only just before and after, but during the period; very unfortunately, as, of course, they cannot then be gratified"; while a refined girl of 19, living a chaste life, without either coitus or masturbation, which she has never practiced, habitually feels very strong sexual excitement about the time of menstruation, and more especially during the period; this desire torments her life, prevents her from sleeping at these times, and she looks upon it as a kind of illness.[2]   I could quote many other similar and equally emphatic statements, and the fact that so cardinal a relationship of the sexual life of women should be ignored or denied by most writers on this matter, is a curious proof of the prevailing ignorance.[3]

sion to coitus during menstruation. On the other hand, the old Hindoo physician, Susruta, appears to have stated that a tendency to run after men is one of the signs of menstruation.

[1] The actual period of the menstrual flow corresponds, in Heape's terminology, to the congestive stage, or *pro-œstrum*, in female animals; the *œstrus*, or period of sexual desire, immediately follows the *pro-œstrum*, and is the direct result of it. See Heape, "The 'Sexual Season' of Mammals," *Quarterly Journal of Microscopical Science*, 1900, vol. xliv, Part I.

[2] It may be noted that (as Barnes, Oliver, and others have pointed out) there is heightened blood-pressure during menstruation. Haig remarks that he has found a tendency for high pressure to be accompanied by increased sexual appetite (*Uric Acid*, 6th edition, p. 155).

[3] Sir W. F. Wade, however, remarked, some years ago, in his Ingleby Lectures (*Lancet*, June 5, 1886): "It is far from exceptional to find that there is an extreme enhancement of concupiscence in the immediate precatamenial period," and adds, "I am satisfied that evidence is obtainable that in some instances, ardor is at its maximum during the actual period, and suspect that cases occur in which it is almost, if not entirely, limited to that time." Long ago, however, the genius of Haller had noted

This ignorance has been fostered by the fact that women often disguise even to themselves the real state of their feelings. One lady remarks that while she would be very ready for coitus during menstruation, the thought that it is impossible during that time makes her put the idea of it out of her mind. I have reason to think that this statement may be taken to represent the real feelings of very many women. The aversion to coitus is real, but it is often due, not to failure of sexual desire, but to the inhibitory action of powerful extraneous causes. The absence of active sexual desire in women during the height of the flow may thus be regarded as, in part, a physiological fact, following from the correspondence of the actual menstrual flow to the period of *pro-œstrum,* and in part, a psychological fact due to the æsthetic repugnance to union when in such a condition, and to the unquestioned acceptance of the general belief that at such a period intercourse is out of the question. Some of the strongest factors of modesty, especially the fear of causing disgust and the sense of the demands of ceremonial ritual, would thus help to hold in check the sexual emotions during this period, and when, under the influence of insanity, these motives are in abeyance, the coincidence of sexual desire with the menstrual flow often becomes more obvious.[1]

---

the same fact. More recently, Icard (*La Femme*, Chapter VI and elsewhere, *e.g.*, p. 125) has brought forward much evidence in confirmation of this view. It may be added that there is considerable significance in the fact that the erotic hallucinations, which are not infrequently experienced by women under the influence of nitrous oxide gas, are more likely to appear at the monthly period than at any other time. (D. W. Buxton, *Anesthetics*, 1892, p. 61.)

[1] Gehrung considers that in healthy young girls amorous sensations are normal during menstruation, and in some women persist, during this period, throughout life. More usually, however, as menstrual period after menstrual period recurs, without the natural interruption of pregnancy, the feeling abates, and gives place to sensations of discomfort or pain. He ascribes this to the vital tissues being sapped of more blood than can be replaced in the intervals. "The vital powers, being thus kept in abeyance, the amative sensations are either not developed, or destroyed. This, superadded by the usual moral and religious teachings, is amply sufficient, by degrees, to extinguish or prevent such feelings with the great majority. The sequestration as 'unclean,' of women during their catamenial period, as practiced in olden times, had the same tendency." (E. C. Gehrung, "The Status of Menstruation," *Transactions American Gynecology Society,* 1901, p. 48.)

It must be added that, especially among the lower social classes, the primitive belief of the savage that coitus during menstruation is bad for the man still persists. Ploss and Bartels mention that among the peasants in some parts of Germany, where it is believed that impregnation is impossible during menstruation, coitus at that time would be frequent were it not thought dangerous for the man.[1] It has also been a common belief both in ancient and modern times that coitus during menstruation engenders monsters.[2]

Notwithstanding all the obstacles that are thus placed in the way of coitus during menstruation, there is nevertheless good reason to believe that the first coitus very frequently takes place at this point of least psychic resistance. When still a student I was struck by the occurrence of cases in which seduction took place during the menstrual flow, though at that time they seemed to me inexplicable, except as evidencing brutality on the part of the seducer. Négrier,[3] in the lying-in wards of the Hôtel-Dieu at Angers, constantly found that the women from the country who came there pregnant as the result of a single coitus had been impregnated at or near the menstrual epoch, more especially when the period coincided with a feast-day, as St. John's Day or Christmas.

Whatever doubt may exist as to the most frequent state of the sexual emotions during the period of menstruation, there can be no doubt whatever that immediately before and immediately after, very commonly at both times,—this varying slightly in different women,—there is usually a marked heightening of actual desire. It is at this period (and sometimes during the menstrual flow) that masturbation may take place

---

[1] It is possible there may be an element of truth in this belief. Diday, of Lyons, found that chronic urethorrhœa is an occasional result of intercourse during menstruation. Raciborski (*Traité de la Menstruation*, 1868, p. 12), who also paid attention to this point, while confirming Diday, came to the conclusion that some special conditions must be present on one or both sides.

[2] See, *e.g.*, Ballantyne, "Teratogenesis, *Transactions of the Edinburgh Obstetrical Society*, 1896, vol. xxi, pp. 324-25.

[3] As quoted by Icard, **La Femme**, etc., p. 194. I have not been able to see Négrier's work.

in women who at other times have no strong auto-erotic impulse. The only women who do not show this heightening of sexual emotion seem to be those in whom sexual feelings have not yet been definitely called into consciousness, or the small minority, usually suffering from some disorder of sexual or general health, in whom there is a high degree of sexual anæsthesia.[1]

The majority of authorities admit a heightening of sexual emotion before or after the menstrual crisis. See *e.g.*, Krafft-Ebing, who places it at the post-menstrual period (*Psychopathia Sexualis*, Eng. translation of tenth edition, p. 27). Adler states that sexual feeling is increased before, during and after menstruation (*Die Mangelhafte Geschlechtsempfindung des Weibes*, 1904, p. 88). Kossmann (Senator and Kaminer, *Health and Disease in Relation to Marriage*, I, 249), advises intercourse just after menstruation, or even during the latter days of the flow, as the period when it is most needed. Guyot says that the eight days after menstruation are the period of sexual desire in women (*Bréviaire de l'Amour Expérimentale*, p. 144). Harry Campbell investigated the periodicity of sexual desire in healthy women of the working classes, in a series of cases, by inquiries made of their husbands who were patients at a London hospital. People of this class are not always skilful in observation, and the method adopted would permit many facts to pass unrecorded; it is, therefore, noteworthy that only in one-third of the cases had no connection between menstruation and sexual feeling been observed; in the other two-thirds, sexual feeling was increased, either before, after, or during the flow, or at all of these times; the proportion of cases in which sexual feeling was increased before the flow, to those in which it was increased after, was as three to two. (H. Campbell, *Nervous Organization of Men and Women*, p. 203.)

Even this elementary fact of the sexual life has, however, been denied, and, strange to say, by two women doctors. Dr. Mary Putnam Jacobi, of New York, who furnished valuable contributions to the physiology of menstruation, wrote some years ago, in a paper on "The Theory of Menstruation," in reference to the question of the connection between œstrus and menstruation: "Neither can any such rhythmical alternation of sexual instinct be demonstrated in women as would lead to the inference that the menstrual crisis was an expression of this," *i.e.*, of œstrus. Dr. Elizabeth Blackwell, again, in her book on *The Human Element in Sex*, asserts that the menstrual flow itself affords

---

[1] I deal with the question of sexual anæsthesia in women in the third volume of these *Studies*: "The Sexual Impulse in Women."

complete relief for the sexual feelings in women (like sexual emissions during sleep in men), and thus practically denies the prevalence of sexual desire in the immediately post-menstrual period, when, on such a theory, sexual feeling should be at its minimum. It is fair to add that Dr. Blackwell's opinion is merely the survival of a view which was widely held a century ago, when various writers (Bordeu, Roussel, Duffieux, J. Arnould, etc.), as Icard has pointed out, regarded menstruation as a device of Providence for safeguarding the virginity of women.

II.

The Question of a Monthly Sexual Cycle in Men—The Earliest Suggestions of a General Physiological Cycle in Men—Periodicity in Disease—Insanity, Heart Disease, etc.—The Alleged Twenty-three Days' Cycle—The Physiological Periodicity of Seminal Emissions during Sleep—Original Observations—Fortnightly and Weekly Rhythms.

FOR some centuries, at least, inquisitive observers here and there have thought they found reason to believe that men, as well as women, present various signs of a menstrual physiological cycle. It would be possible to collect a number of opinions in favor of such a monthly physiological periodicity in men. Precise evidence, however, is, for the most part, lacking. Men have expended infinite ingenuity in establishing the remote rhythms of the solar system and the periodicity of comets. They have disdained to trouble about the simpler task of proving or disproving the cycles of their own organisms.[1] It is over half a century since Laycock wrote that "the *scientific* observation and treatment of disease are impossible without a knowledge of the mysterious revolutions continually taking place in the system"; yet the task of summarizing the whole of our knowledge regarding these "mysterious revolutions" is even to-day no heavy one. As to the existence of a monthly cycle in the sexual instincts of men, with a single exception, I am not aware that any attempt has been made to bring forward definite evidence.[2] A certain interest and novelty attaches, therefore, to the evidence I am able to produce, although that evidence will not suffice to settle the question finally.

The great Italian physician, Sanctorius, who was in so many ways the precursor of our modern methods of physiological re-

---

[1] Even counting the pulse is a comparatively recent method of physiological examination. It was not until 1450 that Nicolas of Cusa advocated counting the pulse-heats. (Binz, *Deutsche medizinische Wochenschrift*, October 6, 1898.)

[2] I leave this statement as it stands, though since the first publication of this book it has ceased to be strictly accurate.

search by the means of instruments of precision, was the first, so far as I am aware, to suggest a monthly cycle of the organism in men. He had carefully studied the weight of the body with reference to the amount of excretions, and believed that a monthly increase in weight to the amount of one or two pounds occurred in men, followed by a critical discharge of urine, this crisis being preceded by feelings of heaviness and lassitude.[1] Gall, another great initiator of modern views, likewise asserted a monthly cycle in men. He insisted that there is a monthly critical period, more marked in nervous people than in others, and that at this time the complexion becomes dull, the breath stronger, digestion more laborious, while there is sometimes disturbance of the urine, together with general *malaise,* in which the temper takes part; ideas are formed with more difficulty, and there is a tendency to melancholy, with unusual irascibility and mental inertia, lasting a few days. More recently Stephenson, who established the cyclical wave-theory of menstruation, argued that it exists in men also, and is really "a general law of vital energy."[2]

Sanctorius does not appear to have published the data on which his belief was founded. Keill, an English follower of Sanctorius, in his *Medicina Statica Britannica* (1718), published a series of daily (morning and evening) body-weights for the year, without referring to the question of a monthly cycle. A period of maximum weight is shown usually, by Keill's figures, to occur about once a month, but it is generally irregular, and cannot usually be shown to occur at definite intervals. Monthly discharges of blood from the sexual organs and other parts of the body in men have been recorded in ancient and modern times, and were treated of by the older medical writers as an affliction peculiar to men with a feminine system. (Laycock, *Nervous Diseases of Women,* p. 79.) A summary of such cases will be found in Gould and Pyle (*Anomalies and Curiosities of Medicine,* 1897, pp. 27-28). Laycock (*Lancet,* 1842-43, vols. i and ii) brought forward cases of monthly and fortnightly cycles in disease, and asserted "the general principle that there are greater and less cycles of movements going on in the system, involving each other, and closely connected with the organization of the individual." He was inclined to accept lunar influ-

---

1 Sanctorius, *Medicina Statica,* Sect. I, aph. lxv.
2 *American Journal of Obstetrics,* xiv, 1882.

ence, and believed that the physiological cycle is made up of definite fractions and multiples of a period of seven days, especially a unit of three and a half days. Albrecht, a somewhat erratic zoölogist, put forth the view a few years ago that there are menstrual periods in men, giving the following reasons: (1) males are rudimentary females, (2) in all males of mammals, a rudimentary masculine uterus (Müller's ducts) still persists, (3) totally hypospadic male individuals menstruate; and believed that he had shown that in man there is a rudimentary menstruation consisting in an almost monthly periodic appearance, lasting for three or four days, of white corpuscles in the urine (*Anomalo*, February. 1890). Dr. Campbell Clark, some years since, made observations on asylum attendants in regard to the temperature, during five weeks, which tended to show that the normal male temperature varies considerably within certain limits, and that "so far as I have been able to observe, there is one marked and prolonged rise every month or five weeks, averaging three days, occasional lesser rises appearing irregularly and of shorter duration. These observations are only made in three cases, and I have no proof that they refer to the sexual appetite" (Campbell Clark, "The Sexual Reproductive Functions," Psychological Section, British Medical Association, Glasgow, 1888; also, private letters). Hammond (*Treatise on Insanity*, p. 114) says: "I have certainly noted in some of my friends, the tendency to some monthly periodic abnormal manifestations. This may be in the form of a headache, or a nasal hæmorrhage, or diarrhœa, or abundant discharge of uric acid, or some other unusual occurrence. I think," he adds, "this is much more common than is ordinarily supposed, and a careful examination or inquiry will generally, if not invariably, establish the existence of a periodicity of the character referred to."

Dr. Harry Campbell, in his book on *Differences in the Nervous Organization of Men and Women*, deals fully with the monthly rhythm (pp. 270 *et seq.*), and devotes a short chapter to the question, "Is the Menstrual Rhythm peculiar to the Female Sex?" He brings forward a few pathological cases indicating such a rhythm, but although he had written a letter to the *Lancet*, asking medical men to supply him with evidence bearing on this question, it can scarcely be said that he has brought forward much evidence of a convincing kind, and such as he has brought forward is purely pathological. He believes, however, that we may accept a monthly cycle in men. "We may," he concludes, "regard the human being—both male and female—as the subject of a monthly pulsation which begins with the beginning of life, and continues till death," menstruation being regarded as a function accidentally ingrafted upon this primordial rhythm.

It is not unreasonable to argue that the possibility of such a menstrual cycle is increased, if we can believe that in women, also, the menstrual cycle persists even when its outward manifestations no longer occur. Aëtius said that menstrual changes take place during gestation; in more modern times, Buffon was of the same opinion. Laycock also maintained that menstrual changes take place during pregnancy (*Nervous Diseases of Women*, p. 47). Fliess considers that it is certainly incorrect to assert that the menstrual process is arrested during pregnancy, and he refers to the frequency of monthly epistaxis and other nasal symptoms throughout this period (W. Fliess, *Beziehungen zwischen Nase und Geschlechts-Organen*, pp. 44 *et seq.*). Beard, who attaches importance to the persistence of a cyclical period in gestation, calls it the muffled striking of the clock. Harry Campbell (*Causation of Disease*, p. 54) has found post-climacteric menstrual rhythm in a fair sprinkling of cases up to the age of sixty.

It is somewhat remarkable that, so far as I have observed, none of these authors refer to the possibility of any heightening of the sexual appetite at the monthly crisis which they believe to exist in men. This omission indicates that, as is suggested by the absence of definite statements on the matter of increase of sexual desire at menstruation, it was an ignored or unknown fact. Of recent years, however, many writers, especially alienists, have stated their conviction that sexual desire in men tends to be heightened at approximately monthly intervals, though they have not always been able to give definite evidence in support of their statements.

Clouston, for instance, has frequently asserted this monthly periodic sexual heightening in men. In the article, "Developmental Insanity," in Tuke's *Psychological Dictionary*, he refers to the periodic physiological heightening of the reproductive *nisus;* and, again, in an article on "Alternation, Periodicity, and Relapse in Mental Diseases" (*Edinburgh Medical Journal*, July, 1882), he records the case of "an insane gentleman, aged 49, who, for the past twenty-six years, has been subject to the most regularly occurring brain-exaltation every four weeks, almost to a day. It sometimes passes off without becoming acutely maniacal, or even showing itself in outward acts; at other times it becomes so, and lasts for periods of from one to four weeks. It is always preceded by an uncomfortable feeling in the head, and pain in the back, mental hebetude, and slight depression. The *nisus generativus* is greatly increased, and he says that, if in that condition, he has full and free seminal emissions during sleep, the excitement passes off; if not, it goes on. A full dose of bromide or iodide of potassium often, but not always, has the effect of stopping the excitement, and a very long walk sometimes does the same. When the excitement gets to a height, it is always followed by about a week of stupid depression." In the same article Clouston remarks: "I have for a long time been impressed with the relationship of the mental and bodily alternations and periodicities in insanity to the great physiological alternations and periodicities, and I have generally been led to the conclusion that they are the same in all essential respects, and only differ in degree of intensity or duration. By far the majority of the cases in women follow the law of the menstrual and sexual periodicity; the majority of the cases in men follow the law of the more irregular periodicities of the *nisus generativus* in that sex. Many of the cases in both sexes follow the seasonal periodicity which perhaps in man is merely a reversion to the seasonal generative activities of the majority of the lower animals." He found that among 338 cases of insanity, chiefly mania and melancholia, 46 per cent. of females and 40 per cent. of males showed periodicity,—diurnal, monthly, seasonal, or annual, and more marked in women than in men, and in mania than in melancholia,—and adds: "I found that the younger the patient, the greater is the tendency to periodic remission and relapse. The phenomenon finds its acme in the cases of pubescent and adolescent insanity."

Conolly Norman, in the article "Mania, Hysterical" (Tuke's *Psychological Dictionary*), states that "the activity of the sexual organs is probably in both sexes fundamentally periodic."

Krafft-Ebing records the case of a neurasthenic Russian, aged 24, who experienced sexual desires of urologinic character, with fair regularity, every four weeks (*Psychopathia Sexualis*), and Näcke mentions the case of a man who had nocturnal emissions at intervals of four weeks (*Archiv für Kriminalanthropologie*, 1908, p. 363), while Moll (*Libido Sexualis*, Bd. I, pp. 621-623) recorded the case of a man, otherwise normal, who had attacks of homosexual feeling every four weeks, and Rohleder (*Zeitschrift für Sexualwissenschaft*, Nov., 1908) gives the case of an unmarried slightly neuropathic physician who for several days every three to five weeks has attacks of almost satyriacal sexual excitement.

Féré, whose attention was called to this point, from time to time noted the existence of sexual periodicity. Thus, in a case of general paralysis, attacks of continuous sexual excitement, with sleeplessness, occurred every twenty-eight days; at other times, the patient, a man of 42, in the stage of dementia, slept well, and showed no signs of sexual excitation (*Société de Biologie*, October 6, 1900). In another case, of a man of sound heredity and good health till middle life, periodic sexual manifestations began from puberty, with localized genital congestion, erotic ideas, and copious urination, lasting for two or three days. These manifestations became menstrual, with a period of intermenstrual excitement appearing regularly, but never became intense. Between the age of 36 and 42, the intermenstrual crises gradually ceased; at about 45, the menstrual crises ceased; the periodic crises continued, however, with the sole manifestation of increased frequency of urination (*Société de Biologie*, July 23, 1904). In a third case, of sexual neurasthenia, Féré found that from puberty, onwards to middle life, there appeared, every twenty-five to twenty-eight days, tenderness and swelling below the nipple, accompanied by slight sexual excitation and erotic dreams, lasting for one or two days (*Revue de Médecine*, March, 1905).

It is in the domain of disease that the most strenuous and, on the whole, the most successful efforts have been made to discover a menstrual cycle in men. Such a field seems promising at the outset, for many morbid exaggerations or defects of the nervous system might be expected to emphasize, or to free from inhibition, fundamental rhythmical processes of the organism which in health, and under the varying conditions of social existence, are overlaid by the higher mental activities and the pressure of external stimuli. In the eighteenth century Erasmus Darwin wrote a remarkable and interesting chapter on "The Periods of Disease," dealing with solar and lunar influence on biological processes.[1] Since then, many writers have brought forward evidence, especially in the domain of nervous and mental disease, which seems to justify a belief that, under pathological conditions, a tendency to a male menstrual rhythm may be clearly laid bare.

We should expect an organ so primitive in character as the heart, and with so powerful a rhythm already stamped upon its nervous organization, to be peculiarly apt to display a menstrual rhythm under the stress of abnormal conditions. This expectation might be strengthened by the menstrual rhythm which Mr. Perry-Coste has found reason to suspect in pulse-frequency during health. I am able to present a case in which such a periodicity seems to be indicated. It is that of a gentleman who suffered severely for some years before his death from valvular disease of the heart, with a tendency to pulmonary congestion, and attacks of "cardiac asthma." His wife, a lady of great

---

[1] *Zoönomia*, Section XXXVI.

intelligence, kept notes of her husband's condition,[1] and at last observed that there was a certain periodicity in the occurrence of the exacerbations. The periods were not quite regular, but show a curious tendency to recur at about thirty days' interval, a few days before the end of every month; it was during one of these attacks that he finally died. There was also a tendency to minor attacks about ten days after the major attacks. It is noteworthy that the subject showed a tendency to periodicity when in health, and once remarked laughingly before his illness: "I am just like a woman, always most excitable at a particular time of the month."

Periodicity has been noted in various disorders of nervous character. Periodic insanity has long been known and studied (see, *e.g.*, Pilcz, *Die periodischen Geistesstörungen*, 1901); it is much commoner in women than in men. Periodicity has been observed in stammering (a six-weekly period in one case), and notably in hemicrania or migraine, by Harry Campbell, Osler, etc. (The periodicity of a case of hemicrania has been studied in detail by D. Fraser Harris, *Edinburgh Medical Journal*, July, 1902.) But the cycle in these cases is not always, or even usually, of a menstrual type.

It is now possible to turn to an investigation which, although of very limited extent, serves to place the question of a male menstrual cycle for the first time on a sound basis. If there is such a cycle analogous to menstruation in women, it must be a recurring period of nervous erethism, and it must be demonstrably accompanied by greater sexual activity. In the *American Journal of Psychology* for 1888, Mr. Julius Nelson, afterward Professor of Biology at the Rutgers College of Agriculture, New Brunswick, published a study of dreams in which he recorded the results of detailed observations of his dreams, and also of seminal emissions during sleep (by him termed "gonekbole" or "ecbole"), during a period of something over two years. Mr. Nelson found that both dreams and ecboles fell into a physiological cycle of 28 days. The climax of maximum dreaming (as determined by the number of words in the dream record) and the climax of

---

[1] I reproduced these notes in full in earlier editions of this volume.

maximum ecbole fell at the same point of the cycle, the ecbolic climax being more distinctly marked than the dream climax.

The question of cyclic physiological changes is considerably complicated by our uncertainty regarding the precise length of the cycle we may expect to find. Nelson finds a 28-day cycle satisfactory. Perry-Coste, as we shall see, accepts a strictly lunar cycle of 29½ days. Fliess has argued that in both women and men, many physiological facts fall into a cycle of 23 days, which he calls male, the 28-day cycle being female. (W. Fliess, *Die Beziehungen zwischen Nase und weiblichen Geschlechts-Organen*, 1897, pp. 113 *et seq.*) Although Fliess brings forward a number of minutely-observed cases, I cannot say that I am yet convinced of the reality of this 23-day cycle. It is somewhat curious, however, that at the same time as Fliess, though in apparent independence, and from a different point of view, another worker also suggested that there is a 23-day physiological cycle (John Beard, *The Span of Gestation and the Cause of Birth*, Jena, 1897). Beard approaches the question from the embryological standpoint, and argues that there is what he terms an "ovulation unit" of about 23½ days, in the interval from the end of one menstruation to the beginning of the next. Two "ovulation units" make up one "critical unit," and the length of pregnancy, according to Beard, is always a multiple of the "critical unit;" in man, the gestation period amounts to six critical units. These attempts to prove a new physiological cycle deserve careful study and further investigation. The possibility of such a cycle should be borne in mind, but at present we are scarcely entitled to accept it.

So far as I am aware, Professor Nelson's very interesting series of observations, which, for the first time, placed the question of a menstrual rhythm in men on a sound and workable basis, have not directly led to any further observations. I am, however, in possession of a much more extended series of ecbolic observations completed before Nelson's paper was published, although the results have only been calculated at a comparatively recent date. I now propose to present a summary of these observations, and consider how far they confirm Nelson's conclusions. These observations cover no less a period than twelve years, between the ages of 17 and 29, the subject, W. K., being a student, and afterward schoolmaster, leading, on the whole, a chaste life. The records were faithfully made throughout the whole of this long period. Here, if anywhere, should be material

for the construction of a menstrual rhythm on an ecbolic basis.
While the results are in many respects instructive, it can scarcely,
perhaps, be said that they absolutely demonstrate a monthly cycle.
When summated in a somewhat similar manner to that adopted by
Nelson in his ecbolic observations, it is not difficult to regard the
maximum, which is reached on the 19th to 21st days of the
summated physiological month, as a real menstrual ecbolic climax,
for no other three consecutive days at all approach these in
number of ecboles, while there is a marked depression occurring
four days earlier, on the 16th day of the month. If, however,
we split up the curve by dividing the period of twelve years into
two nearly equal periods, the earlier of about seven years and the
latter of about four years, and summate these separately, the two
curves do not present any parallel as regards the menstrual cycle.
It scarcely seems to me, therefore, that these curves present any
convincing evidence in this case of a monthly ecbolic cycle (and,
therefore, I refrain from reproducing them), although they seem
to suggest such a cycle. Nor is there any reason to suppose that
by adopting a different cycle of thirty days, or of twenty-three
days, any more conclusive results would be obtained.

It seems, however, when we look at these curves more
closely, that they are not wholly without significance. If I am
justified in concluding that they scarcely demonstrate a monthly
cycle, it may certainly be added that they show a rudimentary
tendency for the ecboles to fall into a fortnightly rhythm, and
a very marked and unmistakable tendency to a weekly rhythm.
The fortnightly rhythm is shown in the curve for the earlier
period, but is somewhat disguised in the curve for the total period,
because the first climax is spread over two days, the 7th and
8th of the month. If we readjust the curve for the total period
by presenting the days in pairs, the fortnightly tendency is more
clearly brought out (Chart 1).

A more pronounced tendency still is traceable to a weekly
rhythm. This is, indeed, the most unquestionable fact brought
out by these curves. All the maxima occur on Saturday or Sunday, with the minima on Tuesday, Wednesday, Thursday, or
Friday. This very pronounced weekly rhythm will serve to

swamp more or less completely any monthly rhythm on a 28-day basis. Although here probably seen in an exaggerated form, it is almost certainly a characteristic of the ecbolic curve generally.[1] I have been told by several young men and women, especially those who work hard during the week, that Saturday, and especially Sunday afternoon, are periods when the thoughts spontaneously go in an erotic direction, and at this time there is a special tendency to masturbation or to spontaneous sexual excitement. It is on Friday, Saturday, Sunday, and Monday, according to Guerry's tables,[2] that the fewest suicides are committed, Tuesday, Wednesday, and Thursday, with, however, a partial fall on Wednesday, those on which most suicides are committed, so that there would appear to be an antagonism between sexual activity and the desire to throw off life. It also appears (in the reports of the Bavarian factory inspectors) that accidents in factories have a tendency to occur chiefly at the beginning of the week, and toward the end rather than in the middle.[3] Even growth, as Fleischmann has shown in the case of children, tends to fall into weekly cycles. It is evident that the nervous system is profoundly affected by the social influences resulting from the weekly cycle.

The analysis of this series of ecbolic curves may thus be said to recall the suggestion of Laycock, that the menstrual cycle is really made up of four weekly cycles, the periodic unit, according to Laycock, being three and one-half days. I think it would, however, be more correct to say that the menstrual cycle, perhaps originally formed with reference to the influence of the moon on the sexual and social habits of men and other animals, tends to break up by a process of segmentation into fortnightly and weekly cycles. If we are justified in assuming that there is a male menstrual cycle, we must conclude that in such a case as

---

[1] Moll refers to the case of a man whose erotic dreams occurred every fortnight, and always on Friday night (*Libido Sexualis*, Band I, p. 136). One is inclined to suspect an element of autosuggestion in such a case; still, the coincidence is noteworthy.

[2] See Durkheim, *Le Suicide*, p. 101.

[3] We must, of course, see here the results of the disorganization produced by holidays, and the exhaustion produced by the week's labor; but such influences are still the social effects of the cosmic week.

that just analyzed, the weekly rhythm has become so marked as almost entirely to obliterate the larger monthly rhythm.

However constituted, there seems little doubt that a physiological weekly cycle really exists. This was, indeed, very clearly indicated many years ago by the observations of Edward Smith, who showed that there are weekly rhythms in pulse, respiration, temperature, carbonic acid evolution, urea, and body-weight, Sunday being the great day of repair and increase of weight.[1]

In an appendix to this volume I am able to present the results of another long series of observations of nocturnal ecbolic manifestations carried out by Mr. Perry-Coste, who has elaborately calculated the results, and has convinced himself that on the basis of a strictly lunar month, thus abolishing the disturbing influence of the weekly rhythm, which in his case also appears, a real menstrual rhythm may be traced.[2]

It does not appear to me, however, even yet, that a final answer to the question whether a menstrual sexual rhythm occurs in men can be decisively given in the affirmative. That such a cycle will be proved in many cases seems to me highly probable, but before this can be decisively affirmed it is necessary that a much larger number of persons should be induced to carry out on themselves the simple, but protracted, series of observations that are required.

Since the first edition of this volume appeared, numerous series of ecbolic records have reached me from different parts of the world. The most notable of these series comes from a professional man, of scientific training, who has for the past six years lived in different parts of India, where the record was kept. Though the record extends over nearly six years, there are two breaks in it, due to a visit to England, and to loss of interest. Both involuntary and voluntary discharges are included in the record. The involuntary discharges occurred during sleep, usually with an erotic dream, in which the subject invariably awaked and frequently made an effort to check the emission. The voluntary discharges in most cases commenced during sleep, or

---

[1] E. Smith, *Health and Disease*, Chapter III. I may remark that, according to Kemsoes (*Deutsche medizinische Wochenschrift*, January 20, 1908, and *British Medical Journal*, January 29, 1898), school-children work best on Monday and Tuesday.

[2] See Appendix B.

in the half-waking state; deliberate masturbation, when fully awake, was comparatively rare. The proportion of involuntary to more or less voluntary ecboles was about 3 to 1. A third kind of sexual manifestation (of frequency intermediate between the other two forms) is also included, in which a high degree of erethism is induced during the half waking state, culminating in an orgasm in which the power of preventing discharge has been artificially acquired. The subject, E. M., was 32 years of age when the record began. He belongs to a healthy family, and is himself physically sound, 5 feet 6 inches in height, but weight low, due to rickets in infancy. In early life he stammered badly; his temperament is emotional and self-conscious, while his work is unusually exacting, and he lives for most of the year in a very trying climate. As a boy he was very religious, and has always felt obliged to resist sexual vice to the utmost, though there have been occasional lapses.

As regards lunar periodicity, E. M., has summated his results in a curve, after the same manner as Mr. Perry-Coste, beginning with the new moon. The periods covered include 54 lunar months, and the total number of discharges is 176; the average frequency is about 3 per month of twenty-eight days. The curve, for the most part, zigzags between a frequency of 4 and 9, but on the twenty-fourth day it falls to 1, and then rises uninterruptedly to a height of 11 on the twenty-seventh day, falling to 2 on the next day. Whether a really menstrual ryhthm is thus indicated I do not undertake to decide, but I am inclined to agree with E. M. himself that there is no definite evidence of it. "It looks to me," he writes, "as if the only real rhythm (putting aside the annual cycle) will be found to be the average period between the ecboles, varying in different persons, but in my case, about nine and one-eighth days. May not the ecbolic period in men be compared to the menstrual period in women, and be an example of the greater katabolic activity of men? There is the period of tumescence, and the ecbole constituting the detumescence. The weekend holiday would hasten the detumescence, but about every third week-end there would tend to be delay to enable the system to get back into its regulation nine or ten days' stride. This might possibly be the explanation of the curves. The recent emissions were nearly all involuntary during sleep. Age may have something to do with the change in character."

E. M.'s curves frequently show the influence of weekly periodicity, in the tendency to ecbole on Sunday, or sometimes on Saturday or Monday. In recent years there has been some tendency for this climax to be thrown towards the middle of the week, but, on the whole, Wednesday is the point of lowest frequency.

In another case, the subject, A. N., who has spent nearly all his

life in the State of Indiana, has kept a record of sexual manifestations between the ages of 30 and 34. The data, which cover four
years, have not been sent to me in a form which enables the possibility of a monthly curve to be estimated, but A. N., who has himself
arranged the data on a lunar monthly basis, considers that a monthly
curve is thus revealed. "My memoranda, he writes, "show that discharges occur most frequently on the first, second, and third days after
new moon. There is also another period on the fourteenth and fifteenth,
which might indicate a semi-lunar rhythm. The days of minimum discharge are the seventh, eighth, twenty-second, and twenty-third." It
may be added that the yearly average of ecbolic manifestations, varying
between 50 and 55, comes out as 52, or exactly one per week.

A weekly periodicity is very definitely shown by A. N.'s data.
Sunday once more stands at the head of the week as regards frequency,
in this case very decisively. The figures are as follows:—

Sun.	Mon.	Tues.	Wed.	Thurs.	Fri.	Sat.
48	21	24	35	28	26	27

In another case which has reached me from the United States,
the data are slighter, but deserve note, as the subject is a trained
psychologist, and I quote the case in his own words. Here, it will be
seen, there appears to be a tendency for the ecbolic cycle to cover a
period of about six weeks. In this case, also, there is a tendency for the
climax to occur about Saturday or Sunday. "X. is 38 years old, unmarried, fair health, pretty good heredity; university trained, and
engaged in academic pursuits. He thinks he may have completed
puberty at about 13, though he has no proof that he was in the
full possession of his sex-powers until he was 15 years 3 months old
(when he had his first emission). His sex life has been normal. He
masturbated somewhat when he slept with other boys (or men) during
early manhood, but not to excess.

"During the autumn of 1889 (when 28 years of age) he observed
that at certain times he had an itching feeling about the testicles; that
he felt slightly irritable; that the penis erected with the slightest provo-
cation, and that this peculiar feeling usually passed away with a
nightly emission. Indeed, so regular was the matter that he usually
wore a loin garment at these times, to prevent the semen getting on
the bedding. This peculiar feeling ordinarily continued for two or three
days. He recalls at these times that he felt that he would like to
wrestle with some one, for there seemed to be a muscular tension.
These states returned with apparent regularity, and the intervals seemed
to be about six weeks, though no effort was made to measure the
periods until 1893. The following notes are taken from the diaries
of X.:—

Thursday, December 29, 1892. The peculiar feeling.
(This is the only entry.)

Thursday, February 9, 1893. The peculiar feeling.
(The diary notes that X. awoke nights to find erections, and that the feeling continued until Sunday night following, when there was an emission.)

Friday, March 27, 1893. The peculiar feeling.
(The diary notes that there was an emission the next night, and that the feeling disappeared.)

Wednesday, May 3, 1893. The peculiar feeling.
(The diary notes that it continued until Saturday night, when X. had sexual relations, and that it then disappeared.)

Wednesday, June 14, 1893. The peculiar feeling.
(The diary states that the next night X. had an emission, and the disappearance of the feeling.)

Thursday, July 27, 1893. The peculiar feeling.
(The diary notes that it was apparent at about 3 o'clock that afternoon. That night at 10 o'clock, X. had sexual intercourse, and the feeling was not noted the next day.)

Friday, September 8, 1893. The peculiar feeling.
(Continued until Tuesday, the 11th, and then disappeared. No sexual intercourse, and no nightly emission.)

Wednesday, October 25, 1893. The peculiar feeling.
(Continued until Saturday night, when there was a nightly emission.)

Saturday, December 9, 1893. The peculiar feeling.
(Continued until Monday night, when there was sexual relations.)

It will be noted that the intervals observed were of about six weeks' duration, excepting one, that from September to October, when it was nearly seven weeks.

"These observations were not recorded after 1893. X. thinks that in 1894 the intervals were longer, an opinion which is based on the fact that for a period of six months he had no sexual intercourse and no nightly emissions. The times during this six months when he had the 'peculiar feeling,' the sensation was so slight as to be scarcely noted. In 1895, the feeling seemed more pronounced than ever before, and X. thinks that it may have recurred as often as once a month. In 1896, 1897, and 1898, the intervals, he thinks, lengthened—at times, he thought, wholly disappeared. During 1899, while they did not recur often, when they did come the sensation was pronounced, although the emission was less common. There was a peculiar 'heavy' feeling about the testicles, and a marked tendency towards erection of the penis, especially at night-time (while sleeping). X. often awoke to find a tense erection. Moreover, these feelings usually continued a week.

"1. In general, X. is of the opinion that as he grows older these intervals lengthen, though this inference is not based on *recorded* data.

"2. He notes that a discharge (through sexual intercourse or in sleep) invariably brings the peculiar feeling to a close for the time being.

3. He notes that sexual intercourse *at the time* stops it; but, when there has been sexual intercourse within a week or ten days of the time (based upon the observations of 1893), that it had no tendency to check the feeling."

In another case, that of F. C., an Irish farmer, born in Waterford, the data are still more meagre, though the periodicity is stated to be very pronounced. He is chaste, steady, with occasional lapses from strict sobriety, healthy and mentally normal, living a regular open-air life, far from the artificial stimuli of towns. The observations refer to a period when he was from 20 to 27 years of age. During this period, nocturnal emissions occurred at regular intervals of exactly a month. They were ushered in by fits of irritability and depression, and usually occurred in dreamless sleep. The discharges were abundant and physically weakening, but they relieved the psychic symptoms, though they occasioned mental distress, since F. C. is scrupulous in a religious sense, and also apprehensive of bad constitutional effects, the result of reading alarmist quack pamphlets.

In another case known to me, a young man leading a chaste life, experienced crises of sexual excitement every ten to fourteen days, the crisis lasting for several days.

Finally, an interesting contribution to this subject, suggested by this *Study,* has been made and published (in the proceedings of the Amsterdam International Congress of Psychology, in 1907) by the well-known Amsterdam neurologist and psychologist, Dr. L. S. A. M. Von Römer under the title, "Ueber das Verhältniss zwischen Mondalter und Sexualität." Von Römer's data are made up not of nocturnal involuntary emissions, but of the voluntary acts of sexual intercourse of an unmarried man, during a period of four years. Von Römer believes that these, to a much greater extent than those of a married man, would be liable to periodic influence, if such exist. On making a curve of exact lunar length (similarly to Perry-Coste), he finds that there are, every month, two maxima and two minima, in a way that approximately resemble Perry-Coste's curve. The main point in Von Römer's results is, however, the correspondence that he finds with the actual lunar phases; the chief maximum occurs at the time of the full moon, and the secondary maximum at the time of the new moon, the minima being at the first and fourth quarters. He hazards no theory in explanation of this coincidence, but insists on the need for further observations. It will be seen that A. N.'s results (*ante* p. 117) seem in the main to correspond to Von Römer's.

III.

The Annual Sexual Rhythm—In Animals—In Man—Tendency of the Sexual Impulse to become Heightened in Spring and Autumn—The Prevalence of Seasonal Erotic Festivals—The Feast of Fools—The Easter and Midsummer Bonfires—The Seasonal Variations in Birthrate—The Causes of those Variations—The Typical Conception-rate Curve for Europe—The Seasonal Periodicity of Seminal Emissions During Sleep—Original Observations—Spring and Autumn the Chief Periods of Involuntary Sexual Excitement—The Seasonal Periodicity of Rapes—Of Outbreaks among Prisoners—The Seasonal Curves of Insanity and Suicide—The Growth of Children According to Season—The Annual Curve of Bread-consumption in Prisons—Seasonal Periodicity of Scarlet Fever—The Underlying Causes of these Seasonal Phenomena.

THAT there are annual seasonal changes in the human organism, especially connected with the sexual function, is a statement that has been made by physiologists and others from time to time, and the statement has even reached the poets, who have frequently declared that spring is the season of love.

Thus, sixty years ago, Laycock, an acute pioneer in the investigation of the working of the human organism, brought together (in a chapter on "The Periodic Movements in the Reproductive Organs of Woman," in his *Nervous Diseases of Women*, 1840, pp. 61-70) much interesting evidence to show that the system undergoes changes about the vernal and autumnal equinoxes, and that these changes are largely sexual.

Edward Smith, also a notable pioneer in this field of human periodicity, and, indeed, the first to make definite observations on a number of points bearing on it, sums up, in his remarkable book, *Health and Disease as Influenced by Daily, Seasonal, and Other Cyclical Changes in the Human System* (1861), to the effect that season is a more powerful influence on the system than temperature or atmospheric pressure; "in the early and middle parts of spring every function of the body is in its highest degree of efficiency," while autumn is "essentially a period of change from the minimum toward the maximum of vital conditions." He found that in April and May most carbonic acid is evolved, there being then a progressive diminution to September, and then a progressive increase; the respiratory rate also fell from a maximum in April to a minimum maintained at exactly the same level throughout August, Sep-

(122)

tember, October, and November; spring was found to be the season of maximum, autumn of minimum, muscular power; sensibility to tactile and temperature impressions was also greater in spring.

Kulischer, studying the sexual customs of various human races, concluded that in primitive times, only at two special seasons—at spring and in harvest-time—did pairing take place; and that, when pairing ceased to be strictly confined to these periods, its symbolical representation was still so confined, even among the civilized nations of Europe. He further argued that the physiological impulse was only felt at these periods. (Kulischer, "Die geschlechtliche Zuchtwahl bei den Menschen in der Urzeit," *Zeitschrift für Ethnologie*, 1876, pp. 152 and 157.) Cohnstein ("Ueber Prädilectionszeiten bei Schwangerschaft," *Archiv für Gynäkologie*, 1879) also suggested that women sometimes only conceive at certain periods of the year.

Wiltshire, who made various interesting observations regarding the physiology of menstruation, wrote: "Many years ago, I concluded that every women had a law peculiar to herself, which governed the times of her bringing forth (and conceiving); that she was more prone to bring forth at certain epochs than at others; and subsequent researches have established the accuracy of the forecast." He further stated his belief in a "primordial seasonal aptitude for procreation, the impress of which still remains, and, to some extent, governs the breeding-times of humanity." (A. Wiltshire, "Lectures on the Comparative Physiology of Menstruation," *British Medical Journal*, March, 1883, pp. 502, etc.)

Westermarck, in a chapter of his *History of Human Marriage*, dealing with the question of "A Human Pairing Season in Primitive Times," brings forward evidence showing that spring, or, rather, early summer, is the time for increase of the sexual instinct, and argues that this is a survival of an ancient pairing season; spring, he points out, is a season of want, rather than abundance, for a frugivorous species, but when men took to herbs, roots, and animal food, spring became a time of abundance, and suitable for the birth of children. He thus considers that in man, as in lower animals, the times of conception are governed by the times most suitable for birth.

Rosenstadt, as we shall see later, also believes that men to-day have inherited a physiological custom of procreating at a certain epoch, and he thus accounts for the seasonal changes in the birthrate.

Heape, who also believes that "at one period of its existence the human species had a special breeding season," follows Wiltshire in suggesting that "there is some reason to believe that the human female is not always in a condition to breed." (W. Heape, "Menstruation and Ovulation of *Macacus rhesus*," *Philosophical Transactions*, 1897; *id.* "The Sexual Season of Mammals," *Quarterly Journal Microscopical Science*, 1900.)

Except, however, in one important respect, with which we shall presently have to deal, few attempts have been made to demonstrate any annual organic sexual rhythm. The supposition of such annual cycle is usually little more than a deduction from the existence of the well-marked seasonal sexual rhythm in animals. Most of the higher animals breed only once or twice a year, and at such a period that the young are born when food is most plentiful. At other periods the female is incapable of breeding, and without sexual desires, while the male is either in the same condition or in a condition of latent sexuality. Under the influence of domestication, animals tend to lose the strict periodicity of the wild condition, and become apt for breeding at more frequent intervals. Thus among dogs in the wild state the bitch only experiences heat once a year, in the spring. Among domesticated dogs, there is not only the spring period of heat, early in the year, but also an autumn period, about six months later; the primitive period, however, remains the most important one, and the best litters of pups are said to be produced in the spring. The mare is in season in spring and summer; sheep take the ram in autumn.[1] Many of the menstruating monkeys also, whether or not sexual desire is present throughout the year, only conceive in spring and in autumn. Almost any time of the year may be an animal's pairing season, this season being apparently in part determined by the economic conditions which will prevail at birth. While it is essential that animals should be born during the season of greatest abundance, it is equally essential that pairing, which involves great expenditure of energy, should also take place at a season of maximum physical vigor.

As an example of the sexual history of an animal through the year, I may quote the following description, by Dr. A. W. Johnstone, of the habits of the American deer: "Our common American deer, in winter-time, is half-starved for lack of vegetation in the woods; the low temperature, snow, and ice, make his conditions of life harder for lack of the proper amount of food, whereby he becomes an easier prey to carnivorous animals. He has difficulty even in preserving life. In spring he sheds his winter coat, and is provided with a suit of lighter hair, and

---

[1] F. Smith, *Veterinary Physiology;* Dalziel, *The Collie.*

while this is going on the male grows antlers for defence. The female about this time is far along in pregnancy, and when the antlers are fully grown she drops the fawn. When the fawns are dropped vegetation is plentiful and lactation sets in. During this time the male is kept fully employed in getting food and guarding his more or less helpless family. As the season advances the vegetation increases and the fawn begins to eat grass. When the summer heat commences the little streams begin to dry up, and the animal once more has difficulty in supporting life because of the enervating heat, the effect of drought on the vegetation, and the distance which has to be traveled to get water; therefore, fully ten months in each year the deer has all he can do to live without extra exertion incident to rutting. Soon after the autumn rains commence vegetation becomes more luxurious, the antlers of the male and new suits of hair for both are fully grown, heat of the summer is gone, food and drink are plentiful everywhere, the fawns are weaned, and both sexes are in the very finest condition. Then, and then only, in the whole year, comes the rut, which, to them as to most other animals, means an unwonted amount of physical exercise besides the everyday runs for life from their natural enemies, and an unusual amount of energy is used up. If a doe dislikes the attention of a special buck, miles of racing result. If jealous males meet, furious battles take place. The strain on both sexes could not possibly be endured at any other season of the year. With approach of cold weather, climatic deprivations and winter dangers commence and rut closes. In all wild animals, rut occurs only when the climatic and other conditions favor the highest physical development. This law holds good in all wild birds, for it is then only that they can stand the strain incident to love-making. The common American crow is a very good study. In the winter he travels around the ricefields of the South, leading a tramp's existence in a country foreign to him, and to which he goes only to escape the rigors of the northern climate. For several weeks in the spring he goes about the fields, gathering up the worms and grubs. After his long flight from the South he experiences several weeks of an almost ideal existence, his food is plentiful, he becomes strong and hearty, and then he turns to thoughts of love. In the pairing season he does more work than at any other time in the year: fantastic dances, racing and chasing after the females, and savage fights with rivals. He endures more than would be possible in his ordinary physical state. Then come the care of the young and the long flights for water and food during the drought of the summer. After the molt, autumn finds him once more in flock, and with the first frosts he is off again to the South. In the wild state, rut is the capstone of perfect physical condition." (A. W. Johnstone, "The Relation of Menstruation to the other Reproductive Functions," *American Journal of Obstetrics*, vol. xxxii, 1895.)

Wiltshire ("Lectures on the Comparative Physiology of Menstruation," *British Medical Journal*, March, 1888) and Westermarck (*History of Human Marriage*, Chapter II) enumerate the pairing season of
a number of different animals.

With regard to the breeding seasons of monkeys, little seems to be
positively known. Heape made special inquiries with reference to the
two species whose sexual life he investigated. He was informed that
Semnopithecus entellus breeds twice a year, in April and in October.
He accepts Aitcheson's statement that the *Macacus rhesus*, in Simla,
copulates in October, and adds that in the very different climate of the
plains it appears to copulate in May. He concludes that the breeding
season varies greatly in dependence on climate, but believes that the
breeding season is always preserved, and that it affects the sexual aptitude of the male. He could not make his monkeys copulate during
February or March, but is unable to say whether or not sexual intercourse is generally admitted outside the breeding season. He quotes the
observation of Breschet that monkeys copulate during pregnancy.

In primitive human races we very frequently trace precisely the same influence of the seasonal impulse as may be witnessed in the higher animals, although among human races it
does not always result that the children are born at the time of
the greatest plenty, and on account of the development of human
skill such a result is not necessary. Thus Dr. Cook found among
the Eskimo that during the long winter nights the secretions
are diminished, muscular power is weak, and the passions are depressed. Soon after the sun appears a kind of rut affects the
young population. They tremble with the intensity of sexual
passion, and for several weeks much of the time is taken up with
courtship and love. Hence, the majority of the children are born
nine months later, when the four months of perpetual night are
beginning. A marked seasonal periodicity of this kind is not
confined to the Arctic regions. We may also find it in the tropics.
In Cambodia, Mondière has found that twice a year, in April
and September, men seem to experience a "veritable rut," and
will sometimes even kill women who resist them.[1]

These two periods, spring and autumn—the season for greet-
ing the appearance of life and the season for reveling in its final

---

[1] Mondière, Art "Cambodgiens," *Dictionnaire des Sciences Anthro-
pologiques.*

fruition—seem to be everywhere throughout the world the most usual seasons for erotic festivals. In classical Greece and Rome, in India, among the Indians of North and South America, spring is the most usual season, while in Africa the yam harvest of autumn is the season chiefly selected. There are, of course, numerous exceptions to this rule, and it is common to find both seasons observed. Taking, indeed, a broad view of festivals throughout the world, we may say that there are four seasons when they are held: the winter solstice, when the days begin to lengthen and primitive man rejoices in the lengthening and seeks to assist it;[1] the vernal equinox, the period of germination and the return of life; the summer solstice, when the sun reaches its height; and autumn, the period of fruition, of thankfulness, and of repose. But it is rarely that we find a people seriously celebrating more than two of these festival seasons.

In Australia, according to Müller as quoted by Ploss and Bartels, marriage and conception take place during the warm season, when there is greatest abundance of food, and to some extent is even confined to that period. Oldfield and others state that the Australian erotic festivals take place only in spring. Among some tribes, Müller adds, such as the Watschandis, conception is inaugurated by a festival called *kaaro,* which takes place in the warm season at the first new moon after the yams are ripe. The leading feature of this festival is a moonlight dance, representing the sexual act symbolically. With their spears, regarded as the symbols of the male organ, the men attack bushes, which

---

[1] This primitive aspect of the festival is well shown by the human sacrifices which the ancient Mexicans offered at this time, in order to enable the sun to recuperate his strength. The custom survives in a symbolical form among the Mokis, who observe the festivals of the winter solstice and the vernal equinox. ("Aspects of Sun-worship among the Moki Indians," *Nature,* July 28, 1898.) The Walpi, a Tusayan people, hold a similar great sun-festival at the winter solstice, and December is with them a sacred month, in which there is no work and little play. This festival, in which there is a dance dramatizing the fructification of the earth and the imparting of virility to the seeds of corn, is fully described by J. Walter Fewkes (*American Anthropologist,* March, 1898). That these solemn annual dances and festivals of North America frequently merge into "a lecherous *saturnalia,*" when "all is joy and happiness," is stated by H. H. Bancroft (*Native Races of Pacific States,* vol. i, p. 352).

represent the female organs. They thus work themselves up to
a state of extreme sexual excitement.[1] Among the Papuans of
New Guinea, also, according to Miklucho-Macleay, conceptions
chiefly occur at the end of harvest, and Guise describes the
great annual festival of the year which takes place at the time of
the yam and banana harvest, when the girls undergo a ceremony
of initiation and marriages are effected.[2] In Central Africa, says
Sir H. H. Johnston, in his *Central Africa,* sexual orgies are
seriously entered into at certain seasons of the year, but he
neglects to mention what these seasons are. The people of New
Britain, according to Weisser (as quoted by Ploss and Bartels),
carefully guard their young girls from the young men. At certain times, however, a loud trumpet is blown in the evening, and
the girls are then allowed to go away into the bush to mix freely
with the young men. In ancient Peru (according to an account
derived from a pastoral letter of Archbishop Villagomez of
Lima), in December, when the fruit of the *paltay* is ripe, a
festival was held, preceded by a five days' fast. During the
festival, which lasted six days and six nights, men and women
met together in a state of complete nudity at a certain spot among
the gardens, and all raced toward a certain hill. Every man who
caught up with a woman in the race was bound at once to have
intercourse with her.

Very instructive, from our present point of view, is the
account given by Dalton, of the festivals of the various Bengal
races. Thus the Hos (a Kolarian tribe), of Bengal, are a purely
agricultural people, and the chief festival of the year with them
is the *mágh parah.* It is held in the month of January, "when
the granaries are full of grain, and the people, to use their own

---

[1] As regards the northern tribes of Central Australia, Spencer and
Gillen state that, during the performance of certain ceremonies which
bring together a large number of natives from different parts, the
ordinary marital rules are more or less set aside (*Northern Tribes of
Central Australia,* p. 136). Just in the same way, among the Siberian
Yakuts, according to Sieroshevski, during weddings and at the great
festivals of the year, the usual oversight of maidens is largely removed.
(*Journal of the Anthropological Institute,* Jan.-June, 1901, p. 96.)

[2] R. E. Guise, *Journal of the Anthropological Institute,* 1899,
pp. 214-216.

expression, full of devilry." It is the festival of the harvest-home, the termination of the year's toil, and is always held at full moon. The festival is a *saturnalia,* when all rules of duty and decorum are forgotten, and the utmost liberty is allowed to women and girls, who become like bacchantes. The people believe that at this time both men and women become overcharged with vitality, and that a safety valve is absolutely necessary. The festival begins with a religious sacrifice made by the village priest or elders, and with prayers for the departed and for the vouchsafing of seasonable rain and good crops. The religious ceremonies over, the people give themselves up to feasting and to drinking the home-made beer, the preparation of which from fermented rice is one of a girl's chief accomplishments. "The Ho population," wrote Dalton, "are at other seasons quiet and reserved in manner, and in their demeanor toward women gentle and decorous; even in their flirtations they never transcend the bounds of decency. The girls, though full of spirits and somewhat saucy, have innate notions of propriety that make them modest in demeanor, though devoid of all prudery, and of the obscene abuse, so frequently heard from the lips of common women in Bengal, they appear to have no knowledge. They are delicately sensitive under harsh language of any kind, and never use it to others; and since their adoption of clothing they are careful to drape themselves decently, as well as gracefully; but they throw all this aside during the *mágh* feast. Their nature appears to undergo a temporary change. Sons and daughters revile their parents in gross language, and parents their children; men and women become almost like animals in the indulgence of their amorous propensities. They enact all that was ever portrayed by prurient artists in a bacchanalian festival or pandean orgy; and as the light of the sun they adore, and the presence of numerous spectators, seems to be no restraint on their indulgence, it cannot be expected that chastity is preserved when the shades of night fall on such a scene of licentiousness and debauchery." While, however, thus representing the festival as a mere debauch, Dalton adds that relationships formed at this time generally end in marriage. There is also a flower festival in April and May,

9

of religious nature, but the dances at this festival are quieter in character.[1]

In Burmah the great festival of the year is the full moon of October, following the Buddhist Lent season (which is also the wet season), during which there is no sexual intercourse. The other great festival is the New Year in March.[2]

In classical times the great festivals were held at the same time as in northern and modern Europe. The *brumalia* took place in midwinter, when the days were shortest, and the *rosalia,* according to early custom in May or June, and at a later time about Easter. After the establishment of Christianity the Church made constant efforts to suppress this latter festival, and it was referred to by an eighth century council as "a wicked and reprehensible holiday-making." These festivals appear to be intimately associated with Dionysus worship, and the flower-festival of Dionysus, as well as the Roman Liberales in honor of Bacchus, was celebrated in March with worship of Priapus. The festivals of the Delian Apollo and of Artemis, both took place during the first week in May and the Roman Bacchanales in October.[3]

The mediæval Feast of Fools was to a large extent a seasonal orgy licensed by the Church. It may be traced directly back through the barbatories of the lower empire to the Roman *saturnalia,* and at Sens, the ancient ecclesiastical metropolis of France, it was held at about the same time as the *saturnalia,* on

---

[1] Dalton, *Ethnology of Bengal*, pp. 196 *et seq.* W. Crooke (*Journal of the Anthropological Institute*, p. 243, 1899) also refers to the annual harvest-tree dance and *saturnalia*, and its association with the seasonal period for marriage. We find a similar phenomenon in the Malay Peninsula: "In former days, at harvest-time, the Jakuns kept an annual festival, at which, the entire settlement having been called together, fermented liquor, brewed from jungle fruits, was drunk; and to the accompaniments of strains of their rude and incondite music, both sexes, crowning themselves with fragrant leaves and flowers, indulged in bouts of singing and dancing, which grew gradually wilder throughout the night, and terminated in a strange kind of sexual orgie." (W. W. Skeat, "The Wild Tribes of the Malay Peninsula," *Journal of the Anthropological Institute*, 1902, p. 133.)

[2] Fielding Hall, *The Soul of a People*, 1898, Chapter XIII.

[3] See *e.g.,* L. Dyer, *Studies of the Gods in Greece*, 1891, pp. 86-89, 375, etc.

the Feast of the Circumcision, *i.e.,* New Year's Day. It was not, however, always held at this time; thus at Evreux it took place on the 1st of May.[1]

The Easter bonfires of northern-central Europe, the Midsummer (St. John's Eve) fires of southern-central Europe, still bear witness to the ancient festivals.[2] There is certainly a connection between these bonfires and erotic festivals; it is noteworthy that they occur chiefly at the period of spring and early summer, which, on other grounds, is widely regarded as the time for the increase of the sexual instinct, while the less frequent period for the bonfires is that of the minor sexual climax. Mannhardt was perhaps the first to show how intimately these spring and early summer festivals—held with bonfires and dances and the music of violin—have been associated with love-making and the choice of a mate.[3] In spring, the first Monday in Lent (Quadrigesima) and Easter Eve were frequent days for such bonfires. In May, among the Franks of the Main, the unmarried women, naked and adorned with flowers, danced on the Blocksberg before the men, as described by Herbels in the tenth century.[4] In the central highlands of Scotland the Beltane fires were kindled on the 1st of May. Bonfires sometimes took place on

---

[1] For a popular account of the Feast of Fools, see Loliée, "La Fête des Fous," *Revue des Revues,* May 15, 1898; also, J. G. Bourke, *Scatologic Rites of all Nations,* pp. 11-23.

[2] J. Grimm (*Teutonic Mythology,* p. 615) points out that the observance of the spring or Easter bonfires marks off the Saxon from the Franconian peoples. The Easter bonfires are held in Lower Saxony, Westphalia, Lower Hesse, Geldern, Holland, Friesland, Jutland, and Zealand. The Midsummer bonfires are held on the Rhine, in Franconia, Thuringia, Swabia, Bavaria, Austria, and Silesia. Schwartz (*Zeitschrift für Ethnologie,* 1896, p. 151) shows that at Lauterberg, in the Harz Mountains, the line of demarcation between these two primitive districts may still be clearly traced.

[3] *Wald und Feldkulte,* 1875, vol. i, pp. 422 *et seq.* He also mentions (p. 458) that St. Valentine's Day (14th of February),—or Ember Day, or the last day of February,—when the pairing of birds was supposed to take place, was associated, especially in England, with love-making and the choice of a mate. In Lorraine, it may be added, on the 1st of May, the young girls chose young men as their valentines, a custom known by this name to Rabelais.

[4] Rochholz, *Drei gaugöttinnen,* p. 37.

Halloween (October 31st) and Christmas. But the great season all over Europe for these bonfires, then often held with erotic ceremonial, is the summer solstice, the 23d of June, the eve of Midsummer, or St. John's Day.[1]

The Bohemians and other Slavonic races formerly had meetings with sexual license. This was so up to the beginning of the sixteenth century on the banks of rivers near Novgorod. The meetings took place, as a rule, the day before the Festival of John the Baptist, which, in pagan times, was that of a divinity known by the name of Jarilo (equivalent to Priapus). Half a century later, a new ecclesiastical code sought to abolish every vestige of the early festivals held on Christmas Day, on the Day of the Baptism of Our Lord, and on John the Baptist's Day. A general feature of all these festivals (says Kowalewsky) was the prevalence of the promiscuous intercourse of the sexes. Among the Ehstonians, at the end of the eighteenth century, thousands of persons would gather around an old ruined church (in the Fellinschen) on the Eve of St. John, light a bonfire, and throw sacrificial gifts into it. Sterile women danced naked among the ruins; much eating and drinking went on, while the young men and maidens disappeared into the woods to do what they would. Festivals of this character still take place at the end of June in

---

[1] Mannhardt, *ibid.*, pp. 466 *et seq.* Also J. G. Frazer, *Golden Bough*, vol ii, Chapter IV. For further facts and references, see K. Pearson (*The Chances of Death*, 1897, vol, ii, "Woman as Witch," "Kindred Group-marriage," and Appendix on "The '*Mailehn*' and '*Kiltgang*,'") who incidentally brings together some of the evidence concerning primitive sex-festivals in Europe. Also, E. Hahn, *Demeter und Baubo*, 1896, pp. 38-40; and for some modern survivals, see Deniker, *Races of Man*, 1900, Chapter III. On a lofty tumulus near the megalithic remains at Carnac, in Brittany, the custom still prevails of lighting a large bonfire at the time of the summer solstice; it is called Tan Heol, or Tan St. Jean. In Ireland, the bonfires also take place on St. John's Eve, and a correspondent, who has often witnessed them in County Waterford, writes that "women, with garments raised, jump through these fires, and conduct which, on ordinary occasions would be reprobated, is regarded as excusable and harmless." Outside Europe, the Berbers of Morocco still maintain this midsummer festival, and in the Rif they light bonfires; here the fires seem to be now regarded as mainly purificatory, but they are associated with eating ceremonies which are still regarded as multiplicative. (Westermarck, "Midsummer Customs in Morocco, *Folk-Lore*, March, 1905.)

some districts. Young unmarried couples jump barefoot over large fires, usually near rivers or ponds. Licentiousness is rare.[1] But in many parts of Russia the peasants still attach little value to virginity, and even prefer women who have been mothers. The population of the Grisons in the sixteenth century held regular meetings not less licentious than those of the Cossacks. These were abolished by law. Kowalewsky regards all such customs as a survival of early forms of promiscuity.[2]

Frazer (*Golden Bough*, 2d ed., 1900, vol. iii, pp. 236-350) fully describes and discusses the dances, bonfires and festivals of spring and summer, of Halloween (October 31), and Christmas. He also explains the sexual character of these festivals. "There are clear indications," he observes (p. 305), "that even human fecundity is supposed to be promoted by the genial heat of the fires. It is an Irish belief that a girl who jumps thrice over the midsummer bonfire will soon marry and become the mother of many children; and in various parts of France they think that if a girl dances round nine fires she will be sure to marry within a year. On the other hand, in Lechrain, people say that if a young man and woman, leaping over the midsummer fire together, escape unsmirched, the young woman will not become a mother within twelve months—the flames have not touched and fertilized her. The rule observed in some parts of France and Belgium, that the bonfires on the first Sunday in Lent should be kindled by the person who was last married, seems to belong to the same class of ideas, whether it be that such a person is supposed to receive from, or impart to, the fire a generative and fertilizing influence. The common practice of lovers leaping over the fires hand-in-hand may very well have originated in a notion that thereby their marriage would be more likely to be blessed with offspring. And the scenes of profligacy which appear to have marked the midsummer celebration among the Ehstonians, as they once marked the celebration of May Day among ourselves, may

---

[1] Mannhardt (*op. cit.*, p. 469) quotes a description of an Ehstonian festival in the Island of Moon, when the girls dance in a circle round the fire, and one of them,—to the envy of the rest, and the pride of her own family,—is chosen by the young men, borne away so violently that her clothes are often torn, and thrown down by a youth, who places one leg over her body in a kind of symbolical coitus, and lies quietly by her side till morning. The spring festivals of the young people of Ukrainia, in which, also, there is singing, dancing, and sleeping together, are described in "Folk-Lore de l'Ukrainie." Κρυπτάδια, vol. v, pp. 2-6, and vol. viii, pp. 303 *et seq.*

[2] M. Kowalewsky, "Marriage Among the Early Slavs," *Folk-Lore*, December, 1890.

have sprung, not from the mere license of holiday-makers, but from a crude notion that such orgies were justified, if not required, by some mysterious bond which linked the life of man to the courses of the heavens at the turning-point of the year."

As regards these primitive festivals, although the evidence is scattered and sometimes obscure, certain main conclusions clearly emerge. In early Europe there were, according to Grimm, only two seasons, sometimes regarded as spring and winter, sometimes as spring and autumn, and for mythical purposes these seasons were alone available.[1] The appearance of each of these two seasons was inaugurated by festivals which were religious and often erotic in character. The Slavonic year began in March, at which time there was formerly, it is believed, a great festival, not only in Slavonic but also in Teutonic countries. In Northern Germany there were Easter bonfires always associated with mountains or hills. The Celtic bonfires were held at the beginning of May, while the Teutonic May-day, or *Walpurgisnacht,* is a very ancient sacred festival, associated with erotic ceremonial, and regarded by Grimm as having a common origin with the Roman *floralia* and the Greek *dionysia.* Thus, in Europe, Grimm concludes: "there are four different ways of welcoming summer. In Sweden and Gothland a battle of winter and summer, a triumphal entry of the latter. In Schonen, Denmark, Lower Saxony, and England, simply May-riding, or fetching of the May-wagon. On the Rhine merely a battle of winter and summer, without immersion, without the pomp of an entry. In Franconia, Thuringia, Meissen, Silesia, and Bohemia only the carrying out of wintry death; no battle, no formal introduction of summer. Of these festivals the first and second fall in May, the third and fourth in March. In the first two, the whole population take part with unabated enthusiasm; in the last two only the lower poorer class. . . . Everything goes to prove that the approach of summer was to our forefathers a holy tide, welcomed

---

[1] A. Tille, however (*Yule and Christmas,* 1899), while admitting that the general Aryan division of the year was dual, follows Tacitus in asserting that the Germanic division of the year (like the Egyptian) was tripartite: winter, spring, and summer.

by sacrifice, feast, and dance, and largely governing and brightening the people's life."[1] The early spring festival of March, the festival of Ostara, the goddess of spring, has become identified with the Christian festival of Resurrection (just as the summer solstice festival has been placed beneath the patronage of St. John the Baptist); but there has been only an amalgamation of closely-allied rites, for the Christian festival also may be traced back to a similar origin. Among the early Arabians the great *ragab* feast, identified by Ewald and Robertson Smith with the Jewish *paschal* feast, fell in the spring or early summer, when the camels and other domestic animals brought forth their young and the shepherds offered their sacrifices.[2] Babylonia, the supreme early centre of religious and cosmological culture, presents a more decisive example of the sex festival. The festival of Tammuz is precisely analogous to the European festival of St. John's Day. Tammuz was the solar god of spring vegetation, and closely associated with Ishtar, also an agricultural deity of fertility. The Tammuz festival was, in the earliest times, held toward the summer solstice, at the time of the first wheat and barley harvest. In Babylonia, as in primitive Europe, there were only two seasons; the festival of Tammuz, coming at the end of winter and the beginning of summer, was a fast followed by a feast, a time of mourning for winter, of rejoicing for summer. It is part of the primitive function of sacred ritual to be symbolical of natural processes, a mysterious representation of natural processes with the object of bringing them about.[3] The Tammuz festival was an appeal to the powers of Nature to exhibit their generative functions; its erotic character is indicated not only by the well-known fact that the priestesses of Ishtar (the Kadishtu, or "holy ones") were prostitutes, but by the statements in Babylonian legends concerning the state of the earth during Ishtar's winter absence, when the bull, the ass, and man

---

[1] Grimm, *Teutonic Mythology* (English translation by Stallybrass), pp. 612-630, 779, 788.

[2] Wellhausen, *Reste Arabischen Heidentums*, 1897, p. 98.

[3] See, *e.g.*, the chapter on ritual in Gérard-Varet's interesting book. *L'Ignorance et l'Irréflexion*, 1899, for a popular account of this and allied primitive conceptions.

ceased to reproduce. It is evident that the return of spring, coincident with the Tammuz festival, was regarded as the period for the return of the reproductive instinct even in man.[1] So that along this line also we are led back to a great procreative festival.

Thus the great spring festivals were held between March and June, frequently culminating in a great orgy on Midsummer's Eve. The next great season of festivals in Europe was in autumn. The beginning of August was a great festival in Celtic lands, and the echoes of it, Rhys remarks, have not yet died out in Wales.[2] The beginning of November, both in Celtic and Teutonic countries, was a period of bonfires.[3] In Germanic countries especially there was a great festival at the time. The Germanic year began at Martinmas (November 11th), and the great festival of the year was then held. It is the oldest Germanic festival on record, and retained its importance even in the Middle Ages. There was feasting all night, and the cattle that were to be killed were devoted to the gods; the goose was associated with this festival.[4] These autumn festivals culminated in the great festival of the winter solstice which we have perpetuated

---

[1] Jastrow, *Religion of Babylonia*, especially pp. 485, 571; regarding the priestesses, Jastrow remarks: "Among many nations, the mysterious aspects of woman's fertility lead to rites that, by a perversion of their original import, appear to be obscene. The prostitutes were priestesses attached to the Ishtar cult, and who took part in ceremonies intended to symbolize fertility." Whether there is any significance in the fact that the first two months of the Babylonian year (roughly corresponding to our March and April), when we should expect births to be at a maximum, were dedicated to Ea and Bel, who, according to varying legends, were the creators of man, and that New Year's Day was the festival of Bau, regarded as the mother of mankind, I cannot say, but the suggestion may be put forward.

[2] *Celtic Heathendom*, p. 421.

[3] Grimm, *Teutonic Mythology*, p. 1465. In England, the November bonfires have become merged into the Guy Fawkes celebrations. In the East, the great primitive autumn festivals seem to have fallen somewhat earlier. In Babylonia, the seventh month (roughly corresponding to September) was specially sacred, though nothing is known of its festivals, and this also was the sacred festival month of the Hebrews, and originally of the Arabs. In Europe, among the southern Slavs, the Reigen, or Kolo—wild dances by girls, adorned with flowers, and with skirts girt high, followed by sexual intercourse—take place in autumn, during the nights following harvest time.

[4] A. Tille, *Yule and Christmas*, p. 21, etc.

in the celebrations of Christmas and New Year. Thus, while the two great primitive culminating festivals of spring and autumn correspond exactly (as we shall see) with the seasons of maximum fecundation, even in the Europe of to-day, the earlier spring (March) and—though less closely—autumn (November) festivals correspond with the periods of maximum spontaneous sexual disturbance, as far as I have been able to obtain precise evidence of such disturbance. That the maximum of physiological sexual excitement should tend to appear earlier than the maximum of fecundation is a result that might be expected.

The considerations so far brought forward clearly indicate that among primitive races there are frequently one or two seasons in the year—especially spring and autumn—during which sexual intercourse is chiefly or even exclusively carried on, and they further indicate that these primitive customs persist to some extent even in Europe to-day. It would still remain to determine whether any such influence affects the whole mass of the civilized population and determines the times at which intercourse, or fecundation, most frequently takes place.

This question can be most conveniently answered by studying the seasonal variation in the birthrate, calculating back to the time of conception. Wargentin, in Sweden, first called attention to the periodicity of the birthrate in 1767.[1] The matter seems to have attracted little further attention until Quetelet, who instinctively scented unreclaimed fields of statistical investigation, showed that in Belgium and Holland there is a maximum of births in February, and, consequently, of conceptions in May, and a minimum of births about July, with consequent minimum of conceptions in October. Quetelet considered that the spring maximum of conceptions corresponded to an increase of vitality after the winter cold. He pointed out that this sexual climax was better marked in the country than in towns, and accounted

---

[1] Long before Wargentin, however, Rabelais had shown some interest in this question, and had found that there were most christenings in October and November, this showing, he pointed out, that the early warmth of spring influenced the number of conceptions (*Pantagruel*, liv. v, Ch. XXIX). The spring maximum of conceptions is not now so early in France.

for this by the consideration that in the country the winter cold is more keenly felt. Later, Wappäus investigated the matter in various parts of northern and southern Europe as well as in Chile, and found that there was a maximum of conceptions in May and June attributable to season, and in Catholic countries strengthened by customs connected with ecclesiastical seasons. This maximum was, he found, followed by a mimimum in September, October, and November, due to gradually increasing exhaustion, and the influence of epidemic diseases, as well as the strain of harvest-work. The minimum is reached in the south earlier than in the north. About November conceptions again become more frequent, and reach the second maximum at about Christmas and New Year. This second maximum is very slightly marked in southern countries, but strongly marked in northern countries (in Sweden the absolute maximum of conceptions is reached in December), and is due, in the opinion of Wappäus, solely to social causes. Villermé reached somewhat similar results. Founding his study on 17,000,000 births, he showed that in France it was in April, May, and June, or from the spring equinox to the summer solstice, and nearer to the solstice than the equinox, that the maximum of fecundations takes place; while the minimum of births is normally in July, but is retarded by a wet and cold summer in such a manner that in August there are scarcely more births than in July, and, on the other hand, a very hot summer, accelerating the minimum of births, causes it to fall in June instead of in July.[1] He also showed that in Buenos Ayres, where the seasons are reversed, the conception-rate follows the reversed seasons, and is also raised by epochs of repose, of plentiful food, and of increased social life. Sormani studied the periodicity of conception in Italy, and found that the spring maximum in the southern provinces occurs in May, and gradually falls later as one proceeds northward, until, in the extreme north of the peninsula, it occurs in July. In southern Italy there is only one maximum and one minimum; in the north there are two. The minimum which follows the spring or sum-

1 Villermé, "De la Distribution par mois des conceptions," *Annales d'Hygiène Publique*, tome v, 1831, pp. 55-155.

mer maximum increases as we approach the south, while the minimum associated with the winter cold increases as we approach the north.[1] Beukemann, who studied the matter in various parts of Germany, found that seasonal influence was specially marked in the case of illegitimate births. The maximum of conceptions of illegitimate children takes place in the spring and summer of Europe generally; in Russia it takes place in the autumn and winter, when the harvest-working months for the population are over, and the period of rest, and also of minimum deathrate (September, October, and November), comes round. In Russia the general conception-rate has been studied by various investigators. Here the maximum number of conceptions is in winter, the minimum varying among different elements of the population. Looked at more closely, there are maxima of conceptions in Russia in January and in April. (In Russian towns, however, the maximum number of conceptions occurs in the autumn.) The special characteristics of the Russian conception-rate are held to be due to the prevalence of marriages in autumn and winter,[2] to the severely observed fasts of spring, and to the exhausting harvest-work of summer.

It is instructive to compare the conception-rate of Europe with that of a non-European country. Such a comparison has been made by S. A. Hill for the Northwest Provinces of India. Here the Holi and other erotic festivals take place in spring; but spring is not the period when conceptions chiefly take place; indeed, the prevalence of erotic festivals in spring appears to Hill an argument in favor of those festivals having originated in a colder climate. The conceptions show a rise through October and November to a maximum in December and January, followed by a steady and prolonged fall to a minimum in September. This curve can be accounted for by climatic and economic conditions. September is near the end of the long and depressing hot season,

---

[1] Sormani, *Giornale di Medicina Militare*, 1870.

[2] Throughout Europe, it may be said, marriages tend to take place either in spring or autumn (Oettinger *Moralstatistik*, p. 181, gives details). That is to say, that there is a tendency for marriages to take place at the season of the great public festivals, during which sexual intercourse was prevalent in more primitive times.

when malarial influences are rapidly increasing to a maximum, the food-supply is nearly exhausted, and there is the greatest tendency to suicide. With October it forms the period of greatest mortality. December, on the other hand, is the month when food is most abundant, and it is also a very healthy month.[1]

For a summary of the chief researches into this question, see Ploss and Bartels, *Das Weib;* also, Rosenstadt, "Zur Frage nach den Ursachen welche die Zahl der Conceptionen, etc," *Mittheilungen aus den embryologischen Institute Universität Wien*, second series, fasc. 4, 1890. Rosenstadt concludes that man has inherited from animal ancestors a "physiological custom" which has probably been further favored by climatic and social conditions. "Primitive man," he proceeds, "had inherited from his ancestors the faculty of only reproducing himself at determined epochs. On the arrival of this period of rut, fecundation took place on a large scale, this being very easy, ·thanks to the promiscuity in which primitive man lived. With the development of civilization, men give themselves up to sexual relations all the year around, but the 'physiological custom' of procreating at a certain epoch has not completely disappeared; it remains as a survival of the animal condition, and manifests itself in the recrudescence of the number of conceptions during certain months of the year." O. Rosenbach ("Bemerkungen über das Problem einer Brunstzeit beim Menschen," *Archiv für Rassen und Gesellschafts-Biologie*, Bd. III, Heft 5) has also argued in favor of a chief sexual period in the year in man, with secondary and even tertiary climaxes, in March, August, and December. He finds that in some families, for several generations, birthdays tend to fall in the same months, but his paper is, on the whole, inconclusive.

Some years ago, Prof. J. B. Haycraft argued, on the basis of data furnished by Scotland, that the conception-rate corresponds to the temperature-curve (Haycraft, "Physiological Results of Temperature Variation, *Transactions of the Royal Society of Edinburgh*, vol. xxix, 1880). "Temperature," he concluded, "is the main factor regulating the variations in the number of conceptions which occur during the year. It increases their number with its elevation, and this on an average of 0.5 per cent. for an elevation of 1° F." Whether or not this theory may fit the facts as regards Scotland, it is certainly altogether untenable when we take a broader view of the phenomena.

Recently Dr. Paul Gaedeken of Copenhagen has argued in a detailed statistical study ("La Réaction de l'Organisme sous l'Influence Physico-Chimiques des Agents Météorologiques," *Archives d'Anthropologie*

[1] Hill, *Nature*, July 12, 1888.

Criminelle, Feb., 1909) that the conception-rate, as well as the periodicity of suicide and allied phenomena, is due to the action of the chemical rays on the unpigmented skin in early spring, this action being physiologically similar to that of alcohol. He seeks thus to account for the marked and early occurrence of such periodic phenomena in Greenland and other northern countries where there is much chemical action (owing to the clear air) in early spring, but little heat. This explanation would not cover an autumnal climax, the existence of which Gaedeken denies.

In order to obtain a fairly typical conception-curve for Europe, and to allow the variations of local habit and custom to some extent to annihilate each other, I have summated the figures given by Mayr for about a quarter of a million births in Germany, France, and Italy,[1] obtaining a curve (Chart 2) of the conception-rate which may be said roughly to be that of Europe generally. If we begin at September as the lowest point, we find an autumn rise culminating in the lesser maximum of Christmas, followed by a minor depression in January and February. Then comes the great spring rise, culminating in May, and followed after June by a rapid descent to the minimum.

In Canada (see *e.g.*, *Report of the Registrar General of the Province of Ontario* for 1904), the maximum and minimum of conceptions alike fall later than in Europe; the months of maximum conception are June, July, and August; of minimum conception, January, February, and March. June is the favorite month for marriage.

It would be of some interest to know the conception-curve for the well-to-do classes, who are largely free from the industrial and social influences which evidently, to a great extent, control the conception-rate. It seems probable that the seasonal influence would here be specially well shown. The only attempt I have made in this direction is to examine a well-filled birthday-book. The entries show a very high and equally maintained maximum of conceptions throughout April, May and June, followed by a marked minimum during the next three months, and an autumn rise very strongly marked, in November. There is no December rise. As will be seen, there is here a fairly exact resemblance to the yearly ecbolic curve of people of the same class. The inquiry needs, however, to be extended to a very much larger number of cases.

---

[1] G. Mayr, *Die Gesetzmässigkeit im Gesellschaftsleben*, 1877, p. 240.

Mr. John Douglass Brown, of Philadelphia, has kindly prepared and sent me, since the above was written, a series of curves showing the annual periodicity of births among the educated classes in the State of Pennsylvania, using the statistics as to 4,066 births contained in the Biographical Catalogue of Matriculates of the College of the University of Pennsylvania. Mr. Brown prepared four curves: the first, covering the earliest period, 1757-1859; the second, the period 1860-1876; the third, 1877-1893; while the fourth presented the summated results for the whole period. (The dates named are those of the entry to classes, and not of actual occurrence of birth.) A very definite and well-marked curve is shown, and the average number of births (not conceptions) per day, for the whole period, is as follows:—

Jan.	Feb.	Mar.	Apr.	May	June	July	Aug.	Sept.	Oct.	Nov.	Dec.
10.5	11.4	11	8.3	10.2	10.5	11.5	12.6	12.3	11.6	12	11.7

There is thus a well-marked minimum of conceptions (a depression appearing here in each of the three periods, separately) about the month of July. (In the second period, however, which contains the smallest number of births, the minimum occurs in September.) From that low minimum there is steady and unbroken rise up to the chief maximum in November. (In the first period, however, the maximum is delayed till January, and in the second period it is somewhat diffused.) There is a tendency to a minor maximum in February, specially well marked in the third and most important period, and in the first period delayed until March.

A very curious and perhaps not accidental coincidence might be briefly pointed out before we leave this part of the subject. It is found[1] by taking 3000 cases of children dying under one year that, among the general population, children born in February and September (and therefore conceived in May and December) appear to possess the greatest vitality, and those born in June, and, therefore, conceived in September, the least vitality.[2] As we have seen, May and December are precisely the periods

---

[1] Edward Smith (*Health and Disease*), who attributes this to the lessened vitality of offspring at that season. Beukemann also states that children born in September have most vitality.

[2] Westermarck has even suggested that the December maximum of conceptions may be due to better chance of survival for September offspring (*Human Marriage*, Chapter II). It may be noted that though the maximum of conceptions is in May, relatively the smallest proportion of boys is conceived at that time. (Rauber, *Der Ueberschuss an Knabengeburten*, p. 39.)

when conceptions in Europe generally are at a maximum, and September is precisely the period when they are at a minimum, so that, if this coincidence is not accidental, the strongest children are conceived when there is the strongest tendency to procreate, and the feeblest children when that tendency is feeblest.

Nelson, in his study of dreams and their relation to seasonal ecbolic manifestations, does not present any yearly ecbolic curve, as the two years and a half over which his observations extend scarcely supply a sufficient basis. On examining his figures, however, I find there is a certain amount of evidence of a yearly rhythm. There are spring and autumn climaxes throughout (in February and in November); there is no December rise. During one year there is a marked minimum from May to September, though it is but slightly traceable in the succeeding year. These figures are too uncertain to prove anything, but, as far as they go, they are in fair agreement with the much more extensive record, that of W. K. (*ante* p. 113), which I have already made use of in discussing the question of a monthly rhythm. This record, covering nearly twelve years, shows a general tendency, when the year is divided into four periods (November-January, February-April, May-July, August-October) and the results summated, to rise steadily throughout, from the minimum in the winter period to the maximum in the autumn period. This steady upward progress is not seen in each year taken separately. In three years there is a fall in passing from the November-January to the February-April quarter (always followed by a rise in the subsequent quarter); in three cases there is a fall in passing from the second to the third quarter (again always followed by a rise in the following quarter), and in two successive years there is a fall in passing from the third to the fourth quarter. If, however, beginning at the second year, we summate the results for each year with those for all previous years, a steady rise from season to season is seen throughout. If we analyze the data according to the months of the year, still more precise and interesting results (as shown in the curve, Chart 3) are obtained; two maximum points are seen, one in spring (March), one in autumn (October, or, rather, August-

October), and each of these maximum points is followed by a steep and sudden descent to the minimum points in April and in December. If we compare this result with Perry-Coste's, also extending over a long series of years, we find a marked similarity. In both alike there are spring and autumn maxima, in both the autumn maximum is the highest, and in both also there is an intervening fall. In both cases, again, the maxima are followed by steep descents, but while in both the spring maximum occurs in March, in Perry-Coste's case the second maximum, though of precisely similar shape, occurs earlier, in June-September instead of August-October. In Perry-Coste's case, also, there is an apparently abnormal tendency, only shown in the more recent years of the record, to an additional maximum in January. The records certainly show far more points of agreement than of discrepancy, and by their harmony, as well with each other as with themselves, when the years are taken separately, certainly go far to prove that there is a very marked annual rhythm in the phenomena of seminal emissions during sleep, or, as Nelson has termed it, the ecbolic curve. We see, also, that the great yearly organic climax of sexual effervescence corresponds with the period following harvest, which, throughout the primitive world, has been a season of sexual erethism and orgy; though those customs have died out of our waking lives, they are still imprinted on our nervous texture, and become manifest during sleep.

The fresh records that have reached me since the first edition of this book was published show well-marked annual curves, though each curve always has some slight personal peculiarities of its own. The most interesting and significant is that of E. M. (see *ante* p. 116), covering four years. It is indicated by the following monthly frequencies, summated for the four years:—

Jan.	Feb.	Mar.	Apr.	May	June	July	Aug.	Sept.	Oct.	Nov.	Dec.
16	13	14	22	19	19	12	12	14	14	12	24

E. M. lives in India. April, May, and June, are hot months, but not unhealthy, and during this season, moreover, he lives in the hills, under favorable conditions, getting plenty of outdoor exercise. July, August, and September, are nearly as hot, but much damper, and more trying; during these months, E. M. is living in the city, and his work is then,

also, more **exacting** than at other times. September is the worst
month of all; he has a short holiday at the end of it. During December, January, and February, the climate is very fine, and E. M.'s
work is easier. It will be seen that his ecbolic curve corresponds to
his circumstances and environment, although until he analyzed the
record he had no idea that any such relationship existed. Unfavorable climatic conditions and hard work, favorable conditions and lighter
work, happen to coincide in his life, and the former depress the frequency
of seminal emissions; the latter increase their frequency. At the same
time, the curve is not out of harmony with the northern curves. There
is what corresponds to a late spring (April) climax, and another still
higher, late autumn (December) climax. A very interesting point
is the general resemblance of the ecbolic curves to the Indian conception-
curves as set forth by Hill (*ante* p. 140). The conception-curve is at
its lowest point in September, and at its highest point in December-
January, and this ecbolic curve follows it, except that both the minimum
and the maximum are reached a little earlier. When compared with the
English annual ecbolic curves (W. K. and Perry-Coste), both spring
and autumn maxima fall rather later, but all agree in representing
the autumn rise as the chief climax.

The annual curve of A. N. (*ante* p. 117), who lives in Indiana,
U. S. A., also covers four years. It presents the usual spring (May-
June, in this case) and autumn (September-October) climaxes. The
exact monthly results, summated for the four years, are given below;
in order to allow for the irregular lengths of the months, I have reduced them to daily averages, for convenience treating the four years
as one year:—

Jan.	Feb.	Mar.	Apr.	May	June	July	Aug.	Sept.	Oct.	Nov.	Dec.
13	9	13	20	23	22	20	20	21	23	9	16
.42	.32	.42	.66	.74	.73	.64	.64	.70	.74	.30	.52

In his book on *Adolescence*, Stanley Hall refers to three ecbolic
records in his possession, all made by men who were doctors of philosophy, and all considering themselves normal. The best of these records
made by "a virtuous, active and able man," covered nearly eight years.
Stanley Hall thus summarizes the records, which are not presented in
detail: "The best of these records averages about three and a half such
experiences per month, the most frequent being 5.14 for July, and the
least frequent 2.28, for September, for all the years taken together.
There appears also a slight rise in April, and another in November, with
a fall in December." The frequency varies in the different individuals.
There was no tendency to a monthly cycle. In the best case, the
minimum number for the year was thirty-seven, and the maximum,
fifty. Fifty-nine per cent. of all were at an interval of a week or less;

forty per cent. at an interval of from one to four days; thirty-four per cent. at an interval of from eight to seventeen days, the longest being forty-two days. Poor condition, overwork, and undersleep, led to infrequency. Early morning was the most common time. Normally there was a sense of distinct relief, but in low conditions, or with over-frequency, depression. (G. S. Hall, *Adolescence*, vol. i, p. 453.) I may add that an anonymous article on "Nocturnal Emissions" (*American Journal of Psychology*, Jan., 1904) is evidently a fuller presentation of the first of Stanley Hall's three cases. It is the history of a healthy, unmarried, chaste man, who kept a record of his nocturnal emissions (and their accompanying dreams) from the age of thirty to thirty-eight. In what American State he lived is not mentioned. He was ignorant of the existence of any previous records. The yearly average was 37 to 50, remaining fairly constant; the monthly average was 3.43. I reproduce the total results summated for the months, separately, and I have worked out the daily average for each month, for convenience counting the summated eight years as one year:—

Jan.	Feb.	Mar.	Apr.	May	June	July	Aug.	Sept.	Oct.	Nov.	Dec.
27	27	27	31	29	28	36	25	18	27	30	24
.87	.94	.87	1.03	.93	.93	1.16	.81	.60	.87	1.00	.77

Here, as in all the other curves we have been able to consider, we may see the usual two points of climax in spring and in autumn; the major climax covers April, May, June, and July, the minor autumnal climax is confined to November. In the light of the evidence which has thus accumulated, we may conclude that the existence of an annual ecbolic curve, with its spring and autumn climaxes, as described in the first edition of this book, is now definitely established.

If we are to believe, as these records tend to show, that the nocturnal and involuntary voice of the sexual impulse usually speaks at least as loudly in autumn as in spring, we are confronted by a certain divergence of the sleeping sexual impulse from the waking sexual instinct, as witnessed by the conception-curve, and also, it may be added, by the general voice of tradition, and, indeed, of individual feeling, which concur, on the whole, in placing the chief epoch of sexual activity in spring and early summer, more especially as regards women.[1] It is not impossible to reconcile the contradiction, assuming it to be real, but I will

---

[1] Krieger found that the great majority of German women investigated by him menstruated for the first time in September, October, or November. In America, Bowditch states that the first menstruation of country girls more often occurs in spring than at any other season.

refrain here from suggesting the various explanations which arise. We need a broader basis of facts.

There are many facts to show that early spring and, to a certain extent, autumn are periods of visible excitement, mainly sexual in character. We have already seen that among the Eskimo menstruation and sexual desire occur chiefly in spring, but cases are known of healthy women in temperate climes who only menstruate twice a year, and in such cases the menstrual epochs appear to be usually in spring and autumn. Such, at all events, was the case in a girl of 20, whose history has been recorded by Dr. Mary Wenck, of Philadelphia.[1] She menstruated first when 15 years old. Six months later the flow again appeared for the second time, and lasted three weeks, without cessation. Since then, for five years, she menstruated during March and September only, each time for three weeks, the flow being profuse, but not exhaustingly so, without pain or systemic disturbance. Examination revealed perfectly normal uterus and ovarian organs. Treatment, accompanied by sitz-baths during the time of month the flow should appear, accomplished nothing. The semi-annual flow continued and the girl seemed in excellent health.

It is a remarkable fact that, as noted by Dr. Hamilton Wey at Elmira, sexual outbursts among prisoners appear to occur at about March and October. "Beginning with the middle of February," writes Dr. Wey in a private letter, "and continuing for about two months, is a season of ascending sexual wave; also the latter half of September and the month of October. We are now (March 30th) in the midst of a wave."

According to Chinese medicine, it is the spring which awakens human passions. In early Greek tradition, spring and summer were noted as the time of greatest wantonness. "In the season of toilsome summer," says Hesiod (*Works and Days*, xi, 569-90), "the goats are fattest, wine is best, women most wanton, and men weakest." It was so, also, in the experience of the Romans. Pliny (*Natural History*, Bk. XII, Ch. XLIII) states that when the asparagus blooms and the cicada sings loudest, is the season when women are most amorous, but

---

1 *Women's Medical Journal*, 1894.

men least inclined to pleasure. Paulus Ægineta said that hysteria specially abounds during spring and autumn in lascivious girls and sterile women, while more recent observers have believed that hysteria is particularly difficult to treat in autumn. Oribasius (*Synopsis*, lib. i, cap. 6) quotes from Rufus to the effect that sexual feeling is most strong in spring, and least so in summer. Rabelais said that it was in March that the sexual impulse is strongest, referring this to the early warmth of spring, and that August is the month least favorable to sexual activity (*Pantagruel*, liv. v, Ch. XXIX). Nipho, in his book on love dedicated to Joan of Aragon, discussed the reasons why "women are more lustful and amorous in summer, and men in winter." Venette, in his *Génération de l'homme*, harmonized somewhat conflicting statements with the observation that spring is the season of love for both men and women; in summer, women are more amorous than men; in autumn, men revive to some extent, but are still oppressed by the heat, which, sexually, has a less depressing effect on women. There is probably a real element of truth in this view, and both extremes of heat and cold may be regarded as unfavorable to masculine virility. It is highly probable that the well-recognized tendency of piles to become troublesome in spring and in autumn, is due to increased sexual activity. Piles are favored by congestion, and sexual excitement is the most powerful cause of sudden congestion in the genito-anal region. Erasmus Darwin called attention to the tendency of piles to recur about the equinoxes (*Zoönomia*, Section XXXVI), and since his days Gant, Bonavia, and Cullimore have correlated this periodicity with sexual activity.

Laycock, quoting the opinions of some earlier authorities as to the prevalence of sexual feeling in spring, stated that that popular opinion "appears to be founded on fact" (*Nervous Diseases of Women*, p. 69). I find that many people, and perhaps especially women, confirm from their own experience, the statement that sexual feeling is strongest in spring and summer. Wichmann states that pollutions are most common in spring (being perhaps the first to make that statement), and also nymphomania. (In the eighteenth century, Schurig recorded a case of extreme and life-long sexual desire in a woman whose salacity was always at its height towards the festival of St. John, *Gynœcologia*, p. 16.) A correspondent in the Argentine Republic writes to me that "on big estancias, where we have a good many shepherds, nearly always married, or, rather, I should say, living with some woman (for our standard of morality is not very high in these parts), we always look out for trouble in springtime, as it is a very common thing at this season for wives to leave their husbands and go and live with some other man." A corresponding tendency has been noted even among children. Thus, Sanford Bell ("The Emotion of Love Between the Sexes," *American Journal Psychology*, July, 1902) remarks: "The season of the year seems to have its effect upon the intensity of the emotion of sex-love among children. One teacher, from Texas, who furnished me with seventy-six cases, said that he had noticed that in the matter of love children seemed 'fairly to break out in the springtime.' Many of the others who reported, incidentally mentioned the love affairs as beginning in the spring. This also agrees with my own observations."

Crichton-Browne remarks that children in springtime exhibit restlessness, excitability, perversity, and indisposition to exertion that are not displayed at other times. This condition, sometimes known as "spring fever," has been studied in over a hundred cases, both children and adults, by Kline. The majority of these report a feeling of tiredness, languor, lassitude, sometimes restlessness, sometimes drowsiness. There is often a feeling of suffocation, and a longing for Nature and fresh air and day-dreams, while work seems distasteful and unsatisfactory. Change is felt to be necessary at all costs, and sometimes there is a desire to begin some new plan of life.[1] In both sexes there is frequently a wave of sexual emotion, a longing for love. Kline also found by examination of a very large number of cases that between the ages of four and seventeen it is in spring that running away from home most often occurs. He suggests that this whole group of phenomena may be due to the shifting of the metabolic processes from the ordinary grooves into reproductive channels, and seeks to bring it into connection with the migrations of animals for reproductive purposes.[2]

It has long been known that the occurrence of insanity follows an annual curve,[3] and though our knowledge of this curve, being founded on the date of admissions to asylums, cannot be said to be quite precise, it fairly corresponds to the outbreaks of

---

[1] It is, perhaps, worth while noting that the wisdom of the mediæval Church found an outlet for this "spring fever" in pilgrimages to remote shrines. As Chaucer wrote, in the *Canterbury Tales:*—

"Whané that Aprille with his showers sote
The droughts of March hath piercèd to the root,
Thaen longen folk to gon on pilgrimages,
And palmers for to seeken strange stronds."

[2] L. W. Kline, "The Migratory Impulse," *American Journal of Psychology,* 1898, vol. x, especially pp. 21-24.

[3] Mania comes to a crisis in spring, said the old physician, Aretæus (Bk. I, Ch. V).

acute insanity.   The curve presented in Chart 4 shows the admissions to the London County Council Lunatic Asylums during the years 1893 to 1897 inclusive; I have arranged it in two-month periods, to neutralize unimportant oscillations.   In order to show that this curve is not due to local or accidental circumstances, we may turn to France and take a special and chronic form of mental disease: Garnier, in his *Folie à Paris,* presents an almost exactly similar curve of the admissions of cases of general paralysis to the Infirmerie Spéciale at Paris during the years 1886-88 (Chart 5).   Both curves alike show a major climax in spring and a minor climax in autumn.

Crime in general in temperate climates tends to reach its maximum at the beginning of the hot season, usually in June.   Thus, in Belgium, the minimum is in February; the maximum in June, thence gradually diminishing (Lentz, *Bulletin Société Médecine Mentale Belgique,* March, 1901).   In France, Lacassagne has summated the data extending over more than 40 years, and finds that for all crimes June is the maximum month, the minimum being reached in November.   He also gives the figures for each class of crime separately, and every crime is found to have its own yearly curve.   Poisonings show a chief maximum in May, with slow fall and a minor climax in December; assassinations have a February and a November climax.   Parricides culminate in May-June, and in October (Lacassagne's tables are given by Laurent, *Les Habitués des Prisons de Paris,* Ch. I).

Notwithstanding the general tendency for crime to reach its maximum in the first hot month (a tendency not necessarily due to the direct influence of heat), we also find, when we consider the statistics of crime generally (including sexual crime), that there is another tendency for minor climaxes in spring and autumn.   Thus, in Italy, Penta, taking the statistics of nearly four thousand crimes (murder, highway robbery, and sexual offences), found the maximum in the first summer months, but there were also minor climaxes in spring and in August and September (Penta, *Rivista Mensile di Psichiatria,* 1899).   In nearly all Europe (as is shown by a diagram given by Lombroso and Laschi, at the end of the first volume of *Le Crime Politique*), while the chief climaxes occur about July, there is, in most countries, a distinct tendency to spring (usually about March) and autumn (September and November) climaxes, though they rarely rise as high as the July climax.

If we consider the separate periodicity of sexual offences, we find that they follow the rule for crimes generally, and usually show a chief maximum in early summer. Aschaffenburg finds that the annual periodicity of the sexual impulse appears more strongly marked the more abnormal its manifestations, which he places in the following order of increasing periodicity: conceptions in marriage, conceptions out of marriage, offences against decency, rape, assaults on children (*Centralblatt für Nervenheilkunde*, January, 1903). In France, rapes and offences against modesty are most numerous in May, June, and July, as Villermé, Lacassagne, and others have shown. Villermé, investigating 1,000 such cases, found a gradual ascent in frequency (only slightly broken in March) to a maximum in June (oscillating between May and July, when the years are considered separately), and then a gradual descent to a minimum in December. Legludic gives, for the 159 cases he had investigated, a table showing a small February-March climax, and a large June-August maximum, the minimum being reached in November-January. (Legludic, *Attentats aux Mœurs*, 1896, p. 16.) In Germany, Aschaffenburg finds that sexual offences begin to increase in March and April, reach a maximum in June or July, and fall to a minimum in winter (*Monatsschrift für Psychiatrie*, 1903, Heft 2). In Italy, Penta shows that sexual offences reach a minor climax in May (corresponding, in his experience, with the maximum for crimes generally, as well as with the maximum for conceptions), and a more marked climax in August-September (Penta, *I Pervertimenti Sessuali*, 1893, p. 115; *id. Rivista Mensile di Psichiatria*, 1899).

Corre, in his *Crime en Pays Créole*, presents charts of the seasonal distribution of crime in Guadeloupe, with relation to temperature, which show that while, in a mild temperature like that of France and England, crime attains its maximum in the hot season, it is not so in a more tropical climate; in July, when in Guadeloupe the heat attains its maximum degree, crime of all kinds falls suddenly to a very low minimum. Even in the United States, where the summer heat is often excessive, it tends to produce a diminution of crime.

Dexter, in an elaborate study of the relationship of conduct to the weather, shows that in the United States assaults present the maximum of frequency in April and October, with a decrease during the summer and the winter. "The unusual and interesting fact demonstrated here with a certainty that cannot be doubted is," he concludes, "that the unseasonably hot days of spring and autumn are the pugnacious ones, even though the actual heat be much less than for summer. We might infer from this that conditions of heat, up to a certain extent, are vitalizing, while, at the same time, irritating, but above that limit, heat is so devitalizing in its effects as to leave hardly energy enough to carry on a fight." (E. G. Dexter, *Conduct and the Weather*, 1899, pp. 63 *et seq.*)

It is not impossible that the phenomena of seasonal periodicity in crimes may possess a real significance in relation to sexual periodicity. If, as is possible, the occurrence of spring and autumn climaxes of criminal activity is due less to any special exciting causes at these seasons than to the depressing influences of heat and cold in summer and winter, it may appear reasonable to ask whether the spring and autumn climaxes of sexual activity are not really also largely due to a like depressing influence of extreme temperatures at the other two seasons.

Not only is there periodicity in criminal conduct, but even within the normal range of good and bad conduct seasonal periodicity may still be traced. In his *Physical and Industrial Training of Criminals,* H. D. Wey gives charts of the conduct of seven prisoners during several years, as shown by the marks received. These charts show that there is a very decided tendency to good behavior during summer and winter, while in spring (February, March, and April) and in autumn (August, September and October) there are very marked falls to bad conduct, each individual tending to adhere to a conduct-curve of his own. Wey does not himself appear to have noticed this seasonal periodicity. Marro, however, has investigated this question in Turin on a large scale and reaches results not very dissimilar from those shown by Wey's figures in New York. He noted the months in which over 4,000 punishments were inflicted on prisoners for assaults, insults, threatening language, etc., and shows the annual curve in Tavola VI of his *Caratteri dei Delinquenti.* There is a marked and isolated climax in May; a still more sudden rise leads to the chief maximum of punishment in August; and from the minimum in October there is rapid ascent during the two following months to a climax much inferior to that of May.

The seasonal periodicity of bad conduct in prisons is of interest as showing that we cannot account for psychic periodicity by invoking exclusively social causes. This theory of psychic periodicity has been seriously put forward, but has been investigated and dismissed, so far as crime in Holland is concerned, by J. R. B. de Roos, in the Transactions of the sixth Congress of Criminal Anthropology, at Turin, in 1906 (*Archivio di Psichiatria* fasc. 3, 1906).

The general statistics of suicides in Continental Europe show a very regular and unbroken curve, attaining a maximum in June and a minimum in December, the curve rising steadily through the first six months, sinking steadily through the last six months, but always reaching a somewhat greater height in May than in July.[1] Morselli shows that in various European countries there is always a rise in spring and in autumn (Ocober or November).[2] Morselli attributes these spring and autumn rises to the influence of the strain of the early heat and the early cold.[3] In England, also, if we take a very large number of statistics, for instance, the figures for London during the twenty years between 1865 and 1884, as given by Ogle (in a paper read before the Statistical Society in 1886), we find that, although the general curve has the same maximum and minimum points, it is interrupted by a break on each side of the maximum, and these two breaks occur precisely at about March and October.[4] This is shown in the curve in Chart 6, which presents the daily average for the different months.

The growth of children follows an annual rhythm. Wahl, the director of an educational establishment for homeless girls in Denmark, who investigated this question, found that the increase of weight for all the ages investigated was constantly about 33 per cent. greater in the summer half-year than in the winter half-year. It was noteworthy that even the children who had

---

[1] This is, at all events, the case in France, Prussia, and Italy. See, for instance, Durkheim's discussion of the cosmic factors of suicide, *Le Suicide*, 1897, Chapter III. In Spain, as Bernaldo de Quirós shows (*Criminologia*, p. 69), there is a slight irregular rise in December, but otherwise the curve is perfectly regular, with maximum in June, and minimum in January.

[2] This holds good of a south European country, taken separately. A chart of the annual incidence of suicide by hanging, in Roumania, presented by Minovici (*Archives d'Anthropologie Criminelle*, 1905, p. 587), shows climaxes of equal height in May and September.

[3] Morselli, *Suicide*, pp. 55-72.

[4] Ogle himself was inclined to think that these breaks were accidental, being unaware of the allied phenomena with which they may be brought into line. It is true that (as Gaedeken objects to me) the autumnal break is very slight, but it is probably real when we are dealing with so large a mass of data.

not reached school-age, and therefore could not be influenced
by school-life, showed a similar, though slighter, difference in
the same direction. It is, however, Malling-Hansen, the director
of an institution for deaf-mutes in Copenhagen, who has most
thoroughly investigated this matter over a great many years. He
finds that there are three periods of growth throughout the year,
marked off in a fairly sharp manner, and that during each of these
periods the growth in weight and height shows constant characteristics. From about the end of November up to about the end
of March is a period when growth, both in height and weight,
proceeds at a medium rate, reaching neither a maximum nor a
minimum; increase in weight is slight, the increase in height,
although trifling, preponderating. After this follows a period
during which the children show a marked increase in height,
while increase in weight is reduced to a minimum. The children
constantly lose in weight during this period of growth in height
almost as much as they gain in the preceding period. This period
lasts from March and April to July and August. Then follows
the third period, which continues until November and December.
During this period increase in height is very slight, being at its
early minimum; increase in weight, on the other hand, at the
beginning of the period (in September and October), is rapid and
to the middle of December very considerable, daily increase in
weight being three times as great as during the winter months.
Thus it may be said that the spring sexual climax corresponds,
roughly, with growth in height and arrest of growth in weight,
while the autumn climax corresponds roughly with a period of
growth in weight and arrest of growth in height. Malling-
Hansen found that slight variations in the growth of the children
were often dependent on changes in temperature, in such a way
that a rise of temperature, even lasting for only a few days, caused
an increase of growth, and a fall of temperature a decrease in
growth. At Halle, Schmid-Monnard found that nearly all
growth in weight took place in the second half of the year, and
that the holidays made little difference. In America, Peckham
has shown that increase of growth is chiefly from the 1st of May

to the 1st of September.[1] Among young girls in St. Petersburg, Jenjko found that increase in weight takes place in summer. Goepel found that increase in height takes place mostly during the first eight months of the year, reaching a maximum in August, declining during the autumn and winter, in February being *nil,* while in March there is sometimes loss in weight even in healthy children.

In the course of a study as to the consumption of bread in Normal schools during each month of the year, as illustrating the relationship between intellectual work and nutrition, Binet presents a number of curves which bring out results to which he makes no allusion, as they are outside his own investigation. Almost without exception, these curves show that there is an increase in the consumption of bread in spring and in autumn, the spring rise being in February, March, and April; the autumn rise in October or November. There are, however, certain fallacies in dealing with institutions like Normal schools, where the conditions are not perfectly regular throughout the year, owing to vacations, etc. It is, therefore, instructive to find that under the monotonous conditions of prison-life precisely the same spring and autumn rises are found. Binet takes the consumption of bread in the women's prison at Clermont, where some four hundred prisoners, chiefly between the ages of thirty and forty, are confined, and he presents two curves for the years 1895 and 1896. The curves for these two years show certain marked disagreements with each other, but both unite in presenting a distinct rise in April, preceded and followed by a fall, and both present a still more marked autumn rise, in one case in September and November, in the other case in October.[2]

Some years ago, Sir J. Crichton-Browne stated that a manifestation of the sexual stimulus of spring is to be found in the large number of novels read during the month of March ("Address in Psychology" at the annual meeting of the British Medical Association, Leeds, 1889;

---

[1] *Pedagogical Seminary,* June, 1891, p. 298. For a very full summary and bibliography of investigations regarding growth, see F. Burk, "Growth of Children in Height and Weight," *American Journal of Psychology,* April, 1898.

[2] *L'Année Psychologique,* 1898.

Lancet, August 14, 1889). The statement was supported by figures furnished by lending libraries, and has since been widely copied. It would certainly be interesting if we could so simply show the connection between love and season, by proving that when the birds began to sing their notes, the young person's fancy naturally turns to brood over the pictures of mating in novels. I accordingly applied to Mr. Capel Shaw, Chief Librarian of the Birmingham Free Libraries (specially referred to by Sir J. Crichton-Browne), who furnished me with the Reports for 1896 and 1897-98 (this latter report is carried on to the end of March, 1898).

The readers who use the Birmingham Free Lending Libraries are about 30,000 in number; they consist very largely of young people between the ages of 14 and 25; somewhat less than half are women. Certainly we seem to have here a good field for the determination of this question. The monthly figures for each of the ten Birmingham libraries are given separately, and it is clear at a glance that without exception the maximum number of readers of prose-fiction at all the libraries during 1897-98 is found in the month of March. (I have chiefly taken into consideration the figures for 1897-98; the figures for 1896 are somewhat abnormal and irregular, probably owing to a decrease in readers, attributed to increased activity in trade, and partly to a disturbing influence caused by the opening of a large new library in the course of the year, suddenly increasing the number of readers, and drafting off borrowers from some of the other libraries.) Not only so, but there is a second, or autumnal climax, almost equaling the spring climax, and occuring with equal certainty, appearing during 1897-98 either in October or November, and during 1896, constantly in October. Thus, the periodicity of the rate of consumption of prose-fiction corresponds with the periodicity which is found to occur in the conception-rate and in sexual ecbolic manifestations.

It is necessary, however, to examine somewhat more closely the tables presented in these reports, and to compare the rate of the consumption of novels with that of other classes of literature. In the first place, if, instead of merely considering the consumption of novels per month, we make allowance for the varying length of the months, and consider the average *daily* consumption per month, the supremacy of March at once vanishes. February is really the month during which most novels were read during the first quarter of 1898, except at two libraries, where February and March are equal. The result is similar if we ascertain the daily averages for the first quarter in 1897, while, in 1896 (which, however, as I have already remarked, is a rather abnormal year), the daily average for March in many of the libraries falls below that for January, as well as for February. Again, when we turn to the other classes of books, we find that this predominance which February possesses, and to some extent shares with March and January, by no means exclusively applies to novels. It is not only shared by both music and poetry,—which would fit in well with the assumption of a sexual *nisus*,—but the department of "history, biography, voyages, and travels" shares it also with considerable regularity; so, also, does that of "arts, sciences, and natural history," and it is quite well marked in "theology, moral philosophy, etc.," and in "juvenile literature." We even have to admit that the promptings of the sexual instinct bring an increased body of visitors to the reference library (where there are no novels), for here, also, both the spring and autumnal climaxes are quite distinct. Certainly this theory carries us a little too far.

The main factor in producing this very marked annual periodicity seems to me to be wholly unconnected with the sexual impulse. The winter half of the year (from the beginning of October to the end of March), when outdoor life has lost its attractions, and much time must be spent in the house, is naturally the season for reading. But during the two central months of winter, December and January, the attraction of reading meets with a powerful counter-attraction in the excitement produced by the approach of Christmas, and the increased activity of social life which accompanies and for several weeks follows Christmas. In this way the other four winter months—October and November at the autumnal end, and February and March at the spring end—must inevitably present the two chief reading climaxes of the year; and so the reports of lending libraries present us with figures which show a striking, but fallacious, resemblance to the curves which are probably produced by more organic causes.

I am far from wishing to deny that the impulse which draws young men and women to imaginative literature is unconnected with the obscure promptings of the sexual instinct. But, until the disturbing influence I have just pointed out is eliminated, I see no evidence here for any true seasonal periodicity. Possibly in prisons—the value of which, as laboratories of experimental psychology we have scarcely yet begun to realize—more reliable evidence might be obtained; and those French and other prisons where novels are freely allowed to the prisoners might yield evidence as regards the consumption of fiction as instructive as that yielded at Clermont concerning the consumption of bread.

Certain diseases show a very regular annual curve. This is notably the case with scarlet fever. Caiger found in a London fever hospital a marked seasonal prevalence: there was a minor climax in May (repeated in July), and a great autumnal climax in October, falling to a minimum in December and January.

This curve corresponds closely to that usually observed in London.[1] It is not peculiar to London, or to urban districts, for in rural districts we find nearly the same spring minor maximum and major autumnal maximum. In Russia it is precisely the same. Many other epidemic diseases show very similar curves.

An annual curve may be found in the expulsive force of the bladder as measured by the distance to which the urinary stream can be projected. This curve, as ascertained for one case, is interesting on account of the close relationship between sexual and vesical activity. After a minimum point in autumn there is a rise through the early part of the year to a height maintained through spring and summer, and reaching its maximum in August.[2] This may be said to correspond with the general tendency found in some cases of nocturnal seminal emissions from a winter minimum to an autumn maximum.

There is an annual curve in voluntary muscle strength. Thus in Antwerp, where the scientific study of children is systematically carried out by a Pedological Bureau, Schuyten found that, measured by the dynamometer, both at the ages of 8 and 9, both boys and girls showed a gradual increase of strength from October to January, a fall from January to March and a rise to June or July. March was the weakest month, June and July the strongest.[3]

Schuyten also found an annual curve for mental ability, as tested by power of attention, which for much of the year corresponded to the curve of muscular strength, being high during the cold winter months. Lobsien, at Kiel, seeking to test Schuyten's results and adopting a different method so as to gauge memory as well as attention, came to conclusions which confirmed those of Schuyten. He found a very marked increase of ability in December and January, with a fall in April; April and May were

---

[1] *Lancet*, June 6, 1891. Edward Smith had pointed out many years earlier that scarlet fever is most fatal in periods of increasing vitality.

[2] Havelock Ellis, "The Bladder as a Dynamometer," *American Journal of Dermatology*, May, 1902.

[3] See, *e.g.*, summary in *Internationales Centrablatt für Anthropologie*, 1902, Heft 4, p. 207.

the minimum months, while July and October also stood low.[1] The inquiries of Schuyten and Lobsien thus seem to indicate that the voluntary aptitudes of muscular and mental force in children reach their maximum at a time of the year when most of the more or less involuntary activities we have been considering show a minimum of energy. If this conclusion should be confirmed by more extended investigations, it would scarcely be matter for surprise and would involve no true contradiction. It would, indeed, be natural to suppose that the voluntary and regulated activities of the nervous system should work most efficiently at those periods when they are least exposed to organic and emotional disturbance.

So persistent a disturbing element in spring and autumn suggests that some physiological conditions underlie it, and that there is a real metabolic disturbance at these times of the year. So few continuous observations have yet been made on the metabolic processes of the body that it is not easy to verify such a surmise with absolute precision. Edward Smith's investigations, so far as they go, support it, and Perry-Coste's long-continued observations of pulse-frequency seem to show with fair regularity a maximum in early spring and another maximum in late autumn.[2] I may also note that Haig, who has devoted many years of observations to the phenomena of uric-acid excretion, finds that uric acid tends to be highest in the spring months, (March, April, May) and lowest at the first onset of cold in October.[3]

Thus, while the sexual climaxes of spring and autumn are rooted in animal procreative cycles which in man have found expression in primitive festivals—these, again, perhaps, strengthening and developing the sexual rhythm—they yet have a wider significance. They constitute one among many manifestations of spring and autumn physiological disturbance corresponding with

---

[1] Summarized in *Zeitschrift für Psychologie der Sinnesorgane*, 1903, p. 135.

[2] Camerer found that from September to November is the period of greatest metabolic activity.

[3] Haig, *Uric Acid*, 6th edition, 1903, p. 33.

fair precision to the vernal and autumnal equinoxes. They resemble those periods of atmospheric tension, of storm and wind, which accompany the spring and autumn phases in the earth's rhythm, and they may fairly be regarded as ultimately a physiological reaction to those cosmic influences.

AUTO-EROTISM: A STUDY OF THE SPONTANEOUS MANIFESTATIONS OF THE SEXUAL IMPULSE.

I.

Definition of Auto-erotism—Masturbation only Covers a Small Portion of the Auto-erotic Field—The Importance of this Study, especially To-day—Auto-erotic Phenomena in Animals—Among Savage and Barbaric Races—The Japanese *rin-no-tama* and other Special Instruments for Obtaining Auto-erotic Gratification—Abuse of the Ordinary Implements and Objects of Daily Life—The Frequency of Hairpin in the Bladder—The Influence of Horse-exercise and Railway Traveling—The Sewing-machine and the Bicycle—Spontaneous Passive Sexual Excitement—*Delectatio Morosa*—Day-dreaming—*Pollutio*—Sexual Excitement During Sleep—Erotic Dreams—The Analogy of Nocturnal Enuresis—Differences in the Erotic Dreams of Men and Women—The Auto-erotic Phenomena of Sleep in the Hysterical—Their Frequently Painful Character.

By "auto-erotism" I mean the phenomena of spontaneous sexual emotion generated in the absence of an external stimulus proceeding, directly or indirectly, from another person. In a wide sense, which cannot be wholly ignored here, auto-erotism may be said to include those transformations of repressed sexual activity which are a factor of some morbid conditions as well as of the normal manifestation of art and poetry, and, indeed, more or less color the whole of life.

Such a definition excludes the normal sexual excitement aroused by the presence of a beloved person of the opposite sex; it also excludes the perverted sexuality associated with an attraction to a person of the same sex; it further excludes the manifold forms of erotic fetichism, in which the normal focus of sexual attraction is displaced, and voluptuous emotions are only aroused by some object—hair, shoes, garments, etc.—which, to the ordinary lover, are of subordinate—though still, indeed, considerable—importance.[1] The auto-erotic field remains extensive; it ranges from occasional voluptuous day-dreams, in which the subject is entirely passive, to the perpetual unashamed efforts at sexual self-manipulation witnessed among the insane. It also includes, though chiefly as curiosities, those cases in which individuals fall in love with themselves. Among auto-erotic phenomena, or on the borderland, we must further include those religious sexual manifestations for an ideal object, of which we may find evidence in the lives of saints and ecstatics.[2] The typical form of auto-erotism is the occurrence of the sexual orgasm during sleep.

I do not know that any apology is needful for the invention of the term "auto-erotism."[3] There is no existing word in current use to indicate the whole range of phenomena I am here concerned with. We are familiar with "masturbation," but that, strictly speaking, only covers a special and arbitrary subdivision of the field, although, it is true, the subdivision with which physicians and alienists have chiefly occupied themselves. "Self-abuse" is somewhat wider, but by no means covers the whole ground, while for various reasons it is an unsatisfactory term. "Onanism" is largely used, especially in France, and some writers even include all forms of homosexual connection under this name; it may be convenient to do so from a physiological point of view,

---

[1] All the above groups of phenomena are dealt with in other volumes of these *Studies*: the manifestations of normal sexual excitement, in vols. iii, iv, and v; homosexuality, in vol. ii, and erotic fetichism, in vol. v.

[2] See Appendix C.

[3] Letamendi, of Madrid, has suggested *"auto-erastia"* to cover what is probably much the same field. In the beginning of the nineteenth century, Hufeland, in his *Makrobiotic*, invented the term *"geistige Onanie,"* to express the filling and heating of the imagination with voluptuous images, without unchastity of body; and in 1844, Kaan, in his *Psychopathia Sexualis*, used, but did not invent, the term *"onania psychica."* Gustav Jaeger, in his *Entdeckung der Seele*, proposed "monosexual idiosyncrasy," to indicate the most animal forms of masturbation taking place without any correlative imaginative element, a condition illustrated by cases given in Moll's *Untersuchungen über die Libido Sexualis*, Bd. I, pp. 13 *et seq.* Dr. Laupts (a pseudonym for the accomplished psychologist, Dr. Saint-Paul) uses the term *autophilie*, for solitary vice. (*Perversion et Perversité Sexuelles*, 1896, p. 337.) But all these terms only cover a portion of the field.

but it is a confusing and antiquated mode of procedure, and from the psychological standpoint altogether illegitimate; "onanism" ought never to be used in this connection, if only on the ground that Onan's device was not auto-erotic, but was an early example of withdrawal before emission, or *coitus interruptus*.

While the name that I have chosen may possibly not be the best, there should be no question as to the importance of grouping all these phenomena together. It seems to me that this field has rarely been viewed in a scientifically sound and morally sane light, simply because it has not been viewed as a whole. We have made it difficult so to view it by directing our attention on the special group of auto-erotic facts—that group included under masturbation—which was most easy to observe and which in an extreme form came plainly under medical observation in insanity and allied conditions, and we have wilfully torn this group of facts away from the larger group to which it naturally belongs. The questions which have been so widely, so diversely, and—it must unfortunately be added—often so mischievously discussed, concerning the nature and evils of masturbation are not seen in their true light and proportions until we realize that masturbation is but a specialized form of a tendency which in some form or in some degree normally affects not only man, but all the higher animals. From a medical point of view it is often convenient to regard masturbation as an isolated fact; but in order to understand it we must bear in mind its relationships. In this study of auto-erotism I shall frequently have occasion to refer to the old entity of "masturbation," because it has been more carefully studied than any other part of the auto-erotic field; but I hope it will always be borne in mind that the psychological significance and even the medical diagnostic value of masturbation cannot be appreciated unless we realize that it is an artificial subdivision of a great group of natural facts.

The study of auto-erotism is far from being an unimportant or merely curious study. Yet psychologists, medical and non-medical, almost without exception, treat its manifestations— when they refer to them at all—in a dogmatic and off-hand manner which is far from scientific. It is not surprising, therefore, that the most widely divergent opinions are expressed. Nor is it surprising that ignorant and chaotic notions among the general population should lead to results that would be ludicrous if they were not pathetic. To mention one instance known to me: a married lady who is a leader in social-purity movements and an enthusiast for sexual chastity, discovered, through reading some pamphlet against solitary vice, that she had herself been practicing masturbation for years without knowing it. The profound anguish and hopeless despair of this woman in face of what she believed to be the moral ruin of her whole life cannot well be described. It would be easy to give further examples, though scarcely a more striking one, to show the utter confusion into which we are thrown by leaving this matter in the hands of blind leaders of the blind. Moreover, the conditions of modern civilization render auto-erotism a matter of increasing social significance. As our marriage-rate declines, and as illicit sexual relationships continue to be openly discouraged, it is absolutely inevitable that auto-erotic phenomena of one kind or another, not only among women but also among men, should increase among us both in amount and intensity. It becomes, therefore, a matter of some importance, both to the moralist and the physician, to investigate the psychological nature of these phenomena and to decide precisely what their attitude should be toward them.

I do not purpose to enter into a thorough discussion of all the aspects of auto-erotism. That would involve a very extensive study indeed. I wish to consider briefly certain salient points concerning auto-erotic phenomena, especially their prevalence, their nature, and their moral, physical, and other effects. I base my study partly on the facts and opinions which during the last thirty years have been scattered through the periodical and other medical literature of Europe and America, and partly on the experience of individuals, especially of fairly normal individuals.

Among animals in isolation, and sometimes in freedom—though this can less often be observed—it is well known that various forms of spontaneous solitary sexual excitement occur. Horses when leading a lazy life may be observed flapping the penis until some degree of emission takes place. Welsh ponies, I learn from a man who has had much experience with these animals, habitually produce erections and emissions in their stalls; they do not bring their hind quarters up during this process, and they close their eyes, which does not take place when they have congress with mares. The same informant observed that bulls and goats produce emissions by using their forelegs as a stimulus, bringing up their hind quarters, and mares rub themselves against objects. I am informed by a gentleman who is a recognized authority on goats, that they sometimes take the penis into the mouth and produce actual orgasm, thus practicing auto-fellatio. As regards ferrets, the Rev. H. Northcote states: "I am informed by a gentleman who has had considerable experience of ferrets, that if the bitch, when in heat, cannot obtain a dog she pines and becomes ill. If a smooth pebble is introduced into the hutch, she will masturbate upon it, thus preserving her normal health for one season. But if this artificial substitute is given to her a second season, she will not, as formerly, be content with it.[1]

Stags in the rutting season, when they have no partners, rub themselves against trees to produce ejaculation. Sheep masturbate; as also do camels, pressing themselves down against convenient objects; and elephants compress the penis between the hind legs to obtain emissions.[2] Blumenbach observed a bear act somewhat similarly on seeing other bears coupling, and hyenas, according to Ploss and Bartels, have been seen practicing mutual masturbation by licking each other's genitals. Mammary masturbation, remarks Féré, is found in certain female and even male animals, like the dog and the cat.[3] Apes are much given to masturbation, even in freedom, according to the evidence of good observers; for while no female apes are celibates, many of

---

[1] H. Northcote, *Christianity and Sex Problems*, p. 231.

[2] Rosse observed two elephants procuring erection by entwining their proboscides, the act being completed by one elephant opening his mouth and allowing the other to tickle the roof of it. (I. Rosse, *Virginia Medical Monthly*, October, 1892.)

[3] Féré, "Perversions sexuelles chez les animaux," *Revue Philosophique*, May, 1897.

the males are obliged to lead a life of celibacy.[1] Male monkeys
use the hand in masturbation, to rub and shake the penis.[2]

In the human species these phenomena are by no means
found in civilization alone. To whatever extent masturbation
may have been developed by the conditions of European life,
which carry to the utmost extreme the concomitant stimulation
and repression of the sexual emotions, it is far from being, as
Mantegazza has declared it to be, one of the moral characteristics
of Europeans.[3] It is found among the people of nearly every
race of which we have any intimate knowledge, however natural
the conditions under which men and women may live.[4] Thus,

---

[1] Tillier, *L'Instinct Sexuel*, 1889, p. 270.

[2] Moll, *Libido Sexualis*, Bd. I, p. 76. The same author mentions
(*ibid.*, p. 373) that parrots living in solitary confinement masturbate
by rubbing the posterior part of the body against some object until
ejaculation occurs. Edmund Selous ("Habits of the Peewit," *Zoologist*,
April, 1902) suggests that the peewit, when rolling on the ground, and
exerting pressure on the anal region, is moved by a sexual impulse to
satisfy desire; he adds that actual orgasm appears eventually to take
place, a spasm of energy passing through the bird.

[3] Dr. J. W. Howe (*Excessive Venery, Masturbation, and Continence*, London and New York, 1883, p. 62) writes of masturbation: "In
savage lands it is of rare occurrence. Savages live in a state of Nature.
No moral obligations exist which compel them to abstain from a natural
gratification of their passions. There is no social law which prevents
them from following the dictates of their lower nature. Hence, they
have no reason for adopting onanism as an outlet for passions. The
moral trammels of civilized society, and ignorance of physiological laws,
give origin to the vice." Every one of these six sentences is incorrect or
misleading. They are worth quoting as a statement of the popular view
of savage life.

[4] I can recall little evidence of its existence among the Australian
aborigines, though there is, in the Wiradyuri language, spoken over a
large part of New South Wales, a word (whether ancient or not, I do
not know) meaning masturbation (*Journal of the Anthropological Institute*, July-Dec., 1904, p. 303). Dr. W. Roth (*Ethnological Studies
Among the Northwest-Central Queensland Aborigines*, p. 184), who has
carefully studied the blacks of his district, remarks that he has no evidence as to the practice of either masturbation or sodomy among them.
More recently (1906) Roth has stated that married men in North
Queensland and elsewhere masturbate during their wives' absence. As
regards the Maori of New Zealand, Northcote adds, there is a rare
word for masturbation (as also at Rarotonga), but according to a
distinguished Maori scholar there are no allusions to the practice in
Maori literature, and it was probably not practiced in primitive times.
The Maori and the Polynesians of the Cook Islands, Northcote remarks,
consider the act unmanly, applying to it a phrase meaning "to make
women of themselves." (Northcote, *loc. cit.*, p. 232.)

among the Nama Hottentots, among the young women at all
events, Gustav Fritsch found that masturbation is so common
that it is regarded as a custom of the country; no secret is made
of it, and in the stories and legends of the race it is treated as
one of the most ordinary facts of life. It is so also among the
Basutos, and the Kaffirs are addicted to the same habit.[1] The
Fuegians have a word for masturbation, and a special word for
masturbation by women.[2] When the Spaniards first arrived at
Vizcaya, in the Philippines, they found that masturbation was
universal, and that it was customary for the women to use an
artificial penis and other abnormal methods of sexual gratification. Among the Balinese, according to Jacobs (as quoted by
Ploss and Bartels), masturbation is general; in the boudoir of
many a Bali beauty, he adds, and certainly in every harem, may
be found a wax penis to which many hours of solitude are
devoted. Throughout the East, as Eram, speaking from a long
medical experience, has declared, masturabtion is very prevalent,
especially among young girls. In Egypt, according to Sonnini, it is prevalent in harems. In India, a medical correspondent tells me, he once treated the widow of a wealthy Mohammedan, who informed him that she began masturbation at an
early age, "just like all other women." The same informant tells
me that on the *façade* of a large temple in Orissa are bas-reliefs,
representing both men and women, alone, masturbating, and also
women masturbating men. Among the Tamils of Ceylon masturbation is said to be common. In Cochin China, Lorion remarks,
it is practiced by both sexes, but especially by the married
women.[3] Japanese women have probably carried the mechanical
arts of auto-erotism to the highest degree of perfection. They
use two hollow balls about the size of a pigeon's egg (sometimes

---

1 Greenlees, *Journal of Mental Science*, July, 1895. A gentleman
long resident among the Kaffirs of South Natal, told Northcote, however,
that he had met with no word for masturbation, and did not believe the
practice prevailed there.

2 Hyades and Deniker, *Mission Scientifique du Cap Horn*, vol. vii,
p. 295.

3 *La Criminalité en Cochin-Chine*, 1887, p. 116; also Mondière,
"Monographie de la Femme Annamite," *Mémoires Société d'Anthropologie*, tome ii, p. 465.

one alone is used), which, as described by Joest, Christian, and others,[1] are made of very thin leaf of brass; one is empty, the other (called the little man) contains a small heavy metal ball, or else some quicksilver, and sometimes metal tongues which vibrate when set in movement; so that if the balls are held in the hand side by side there is a continuous movement. The empty one is first introduced into the vagina in contact with the uterus, then the other; the slightest movement of the pelvis or thighs, or even spontaneous movement of the organs, causes the metal ball (or the quicksilver) to roll, and the resulting vibration produces a prolonged voluptuous titillation, a gentle shock as from a weak electric inductive apparatus; the balls are called *rin-no-tama*, and are held in the vagina by a paper tampon. The women who use these balls delight to swing themselves in a hammock or rocking-chair, the delicate vibration of the balls slowly producing the highest degree of sexual excitement. Joest mentions that this apparatus, though well known by name to ordinary girls, is chiefly used by the more fashionable *geishas,* as well as by prostitutes. Its use has now spread to China, Annam, and India. Japanese women also, it is said, frequently use an artificial penis of paper or clay, called *engi.* Among the Atjeh, again, according to Jacobs (as quoted by Ploss), the young of both sexes masturbate and the elder girls use an artificial penis of wax. In China, also, the artificial penis—made of rosin, supple and (like the classical instrument described by Herondas) rose-colored—is publicly sold and widely used by women.[2]

---

[1] Christian, article on "Onanisme," *Dictionnaire encyclopédique des sciences médicales;* Ploss and Bartels, *Das Weib;* Moraglia, "Die Onanie beim normalen Weibe," *Zeitschrift für Criminal-Anthropologie,* 1897; Dartigues, *De la Procréation Volontaire des Sexes,* p. 32. In the eighteenth century, the *rin-no-tama* was known in France, sometimes as "pommes d'amour." Thus Bachaumont, in his Journal (under date July 31, 1773), refers to "a very extraordinary instrument of amorous mystery," brought by a traveler from India; he describes this "boule erctique" as the size of a pigeon's egg, covered with soft skin, and gilded. *Cf.* F. S. Krauss, *Geschlechtsleben in Brauch und Sitte der Japaner,* Leipzig, 1907.

[2] It may be worth mentioning that the Salish Indians of British Columbia have a myth of an old woman having intercourse with young women, by means of a horn worn as a penis (*Journal of the Anthropological Institute,* July-Dec., 1904, p. 342).

It may be noticed that among non-European races it is among women, and especially among those who are subjected to the excitement of a life professionally devoted to some form of pleasure, that the use of the artificial instruments of auto-erotism is chiefly practiced. The same is markedly true in Europe. The use of an artificial penis in solitary sexual gratification may be traced down from classic times, and doubtless prevailed in the very earliest human civilization, for such an instrument is said to be represented in old Babylonian sculptures, and it is referred to by Ezekiel (Ch. XVI. v. 17). The Lesbian women are said to have used such instruments, made of ivory or gold with silken stuffs and linen. Aristophanes (*Lysistrata*, v. 109) speaks of the manufacture by the Milesian women of a leather artificial penis, or olisbos. In the British Museum is a vase representing a *hetaira* holding such instruments, which, as found at Pompeii, may be seen in the museum at Naples. One of the best of Herondas's mimes, "The Private Conversation," presents a dialogue between two ladies concerning a certain olisbos (or νβών), which one of them vaunts as a dream of delight. Through the Middle Ages (when from time to time the clergy reprobated the use of such instruments[1]) they continued to be known, and after the fifteenth century the references to them became more precise. Thus Fortini, the Siennese novelist of the sixteenth century, refers in his *Novelle dei Novizi* (7th Day, Novella XXXIX) to "the glass object filled with warm water which nuns use to calm the sting of the flesh and to satisfy themselves as well as they can"; he adds that widows and other women anxious to avoid pregnancy availed themselves of it. In Elizabethan England, at the same time, it appears to have been of similar character and Marston in his satires tells how Lucea prefers "a glassy instru-

---

[1] In Burchard's Penitential (cap. 142-3), penalties are assigned to the woman who makes a phallus for use on herself or other women. (Wasserschleben, *Bussordnungen der abendländlichen Kirche*, p. 658.) The *penis succedaneus*, the Latin *phallus* or *fascinum*, is in France called *godemiche;* in Italy, *passatempo*, and also *diletto*, whence *dildo*, by which it is most commonly known in England. For men, the corresponding *cunnus succedaneus* is, in England, called *merkin*, which meant originally (as defined in old editions of Bailey's *Dictionary*) "counterfeit hair for women's privy parts."

ment" to "her husband's lukewarm bed." In sixteenth century France, also, such instruments were sometimes made of glass, and Brantôme refers to the godemiche; in eighteenth century Germany they were called *Samthanse,* and their use, according to Heinse, as quoted by Dühren, was common among aristocratic women. In England by that time the dildo appears to have become common. Archemholtz states that while in Paris they are only sold secretly, in London a certain Mrs. Philips sold them openly on a large scale in her shop in Leicester Square. John Bee in 1835, stating that the name was originally dil-dol, remarks that their use was formerly commoner than it was in his day. In France, Madame Gourdan, the most notorious brothel-keeper of the eighteenth century, carried on a wholesale trade in *consolateurs,* as they were called, and "at her death numberless letters from abbesses and simple nuns were found among her papers, asking for a 'consolateur' to be sent."[1] The modern French instrument is described by Garnier as of hardened red rubber, exactly imitating the penis and capable of holding warm milk or other fluid for injection at the moment of orgasm; the compressible scrotum is said to have been first added in the eighteenth century.[2]

In Islam the artificial penis has reached nearly as high a development as in Christendom. Turkish women use it and it is said to be openly sold in Smyrna. In the harems of Zanzibar, according to Baumann, it is of considerable size, carved out of ebony or ivory, and commonly bored through so that warm water may be injected. It is here regarded as an Arab invention.[3]

Somewhat similar appliances may be traced in all centres of civilization. But throughout they appear to be frequently confined to the world of prostitutes and to those women who live on the fashionable or semi-artistic verge of that world. Ignorance and delicacy combine with a less versatile and perverted concentration on the sexual impulse to prevent any general recourse to such highly specialized methods of solitary gratification.

---

[1] Dühren, *Der Marquis de Sade und Seine Zeit,* 3d ed., pp. 130, 232; *id. Geschlechtsleben in England,* Bd. II, pp. 284 *et seq.*

[2] Garnier, *Onanisme,* p. 378.

[3] *Zeitschrift für Ethnologie,* 1899, p. 669.

On the other hand, the use, or rather abuse, of the ordinary objects and implements of daily life in obtaining auto-erotic gratification, among the ordinary population in civilized modern lands, has reached an extraordinary degree of extent and variety we can only feebly estimate by the occasional resulting mischances which come under the surgeon's hands, because only a certain proportion of such instruments are dangerous. Thus the banana seems to be widely used for masturbation by women, and appears to be marked out for the purpose by its size and shape[1]; it is, however, innocuous, and never comes under the surgeon's notice; the same may probably be said of the cucumbers and other vegetables more especially used by country and factory girls in masturbation; a lady living near Vichy told Pouillet that she had often heard (and had herself been able to verify the fact) that the young peasant women commonly used turnips, carrots, and beet-roots. In the eighteenth century Mirabeau, in his *Erotika Biblion* gave a list of the various objects used in convents (which he describes as "vast theatres" of such practices) to obtain solitary sexual excitement. In more recent years the following are a few of the objects found in the vagina or bladder whence they could only be removed by surgical interference[2]:

---

[1] The mythology of Hawaii, one may note, tells of goddesses who were impregnated by bananas they had placed beneath their garments. B. Stern mentions (*Medizin in der Türki*, Bd. II, p. 24) that the women of Turkey and Egypt use the banana, as well as the cucumber, etc., for masturbation. In a poem in the *Arabian Nights*, also ("History of the Young Nour with the Frank"), we read: "O bananas, of soft and smooth skins, which dilate the eyes of young girls . . . you, alone among fruits are endowed with a pitying heart, O consolers of widows and divorced women." In France and England they are not uncommonly used for the same purpose.

[2] See, *e.g.*, Winckel, *Die Krankheiten der weiblichen Harnrohre und Blase*, 1885, p. 211; and "Lehrbuch der Frauenkrankheiten," 1886, p. 210; also, Hyrtl, *Handbuch du Topographischen Anatomie*, 7th ed., Bd. II, pp. 212-214. Grünfeld (*Wiener medizinische Blätter*, November 26, 1896), collected 115 cases of foreign body in the bladder—68 in men, 47 in women; but while those found in men were usually the result of a surgical accident, those found in women were mostly introduced by the patients themselves. The patient usually professes profound ignorance as to how the object came there; or she explains that she accidentally sat down upon it, or that she used it to produce freer urination. The earliest surgical case of this kind I happen to have met with, was recorded by Plazzon, in Italy, in 1621 (*De Partibus Generationi Inservien-*

Pencils, sticks of sealing-wax, cotton-reels, hair-pins (and in
Italy very commonly the bone-pins used in the hair), bodkins,
knitting-needles, crochet-needles, needle-cases, compasses, glass
stoppers, candles, corks, tumblers, forks, tooth-picks, tooth-
brushes, pomade-pots (in a case recorded by Schroeder with a
cockchafer inside, a makeshift substitute for the Japanese *rin-no-
tama*), while in one recent English case a full-sized hen's egg was
removed from the vagina of a middle-aged married woman.
More than nine-tenths of the foreign bodies found in the female
bladder or urethra are due to masturbation. The age of the
individuals in whom such objects have been found is usually from
17 to 30, but in a few cases they have been found in girls below
14, infrequently in women between 40 and 50; the large objects,
naturally, are found chiefly in the vagina, and in married women.[1]

Hair-pins have, above all, been found in the female bladder
with special frequency; this point is worth some consideration
as an illustration of the enormous frequency of this form of auto-
erotism. The female urethra is undoubtedly a normal centre
of sexual feeling, as Pouillet pointed out many years ago; a
woman medical correspondent, also, writes that in some women
the maximum of voluptuous sensation is at the vesical sphincter
or orifice, though not always so limited. E. H. Smith, indeed,
considers that "the urethra is the part in which the orgasm
occurs," and remarks that in sexual excitement mucus always
flows largely from the urethra.[2] It should be added that when
once introduced the physiological mechanism of the bladder
apparently causes the organ to tend to "swallow" the foreign
object. Yet for every case in which the hair-pin disappears and

tibus, lib. ii, Ch. XIII); it was that of a certain honorable maiden
with a large clitoris, who, seeking to lull sexual excitement with the aid
of a bone needle, inserted it in the bladder, whence it was removed by
Aquapendente.

[1] A. Poulet, *Traité des Corps étrangers en Chirurgie*, 1879. English
translation, 1881, vol. ii, pp. 209, 230. Rohleder (*Die Masturbation*, 1899,
pp. 24-31) also gives examples of strange objects found in the sexual
organs.

[2] E. H. Smith, "Signs of Masturbation in the Female," *Pacific
Medical Journal*," February, 1903, quoted by R. W. Taylor, *Practical
Treatise on Sexual Disorders*, 3d ed., p. 418.

is lost in the bladder, from carelessness or the oblivion of the sexual spasm, there must be a vast number of cases in which the instrument is used without any such unfortunate result. There is thus great significance in the frequency with which cases of hair-pin in the bladder are strewn through the medical literature of all countries.

In 1862, a German surgeon found the accident so common that he invented a special instrument for extracting hair-pins from the female bladder, as, indeed, Italian and French surgeons have also done. In France, Denucé, of Bordeaux, came to the conclusion that hair-pin in the bladder is the commonest result of masturbation as known to the surgeon. In England cases are constantly being recorded. Lawson Tait, stating that most cases of stone in the bladder in women are due to the introduction of a foreign body, very often a hair-pin, adds: "I have removed hair-pins encrusted with phosphates from ten different female bladders, and not one of the owners of these bladders would give any account of the incident."[1] Stokes, again, records that during four years he had four cases of hair-pin in the female urethra.[2] In New York one physician met with four cases in a short experience.[3] In Switzerland Professor Reverdin had a precisely similar experience.[4]

There is, however, another class of material objects, widely employed for producing physical auto-erotism, which in the

[1] L. Tait, *Diseases of Women*, 1889, vol. i, p. 100.

[2] *Obstetric Journal*, vol. i, 1873, p. 558. *Cf.* G. J. Arnold, *British Medical Journal*, January 6, 1906, p. 21.

[3] Dudley, *American Journal of Obstetrics*, July, 1889, p. 758.

[4] A. Reverdin, "Épingles à Cheveux dans la Vessie, *Revue Médicale de la Suisse Romande*, January 20, 1888. His cases are fully recorded, and his paper is an able and interesting contribution to this by-way of sexual psychology. The first case was a school-master's wife, aged 22, who confessed in her husband's presence, without embarrassment or hesitation, that the manœuvre was habitual, learned from a school-companion, and continued after marriage. The second was a single woman of 42, a *curé's* servant, who attempted to elude confession, but on leaving the doctor's house remarked to the house-maid, "Never go to bed without taking out your hairpins; accidents happen so easily." The third was an English girl of 17 who finally acknowledged that she had lost two hairpins in this way. The fourth was a child of 12, driven by the pain to confess that the practice had become a habit with her.

nature of things never reaches the surgeon.   I refer to the effects
that, naturally or unnaturally, may be produced by many of the
objects and implements of daily life that do not normally come
in direct contact with the sexual organs.   Children sometimes,
even when scarcely more than infants, produce sexual excitement
by friction against the corner of a chair or other piece of furniture, and women sometimes do the same.[1]   Guttceit, in Russia,
knew women who made a large knot in their chemises to rub
against, and mentions a woman who would sit on her naked heel
and rub it against her.   Girls in France, I am informed, are
fond of riding on the *chevaux-de-bois,* or hobby-horses, because of
the sexual excitement thus aroused; and that the sexual emotions
play a part in the fascination exerted by this form of amusement
everywhere is indicated by the ecstatic faces of its devotees.[2]   At
the temples in some parts of Central India, I am told, swings are
hung up in pairs, men and women swinging in these until sexually
excited; during the months when the men in these districts have
to be away from home the girls put up swings to console themselves for the loss of their husbands.

It is interesting to observe the very wide prevalence of swinging,
often of a religious or magic character, and the evident sexual significance underlying it, although this is not always clearly brought out.
Groos, discussing the frequency of swinging (*Die Spiele der Menschen,*
p. 114) refers, for instance, to the custom of the Gilbert Islanders for
a young man to swing a girl from a coco palm, and then to cling on
and swing with her.   In ancient Greece, women and grown-up girls were
fond of see-saws and swings.   The Athenians had, indeed, a swinging
festival (Athenæus, Bk. XIV, Ch. X).   Songs of a voluptuous character,
we gather from Athenæus, were sung by the women at this festival.

---

1 "One of my patients," remarks Dr. R. T. Morris, of New York,
(*Transactions of the American Association of Obstetricians,* for 1892,
Philadelphia, vol. v), "who is a devout church-member, had never allowed
herself to entertain sexual thoughts referring to men, but she masturbated every morning, when standing before the mirror, by rubbing
against a key in the bureau-drawer.   A man never excited her passions,
but the sight of a key in any bureau-drawer aroused erotic desires."

2 Freud (*Drei Abhandlungen zur Sexualtheorie,* p. 118) refers to the
sexual pleasure of swinging.   Swinging another person may be a source of
voluptuous excitement, and one of the 600 forms of sexual pleasure
enumerated in De Sade's *Les 120 Journées de Sodome* is (according to
Dühren) to propel a girl vigorously in a swing.

J. G. Frazer (*The Golden Bough*, vol. ii, note A, "Swinging as a Magical Rite") discusses the question, and brings forward instances in which men, or, especially, women swing. "The notion seems to be," he states, "that the ceremony promotes fertility, whether in the vegetable or in the animal kingdom; though why it should be supposed to do so, I confess myself unable to explain" (*loc. cit.*, p. 450). The explanation seems, however, not far to seek, in view of the facts quoted above, and Frazer himself refers to the voluptuous character of the songs sometimes sung.

Even apart from actual swinging of the whole body, a swinging movement may suffice to arouse sexual excitement, and may,—at all events, in women,—constitute an essential part of methods of attaining solitary sexual gratification. Kiernan thus describes the habitual auto-erotic procedure of a young American woman: "The patient knelt before a chair, let her elbows drop on its seat, grasping the arms with a firm grip, then commenced a swinging, writhing motion, seeming to fix her pelvis, and moving her trunk and limbs. The muscles were rigid, the face took on a passionate expression; the features were contorted, the eyes rolled, the teeth were set, and the lips compressed, while the cheeks were purple. The condition bore a striking resemblance to the passional stage of grand hysteria. The reveling took only a moment to commence, but lasted a long time. Swaying induced a pleasurable sensation, accompanied with a feeling of suction upon the clitoris. Almost immediately after, a sensation of bursting, caused by discharge from the vulvo-vaginal glands, occurs, followed by a rapture prolonged for an indefinite time." The accompanying sexual imagery is so vivid as almost to become hallucinatory. (J. G. Kiernan, "Sex Transformation and Psychic Impotence," *American Journal of Dermatology*, vol. ix, No. 2.)

Somewhat similarly sensations of sexual character are sometimes experienced by boys when climbing up a pole. It is not even necessary that there should be direct external contact with the sexual organs, and Howe states that gymnastic swinging poles around which boys swing while supporting the whole weight on the hands, may suffice to produce sexual excitement.

Several writers have pointed out that riding, especially in women, may produce sexual excitement and orgasm.[1] It is well-

---

[1] The fact that horse exercise may produce pollutions was well recognized by Catholic theologians, and Sanchez states that this fact need not be made a reason for traveling on foot. Rolfincius, in 1667, pointed out that horse-riding, in those unaccustomed to it, may lead

known, also, that both in men and women the vibratory motion
of a railway-train frequently produces a certain degree of sexual
excitement, especially when sitting forward. Such excitement
may remain latent and not become specifically sexual.[1] I am not
aware that this quality of railway traveling has ever been fostered
as a sexual perversion, but the sewing-machine has attracted considerable attention on account of its influence in exciting
auto-erotic manifestations. The early type of sewing-machine,
especially, was of very heavy character and involved much up
and down movement of the legs; Langdon Down pointed out
many years ago that this frequently produced great sexual
erethism which led to masturbation.[2] According to one French
authority, it is a well-recognized fact that to work a sewing-
machine with the body in a certain position produces sexual
excitement leading to the orgasm. The occurrence of the
orgasm is indicated to the observer by the machine being worked
for a few seconds with uncontrollable rapidity. This sound is
said to be frequently heard in large French workrooms, and it
is part of the duty of the superintendents of the rooms to make
the girls sit properly.[3]

"During a visit which I once paid to a manufactory of military
clothing," Pouillet writes, "I witnessed the following scene. In the
midst of the uniform sound produced by some thirty sewing-machines,
I suddenly heard one of the machines working with much more velocity
than the others. I looked at the person who was working it, a brunette
of 18 or 20. While she was automatically occupied with the trousers
she was making on the machine, her face became animated, her mouth
opened slightly, her nostrils dilated, her feet moved the pedals with
constantly increasing rapidity. Soon I saw a convulsive look in her

to nocturnal pollutions. Rohleder (*Die Masturbation*, pp. 133-134)
brings together evidence regarding the influence of horse exercise in
producing sexual excitement.

[1] A correspondent, to whom the idea was presented for the first
time, wrote: "Henceforward I shall know to what I must attribute the
bliss—almost the beatitude—I so often have experienced after traveling
for four or five hours in a train." Penta mentions the case of a young
girl who first experienced sexual desire at the age of twelve, after a railway journey.

[2] Langdon Down, *British Medical Journal*. January 12, 1867.

[3] Pouillet, *L'Onanisme chez la Femme*, Paris, 1880; Fournier, *De
l'Onanisme*, 1885; Rohleder, *Die Masturbation*, p. 132.

eyes, her eyelids were lowered, her face turned pale and was thrown backward; hands and legs stopped and became extended; a suffocated cry, followed by a long sigh, was lost in the noise of the workroom. The girl remained motionless a few seconds, drew out her handkerchief to wipe away the pearls of sweat from her forehead, and, after casting a timid and ashamed glance at her companions, resumed her work. The forewoman, who acted as my guide, having observed the direction of my gaze, took me up to the girl, who blushed, lowered her face, and murmured some incoherent words before the forewoman had opened her mouth, to advise her to sit fully on the chair, and not on its edge.

"As I was leaving, I heard another machine at another part of the room in accelerated movement. The forewoman smiled at me, and re-marked that that was so frequent that it attracted no notice. It was specially observed, she told me, in the case of young work-girls, ap-prentices, and those who sat on the edge of their seats, thus much facili-tating friction of the labia."

In cases where the sewing-machine does not lead to direct self-excitement it has been held, as by Fothergill,[1] to predispose to frequency of involuntary sexual orgasm during sleep, from the irritation set up by the movement of the feet in the sitting posture during the day. The essential movement in working the sewing-machine is the flexion and extension of the ankle, but the muscles of the thighs are used to maintain the feet firmly on the treadle, the thighs are held together, and there is a con-siderable degree of flexion or extension of the thighs on the trunk; by a special adjustment of the body, and sometimes per-haps merely in the presence of sexual hyperæsthesia, it is thus possible to act upon the sexual organs; but this is by no means a necessary result of using the sewing-machine, and inquiry of various women, with well-developed sexual feelings, who are ac-customed to work the treadle, has not shown the presence of any tendency in this direction.

Sexual irritation may also be produced by the bicycle in women. Thus, Moll[2] remarks that he knows many married women, and some unmarried, who experience sexual excitement when cycling; in several cases he has ascertained that the excite-ment is carried as far as complete orgasm. This result cannot,

1 *West-Riding Asylum Reports*, 1876, vol. **vi.**
2 *Das Nervöse Weib*, 1898, p. 193.

12

however, easily happen unless the seat is too high, the peak in contact with the organs, and a rolling movement is adopted; in the absence of marked hyperæsthesia these results are only effected by a bad seat or an improper attitude, the body during cycling resting under proper conditions on the buttocks, and the work being mainly done by the muscles of the thighs and legs which control the ankles, flexion of the thigh on the pelvis being very small. Most medical authorities on cycling are of opinion that when cycling leads to sexual excitement the fault lies more with the woman than with the machine. This conclusion does not appear to me to be absolutely correct. I find on inquiry that with the old-fashioned saddle, with an elevated peak rising toward the pubes, a certain degree of sexual excitement, not usually producing the orgasm (but, as one lady expressed it, making one feel quite ready for it), is fairly common among women. Lydston finds that irritation of the genital organs may unquestionably be produced in both males and females by cycling. The aggravation of hæmorrhoids sometimes produced by cycling indicates also the tendency to local congestion. With the improved flat saddles, however, constructed with more definite adjustment to the anatomical formation of the parts, this general tendency is reduced to a negligible minimum.

Reference may be made at this point to the influence of tight-lacing. This has been recognized by gynæcologists as a factor of sexual excitement and a method of masturbation.[1] Women who have never worn corsets sometimes find that, on first putting them on, sexual feeling is so intensified that it is necessary to abandon their use.[2] The reason of this (as Siebert points out in his *Buch für Eltern*) seems to be that the corset both favors pelvic congestion and at the same time exerts a pressure on the abdominal muscles which brings them into the state produced during coitus. It is doubtless for the same

---

[1] In the Appendix to volume iii of these *Studies*, I have recorded the experience of a lady who found sexual gratification in this manner.

[2] Dr. J. G. Kiernan, to whom I am indebted for a note on this point, calls my attention also to the case of a homosexual and masochistic man (*Medical Record*, vol. xix) whose feelings were intensified by tight-lacing.

reason that, as some women have found, more distension of the bladder is possible without corsets than with them.

In a further class of cases no external object whatever is used to procure the sexual orgasm, but the more or less voluntary pressure of the thighs alone is brought to bear upon the sexual regions. It is done either when sitting or standing, the thighs being placed together and firmly crossed, and the pelvis rocked so that the sexual organs are pressed against the inner and posterior parts of the thighs.[1] This is sometimes done by men, and is fairly common among women, especially, according to Martineau,[2] among those who sit much, such as dressmakers and milliners, those who use the sewing-machine, and those who ride. Vedeler remarks that in his experience in Scandinavia, thigh-friction is the commonest form of masturbation in women. The practice is widespread, and a medical correspondent in India tells me of a Brahmin widow who confessed to this form of masturbation. I am told that in London Board Schools, at the present time, thigh-rubbing is not infrequent among the girl scholars; the proportion mentioned in one school was about ten per cent. of the girls over eleven; the thigh-rubbing is done more or less openly and is interpreted by the uninitiated as due merely to a desire to relieve the bladder. It is found in female infants. Thus, Townsend records the case of an infant, 8 months old, who would cross her right thigh over the left, close her eyes and clench her fists; after a minute or two there would be complete relaxation, with sweating and redness of face; this would occur about once a week or oftener; the child was quite healthy, with no abnormal condition of the genital organs.[3] The frequency of

---

[1] Some women are also able to produce the orgasm, when in a state of sexual excitement, by placing a cushion between the knees and pressing the thighs firmly together.

[2] *Leçons sur les Déformations Vulvaires*, p. 64. Martineau was informed by a dressmaker that it is very frequent in workrooms and can usually be done without attracting attention. An ironer informed him that while standing at her work, she crossed her legs, slightly bending the trunk forward and supporting herself on the table by the hands; then a few movements of contraction of the adductor muscles of the thigh would suffice to produce the orgasm.

[3] C. W. Townsend, "Thigh-friction in Children under one Year," Annual Meeting of the American Pediatric Society, Montreal, 1896. Five cases are recorded by this writer, all in female infants.

thigh-friction among women as a form of masturbation is due to
the fact that it is usually acquired innocently and it involves no
indecorum.   Thus Soutzo reports the case of a girl of 12 who at
school, when having to wait her turn at the water-closet, for fear
of wetting herself would put her clothes between her legs and
press her thighs together, moving them backwards and forwards
in the effort to control the bladder; she discovered that a pleasurable sensation was thus produced and acquired the habit of practicing the manœuvre for its own sake; at the age of 17 she
began to vary it in different ways; thus she would hang from a
tree with her legs swinging and her chemise pressed between her
thighs which she would rub together.[1]   Thigh-friction in some
of its forms is so comparatively decorous a form of masturbation
that it may even be performed in public places; thus, a few
years ago, while waiting for a train at a station on the outskirts
of a provincial town, I became aware of the presence of a young
woman, sitting alone on a seat at a little distance, whom I could
observe unnoticed.   She was leaning back with legs crossed,
swinging the crossed foot vigorously and continuously; this continued without interruption for some ten minutes after I first
observed her; then the swinging movement reached a climax;
she leant still further back, thus bringing the sexual region still
more closely in contact with the edge of the bench and straight-
ened and stiffened her body and legs in what appeared to be a
momentary spasm; there could be little doubt as to what had
taken place.   A few moments later she slowly walked from her
solitary seat into the waiting-room and sat down among the
other waiting passengers, quite still now and with uncrossed legs,
a pale quiet young woman, possibly a farmer's daughter, serenely
unconscious that her manœuvre had been detected, and very
possibly herself ignorant of its true nature.

There are many other forms in which the impulse of auto-
erotism presents itself.   Dancing is often a powerful method of
sexual excitement, not only among civilized but among savage
peoples, and Zache describes the erotic dances of Swaheli women

---

[1] Soutzo, *Archives de Neurologie*, February, 1903, p. 167.

as having a masturbatory object.[1] Stimulation of the nates is a potent adjuvant to the production of self-excitement, and self-flagellation with rods, etc., is practiced by some individuals, especially young women.[2] Urtication is another form of this stimulation; Reverdin knew a young woman who obtained sexual gratification by flogging herself with chestnut burrs, and it is stated that in some parts of France (departments of the Ain and Côte d'Or) it is not uncommon for young girls to masturbate by rubbing the leaves of the *Linaria cymbalaria* (here called "pinton" or "timbarde") on to the sexual parts, thus producing a burning sensation.[3] Stimulation of the mamma, normally an erogenous centre in women, may occasionally serve as a method for obtaining auto-erotic satisfaction, including the orgasm, in both sexes. I have been told of a case in a man, and a medical correspondent in India informs me that he knows a Eurasian woman, addicted to masturbation, who can only obtain the orgasm by rubbing the genitals with one hand while with the other she rubs and finally squeezes her breasts. The tactile stimulation even of regions of the body which are not normally erogenous zones in either sex may sometimes lead on to sexual excitement; Hirschsprung, as well as Freud, believes that this is often the case as regards finger-sucking and toe-sucking in infancy. Even stroking the chin, remarks Debreyne, may produce a pollution.[4] Taylor refers to the case of a young woman of 22, who was liable to attacks of choreic movements of the hands which would terminate in alternately pressing the middle finger on the tip of the nose and the tragus of the ear, when a "far-away, pleased expression" would appear on her face; she thus produced sexual excitement and satisfaction. She had no

---

[1] Zache, *Zeitschrift für Ethnologie*, 1899, p. 72. I have discussed what may be regarded as the normally sexual influence of dancing, in the third volume of these *Studies*, "The Analysis of the Sexual Impulse."

[2] The case has been recorded of a Russian who had the spontaneous impulse to self-flagellation on the nates with a rod, for the sake of sexual excitement, from the age of 6. (*Rivista Mensile di Psichiatria* April, 1900, p. 102.)

[3] Κρυπταδια, vol. v, p. 358. As regards the use of nettles, see Dühren, *Geschlechtsleben in England*, Bd. II, p. 392.

[4] Debreyne, *Mœchialogie*, p. 177.

idea of wrong-doing and was surprised and ashamed when she realized the nature of her act.[1]

Most of the foregoing examples of auto-erotism are commonly included, by no means correctly, under the heading of "masturbation." There are, however, a vast number of people, possessing strong sexual emotions and living a solitary life, who experience, sometimes by instinct and sometimes on moral grounds, a strong repugnance for these manifestations of auto-erotism. As one highly intelligent lady writes: "I have sometimes wondered whether I could produce it (complete sexual excitement) mechanically, but I have a curious unreasonable repugnance to trying the experiment. It would materialize it too much." The same repugnance may be traced in the tendency to avoid, so far as possible, the use of the hands. It is quite common to find this instinctive unreasoning repugnance among women, a healthy repugnance, not founded on any moral ground. In men the same repugnance exists, more often combined with, or replaced by, a very strong moral and æsthetic objection to such practices. But the presence of such a repugnance, however invincible, is very far from carrying us outside the auto-erotic field. The production of the sexual orgasm is not necessarily dependent on any external contact or voluntary mechanical cause.

As an example, though not of specifically auto-erotic manifestations, I may mention the case of a man of 57, a somewhat eccentric preacher, etc., who writes: "My whole nature goes out so to some persons, and they thrill and stir me so that I have an emission while sitting by them with no thought of sex, only the gladness of soul found its way out thus, and a glow of health suffused the whole body. There was no spasmodic conclusion, but a pleasing gentle sensation as the few drops of semen passed." (In reality, no doubt, not semen, but urethral fluid.) This man's condition may certainly be considered somewhat morbid; he is attracted to both men and women, and the sexual impulse seems to be irritable and weak; but a similar state of things exists so often in women, no doubt due to sexual repression, and in individ-

[1] R. W. Taylor, *A Practical Treatise on Sexual Disorders*, 3rd ed., Ch. XXX.

uals who are in a general state of normal and good health, that in these it can scarcely be called morbid. Brooding on sexual images, which the theologians termed *delectatio morosa*, may lead to spontaneous orgasm in either sex, even in perfectly normal persons. Hammond described as a not uncommon form of "psychic coitus," a condition in which the simple act of imagination alone, in the presence of the desired object, suffices to produce orgasm. In some public conveyance, theatre, or elsewhere, the man sees a desirable woman and by concentrating his attention on her person and imagining all the stages of intimacy he quickly succeeds in producing orgasm.[1] Niceforo refers to an Italian work-girl of 14 who could obtain ejaculation of mucus four times a day, in the workroom in the presence of the other girls, without touching herself or moving her body, by simply thinking of sexual things.[2]

If the orgasm occurs spontaneously, without the aid of mental impressions, or any manipulations *ad hoc,* though under such conditions it ceases to be sinful from the theological standpoint, it certainly ceases also to be normal. Sérieux records the case of a somewhat neurotic woman of 50, who had been separated from her husband for ten years, and since lived a chaste life; at this age, however, she became subject to violent crises of sexual orgasm, which would come on without any accompaniment of voluptuous thoughts. MacGillicuddy records three cases of spontaneous orgasm in women coming under his notice.[3] Such crises are frequently found in both men and women, who, from moral reasons, ignorance, or on other grounds are restrained from attaining the complete sexual orgasm, but whose sexual emotions are, literally, continually dribbling from them. Schrenck-Notzing knows a lady who is spontaneously sexually excited on hearing music or seeing pictures without anything lascivious in them; she knows nothing of sexual relationships. Another lady is sexually excited on seeing beautiful and natural scenes, like the sea; sexual ideas are mixed up in her mind with

[1] Hammond, *Sexual Impotence*, pp. 70 *et seq.*

[2] Niceforo, *Il Gergo*, p. 98.

[3] *Functional Disorders of the Nervous System in Women*, p. 114.

these things, and the contemplation of a specially strong and sympathetic man brings the orgasm on in about a minute. Both these ladies "masturbate" in the streets, restaurants, railways, theatres, without anyone perceiving it.[1] A Brahmin woman informed a medical correspondent in India that she had distinct though feeble orgasm, with copious outflow of mucus, if she stayed long near a man whose face she liked, and this is not uncommon among European women. Evidently under such conditions there is a state of hyperæsthetic weakness. Here, however, we are passing the frontiers of strictly auto-erotic phenomena.

Delectatio morosa, as understood by the theologians, is distinct from desire, and also distinct from the definite intention of effecting the sexual act, although it may lead to those things. It is the voluntary and complacent dallying in imagination with voluptuous thoughts, when no effort is made to repel them. It is, as Aquinas and others point out, constituted by this act of complacent dallying, and has no reference to the duration of the imaginative process. Debreyne, in his *Mœchialogie* (pp. 149-163), deals fully with this question, and quotes the opinions of theologians. I may add that in the early Penitentials, before the elaboration of Catholic theology, the voluntary emission of semen through the influence of evil thoughts, was recognized as a sin, though usually only if it occurred in church. In Egbert's Penitential of the eighth or ninth century (cap. IX, 12), the penance assigned for this offence in the case of a deacon, is 25 days; in the case of a monk, 30 days; a priest, 40 days; a bishop, 50. (Haddon and Stubbs, *Councils and Ecclesiastical Documents*, vol. iii, p. 426.)

The frequency of spontaneous orgasm in women seems to have been recognized in the seventeenth century. Thus, Schurig (*Syllepsilogia*, p. 4), apparently quoting Riolan, states that some women are so wanton that the sight of a handsome man, or of their lover, or speech with such a one, will cause them to ejaculate their semen.

There is, however, a closely allied, and, indeed, overlapping form of auto-erotism which may be considered here: I mean that associated with revery, or day-dreaming. Although this is a

---

[1] Schrenck-Notzing, *Suggestions-therapie*, p. 13. A. Kind (*Jahrbuch für Sexuelle Zwischenstufen*, Jahrgang ix, 1908, p. 58) gives the case of a young homosexual woman, a trick cyclist at the music halls, who often, when excited by the sight of her colleague in tights, would experience the orgasm while cycling before the public.

very common and important form of auto-erotism, besides being in a large proportion of cases the early stage of masturbation, it appears to have attracted little attention.[1] The day-dream has, indeed, been studied in its chief form, in the "continued story," by Mabel Learoyd, of Wellesley College. The continued story is an imagined narrative, more or less peculiar to the individual, by whom it is cherished with fondness, and regarded as an especially sacred mental possession, to be shared only, if at all, with very sympathizing friends. It is commoner among girls and young women than among boys and young men; among 352 persons of both sexes, 47 per cent. among the women and only 14 per cent. among the men, have any continued story. The starting-point is an incident from a book, or, more usually, some actual experience, which the subject develops; the subject is nearly always the hero or the heroine of the story. The growth of the story is favored by solitude, and lying in bed before going to sleep is the time specially sacred to its cultivation.[2] No distinct reference, perhaps naturally enough, is made by Miss Learoyd to the element of sexual emotion with which these stories are often strongly tinged, and which is frequently their real motive. Though by no means easy to detect, these elaborate

---

[1] Janet has, however, used day-dreaming—which he calls *"reveries subconscients"*—to explain a remarkable case of demon-possession, which he investigated and cured. (*Névroses et Idées fixes*, vol. i, pp. 390 *et seq.*)

[2] "Minor Studies from the Psychological Laboratory of Wellesley College," *American Journal of Psychology*, vol. vii, No. 1. G. E. Partridge ("Reverie," *Pedagogical Seminary*, April, 1898) well describes the physical accompaniments of day-dreaming, especially in Normal School girls between sixteen and twenty-two. Pick ("Clinical Studies in Pathological Dreaming," *Journal of Mental Sciences*, July, 1901) records three more or less morbid cases of day-dreaming, usually with an erotic basis, all in apparently hysterical men. An important study of day-dreaming, based on the experiences of nearly 1,500 young people (more than two-thirds girls and women), has been published by Theodate L. Smith ("The Psychology of Day Dreams," *American Journal Psychology*, October, 1904). Continued stories were found to be rare—only one per cent. Healthy boys, before fifteen, had day-dreams in which sports, athletics, and adventure had a large part; girls put themselves in the place of their favorite heroines in novels. After seventeen, and earlier in the case of girls, day-dreams of love and marriage were found to be frequent. A typical confession is that of a girl of nineteen: "I seldom have time to build castles in Spain, but when I do, I am not different from most Southern girls; *i.e.*, my dreams are usually about a pretty fair specimen of a six-foot three-inch biped."

and more or less erotic day-dreams are not uncommon in young
men and especially in young women. Each individual has his
own particular dream, which is always varying or developing, but,
except in very imaginative persons, to no great extent. Such a
day-dream is often founded on a basis of pleasurable personal
experience, and develops on that basis. It may involve an element of perversity, even though that element finds no expression
in real life. It is, of course, fostered by sexual abstinence;
hence its frequency in young women. Most usually there is
little attempt to realize it. It does not necessarily lead to
masturbation, though it often causes some sexual congestion or
even spontaneous sexual orgasm. The day-dream is a strictly
private and intimate experience, not only from its very nature,
but also because it occurs in images which the subject finds great
difficulty in translating into language, even when willing to do
so. In other cases it is elaborately dramatic or romantic in
character, the hero or heroine passing through many experiences
before attaining the erotic climax of the story. This climax
tends to develop in harmony with the subject's growing knowledge or experience; at first, merely a kiss, it may develop into any
refinement of voluptuous gratification. The day-dream may
occur either in normal or abnormal persons. Rousseau, in his
Confessions, describes such dreams, in his case combined with
masochism and masturbation. A distinguished American novelist, Hamlin Garland, has admirably described in *Rose of
Dutcher's Coolly* the part played in the erotic day-dreams of a
healthy normal girl at adolescence by a circus-rider, seen on the
first visit to a circus, and becoming a majestic ideal to dominate
the girl's thoughts for many years.[1] Raffalovich[2] describes the
process by which in sexual inverts the vision of a person of the
same sex, perhaps seen in the streets or the theatre, is evoked in

[1] The case has been recorded of a married woman, in love with her
doctor, who kept a day-dream diary, at last filling three bulky volumes,
when it was discovered by her husband, and led to an action for divorce;
it was shown that the doctor knew nothing of the romance in which he
played the part of hero. Kiernan, in referring to this case (as recorded
in John Paget's *Judicial Puzzles*), mentions a similar case in Chicago.
[2] *Uranisme,* p. 125.

solitary reveries, producing a kind of "psychic onanism," whether or not it leads on to physical manifestations.

Although day-dreaming of this kind has at present been very little studied, since it loves solitude and secrecy, and has never been counted of sufficient interest for scientific inquisition, it is really a process of considerable importance, and occupies a large part of the auto-erotic field. It is frequently cultivated by refined and imaginative young men and women who lead a chaste life and would often be repelled by masturbation. In such persons, under such circumstances, it must be considered as strictly normal, the inevitable outcome of the play of the sexual impulse. No doubt it may often become morbid, and is never a healthy process when indulged in to excess, as it is liable to be by refined young people with artistic impulses, to whom it is in the highest degree seductive and insidious.[1] As we have seen, however, day-dreaming is far from always colored by sexual emotion; yet it is a significant indication of its really sexual origin that, as I have been informed by persons of both sexes, even in these apparently non-sexual cases it frequently ceases altogether on marriage.

Even when we have eliminated all these forms of auto-erotic activity, however refined, in which the subject takes a voluntary part, we have still left unexplored an important portion of the auto-erotic field, a portion which many people are alone inclined to consider normal: sexual orgasm during sleep. That under conditions of sexual abstinence in healthy individuals there must inevitably be some auto-erotic manifestations during waking life, a careful study of the facts compels us to believe. There can be no doubt, also, that, under the same conditions, the occurrence

---

[1] The acute Anstie remarked, more than thirty years ago, in his work on *Neuralgia:* "It is a comparatively frequent thing to see an unsocial, solitary life (leading to the habit of masturbation) joined with the bad influence of an unhealthy ambition, prompting to premature and false work in literature and art." From the literary side, M. Léon Bazalgette has dealt with the tendency of much modern literature to devote itself to what he calls "mental onanism," of which the probable counterpart, he seems to hint, is a physical process of auto-erotism. (Léon Bazalgette, "L'onanisme considéré comme principe createur en art," *L'Esprit Nouveau*, 1898.)

of the complete orgasm during sleep with, in men, seminal emissions, is altogether normal.   Even Zeus himself, as Pausanias has recorded, was liable to such accidents : a statement which, at all events, shows that to the Greek mind there was nothing derogatory in such an occurrence.[1]   The Jews, however, regarded it as an impurity,[2] and the same idea was transmitted to the Christian church and embodied in the word *pollutio,* by which the phenomenon was designated in ecclesiastical phraseology.[3]   According to Billuart and other theologians, pollution in sleep is not sin, unless voluntarily caused; if, however, it begins in sleep, and is completed in the half-waking state, with a sense of pleasure, it is a venial sin.   But it seems allowable to permit a nocturnal pollution to complete itself on awaking, if it occurs without intention; and St. Thomas even says *"Si pollutio placeat ut naturæ exoneratio vel alleviatio, peccatum non creditur."*

----

[1] Pausanias, *Achaia,* Chapter XVII. The ancient Babylonians believed in a certain "maid of the night," who appeared to men in sleep and roused without satisfying their passions. (Jastrow, *Religion of Babylonia,* p. 262.)   This succubus was the Assyrian Liler, connected with the Hebrew Lilith. There was a corresponding incubus, "the little night man," who had nocturnal intercourse with women. (*Cf.* Ploss, *Das Weib,* 7th ed., pp. 521 *et seq.*)   The succubus and the incubus (the latter being more common) were adopted by Christendom; St. Augustine (*De Civitate Dei,* Bk. XV, Ch. XXIII) said that the wicked assaults of sylvans and fauns, otherwise called incubi, on women, are so generally affirmed that it would be impudent to deny them. Incubi flourished in mediæval belief, and can scarcely, indeed, be said to be extinct even to-day. They have been studied by many authors; see, *e.g.,* Dufour, *Histoire de la Prostitution,* vol. v, Ch. XXV. Saint-André, physician-in-ordinary to the French King, pointed out in 1725 that the incubus was a dream. It may be added that the belief in the succubus and incubus appears to be widespread. Thus, the West African Yorubas (according to A. B. Ellis) believe that erotic dreams are due to the god Eleghra, who, either as a male or a female, consorts with men and women in sleep.

[2] "If any man's seed of copulation go out from him, then he shall bathe all his flesh in water and be unclean until the even. And every garment, and every skin, whereon is the seed of copulation, shall be washed with water and be unclean until the even." Leviticus, XV, v. 16-17.

[3] It should be added that the term *pollutio* also covers voluntary effusion of semen outside copulation. (Debreyne, *Mœchialogie,* p. 8; for a full discussion of the opinions of theologians concerning nocturnal and diurnal pollutions, see the same author's *Essai sur la Théologie Morale,* pp. 100-149.)

Notwithstanding the fair and logical position of the more distinguished Latin theologians, there has certainly been a widely prevalent belief in Catholic countries that pollution during sleep is a sin. In the "Parson's Tale," Chaucer makes the parson say: "Another sin appertaineth to lechery that cometh in sleeping; and the sin cometh oft to them that be maidens, and eke to them that be corrupt; and this sin men clepe pollution, that cometh in four manners;" these four manners being (1) languishing of body from rank and abundant humors, (2) infirmity, (3) surfeit of meat and drink, and (4) villainous thoughts. Four hundred years later, Madame Roland, in her *Mémoires Particulières*, presented a vivid picture of the anguish produced in an innocent girl's mind by the notion of the sinfulness of erotic dreams. She menstruated first at the age of 14. "Before this," she writes, "I had sometimes been awakened from the deepest sleep in a surprising manner. Imagination played no part; I exercised it on too many serious subjects, and my timorous conscience preserved it from amusement with other subjects, so that it could not represent what I would not allow it to seek to understand. But an extraordinary effervescence aroused my senses in the heat of repose, and, by virtue of my excellent constitution, operated by itself a purification which was as strange to me as its cause. The first feeling which resulted was, I know not why, a sort of fear. I had observed in my *Philotée*, that we are not allowed to obtain any pleasure from our bodies except in lawful marriage. What I had experienced could be called a pleasure. I was then guilty, and in a class of offences which caused me the most shame and sorrow, since it was that which was most displeasing to the Spotless Lamb. There was great agitation in my poor heart, prayers and mortifications. How could I avoid it? For, indeed, I had not foreseen it, but at the instant when I experienced it, I had not taken the trouble to prevent it. My watchfulness became extreme. I scrupulously avoided positions which I found specially exposed me to the accident. My restlessness became so great that at last I was able to awake before the catastrophe. When I was not in time to prevent it, I would jump out of bed, with naked feet on to the polished floor, and with crossed arms pray to the Saviour to preserve me from the wiles of the devil. I would then impose some penance on myself, and I have carried out to the letter what the prophet King probably only transmitted to us as a figure of Oriental speech, mixing ashes with my bread and watering it with my tears."

To the early Protestant mind, as illustrated by Luther, there was something diseased, though not impure, in sexual excitement during sleep; thus, in his *Table Talk* Luther remarks that girls who have such dreams should be married at once, "taking the medicine which God has given." It is only of comparatively recent years that medical science has obtained currency for the belief that this auto-erotic process is entirely normal. Blumenbach stated that nocturnal emissions are normal.[1] Sir James Paget declared that he had never known celibate men who had not such emissions from once or twice a week to twice every three months, both extremes being within the limits of good health, while Sir Lauder Brunton considers once a fortnight or once a month about the usual frequency, at these periods the emissions often following two nights in succession. Rohleder believes that they may normally follow for several nights in succession. Hammond considers that they occur about once a fortnight.[2] Ribbing regards ten to fourteen days as the normal interval.[3] Löwenfeld puts the normal frequency at about once a week;[4] this seems to be nearer the truth as regards most fairly healthy young men. In proof of this it is only necessary to refer to the exact records of healthy young adults summarized in the study of periodicity in the present volume. It occasionally happens, however, that nocturnal emissions are entirely absent. I am acquainted with some cases. In other fairly healthy young men they seldom occur except at times of intellectual activity or of anxiety and worry.

Lately there has been some tendency for medical opinion to revert to the view of Luther, and to regard sexual excitement during sleep as a somewhat unhealthy phenomenon. Moll is a distinguished advocate of this view. Sexual excitement during sleep is the normal result of celibacy, but it is another thing to say that it is, on that account, satisfactory. We might, then, Moll remarks, maintain that nocturnal incontinence of urine is satisfactory, since the bladder is thus emptied. Yet, we take every precaution against this by insisting that the bladder shall be emptied before going to sleep. (*Libido Sexualis*, Bd. I, p. 552.) This remark is supported by the fact, to which I find that both men and women can bear witness, that sexual excitement during sleep is more fatiguing than in the waking state, though this is not an invariable

---

1 *Memoirs*, translated by Bendyshe, p. 182.

2 *Sexual Impotence*, p. 137.

3 *L'Hygiène Sexuelle*, p. 169.

4 *Sexualleben und Nervenleiden*, p. 164.

rule, and it is sometimes found to be refreshing. In a similar way, Eulenburg (*Sexuale Neuropathie*, p. 55) states that nocturnal emissions are no more normal than coughing or vomiting.

Nocturnal emissions are usually, though not invariably, accompanied by dreams of a voluptuous character in which the dreamer becomes conscious in a more or less fantastic manner of the more or less intimate presence or contact of a person of the opposite sex. It would seem, as a general rule, that the more vivid and voluptuous the dream, the greater is the physical excitement and the greater also the relief experienced on awakening. Sometimes the erotic dream occurs without any emission, and not infrequently the emission takes place after the dreamer has awakened.

The widest and most comprehensive investigation of erotic dreams is that carried out by Gualino, in northern Italy, and based on inquiries among 100 normal men—doctors, teachers, lawyers, etc.—who had all had experience of the phenomenon. (L. Gualino, "Il Sogno Erotico nell' Uomo Normale," *Rivista di Psicologia*, Jan.-Feb., 1907.) Gualino shows that erotic dreams, with emissions (whether or not seminal), began somewhat earlier than the period of physical development as ascertained by Marro for youths of the same part of northern Italy. Gualino found that all his cases had had erotic dreams at the age of seventeen; Marro found 8 per cent. of youths still sexually undeveloped at that age, and while sexual development began at thirteen years, erotic dreams began at twelve. Their appearance was preceded, in most cases for some months, by erections. In 37 per cent. of the cases there had been no actual sexual experiences (either masturbation or intercourse); in 23 per cent. there had been masturbation; in the rest, some form of sexual contact. The dreams are mainly visual, tactual elements coming second, and the *dramatis persona* is either an unknown woman (27 per cent. cases), or only known by sight (56 per cent.), and in the majority is, at all events in the beginning, an ugly or fantastic figure, becoming more attractive later in life, but never identical with the woman loved during waking life. This, as Gualino points out, accords with the general tendency for the emotions of the day to be latent in sleep. Masturbation only formed the subject of the dream in four cases. The emotional state in the pubertal stage, apart from pleasure, was anxiety (37 per cent.), desire (17 per cent.), fear (14 per cent.). In the adult stage, anxiety and fear receded to 7 per cent. and 6 per cent., respectively. Thirty-three of the subjects, as a result of sexual or general disturbances, had had nocturnal emissions

without dreams; these were always found exhausting. Normally (in
more than 90 per cent.) erotic dreams are the most vivid of all dreams.
In no case was there knowledge of any monthly or other cyclic periodicity in the occurrence of the manifestations. In 34 per cent. of cases,
they tended to occur very soon after sexual intercourse. In numerous
cases they were peculiarly frequent (even three in one night) during
courtship, when the young man was in the habit of kissing and caressing
his betrothed, but ceased after marriage. It was not noted that position
in bed or a full bladder exerted any marked influence in the occurrence
of erotic dreams; repletion of the seminal vesicles is regarded as the
main factor.

In Germany erotic dreams have been discussed by Volkelt (*Die
Traum-Phantasie*, 1875, pp. 78-82), and especially by Löwenfeld
(*Sexual-Probleme*, Oct., 1908), while in America, Stanley Hall thus
summarizes the general characteristics of erotic dreams in men: "In
by far the most cases, consciousness, even when the act causes full
awakening from sleep, finds only scattered images, single words, gestures,
and acts, many of which would perhaps normally constitute no pro-
vocation. Many times the mental activity seems to be remote and
incidental, and the mind retains in the morning nothing except, perhaps,
a peculiar dress pattern, the shape of a finger-nail, the back of a neck,
the toss of a head, the movement of a foot, or the dressing of the hair.
In such cases, these images stand out for a time with the distinctness
of a cameo, and suggest that the origin of erotic fetichisms is largely
to be found in sexual dreams. Very rarely is there any imagery of the
organs themselves, but the tendency to irradiation is so strong as to
re-enforce the suggestion of so many other phenomena in this field, that
nature designs this experience to be long circuited, and that it may give
a peculiar ictus to almost any experience. When waking occurs just
afterward, it seems at least possible that there may be much imagery
that existed, but failed to be recalled to memory, possibly because the
flow of psychic impressions was over very familiar fields, and this,
therefore, was forgotten, while any eruption into new or unwonted
channels, stood out with distinctness. All these psychic phenomena, although very characteristic of man in his prime, are not so of the dreams
of dawning puberty, which are far more vivid." (G. Stanley Hall,
Adolescence, vol. i, p. 455.)

I may, further, quote the experience of an anonymous contributor—
a healthy and chaste man between 30 and 38 years of age—to the
American Journal of Psychology ("Nocturnal Emissions," Jan., 1904):
"Legs and breasts often figured prominently in these dreams, the other
sexual parts, however, very seldom, and then they turned out to be
male organs in most cases. There were but two instances of copulation dreamt. Girls and young women were the usual *dramatis personæ*,

and, curiously enough, often the aggressors. Sometimes the face or faces were well known; sometimes, only once seen; sometimes, entirely unknown. The orgasm occurs at the most erotic part of the dream, the physical and psychical running parallel. This most erotic or suggestive part of the dream was very often quite an innocent looking incident enough. As, for example: while passing a strange young woman, overtaken on the street, she calls after me some question. At first, I pay no heed, but when she calls again, I hesitate whether to turn back and answer or not—emission. Again, walking beside a young woman, she said, 'Shall I take your arm?' I offered it, and she took it, entwining her arm around it, and raising it high—emission. I could feel stronger erection as she asked the question. Sometimes, a word was enough; sometimes, a gesture. Once emission took place on my noticing the young woman's diminished finger-nails. Another example of fetichism was my being curiously attracted in a dream by the pretty embroidered figure on a little girl's dress. As an illustration of the strange metamorphoses that occur in dreams, I one night, in my dream (I had been observing partridges in the summer) fell in love with a partridge, which changed under my caresses to a beautiful girl, who yet retained an indescribable wild-bird innocence, grace, and charm—a sort of Undina!"

These experiences may be regarded as fairly typical of the erotic dreams of healthy and chaste young men. The bird, for instance, that changes into a woman while retaining some elements of the bird, has been encountered in erotic dreams by other young men. It is indeed remarkable that, as De Gubernatis observes, "the bird is a well-known phallic symbol," while Maeder finds ("Interprétations de Quelques Rêves," *Archives de Psychologie*, April, 1907) that birds have a sexual significance both in life and in dreams. The appearance of male organs in the dream-woman is doubtless due to the dreamer's greater familiarity with those organs; but, though it occurs occasionally, it can scarcely be said to be the rule in erotic dreams. Even men who have never had connection with a woman, are quite commonly aware of the presence of a woman's sexual organs in their erotic dreams.

Moll's comparison of nocturnal emissions of semen with nocturnal incontinence of urine suggests an interesting resemblance, and at the same time seeming contrast. In both cases we are concerned with viscera which, when overfilled or unduly irritable, spasmodically eject their contents during sleep. There is a further resemblance which usually becomes clear when, as occasionally happens, nocturnal incontinence of urine persists on to late childhood or adolescence: both phenomena are frequently accompanied by vivid dreams of appropriate character. (See *e.g.* Ries, "Ueber Enuresis Nocturna," *Monatsschrift für Harnkrankheiten und Sexuelle Hygiene*, 1904; A. P. Buchan, nearly a century ago, pointed out the psychic element in the experiences of young persons who wetted the bed, *Venus sine Concubitu*, 1816, p. 47.) Thus, in one case known to me, a child of seven, who occasionally wetted the bed, usually dreamed at the same time that she wanted to make water, and was out of doors, running to find a suitable spot, which she at last found, and, on awaking, discovered that she had wetted the bed; fifteen years later she still sometimes had similar dreams, which caused her much alarm until, when thoroughly awake, she realized that no accident had happened; these later dreams were not the result of any actual strong desire to urinate. In another case with which I am acquainted, a little girl of eight, after mental excitement or indigestible meals, occasionally wetted the bed, dreaming that she was frightened by some one running after her, and wetted herself in consequence, after the manner of the Ganymede in the eagle's clutch, as depicted by Rembrandt. These two cases, it may be noted, belong to two quite different types. In the first case, the full bladder suggests to imagination the appropriate actions for relief, and the bladder actually accepts the imaginative solution offered; it is, according to Fiorani's phrase, "somnambulism of the bladder." In the other case, there is no such somnambulism, but a psychic and nervous disturbance, not arising in the bladder at all, irradiates convulsively, and whether or not the bladder is overfull, attacks a vesical nervous system which is not yet sufficiently well-balanced to withstand the inflow of excitement. In children of somewhat nervous temperament, manifestations of this kind may occur as an occasional accident, up to about the age of seven or eight; and thereafter, the nervous control of the bladder having become firmly established, they cease to happen, the nervous energy required to affect the bladder sufficing to awake the dreamer. In very rare cases, however, the phenomenon may still occasionally happen, even in adolescence or later, in individuals who are otherwise quite free from it. This is most apt to occur in young women even in waking life. In men it is probably extremely rare.

The erotic dream seems to differ flagrantly from the vesical dream, in that it occurs in adult life, and is with difficulty brought under control. The contrast is, however, very superficial. When we remember that sexual activity only begins normally at puberty, we realize that the youth of twenty is, in the matter of sexual control, scarcely much older than in the matter of vesical control he was at the age of six. Moreover, if we were habitually, from our earliest years, to go to bed with a full bladder, as the chaste man goes to bed with unrelieved sexual system, it would be fully as difficult to gain vesical control during sleep as it now is to gain sexual control. Ultimately, such sexual control is attained; after the age of forty, it seems that erotic dreams with emission become more and more rare; either the dream occurs without actual emission, exactly as dreams of urination occur in adults with full bladder, or else the organic stress, with or without dreams, serves to awaken the sleeper before any emission has occurred. But this stage is not easily or completely attained. St. Augustine, even at the period when he wrote his *Confessions*, mentions, as a matter of course, that sexual dreams "not merely arouse pleasure, but gain the consent of the will." (X. 41.) Not infrequently there is a struggle in sleep, just as the hypnotic subject may resist suggestions; thus, a lady of thirty-five dreamed a sexual dream, and awoke without excitement; again she fell asleep, and had another dream of sexual character, but resisted the tendency to excitement, and again awoke; finally, she fell asleep and had a third sexual dream, which was this time accompanied by the orgasm. (This has recently been described also by Näcke, who terms it *pollutio interrupta, Neurologisches Centralblatt*, Oct. 16, 1909; the corresponding voluntary process in the waking state is described by Rohleder and termed *masturbatio interrupta, Zeitschrift für Sexualwissenschaft*, Aug., 1908.) The factors involved in the acquirement of vesical and sexual control during sleep are the same, but the conditions are somewhat different.

There is a very intimate connection between the vesical and the sexual spheres, as I have elsewhere pointed out (see *e.g.* in the third volume of these *Studies*, "Analysis of the Sexual Impulse"). This connection is psychic as well as organic. Both in men and women, a full bladder tends to develop erotic dreams. (See *e.g.* K. A. Scherner, *Das Leben des Traums*, 1861, pp. 187 *et seq.;* Spitta also points out the connection between vesical and erotic dreams, *Die Schlaf und Traumzustände*, 2d ed., 1882, pp. 250 *et seq.*) Raymond and Janet state (*Les Obsessions*, vol. ii, p. 135) that nocturnal incontinence of urine, accompanied by dreams of urination, may be replaced at puberty by masturbation. In the reverse direction, Freud believes (*Monatsschrift für Psychiatrie*, Bd. XVIII, p. 433) that masturbation plays a large part in causing the bed-wetting of children who have passed the age when that usually ceases, and he even finds that children are themselves aware of the connection.

The diagnostic value of sexual dreams, as an indication of the sexual nature of the subject when awake, has been emphasized by various writers. (*E.g.*, Moll, *Die Konträre Sexualempfindung*, Ch. IX; Näcke, "Der Traum als feinstes Reagens für die Art des sexuellen Empfindens," *Monatsschrift für Kriminalpsychologie*, 1905, p. 500.) Sexual dreams tend to reproduce, and even to accentuate, those characteristics which make the strongest sexual appeal to the subject when awake.

At the same time, this general statement has to be qualified, more especially as regards inverted dreams. In the first place, a young man, however normal, who is not familiar with the feminine body when awake, is not likely to see it when asleep, even in dreams of women; in the second place, the confusions and combinations of dream imagery often tend to obliterate sexual distinctions, however free from perversions the subjects may be. Thus, a correspondent tells me of a healthy man, of very pure character, totally inexperienced in sexual matters, and never having seen a woman naked, who, in his sexual dreams, always sees the woman with male organs, though he has never had any sexual inclinations for men, and is much in love with a lady. The confusions and associations of dream imagery, leading to abnormal combinations, may be illustrated by a dream which once occurred to me after reading Joest's account of how a young negress, whose tattoo-marks he was sketching, having become bored, suddenly pressed her hands to her breasts, spirting two streams of lukewarm milk into his face, and ran away laughing; I dreamed of a woman performing a similar action, not from her breasts, however, but from a penis with which she was furnished. Again, by another kind of confusion, a man dreams sexually that he is with a man, although the figure of the partner revealed in the dream is a woman. The following dream, in a normal man who had never been, or wished to be,. in the position shown by the dream, may be quoted: "I dreamed that I was a big boy, and that a younger boy lay close beside me, and that we (or, certainly, he) had seminal emissions; I was complacently passive, and had a feeling of shame when the boy was discovered. On awaking I found I had had no emission, but was lying very close to my wife. The day before, I had seen boys in a swimming-match." This was, it seems to me, an example of dream confusion, and not an erotic inverted dream. (Näcke also brings forward inverted dreams by normal persons; see *e.g.* his "Beiträge zu den sexuellen Träumen," *Archiv für Kriminalanthropologie*, Bd. XX, 1908, p. 366.)

So far as I have been able to ascertain, there seem to be, generally speaking, certain differences in the manifestations of auto-erotism during sleep in men and women which I believe to be not without psychological significance. In men the phenomenon is fairly simple; it usually appears about puberty, continues at intervals of varying duration during sexual life provided the individual is living chastely, and is generally, though not always, accompanied by erotic dreams which lead up to the climax, its occurrence being, to some extent, influenced by a variety of circumstances: physical, mental, or emotional excitement, alcohol taken before retiring, position in bed (as lying on the back), the state of the bladder, sometimes the mere fact of being in a strange bed, and to some extent apparently by the existence of monthly and yearly rhythms. On the whole, it is a fairly definite and regular phenomenon which usually leaves little conscious trace on awaking, beyond probably some sense of fatigue and, occasionally, a headache. In women, however, the phenomena of auto-erotism during sleep seem to be much more irregular, varied, and diffused. So far as I have been able to make inquiries, it is the exception rather than the rule for girls to experience definitely erotic dreams about the period of puberty or adolescence.[1] Auto-erotic phenomena during sleep in women who have never experienced the orgasm when awake are usually of a very vague kind; while it is the rule in a chaste youth for the orgasm thus to manifest itself, it is the exception in a chaste girl. It is not, as a rule, until the orgasm has been definitely produced in the waking state—under whatever conditions it may have been produced—that it begins to occur during sleep, and even in a strongly sexual woman living a repressed life it is often comparatively infrequent.[2] Thus, a young medical woman who endeavors to deal strenuously with her physical sexual emotions writes: "I sleep soundly, and do not dream at all. Occasionally, but very rarely, I have had sensations which awakened me suddenly. They can scarcely be called dreams, for they are mere impulses, nothing connected or coherent, yet prompted, I know, by sexual feeling. This is probably an experience common to all." Another lady (with a restrained psycho-sexual tendency to be attracted to both sexes), states that her first sexual sensations with orgasm were felt in dreams at the age of 16, but these dreams, which she has now forgotten, were not agreeable and not erotic; two or three years later spontaneous orgasm began to

---

[1] I may here refer to the curious opinion expressed by Dr. Elizabeth Blackwell, that, while the sexual impulse in man is usually relieved by seminal emissions during sleep, in women it is relieved by the occurrence of menstruation. This latter statement is flagrantly at variance with the facts; but it may perhaps be quoted in support of the view expressed above as to the comparative rarity of sexual excitement during sleep in young girls.

[2] Löwenfeld has recently expressed the same opinion. Rohleder believes that pollutions are physically impossible in a *real* virgin, but that opinion is too extreme.

occur occasionally when awake, and after this, orgasm took place regularly once or twice a week in sleep, but still without erotic dreams; she merely dreamt that the orgasm was occurring and awoke as it took place.

It is possible that to the comparative rarity in chaste women of complete orgasm during sleep, we may in part attribute the violence with which repressed sexual emotion in women often manifests itself.[1]   There is thus a difference here between men and women which is of some significance when we are considering the natural satisfaction of the sexual impulse in chaste women.

In women, who have become accustomed to sexual intercourse, erotic dreams of fully developed character occur, with complete orgasm and accompanying relief—as may occasionally be the case in women who are not acquainted with actual intercourse;[2] some women, however, even when familiar with actual coitus, find that sexual dreams, though accompanied by emissions, are only the symptoms of desire and do not produce actual relief.

Some interest attaches to cases in which young women, even girls at puberty, experience dreams of erotic character, or at all events dream concerning coitus or men in erection, although they

---

[1] It may be added that in more or less neurotic women and girls, erotic dreams may be very frequent and depressing. Thus, J. M. Fothergill (*West-Riding Asylum Report*, 1876, vol. vi) remarks: "These dreams are much more frequent than is ordinarily thought, and are the cause of a great deal of nervous depression among women. Women of a highly-nervous diathesis suffer much more from these drains than robust women. Not only are these involuntary orgasms more frequent among such women, but they cause more disturbance of the general health in them than in other women."

[2] I may remark here that a Russian correspondent considers that I have greatly underestimated the frequency of erotic manifestations during sleep in young girls. "All the women I have interrogated on this point," he informs me, "say that they have had such pollutions from the time of puberty, or even earlier, accompanied by erotic dreams. I have put the question to some twenty or thirty women. It is true that they were of southern race (Italian, Spanish, and French), and I believe that Southerners are, in this matter, franker than northern women, who consider the activity of the flesh as shameful, and seek to conceal it." My correspondent makes no reference to the chief point of sexual difference, so far as my observation goes, which is that erotic dreams are comparatively rare in those women *who have yet had no sort of sexual experience in waking life.*" Whether or not this is correct, I do not question the frequency of erotic dreams in girls who have had such experience.

profess, and almost certainly with truth, to be quite ignorant of
sexual phenomena. Several such dreams of remarkable character
have been communicated to me. One can imagine that the
psychologists of some schools would see in these dreams the
spontaneous eruption of the experiences of the race. I am
inclined to regard them as forgotten memories, such as we know
to occur sometimes in sleep. The child has somehow seen or
heard of sexual phenomena and felt no interest, and the memory
may subsequently be aroused in sleep, under the stimulation of
new-born sexual sensations.

It is a curious proof of the ignorance which has prevailed in recent times concerning the psychic sexual nature of women that, although in earlier ages the fact that women are normally liable to
erotic dreams was fully recognized, in recent times it has been denied,
even by writers who have made a special study of the sexual impulse
in women. Eulenburg (*Sexuale Neuropathie*, 1895, pp. 31, 79) appears
to regard the appearances of sexual phenomena during sleep, in women,
as the result of masturbation. Adler, in what is in many respects an
extremely careful study of sexual phenomena in women (*Die Mangelhafte
Geschlechtsempfindung des Weibes*, 1904, p. 130), boldly states that they
do not have erotic dreams. In 1847, E. Guibout ("Des Pollutions In-
volontaires chez la Femme," *Union Médicale*, p. 260) presented the case
of a married lady who masturbated from the age of ten, and continued
the practice, even after her marriage at twenty-four, and at twenty-
nine began to have erotic dreams with emissions every few nights, and
later sometimes even several times a night, though they ceased to be
voluptuous; he believed the case to be the first ever reported of such
a condition in a woman. Yet, thousands of years ago, the Indian of
Vedic days recognized erotic dreams in women as an ordinary and normal
occurrence. (Löwenfeld quotes a passage to this effect from the
Oupnek'hat, *Sexualleben und Nervenleiden*, 2d ed., p. 114.) Even savages recognize the occurrence of erotic dreams in women as normal,
for the Papuans, for instance, believe that a young girl's first menstruation is due to intercourse with the moon in the shape of a man, the
girl dreaming that a man is embracing her. (*Reports Cambridge Expedition to Torres Straits*, vol. v, p. 206.) In the seventeenth century,
Rolfincius, in a well-informed study (*De Pollutione Nocturna*, a Jena
Inaugural Dissertation, 1667), concluded that women experience such
manifestations, and quotes Aristotle, Galen, and Fernelius, in the same
sense. Sir Thomas Overbury, in his *Characters*, written in the early
part of the same century, describing the ideal milkmaid, says that "her

dreams are so chaste that she dare tell them," clearly implying that it was not so with most women. The notion that women are not subject to erotic dreams thus appears to be of comparatively recent origin.

One of the most interesting and important characters by which the erotic dreams of women—and, indeed, their dreams generally—differ from those of men is in the tendency to evoke a repercussion on the waking life, a tendency more rarely noted in men's erotic dreams, and then only to a minor extent. This is very common, even in healthy and normal women, and is exaggerated to a high degree in neurotic subjects, by whom the dream may even be interpreted as a reality, and so declared on oath, a fact of practical importance.

Hersman—having met with a case in which a school-girl with chorea, after having dreamed of an assault, accused the principal of a school of assault, securing his conviction—obtained the opinions of various American alienists as to the frequency with which such dreams in unstable mental subjects lead to delusions and criminal accusations. Dercum, H. C. Wood, and Rohé had not personally met with such cases; Burr believed that there was strong evidence "that a sexual dream may be so vivid as to make the subject believe she has had sexual congress"; Kiernan knew of such cases; C. H. Hughes, in persons with every appearance of sanity, had known the erotic dreams of the night to become the erotic delusions of the day, the patient protesting violently the truth of her story; while Hersman reports the case[1] of a young lady in an asylum who had nightly delusions that a medical officer visited her every night, and had to do with her,

----

[1] C. C. Hersman, "Medico-legal Aspects of Eroto-Choreic Insanities," *Alienist and Neurologist*, July, 1897. I may mention that Pitres (*Leçons cliniques sur l'Hystérie*, vol. ii, p. 34) records the almost identical case of a hysterical girl in one of his wards, who was at first grateful to the clinical clerk to whom her case was intrusted, but afterward changed her behavior, accused him of coming nightly through the window, lying beside her, caressing her, and then exerting violent coitus three or four times in succession, until she was utterly exhausted. I may here refer to the tendency to erotic excitement in women under the influence of chloroform and nitrous oxide, a tendency rarely or never noted in men, and of the frequency with which the phenomenon is attributed by the subject to actual assault. See H. Ellis, *Man and Woman*, pp. 269-274.

coming up the hot-air flue. I am acquainted with a similar case in a clever, but highly neurotic, young woman, who writes: "For years I have been trying to stamp out my passional nature, and was beginning to succeed when a strange thing happened to me last autumn. One night, as I lay in bed, I felt an influence so powerful that a man seemed present with me. I crimsoned with shame and wonder. I remember that I lay upon my back, and marveled when the spell had passed. The influence, I was assured, came from a priest whom I believed in and admired above everyone in the world. I had never dreamed of love in connection with him, because I always thought him so far above me. The influence has been upon me ever since—sometimes by day and nearly always by night; from it I generally go into a deep sleep, which lasts until morning. I am always much refreshed when I awake. This influence has the best effect upon my life that anything has ever had as regards health and mind. It is the knowledge that I am loved *fittingly* that makes me so indifferent to my future. What worries me is that I sometimes wonder if I suffer from a nervous disorder merely." The subject thus seemed to regard these occurrences as objectively caused, but was sufficiently sane to wonder whether her experiences were not due to mental disorder.[1]

The tendency of the auto-erotic phenomena of sleep to be manifested with such energy as to flow over into the waking life and influence conscious emotion and action, while very well marked in normal and healthy women, is seen to an exaggerated extent in hysterical women, in whom it has, therefore, chiefly been studied. Sante de Sanctis, who has investigated the dreams of many classes of people, remarks on the frequently sexual character of the dreams of hysterical women, and the repercussion of

---

[1] In Australia, some years ago, a man was charged with rape, found guilty of "attempt," and sentenced to eighteen months' imprisonment, on the accusation of a girl of 13, who subsequently confessed that the charge was imaginary; in this case, the jury found it impossible to believe that so young a girl could have been lying, or hallucinated, because she narrated the details of the alleged offence with such circumstantial detail. Such cases are not uncommon, and in some measure, no doubt, they may be accounted for by auto-erotic nocturnal hallucinations.

such dreams on the waking life of the following day; he gives
a typical case of hysterical erotic dreaming in an uneducated
servant-girl of 23, in whom such dreams occur usually a few days
before the menstrual period; her dreams, especially if erotic,
make an enormous impression on her; in the morning she is
bad-tempered if they were unpleasant, while she feels lascivious
and gives herself up to masturbation if she has had erotic dreams
of men; she then has a feeling of pleasure throughout the day,
and her sexual organs are bathed with moisture.[1]   Pitres and
Gilles de la Tourette, two of Charcot's most distinguished pupils,
in their elaborate works on hysteria, both consider that dreams
generally have a great influence on the waking life of the hysterical, and they deal with the special influence of erotic dreams,
to which, doubtless, we must refer those conceptions of *incubi*
and *succubi* which played so vast and so important a part in
the demonology of the Middle Ages, and while not unknown
in men were most frequent in women.   Such erotic dreams—
as these observers, confirming the experience of old writers, have
found among the hysterical to-day—are by no means always, or
even usually, of a pleasurable character.   "It is very rare." Pitres
remarks, when insisting on the sexual character of the hallucinations of the hysterical, "for these erotic hallucinations to be accompanied by agreeable voluptuous sensations.   In most cases
the illusion of sexual intercourse even provokes acute pain.   The
witches of old times nearly all affirmed that in their relations with
the devil they suffered greatly.[2]   They said that his organ was
long and rough and pointed, with scales which lifted on with-

---

[1] Sante de Sanctis, *I sogni e il sonno nell'isterismo e nella epilessia,*
Rome, 1896, p. 101.

[2] Pitres, *Leçons cliniques sur l'Hystérie,* vol. ii, pp. 37 *et seq.*   The
Lorraine inquisitor, Nicolas Remy, very carefully investigated the question of the feelings of witches when having intercourse with the Devil,
questioning them minutely. and ascertained that such intercourse was
usually extremely painful, filling them with icy horror (See, *e.g.,* Dufour,
Histoire de la Prostitution, vol. v, p. 127: the same author presents an
interesting summary of the phenomena of the Witches' Sabbath).   But
intercourse with the Devil was by no means always painful.   Isabel
Gowdie, a Scotch witch, bore clear testimony to this point: "The
youngest and lustiest women," she stated, "will have very great pleasure
in their carnal copulation with him, yea, much more than with their
own husbands. . . . He is abler for us than any man can be.

drawal and tore the vagina." (It seems probable, I may remark, that the witches' representations, both of the devil and of sexual intercourse, were largely influenced by familiarity with the coupling of animals). As Gilles de la Tourette is careful to warn his readers, we must not too hastily assume, from the prevalence of nocturnal auto-erotic phenomena in hysterical women, that such women are necessarily sexual and libidinous in excess; the disorder is in them psychic, he points out, and not physical, and they usually receive sexual approaches with indifference and repugnance, because their sexual centres are anæsthetic or hyperæsthetic. "During the period of sexual activity they seek much more the care and delicate attention of men than the genital act, which they often only tolerate. Many households, begun under the happiest auspices—the bride all the more apt to believe that she loves her betrothed in virtue of her suggestibility, easily exalted, perhaps at the expense of the senses—become hells on earth. The sexual act has for the hysterical woman more than one disillusion; she cannot understand it; it inspires her with insurmountable repugnance."[1] I refer to these hysterical phenomena because they present to us, in an extreme form, facts which are common among women whom, under the artificial conditions of civilized life, we are compelled to regard as ordinarily healthy and normal. The frequent painfulness of auto-erotic phenomena is by no means an exclusively hysterical phenomenon, although often seen in a heightened form in hysterical conditions. It is probably to some extent simply the result of a conflict in consciousness with a merely physical impulse which is strong enough to assert itself in spite of the emotional and intellectual abhorrence of the subject. It is thus but an extreme

(Alack! that I should compare him to a man!)" Yet her description scarcely sounds attractive; he was a "large, black, hairy man, very cold, and I found his nature as cold within me as spring well-water." His foot was forked and cloven; he was sometimes like a deer, or a roe; and he would hold up his tail while the witches kissed that region (Pitcairn, *Criminal Trials in Scotland*, vol. iii, Appendix VII; see, also, the illustrations at the end of Dr. A. Marie's *Folie et Mysticisme*, 1907).

[1] Gilles de la Tourette, *loc. cit.*, p. 518. Erotic hallucinations have also been studied by Bellamy, in a Bordeaux thesis, *Hallucinations Erotiques*, 1900-1901.

form of the disgust which all sexual physical manifestations tend
to inspire in a person who is not inclined to respond to them.
Somewhat similar psychic disgust and physical pain are produced in the attempts to stimulate the sexual emotions and organs
when these are exhausted by exercise. In the detailed history
which Moll presents, of the sexual experiences of a sister in an
American nursing guild,—a most instructive history of a woman
fairly normal except for the results of repressed sexual emotion,
and with strong moral tendencies,—various episodes are narrated
well illustrating the way in which sexual excitement becomes
unpleasant or even painful when it takes place as a physical reflex which the emotions and intellect are all the time struggling
against.[1] It is quite probable, however, that there is a physiological, as well as a psychic, factor in this phenomenon, and
Sollier, in his elaborate study of the nature and genesis of
hysteria, by insisting on the capital importance of the disturbance of sensibility in hysteria, and the definite character of the
phenomena produced in the passage between anæsthesia and normal sensation, has greatly helped to reveal the mechanism of·this
feature of auto-erotic excitement in the hysterical.

No doubt there has been a tendency to exaggerate the unpleasant character of the auto-erotic phenomena of hysteria.
That tendency was an inevitable reaction against an earlier view,
according to which hysteria was little more than an unconscious
expression of the sexual emotions and as such was unscientifically
dismissed without any careful investigation. I agree with Breuer
and Freud that the sexual needs of the hysterical are just as individual and various as those of normal women, but that they
suffer from them more, largely through a moral struggle with

---

[1] On one occasion, when still a girl, whenever an artist whom she
admired touched her hand she felt erection and moisture of the sexual
parts, but without any sensation of pleasure; a little later, when an
uncle's knee casually came in contact with her thigh, ejaculation of
mucus took place, though she disliked the uncle; again, when a nurse,
on casually seeing a man's sexual organs, an electric shock went through
her, though the sight was disgusting to her; and when she had once to
assist a man to urinate, she became in the highest degree excited, though
without pleasure, and lay down on a couch in the next room, while a
conclusive ejaculation took place. (Moll, *Libido Sexualis*, Bd. I, p. 354.)

their own instincts, and the attempt to put them into the background of consciousness.[1] In many hysterical and psychically abnormal women, auto-erotic phenomena, and sexual phenomena generally, are highly pleasurable, though such persons may be quite innocent of any knowledge of the erotic character of the experience. I have come across interesting and extreme examples of this in the published experiences of the women followers of the American religious leader, T. L. Harris, founder of the "Brotherhood of the New Life." Thus, in a pamphlet entitled "Internal Respiration," by Respiro, a letter is quoted from a lady physician, who writes: "One morning I awoke with a strange new feeling in the womb, which lasted for a day or two; I was so very happy, but the joy was in my womb, not in my heart."[2] "At last," writes a lady quoted in the same pamphlet, "I fell into a slumber, lying on my back with arms and feet folded, a position I almost always find myself in when I awake, no matter in which position I may go to sleep. Very soon I awoke from this slumber with a most delightful sensation, every fibre tingling with an exquisite glow of warmth. I was lying on my left side (something I am never able to do), and was folded in the arms of my counterpart. Unless you have seen it, I cannot give you an idea of the beauty of his flesh, and with what joy I beheld and felt it. Think of it, luminous flesh; and Oh! such tints, you never could imagine without seeing. He folded me so closely in his arms," etc. In such cases there is no conflict between the physical and the psychic, and therefore the resulting excitement is pleasurable and not painful.

At this point our study of auto-erotism brings us into the sphere of mysticism. Leuba, in a penetrating and suggestive essay on Christian mysticism, after quoting the present *Study,* refers to the famous passages in which St. Theresa describes how a beautiful little angel inserted a flame-tipped dart into her

---

[1] Breuer and Freud, *Studien über Hysterie,* 1895, p. 217.

[2] Calmeil (*De la Folie,* vol. i, p. 252) called attention to the large part played by uterine sensations in the hallucinations of some famous women ascetics, and added: "It is well recognized that the narrative of such sensations nearly always occupies the first place in the divagations of hysterical virgins."

heart until it descended into her bowels and left her inflamed with divine love. "What physiological difference," he asks, "is there between this voluptuous sensation and that enjoyed by the disciple of the Brotherhood of New Life? St. Theresa says bowels,' the woman doctor says 'womb,' that is all."[1]

The extreme form of auto-erotism is the tendency for the sexual emotion to be absorbed and often entirely lost in self-admiration. This Narcissus-like tendency, of which the normal germ in women is symbolized by the mirror, is found in a minor degree in some men, and is sometimes well marked in women, usually in association with an attraction for other persons, to which attraction it is, of course, normally subservient. "The mirror," remarks Bloch (*Beiträge* I, p. 201), "plays an important part in the genesis of sexual aberration. . . . It cannot be doubted that many a boy and girl have first experienced sexual excitement at the sight of their own bodies in a mirror."

Valera, the Spanish novelist, very well described this impulse in his *Genio y Figura*. Rafaela, the heroine of this novel, says that, after her bath: "I fall into a puerility which may be innocent or vicious, I cannot decide. I only know that it is a purely contemplative act, a disinterested admiration of beauty. It is not coarse sensuality, but æsthetic platonism. I imitate Narcissus; and I apply my lips to the cold surface of the mirror and kiss my image. It is the love of beauty, the expression of tenderness and affection for what God has made manifest, in an ingenuous kiss imprinted on the empty and incorporeal reflection." In the same spirit the real heroine of the *Tagebuch einer Verlorenen* (p. 114), at the point when she was about to become a prostitute, wrote: "I am pretty. It gives me pleasure to throw off my clothes, one by one, before the mirror, and to look at myself, just as I am, white as snow and straight as a fir, with my long, fine, hair, like a cloak of black silk. When I spread abroad the black stream of it, with both hands, I am like a white swan with black wings."

A typical case known to me is that of a lady of 28, brought up on a farm. She is a handsome woman, of very large and fine proportions, active and healthy and intelligent, with, however, no marked sexual attraction to the opposite sex; at the same time she is not inverted, though she would like to be a man, and has a considerable degree of contempt for women. She has an intense admiration for her own

---

[1] H. Leuba, "Les Tendances Religieuses chez les Mystiques Chrétiens," *Revue Philosophique*, November. 1902, p. 465. St. Theresa herself states that physical sensations played a considerable part in this experience.

person, especially her limbs; she is never so happy as when alone and naked in her own bedroom, and, so far as possible, she cultivates nakedness. She knows by heart the various measurements of her body, is proud of the fact that they are strictly in accordance with the canons of proportion, and she laughs proudly at the thought that her thigh is larger than many a woman's waist. She is frank and assured in her manners, without sexual shyness, and, while willing to receive the attention and admiration of others, she makes no attempt to gain it, and seems never to have experienced any emotions stronger than her own pleasure in herself. I should add that I have had no opportunity of detailed examination, and cannot speak positively as to the absence of masturbation.

In the extreme form in which alone the name of Narcissus may properly be invoked, there is comparative indifference to sexual intercourse or even the admiration of the opposite sex. Such a condition seems to be rare, except, perhaps, in insanity. Since I called attention to this form of auto-erotism (*Alienist and Neurologist*, April, 1898), several writers have discussed the condition, especially Näcke, who, following out the suggestion, terms the condition Narcissism. Among 1,500 insane persons, Näcke has found it in four men and one woman (*Psychiatrische en Neurologische Bladen*, No. 2, 1899). Dr. C. H. Hughes writes (in a private letter) that he is acquainted with such cases, in which men have been absorbed in admiration of their own manly forms, and of their sexual organs, and women, likewise, absorbed in admiration of their own mammæ and physical proportions, especially of limbs. "The whole subject," he adds, "is a singular phase of psychology, and it is not all morbid psychology, either. It is closely allied to that æsthetic sense which admires the nude in art."

Féré (*L'Instinct Sexuel*, 2d ed., p. 271) mentions a woman who experienced sexual excitement in kissing her own hand. Näcke knew a woman in an asylum who, during periodical fits of excitement, would kiss her own arms and hands, at the same time looking like a person in love. He also knew a young man with dementia præcox, who would kiss his own image ("Der Kuss bei Geisteskranken," *Allgemeine Zeitschrift für Psychiatrie*, Bd. LXIII, p. 127). Moll refers to a young homosexual lawyer, who experienced great pleasure in gazing at himself in a mirror (*Konträre Sexualempfindung*, 3d ed., p. 228), and mentions another inverted man, an admirer of the nates of men, who, chancing to observe his own nates in a mirror, when changing his shirt, was struck by their beauty, and subsequently found pleasure in admiring them (*Libido Sexualis*, Bd. I, Theil I, p. 60). Krafft-Ebing knew a man who masturbated before a mirror, imagining, at the same time, how much better a real lover would be.

The best-observed cases of Narcissism have, however, been recorded by Rohleder, who confers upon this condition the ponderous name of automonosexualism, and believes that it has not been previously observed (H. Rohleder, *Der Automonosexualismus*, being Heft 225 of *Berliner Klinik*, March, 1907). In the two cases investigated by Rohleder, both men, there was sexual excitement in the contemplation of the individual's own body, actually or in a mirror, with little or no sexual attraction to other persons. Rohleder is inclined to regard the condition as due to a congenital defect in the "sexual centre" of the brain.

II.

Hysteria and the Question of Its Relation to the Sexual Emotions
—The Early Greek Theories of its Nature and Causation—The Gradual
Rise of Modern Views—Charcot—The Revolt Against Charcot's Too
Absolute Conclusions—Fallacies Involved—Charcot's Attitude the Out-
come of his Personal Temperament—Breuer and Freud—Their Views
Supplement and Complete Charcot's—At the Same Time they Furnish
a Justification for the Earlier Doctrine of Hysteria—But They Must
Not be Regarded as Final—The Diffused Hysteroid Condition in Nor-
mal Persons—The Physiological Basis of Hysteria—True Pathological
Hysteria is Linked on to almost Normal States, especially to Sex-
hunger.

THE nocturnal hallucinations of hysteria, as all careful
students of this condition now seem to agree, are closely allied
to the hysterical attack proper. Sollier, indeed, one of the ablest
of the more recent investigators of hysteria, has argued with
much force that the subjects of hysteria really live in a state of
pathological sleep, of vigilambulism.[1] He regards all the various
accidents of hysteria as having a common basis in disturbances
of sensibility, in the widest sense of the word "sensibility,"—as
the very foundation of personality,—while anæsthesia is "the
real *sigillum hysteriæ.*" Whatever the form of hysteria, we are
thus only concerned with a more or less profound state of
vigilambulism: a state in which the subject seems, often even
to himself, to be more or less always asleep, whether the sleep
may be regarded as local or general. Sollier agrees with Féré
that the disorder of sensibility may be regarded as due to an
exhaustion of the sensory centres of the brain, whether as the

---

[1] *Genèse et Nature de l'Hystérie*, 1898; and, for Sollier's latest
statement, see "Hystérie et Sommeil," *Archives de Neurologie*, May and
June, 1907. Lombroso (*L'Uomo Delinquente*, 1889, vol. ii, p. 329), referring to the diminished metabolism of the hysterical, had already compared them to hibernating animals, while Babinsky states that the
hysterical are in a state of subconsciousness, a state, as Metchnikoff remarks (*Essais optimistes*, p. 270), reminiscent of our prehistoric past.

14 (209)

result of constitutional cerebral weakness, of the shock of a violent emotion, or of some toxic influence on the cerebral cells.

We may, therefore, fitly turn from the auto-erotic phenomena of sleep which in women generally, and especially in hysterical women, seem to possess so much importance and significance, to the question—which has been so divergently answered at different periods and by different investigators— concerning the causation of hysteria, and especially concerning its alleged connection with conscious or unconscious sexual emotion.[1]

It was the belief of the ancient Greeks that hysteria came from the womb; hence its name. We first find that statement in Plato's *Timæus*: "In men the organ of generation—becoming rebellious and masterful, like an animal disobedient to reason, and maddened with the sting of lust—seeks to gain absolute sway; and the same is the case with the so-called womb, or uterus, of women; the animal within them is desirous of procreating children, and, when remaining unfruitful long beyond its proper time, gets discontented and angry, and, wandering in every direction through the body, closes up the passages of the breath, and, by obstructing respiration,[2] drives them to extremity, causing all varieties of disease."

Plato, it is true, cannot be said to reveal anywhere a very scientific attitude toward Nature. Yet he was here probably only giving expression to the current medical doctrine of his day. We find precisely the same doctrine attributed to Hippocrates,

---

[1] Professor Freud, while welcoming the introduction of the term "auto-erotism," remarks that it should not be made to include the whole of hysteria. This I fully admit, and have never questioned. Hysteria is far too large and complex a phenomenon to be classed as entirely a manifestation of auto-erotism, but certain aspects of it are admirable illustrations of auto-erotic transformation.

[2] The hysterical phenomenon of *globus hystericus* was long afterward attributed to obstruction of respiration by the womb. The interesting case has been recorded by E. Bloch (*Wiener Klinische Wochenschrift*, 1907, p. 1649) of a lady who had the feeling of a ball rising from her stomach to her throat, and then sinking. This feeling was associated with thoughts of her husband's rising and falling penis, and was always most liable to occur when she wished for coitus.

though without a clear distinction between hysteria and epilepsy.[1]
If we turn to the best Roman physicians we find again that
Aretæus, "the Esquirol of antiquity," has set forth the same view,
adding to his description of the movements of the womb in
hysteria: "It delights, also, in fragrant smells, and advances
toward them; and it has an aversion to fœtid smells, and flies
from them; and, on the whole, the womb is like an animal within
an animal."[2]   Consequently, the treatment was by applying fœtid
smells to the nose and rubbing fragrant ointments around the
sexual parts.[3]

The Arab physicians, who carried on the traditions of Greek
medicine, appear to have said nothing new about hysteria, and
possibly had little knowledge of it.   In Christian mediæval Europe, also, nothing new was added to the theory of hysteria; it
was, indeed, less known medically than it had ever been, and,
in part it may be as a result of this ignorance, in part as a result
of general wretchedness (the hysterical phenomena of witchcraft
reaching their height, Michelet points out, in the fourteenth
century, which was a period of special misery for the poor), it
flourished more vigorously.   Not alone have we the records of
nervous epidemics, but illuminated manuscripts, ivories, miniatures, bas-reliefs, frescoes, and engravings furnish the most vivid
iconographic evidence of the prevalence of hysteria in its most
violent forms during the Middle Ages.   Much of this evidence is

---

[1] As Gilles de la Tourette points out, it is not difficult to show that
epilepsy, the *morbus sacer* of the ancients, owed much of its sacred
character to this confusion with hysteria.   Those priestesses who, struck
by the *morbus sacer*, gave forth their oracles amid convulsions, were
certainly not the victims of epilepsy, but of hysteria (*Traité de
l'Hystérie*, vol. i, p. 3).

[2] Aretæus, *On the Causes and Symptoms of Acute Diseases*, Book
ii, Chapter II.

[3] It may be noted that this treatment furnishes another instance
of the continuity of therapeutic methods, through all changes of theory,
from the earliest to the latest times.   Drugs of unpleasant odor, like
asafœtida, have always been used in hysteria, and scientific medicine
to-day still finds that asafœtida is a powerful sedative to the uterus, con-
trolling nervous conditions during pregnancy and arresting uterine irritation when abortion is threatened (see, *e.g.*, Warman, *Der Frauenarzt*,
August, 1895).   Again, the rubbing of fragrant ointments into the sexual
regions is but a form of that massage which is one of the modern methods
of treating the sexual disorders of women.

brought to the service of science in the fascinating works of Dr. P. Richer, one of Charcot's pupils.[1]

In the seventeenth century Ambroise Paré was still talking, like Hippocrates, about "suffocation of the womb"; Forestus was still, like Aretæus, applying friction to the vulva; Fernel was still reproaching Galen, who had denied that the movements of the womb produced hysteria.

It was in the seventeenth century (1618) that a French physician, Charles Lepois (Carolus Piso), physician to Henry II, trusting, as he said, to experience and reason, overthrew at one stroke the doctrine of hysteria that had ruled almost unquestioned for two thousand years, and showed that the malady occurred at all ages and in both sexes, that its seat was not in the womb, but in the brain, and that it must be considered a nervous disease.[2] So revolutionary a doctrine could not fail to meet with violent opposition, but it was confirmed by Willis, and in 1681, we owe to the genius of Sydenham a picture of hysteria which for lucidity, precision, and comprehensiveness has only been excelled in our own times.

It was not possible any longer to maintain the womb theory of Hippocrates in its crude form, but in modified forms, and especially with the object of preserving the connection which many observers continued to find between hysteria and the sexual emotions, it still found supporters in the eighteenth and even the nineteenth centuries. James, in the middle of the eighteenth century, returned to the classical view, and in his *Dictionary of Medicine* maintained that the womb is the seat of hysteria. Louyer Villermay in 1816 asserted that the most frequent causes of hysteria are deprivation of the pleasures of love, griefs connected with this passion, and disorders of menstruation. Foville in 1833 and Landouzy in 1846 advocated somewhat similar views. The acute Laycock in 1840 quoted as "almost a medical proverb"

[1] *Les Démoniaques dans l'Art*, 1887; *Les Malades et les Difformes dans l'Art*, 1889.

[2] Glafira Abricosoff, of Moscow, in her Paris thesis, *L'Hystérie aux xvii et xviii siécles*, 1897, presents a summary of the various views held at this time; as also Gilles de la Tourette, *Traité de l'Hystérie*, vol. i, Chapter I.

the saying, *"Salacitas major, major ad hysteriam proclivitas,"* fully indorsing it. More recently still Clouston has defined hysteria as "the loss of the inhibitory influence exercised on the reproductive and sexual instincts of women by the higher mental and moral functions" (a position evidently requiring some modification in view of the fact that hysteria is by no means confined to women), while the same authority remarks that more or less concealed sexual phenomena are the chief symptoms of "hysterical insanity."[1] Two gynæcologists of high position in different parts of the world, Hegar in Germany and Balls-Headley in Australia, attribute hysteria, as well as anæmia, largely to unsatisfied sexual desire, including the non-satisfaction of the "ideal feelings."[2] Lombroso and Ferrero, again, while admitting that the sexual feelings might be either heightened or depressed in hysteria, referred to the frequency of what they termed "a paradoxical sexual instinct" in the hysterical, by which, for instance, sexual frigidity is combined with intense sexual preoccupations; and they also pointed out the significant fact that the crimes of the hysterical nearly always revolve around the sexual sphere.[3] Thus, even up to the time when the conception of hysteria which absolutely ignored and excluded any sexual relationship whatever had reached its height, independent views favoring such a relationship still found expression.

Of recent years, however, such views usually aroused violent antagonism. The main current of opinion was with Briquet (1859), who, treating the matter with considerable ability and a wide induction of facts, indignantly repelled the idea that there is any connection between hysteria and the sexual facts of life, physical or psychic. As he himself admitted, Briquet was moved to deny a sexual causation of hysteria by the thought that such

---

[1] *Edinburgh Medical Journal*, June, 1883, p. 1123, and *Mental Diseases*, 1887, p. 488.

[2] Hegar, *Zusammenhang der Geschlechtskrankheiten mit nervösen Leiden*, Stuttgart, 1885. (Hegar, however, went much further than this, and was largely responsible for the surgical treatment of hysteria now generally recognized as worse than futile.) Balls-Headley, "Etiology of Nervous Diseases of the Female Genital Organs," Allbutt and Playfair, *System of Gynecology*, 1896, p. 141.

[3] Lombroso and Ferrero, *La Donna Delinquente*, 1893, pp. 613-14.

an origin would be degrading for women ("*a quelque chose de dégradant pour les femmes*").

It was, however, the genius of Charcot, and the influence of his able pupils, which finally secured the overthrow of the sexual theory of hysteria. Charcot emphatically anathematized the visceral origin of hysteria; he declared that it is a psychic disorder, and to leave no loop-hole of escape for those who maintained a sexual causation he asserted that there are no varieties of hysteria, that the disease is one and indivisible. Charcot recognized no primordial cause of hysteria beyond heredity, which here plays a more important part than in any other neuropathic condition. Such heredity is either direct or more occasionally by transformation, any deviation of nutrition found in the ancestors (gout, diabetes, arthritis) being a possible cause of hysteria in the descendants. "We do not know anything about the nature of hysteria," Charcot wrote in 1892; "we must make it objective in order to recognize it. The dominant idea for us in the etiology of hysteria is, in the widest sense, its hereditary predisposition. The greater number of those suffering from this affection are simply born *hystérisables,* and on them the occasional causes act directly, either through autosuggestion or by causing derangement of general nutrition, and more particularly of the nutrition of the nervous system."[1] These views were ably and decisively stated in Gilles de la Tourette's *Traité de l'Hystérie,* written under the inspiration of Charcot.

While Charcot's doctrine was thus being affirmed and generally accepted, there were at the same time workers in these fields who, though they by no means ignored this doctrine of hysteria or even rejected it, were inclined to think that it was too absolutely stated. Writing in the *Dictionary of Psychological Medicine* at the same time as Charcot, Donkin, while deprecating any exclusive emphasis on the sexual causation, pointed out the enormous part played by the emotions in the production of hysteria, and the great influence of puberty in women due to the greater extent of the sexual organs, and the

___

[1] Charcot and Marie, article on "Hysteria," Tuke's *Dictionary of Psychological Medicine.*

consequently large area of central innervation involved, and thus rendered liable to fall into a state of unstable equilibrium. Enforced abstinence from the gratification of any of the inherent and primitive desires, he pointed out, may be an adequate exciting cause. Such a view as this indicated that to set aside the ancient doctrine of a physical sexual cause of hysteria was by no means to exclude a psychic sexual cause. Ten years earlier Axenfeld and Huchard had pointed out that the reaction against the sexual origin of hysteria was becoming excessive, and they referred to the evidence brought forward by veterinary surgeons showing that unsatisfied sexual desire in animals may produce nervous symptoms very similar to hysteria.[1] The present writer, when in 1894 briefly discussing hysteria as an element in secondary sexual characterization, ventured to reflect the view, confirmed by his own observation, that there was a tendency to unduly minimize the sexual factor in hysteria, and further pointed out that the old error of a special connection between hysteria and the female sexual organs, probably arose from the fact that in woman the organic sexual sphere is larger than in man.[2]

When, indeed, we analyze the foundation of the once predominant opinions of Charcot and his school regarding the sexual relationships of hysteria, it becomes clear that many fallacies and misunderstandings were involved. Briquet, Charcot's chief predecessor, acknowledged that his own view was that a sexual origin of hysteria would be "degrading to women"; that is to say, he admitted that he was influenced by a foolish and improper prejudice, for the belief that the unconscious and involuntary morbid reaction of the nervous system to any disturbance of a great

---

[1] Axenfeld and Huchard, *Traité des Névroses*, 1883, pp. 1092-94. Icard (*La Femme pendant la Période Menstruelle*, pp. 120-21) has also referred to recorded cases of hysteria in animals (Coste's and Peter's cases), as has Gilles de la Tourette (*op. cit.*, vol. i, p. 123). See also, for references, Féré, *L'Instinct Sexuel*, p. 59.

[2] *Man and Woman*, 4th ed., p. 326. A distinguished gynecologist, Matthews Duncan, had remarked some years earlier (*Lancet*, May 18, 1889) that hysteria, though not a womb disease, "especially attaches itself to the generative system, because the genital system, more than any other, exerts emotional power over the individual, power also in morals, power in social questions."

primary instinct can have *"quelque chose de dégradant"* is itself
an immoral belief; such disturbance of the nervous system
might or might not be caused, but in any case the alleged
"degradation" could only be the fiction of a distorted imagination. Again, confusion had been caused by the ancient error of
making the physical sexual organs responsible for hysteria, first
the womb, more recently the ovaries; the outcome of this belief
was the extirpation of the sexual organs for the cure of hysteria.
Charcot condemned absolutely all such operations as unscientific
and dangerous, declaring that there is no such thing as hysteria
of menstrual origin.[1] Subsequently, Angelucci and Pierracini
carried out an international inquiry into the results of the
surgical treatment of hysteria, and condemned it in the most
unqualified manner.[2] It is clearly demonstrated that the physical sexual organs are not the seat of hysteria. It does not, however, follow that even physical sexual desire, when repressed, is
not a cause of hysteria. The opinion that it was so formed an
essential part of the early doctrine of hysteria, and was embodied
in the ancient maxim: *"Nubat illa et morbus effugiet."* The
womb, it seemed to the ancients, was crying out for satisfaction,
and when that was received the disease vanished.[3] But when it
became clear that sexual desire, though ultimately founded on
the sexual apparatus, is a nervous and psychic fact, to put the
sexual organs out of count was not sufficient; for the sexual
emotions may exist before puberty, and persist after complete
removal of the sexual organs. Thus it has been the object of
many writers to repel the idea that unsatisfied sexual desire can
be a cause of hysteria. Briquet pointed out that hysteria is rare
among nuns and frequent among prostitutes. Krafft-Ebing

---

[1] Gilles de la Tourette, *Archives de Tocologie et de Gynécologie,*
June, 1895.

[2] *Rivista Sperimentale di Freniatria,* 1897, p. 290; summarized in
the *Journal of Mental Science,* January, 1898.

[3] From the earliest times it was held that menstruation favors
hysteria; more recently, Landouzy recorded a number of observations
showing that hysterical attacks coincide with perfectly healthy menstruation; while Ball has maintained that it is only during menstruation
that hysteria appears in its true color. See the opinions collected by
Icard, *La Femme pendant la Période Menstruelle,* pp. 75-81.

believed that most hysterical women are not anxious for sexual satisfaction, and declared that "hysteria caused through the non-satisfaction of the coarse sensual sexual impulse I have never seen,"[1] while Pitres and others refer to the frequently painful nature of sexual hallucinations in the hysterical. But it soon becomes obvious that the psychic sexual sphere is not confined to the gratification of conscious physical sexual desire. It is not true that hysteria is rare among nuns, some of the most tremendous epidemics of hysteria, and the most carefully studied, having occurred in convents,[2] while the hysterical phenomena sometimes associated with revivals are well known. The supposed prevalence among prostitutes would not be evidence against the sexual relationships of hysteria; it has, however, been denied, even by so great an authority as Parent-Duchâtelet who found it very rare, even in prostitutes in hospitals, when it was often associated with masturbation; in prostitutes, however, who returned to a respectable life, giving up their old habits, he found hysteria common and severe.[3] The frequent absence of physical sexual feeling, again, may quite reasonably be taken as evidence of a disorder of the sexual emotions, while the undoubted fact that sexual intercourse usually has little beneficial effect on pronounced hysteria, and that sexual excitement during sleep and

---

[1] Krafft-Ebing, "Ueber Neurosen und Psychosen durch sexuelle Abstinenz," *Jahrbücher für Psychiatrie*, vol. iii, 1888. It must, however, be added that the relief of hysteria by sexual satisfaction is not rare, and that Rosenthal finds that the convulsions are thus diminished. (*Allgemeine Wiener Medizinal-Zeitung*, Nos. 46 and 47, 1887.) So they are also, in simple and uncomplicated cases, according to Mongeri, by pregnancy.

[2] "All doctors who have patients in convents," remarks Marro (*La Pubertà*, p. 338), "know how hysteria dominates among them;" he adds that his own experience confirms that of Raciborski, who found that nuns devoted to the contemplative life are more liable to hysteria than those who are occupied in teaching or in nursing. It must be added, however, that there is not unanimity as to the prevalence of hysteria in convents. Brachet was of the same opinion as Briquet, and so considered it rare. Imbert-Goubeyre, also (*La Stigmatisation*, p. 436) states that during more than forty years of medical life, though he has been connected with a number of religious communities, he has not found in them a single hysterical subject, the reason being, he remarks, that the unbalanced and extravagant are refused admission to the cloister.

[3] Parent-Duchâtelet, *De la Prostitution*, vol. i, p. 242.

sexual hallucinations are often painful in the same condition, is far from showing that injury or repression of the sexual emotions had nothing to do with the production of the hysteria. It would be as reasonable to argue that the evil effect of a heavy meal on a starving man must be taken as evidence that he was not suffering from starvation. The fact, indeed, on which Gilles de la Tourette and others have remarked, that the hysterical often desire not so much sexual intercourse as simple affection, would tend to show that there is here a real analogy, and that starvation or lesion of the sexual emotions may produce, like bodily starvation, a rejection of those satisfactions which are demanded in health. Thus, even a mainly *a priori* examination of the matter may lead us to see that many arguments brought forward in favor of Charcot's position on this point fall to the ground when we realize that the sexual emotions may constitute a highly complex sphere, often hidden from observation, sometimes not conscious at all, and liable to many lesions besides that due to the non-satisfaction of sexual desire. At the same time we are not thus enabled to overthrow any of the positive results attained by Charcot and his school.

It may, however, be pointed out that Charcot's attitude toward hysteria was the outcome of his own temperament. He was primarily a neurologist, the bent of his genius was toward the investigation of facts that could be objectively demonstrated. His first interest in hysteria, dating from as far back as 1862, was in hystero-epileptic convulsive attacks, and to the last he remained indifferent to all facts which could not be objectively demonstrated. That was the secret of the advances he was enabled to make in neurology. For purely psychological investigation he had no liking, and probably no aptitude. Anyone who was privileged to observe his methods of work at the Salpêtrière will easily recall the great master's towering figure; the disdainful expression, sometimes, even, it seemed, a little sour; the lofty bearing which enthusiastic admirers called Napoleonic. The questions addressed to the patient were cold, distant, sometimes impatient. Charcot clearly had little faith in the value of any results so attained. One may well believe, also, that a man whose superficial personality was so haughty and awe-inspiring to strangers would, in any case, have had the greatest difficulty in penetrating the mysteries of a psychic world so obscure and elusive as that presented by the hysterical.[1]

The way was thus opened for further investigations on the psychic side. Charcot had affirmed the power, not only of physical traumatism, but even of psychic lesions—of moral shocks—to provoke its manifestations, but his sole contribution to the psychology of this psychic malady,—and this was borrowed from the Nancy school,—lay in the one word "suggestibility"; the nature and mechanism of this psychic process he left wholly unexplained. This step has been taken by others, in part by Janet, who, from 1889 onward, has not only insisted that the emotions stand in the first line among the causes of hysteria, but has also pointed out some portion of the mechanism of this process; thus, he saw the significance of the fact, already recognized, that strong emotions tend to produce anæsthesia and to lead to a condition of mental disaggregation, favorable to abulia, or abolition of will-power. It remained to show in detail the mechanism by which the most potent of all the emotions effects its influence, and, by attempting to do this, the Viennese investigators, Breuer and especially Freud, have greatly aided the study of hysteria.[2] They have not, it is important to remark, overturned the positive elements in their great forerunner's work. Freud began as a disciple of Charcot, and he himself remarks that, in his earlier investigations of hysteria, he had no thought

---

[1] It may not be unnecessary to point out that here and throughout, in speaking of the psychic mechanism of hysteria, I do not admit that any process can be *purely* psychic. As Féré puts it in an admirable study of hysteria (*Twentieth Century Practice of Medicine*, 1897, vol. x, p. 556): "In the genesis of hysterical troubles everything takes place as if the psychical and the somatic phenomena were two aspects of the same biological fact."

[2] Pierre Janet, *L'Automatisme Psychologique*, 1889; *L'Etat mental des Hystériques*, 1894; *Névroses et Idées fixes*, 1898; Breuer und Freud, *Studien über Hysterie*, Vienna, 1895; the best introduction to Freud's work is, however, to be found in the two series of his *Sammlung Kleiner Schriften zur Neurosenlehre*, published in a collected form in 1906 and 1909. It may be added that a useful selection of Freud's papers has lately (1909) been published in English.

of finding any sexual etiology for that malady; he would have regarded any such suggestion as an insult to his patient. The results reached by these workers were the outcome of long and detailed investigation. Freud has investigated many cases of hysteria in minute detail, often devoting to a single case over a hundred hours of work. The patients, unlike those on whom the results of the French school have been mainly founded, all belonged to the educated classes, and it was thus possible to carry out an elaborate psychic investigation which would be impossible among the uneducated. Breuer and Freud insist on the fine qualities of mind and character frequently found among the hysterical. They cannot accept suggestibility as an invariable characteristic of hysteria, only abnormal excitability; they are far from agreeing with Janet (although on many points at one with him), that psychic weakness marks hysteria; there is merely an appearance of mental weakness, they say, because the mental activity of the hysterical is split up, and only a part of it is conscious.[1] The superiority of character of the hysterical is indicated by the fact that the conflict between their ideas of right and the bent of their inclinations is often an element in the constitution of the hysterical state. Breuer and Freud are prepared to assert that the hysterical are among "the flower of humanity," and they refer to those qualities of combined imaginative genius and practical energy which characterized St. Theresa, "the patron saint of the hysterical."

To understand the position of Breuer and Freud we may start from the phenomenon of "nervous shock" produced by physical traumatism, often of a very slight character. Charcot had shown that such "nervous shock," with the chain of resulting symptoms, is nothing more or less than hysteria. Breuer and Freud may be linked on to Charcot at this point. They began by regarding the most typical hysteria as really a *psychic traumatism;* that is to say, that it starts in a lesion, or rather in

---

[1] We might, perhaps, even say that in hysteria the so-called higher centres have an abnormally strong inhibitory influence over the lower centres. Gioffredi (*Gazzetta degli Ospedali.* October 1, 1895) has shown that some hysterical symptoms, such as mutism, can be cured by etherization, thus loosening the control of the higher centres.

repeated lesions, of the emotional organism. It is true that the school of Charcot admitted the influence of moral shock, especially of the emotion of fear, but that merely as an *"agent provocateur,"* and with a curious perversity Gilles de la Tourette, certainly reflecting the attitude of Charcot, in his elaborate treatise on hysteria fails to refer to the sphere of the sexual emotions even when enumerating the *"agents provocateurs."*[1]

The influence of fear is not denied by Breuer and Freud, but they have found that careful psychic analysis frequently shows that the shock of a commonplace "fear" is really rooted in a lesion of the sexual emotions. A typical and very simple illustration is furnished in a case, recorded by Breuer, in which a young girl of seventeen had her first hysterical attack after a cat sprang on her shoulders as she was going downstairs. Careful investigation showed that this girl had been the object of somewhat ardent attentions from a young man whose advances she had resisted, although her own sexual emotions had been aroused. A few days before, she had been surprised by this young man on these same dark stairs, and had forcibly escaped from his hands. Here was the real psychic traumatism, the operation of which merely became manifest in the cat. "But in how many cases," asks Breuer, "is a cat thus reckoned as a completely sufficient *causa efficiens?*"

In every case that they have investigated Breuer and Freud have found some similar secret lesion of the psychic sexual sphere. In one case a governess, whose training has been severely upright, is, in spite of herself and without any encouragement, led to experience for the father of the children under her care an affection which she refuses to acknowledge even to herself; in another, a young woman finds herself falling in love with her brother-in-law; again, an innocent girl suddenly discovers

---

[1] Charcot's school could not fail to recognize the erotic tone which often dominates hysterical hallucinations. Gilles de la Tourette seeks to minimize it by the remark that "it is more mental than real." He means to say that it is more psychic than physical, but he implies that the physical element in sex is alone "real," a strange assumption in any case, as well as destructive of Gilles de la Tourette's own fundamental assertion that hysteria is a real disease and yet purely psychic.

her uncle in the act of sexual intercourse with her playmate, and
a boy on his way home from school is subjected to the coarse advances of a sexual invert. In nearly every case, as Freud eventually found reason to believe, a primary lesion of the sexual emotions dates from the period of puberty and frequently of childhood, and in nearly every case the intimately private nature of
the lesion causes it to be carefully hidden from everyone, and
even to be unacknowledged by the subject of it. In the earlier
cases Breuer and Freud found that a slight degree of hypnosis is
necessary to bring the lesion into consciousness, and the accuracy
of the revelations thus obtained has been tested by independent
witness. Freud has, however, long abandoned the induction of
any degree of hypnosis; he simply tries to arrange that the
patient shall feel absolutely free to tell her own story, and so
proceeds from the surface downwards, slowly finding and piecing
together such essential fragments of the history as may be
recovered, in the same way he remarks, as the archæologist ex-
cavates below the surface and recovers and puts together the fragments of an antique statue. Much of the material found, however, has only a symbolic value requiring interpretation and is
sometimes pure fantasy. Freud now attaches great importance
to dreams as symbolically representing much in the subject's
mental history which is otherwise difficult to reach.[1] The subtle
and slender clues which Freud frequently follows in interpreting
dreams cannot fail sometimes to arouse doubt in his readers'
minds, but he certainly seems to have been often successful in
thus reaching latent facts in consciousness. The primary lesion
may thus act as "a foreign body in consciousness." Something is
introduced into psychic life which refuses to merge in the general flow of consciousness. It cannot be accepted simply as
other facts of life are accepted; it cannot even be talked about,
and so submitted to the slow usure by which our experiences are
worn down and gradually transformed. Breuer illustrates what
happens by reference to the sneezing reflex. "When an irritation
to the nasal mucous membrane for some reason fails to liberate

[1] See, e.g., his substantial volume, Die Traumdeutung, 1900, 2d
ed. 1909.

this reflex, a feeling of excitement and tension arises. This excitement, being unable to stream out along motor channels, now spreads itself over the brain, inhibiting other activities. . . . *In the highest spheres of human activity we may watch the same process."* It is a result of this process that, as Breuer and Freud found, the mere act of confession may greatly relieve the hysterical symptoms produced by this psychic mechanism, and in some cases may wholly and permanently remove them. It is on this fact that they founded their method of treatment, devised by Breuer and by him termed the cathartic method, though Freud prefers to call it the "analytic" method. It is, as Freud points out, the reverse of the hypnotic method of suggestive treatment; there is the same difference, Freud remarks, between the two methods as Leonardo da Vinci found for the two technical methods of art, *per via di porre* and *per via di levare;* the hypnotic method, like painting, works by putting in, the cathartic or analytic method, like sculpture, works by taking out.[1]

It is part of the mechanism of this process, as understood by these authors, that the physical symptoms of hysteria are constituted, by a process of conversion, out of the injured emotions, which then sink into the background or altogether out of consciousness. Thus, they found the prolonged tension of nursing a near and dear relative to be a very frequent factor in the production of hysteria. For instance, an originally rheumatic pain experienced by a daughter when nursing her father becomes the symbol in memory of her painful psychic excitement, and this perhaps for several reasons, but chiefly because *its presence in consciousness almost exactly coincided with that excitement.* In another way, again, nausea and vomiting may become a symbol through the profound sense of disgust with which some emotional shock was associated. Then the symbol begins to have a life of its own, and draws hidden strength from the emotion with which it is correlated. Breuer and Freud have found by careful investigation that the pains and physical troubles of hysteria are far from being capricious, but may be traced in a varying manner

---

[1] *Sammlung,* first series, p. 208.

to an origin in some incident, some pain, some action, which was associated with a moment of acute psychic agony. The process of conversion was an involuntary escape from an intolerable emotion, comparable to the physical pain sometimes sought in intense mental grief, and the patient wins some relief from the tortured emotions, though at the cost of psychic abnormality, of a more or less divided state of consciousness and of physical pain, or else anæsthesia. In Charcot's third stage of the hysterical convulsion, that of *"attitudes passionnelles,"* Breuer and Freud see the hallucinatory reproduction of a recollection which is full of significance for the origin of the hysterical manifestations.

The final result reached by these workers is clearly stated by each writer. "The main observation of our predecessors," states Breuer,[1] "still preserved in the word 'hysteria,' is nearer to the truth than the more recent view which puts sexuality almost in the last line, with the object of protecting the patient from moral reproaches. Certainly the sexual needs of the hysterical are just as individual and as various in force as those of the healthy. But they suffer from them, and in large measure, indeed, they suffer precisely through the struggle with them, through the effort to thrust sexuality aside." "The weightiest fact," concludes Freud,[2] "on which we strike in a thorough pursuit of the analysis is this: From whatever side and from whatever symptoms we start, we always unfailingly reach the region of the sexual life. Here, first of all, an etiological condition of hysterical states is revealed. . . . At the bottom of every case of hysteria—and reproducible by an analytical effort after even an interval of long years—may be found one or more facts of precocious sexual experience belonging to earliest youth. I regard this as an important result, as the discovery of a *caput Nili* of neuropathology." Ten years later, enlarging rather than restricting his conception, Freud remarks: "Sexuality is not a mere *deus ex machina* which intervenes but once in the hysterical process; it is the motive force of every separate symptom and every expression of a symptom. The morbid phenomena constitute, to speak

---

[1] *Studien über Hysterie*, p. 217.
[2] *Sammlung*, first series, p. 162.

plainly, the patient's sexual activity."[1] The actual hysterical fit, Freud now states, may be regarded as "the substitute for a once practiced and then abandoned *auto-erotic* satisfaction," and similarly it may be regarded as an equivalent of coitus.[2]

It is natural to ask how this conception affects that elaborate picture of hysteria laboriously achieved by Charcot and his school. It cannot be said that it abolishes any of the positive results reached by Charcot, but it certainly alters their significance and value; it presents them in a new light and changes the whole perspective. With his passion for getting at tangible definite physical facts, Charcot was on very safe ground. But he was content to neglect the psychic analysis of hysteria, while yet proclaiming that hysteria is a purely psychic disorder. He had no cause of hysteria to present save only heredity. Freud certainly admits heredity, but, as he points out, the part it plays has been overrated. It is too vague and general to carry us far, and when a specific and definite cause can be found, the part played by heredity recedes to become merely a condition, the soil on which the "specific etiology" works. Here probably Freud's enthusiasm at first carried him too far and the most important modification he has made in his views occurs at this point: he now attaches a preponderant influence to heredity. He has realized that sexual activity in one form or another is far too common in childhood to make it possible to lay very great emphasis on "traumatic lesions" of this character, and he has also realized that an outcrop of fantasies may somewhat later develop on these childish activities, intervening between them and the subsequent morbid symptoms. He is thus led to emphasize anew the significance of heredity, not, however, in Charcot's sense, as general neuropathic disposition but as "sexual constitution." The significance of "infantile sexual lesions" has also tended to give place to that of "infantilism of sexuality."[3]

The real merit of Freud's subtle investigations is that

---

[1] *Sammlung*, second series, p. 102.

[2] *Ib.* p. 146.

[3] *Sammlung*, first series, p. 229. Freud has developed his conception of sexual constitution in *Drei Abhandlungen zui Sexualtheorie*, 1905.

—while possibly furnishing a justification of the imperfectly understood idea that had floated in the mind of observers ever since the name "hysteria" was first invented—he has certainly supplied a definite psychic explanation of a psychic malady. He has succeeded in presenting clearly, at the expense of much labor, insight, and sympathy, a dynamic view of the psychic processes involved in the constitution of the hysterical state, and such a view seems to show that the physical symptoms laboriously brought to light by Charcot are largely but epiphenomena and by-products of an emotional process, often of tragic significance to the subject, which is taking place in the most sensitive recess of the psychic organism. That the picture of the mechanism involved, presented to us by Professor Freud, cannot be regarded as a final and complete account of the matter, may readily be admitted. It has developed in Freud's own hands, and some of the developments will require very considerable confirmation before they can be accepted as generally true.[1] But these investigations have at least served to open the door, which Charcot had inconsistently held closed, into the deeper mysteries of hysteria, and have shown that here, if anywhere, further research will be profitable. They have also served to show that hysteria may be definitely regarded as, in very many cases at least, a manifestation of the sexual emotions and their lesions; in other words, a transformation of auto-erotism.

The conception of hysteria so vigorously enforced by Charcot and his school is thus now beginning to appear incomplete. But we have to recognize that that incompleteness was right and necessary. A strong reaction was needed against a widespread view of hysteria that was in large measure scientifically false. It was necessary to show clearly that hysteria is a definite disorder, even when the sexual organs and emotions are swept wholly out of consideration; and it was also necessary to show that the lying and dissimulation so widely attributed to the hysterical

---

1 As Moll remarks, Freud's conceptions are still somewhat subjective, and in need of objective demonstration; but whatever may be thought of their theories, he adds, there can be no doubt that Breuer and Freud have done a great service by calling attention to the important action of the sexual life on the nervous system.

were merely the result of an ignorant and unscientific misinterpretation of psychic elements of the disease. This was finally and triumphantly achieved by Charcot's school.

There is only one other point in the explanation of hysteria which I will here refer to, and that because it is usually ignored, and because it has relationship to the general psychology of the sexual emotions. I refer to that physiological hysteria which is the normal counterpart of the pathological hysteria which has been described in its physical details by Charcot, and to which alone the term should strictly be applied. Even though hysteria as a disease may be described as one and indivisible, there are yet to be found, among the ordinary and fairly healthy population, vague and diffused hysteroid symptoms which are dissipated in a healthy environment, or pass nearly unnoted, only to develop in a small proportion of cases, under the influence of a more pronounced heredity, or a severe physical or psychic lesion, into that definite morbid state which is properly called hysteria.

This diffused hysteroid condition may be illustrated by the results of a psychological investigation carried on in America by Miss Gertrude Stein among the ordinary male and female students of Harvard University and Radcliffe College. The object of the investigation was to study, with the aid of a planchette, the varying liability to automatic movements among normal individuals. Nearly one hundred students were submitted to experiment. It was found that automatic responses could be obtained in two sittings from all but a small proportion of the students of both sexes, but that there were two types of individual who showed a special aptitude. One type (probably showing the embryonic form of neurasthenia) was a nervous, high-strung, imaginative type, not easily influenced from without, and not so much suggestible as autosuggestible. The other type, which is significant from our present point of view, is thus described by Miss Stein: "In general the individuals, often blonde and pale, are distinctly phlegmatic. If emotional, decidedly of the weakest, sentimental order. They may be either large, healthy, rather heavy, and lacking in vigor or they may be what we call anæmic and phlegmatic. Their power of concen-

trated attention is very small. They describe themselves as
never being held by their work; they say that their minds
wander easily; that they work on after they are tired, and just
keep pegging away. They are very apt to have premonitory conversations, they anticipate the words of their friends, they imagine whole conversations that afterward come true. The feeling of having been there is very common with them; that is,
they feel under given circumstances that they have had that
identical experience before in all its details. They are often
fatalistic in their ideas. They indulge in day-dreams. As a
rule, they are highly suggestible."[1]

There we have a picture of the physical constitution and
psychic temperament on which the classical symptoms of hysteria might easily be built up.[2] But these persons were ordinary
students, and while a few of their characteristics are what is commonly and vaguely called "morbid," on the whole they must be
regarded as ordinarily healthy individuals. They have the congenital constitution and predisposition on which some severe
psychic lesion at the "psychological moment" might develop the
most definite and obstinate symptoms of hysteria, but under
favorable circumstances they will be ordinary men and women,
of no more than ordinary abnormality or ordinary power. They
are among the many who have been called to hysteria at birth;
they may never be among the few who are chosen.

We may have to recognize that on the side of the sexual
emotions, as well as in general constitution, a condition may be
traced among normal persons that is hysteroid in character, and
serves as the healthy counterpart of a condition which in hys-

---

1 Gertrude Stein, "Cultivated Motor Automatism," *Psychological
Review*, May, 1898.

2 Charcot's most faithful followers refuse to recognize a "hysteric
temperament," and are quite right, if such a conception is used to de-
stroy the conception of hysteria as a definite disease. We cannot, however, fail to recognize a diathesis which, while still apparently healthy,
is predisposed to hysteria. So distinguished a disciple of Charcot as
Janet thoroughly recognizes this, and argues (*L'Etat mental*, etc., p.
298) that "we may find in the habits, the passions, the psychic
automatism of the normal man, the germ of all hysterical phenomena."
Féré held a somewhat similar view.

teria is morbid. In women such a condition has been traced (though misnamed) by Dr. King.[1]

Dr. King describes what he calls "sexual hysteria in women," which he considers a chief variety of hysteria. He adds, however, that it is not strictly a disease, but simply an automatic reaction of the reproductive system, which tends to become abnormal under conditions of civilization, and to be perpetuated in a morbid form. In this condition he finds twelve characters: 1. Time of life, usually between puberty and climacteric. 2. Attacks rarely occur when subject is alone. 3. Subject appears unconscious, but is not really so. 4. She is instinctively ashamed afterward. 5. It occurs usually in single women, or in those, single or married, whose sexual needs are unsatisfied. 6. No external evidence of disease, and (as Aitken pointed out) the nates are not flattened; the woman's physical condition is not impaired, and she may be specially attractive to men. 7. Warmth of climate and the season of spring and summer are conducive to the condition. 8. The paroxysm is short and temporary. 9. While light touches are painful, firm pressure and rough handling give relief. 10. It may occur in the occupied, but an idle, purposeless life is conducive. 11. The subject delights in exciting sympathy and in being fondled and caressed. 12. There is defect of will and a strong stimulus is required to lead to action.

Among civilized women, the author proceeds, this condition does not appear to subserve any useful purpose. "Let us, however, go back to aboriginal woman—to woman of the woods and the fields. Let us picture ourselves a young aboriginal Venus in one of her earliest hysterical paroxysms. In doing so, let us not forget some of the twelve characteristics previously mentioned. She will not be 'acting her part' alone, or, if alone, it will be in a place where someone else is likely soon to discover her. Let this Venus be now discovered by a youthful Apollo of the woods, a man with fully developed animal instincts. He and she, like any other animals, are in the free field of Nature. He cannot but observe to himself: 'This woman is not dead; she breathes and is warm; she does not look ill; she is plump and rosy.' He speaks to her; she neither hears (apparently) nor responds. Her eyes are closed. He touches, moves, and handles her at his pleasure. She makes no resistance. What will this primitive Apollo do next? He will cure the fit, and bring the woman back to consciousness, satisfy her emotions, and restore her volition—not by delicate touches that might be 'agonizing' to her hyperesthetic skin, but by vigorous massage, passive motions, and succussion that would be painless. The emotional process on the

---

[1] A. F. A. King, "Hysteria," *American Journal of Obstetrics*, May 18, 1891.

part of the woman would end, perhaps, with mingled laughter, tears, and shame; and when accused afterward of the part which the ancestrally acquired properties of her nervous system had compelled her to act, as a preliminary to the event, what woman would not deny it and be angry? But the course of Nature having been followed, the natural purpose of the hysterical paroxysm accomplished, there would remain as a result of the treatment—instead of one discontented woman—two happy people, and the possible beginning of a third."

"Natural, primary sexual hysteria in woman," King concludes, "is a temporary modification of the nervous government of the body and the distribution of nerve-force (occurring for the most part, as we see it to-day, in prudish women of strong moral principle, whose volition has disposed them to resist every sort of liberty or approach from the other sex), consisting in a transient abdication of the general, volitional, and self-preservational ego, while the reins of government are temporarily assigned to the usurping power of the reproductive ego, so that the reproductive government overrules the government by volition, and thus, as it were, forcibly compels the woman's organism to so dispose itself, at a suitable time and place, as to allow, invite, and secure the approach of the other sex, whether she will or not, to the end that Nature's imperious demand for reproduction shall be obeyed."

This perhaps rather fantastic description is not a presentation of hysteria in the technical sense, but we may admit that it presents a state which, if not the real physiological counterpart of the hysterical convulsion, is yet distinctly analogous to the latter. The sexual orgasm has this correspondence with the hysterical fit, that they both serve to discharge the nervous centres and relieve emotional tension. It may even happen, especially in the less severe forms of hysteria, that the sexual orgasm takes place during the hysterical fit; this was found by Rosenthal, of Vienna, to be always the case in the semiconscious paroxysms of a young girl whose condition was easily cured;[1] no doubt such cases would be more frequently found if they were sought for. In severe forms of hysteria, however, it frequently happens, as so many observers have noted, that normal sexual excitement has

---

[1] M. Rosenthal, *Diseases of the Nervous System*, vol. ii, p. 44. Féré notes similar cases (*Twentieth Century Practice of Medicine*, vol. x, p. 551). Long previously, Gall had recorded the case of a young widow of ardent temperament who had convulsive attacks, apparently of hysterical nature, which always terminated in sexual orgasm (*Fonctions du Cerveau*, 1825, vol. iii, p. 245).

ceased to give satisfaction, has become painful, perverted, paradoxical. Freud has enabled us to see how a shock to the sexual emotions, injuring the emotional life at its source, can scarcely fail sometimes to produce such a result. But the necessity for nervous explosion still persists.[1] It may, indeed, persist, even in an abnormally strong degree, in consequence of the inhibition of normal activities generally. The convulsive fit is the only form of relief open to the tension. "A lady whom I long attended," remarks Ashwell, "always rejoiced when the fit was over, since it relieved her system generally, and especially her brain, from painful irritation which had existed for several previous days." That the fit mostly fails to give real satisfaction, and that it fails to cure the disease, is due to the fact that it is a morbid form of relief. The same character of hysteria is seen, with more satisfactory results for the most part, in the influence of external nervous shock. It was the misunderstood influence of such shocks in removing hysteria which in former times led to the refusal to regard hysteria as a serious disease. During the Rebellion of 1745-46 in Scotland, Cullen remarks that there was little hysteria. The same was true of the French Revolution and of the Irish Rebellion, while Rush (in a study *On the Influence of the American Revolution on the Human Body*) observed that many hysterical women were "restored to perfect health by the events of the time." In such cases the emotional tension is given an opportunity of explosion in new and impersonal channels, and the chain of morbid personal emotions is broken.

It has been urged by some that the fact that the sexual orgasm usually fails to remove the disorder in true hysteria excludes a sexual factor of hysteria. It is really, one may point out, an argument in favor of such an element as one of the factors of hysteria. If there were no initial lesion of the sexual emotions, if the natural healthy sexual channel still remained free for the passage of the emotional overflow, then we should expect that it

---

[1] There seems to be a greater necessity for such explosive manifestations in women than in men, whatever the reason may be. I have brought together some of the evidence pointing in this direction in *Man and Woman*, 4th ed., revised and enlarged, Chapters xii and xiii.

would much oftener come into play in the removal of hysteria.
In the more healthy, merely hysteroid condition, the psychic
sexual organism is not injured, and still responds normally, removing the abnormal symptoms when allowed to do so.   It is the
confusion between this almost natural condition and the truly
morbid condition, alone properly called hysteria, which led to
the ancient opinion, inaugurated by Plato and Hippocrates, that
hysteria may be cured by marriage.[1]   The difference may be illustrated by the difference between a distended bladder which is
still able to contract normally on its contents when at last an
opportunity of doing so is afforded and the bladder in which distension has been so prolonged that nervous control had been lost
and spontaneous expulsion has become impossible.   The first condition corresponds to the constitution, which, while simulating
the hysterical condition, is healthy enough to react normally in
spite of psychic lesions; the second corresponds to a state in
which, owing to the prolonged stress of psychic traumatism,—
sexual or not,—a definite condition of hysteria has arisen.   The
one state is healthy, though abnormal; the other is one of pronounced morbidity.

The condition of true hysteria is thus linked on to almost
healthy states, and especially to a condition which may be
described as one of sex-hunger.   Such a suggestion may help us

---

[1] There is no doubt an element of real truth in this ancient belief,
though it mainly holds good of minor cases of hysteria.   Many excellent authorities accept it.   "Hysteria is certainly common in the single,"
Herman remarks (*Diseases of Women*, 1898, p. 33), "and is generally
cured by a happy marriage."   Löwenfeld (*Sexualleben und Nervenleiden*,
p. 153) says that "it cannot be denied that marriage produces a beneficial change in the general condition of many hysterical patients,"
though, he adds, it will not remove the hysterical temperament.   The
advantage of marriage for the hysterical is not necessarily due, solely
or at all, to the exercise of sexual functions.   This is pointed out by
Mongeri, who observes (*Allgemeine Zeitschrift für Psychiatrie*, 1901,
Heft 5, p. 917):   "I have known and treated several hysterical girls
who are now married, and do not show the least neuropathic indications.
Some of these no longer have any wish for sexual gratification, and even ful-
fil their marital duties unwillingly, though loving their husbands and living with them in an extremely happy way.   In my opinion, marriage
is a sovereign remedy for neuropathic women, who need to find a support
in another personality, able to share with them the battle of life."

to see these puzzling phenomena in their true nature and perspective.

At this point I may refer to the interesting parallel, and probable real relationship, between hysteria and chlorosis. As Luzet has said, hysteria and chlorosis are sisters. We have seen that there is some ground for regarding hysteria as an exaggerated form of a normal process which is really an auto-erotic phenomenon. There is some ground, also, for regarding chlorosis as the exaggeration of a physiological state connected with sexual conditions, more specifically with the preparation for maternity. Hysteria is so frequently associated with anæmic conditions that Biernacki has argued that such conditions really constitute the primary and fundamental cause of hysteria (*Neurologisches Centralblatt*, March, 1898). And, centuries before Biernacki, Sydenham had stated his belief that poverty of the blood is the chief cause of hysteria.

It would be some confirmation of this position if we could believe that chlorosis, like hysteria, is in some degree a congenital condition. This was the view of Virchow, who regarded chlorosis as essentially dependent on a congenital hyoplasia of the arterial system. Stieda, on the basis of an elaborate study of twenty-three cases, has endeavored to prove that chlorosis is due to a congenital defect of development *Zeitschrift für Geburtshülfe und Gynäkologie,* vol. xxxii, Part I, 1895). His facts tend to prove that in chlorosis there are signs of general ill-development, and that, in particular, there is imperfect development of the breasts and sexual organs, with a tendency to contracted pelvis. Charrin, again, regards utero-ovarian inadequacy as at least one of the factors of chlorosis. Chlorosis, in its extreme form, may thus be regarded as a disorder of development, a sign of physical degeneracy. Even if not strictly a cause, a congenital condition may, as Stockman believes (*British Medical Journal*, December 14, 1895), be a predisposing influence.

However it may be in extreme cases, there is very considerable evidence to indicate that the ordinary anæmia of young women may be due to a storing up of iron in the system, and is so far normal, being a preparation for the function of reproduction. Some observations of Bunge's seem to throw much light on the real cause of what may be termed physiological chlorosis. He found by a series of experiments on animals of different ages that young animals contain a much greater amount of iron in their tissues than adult animals; that, for instance, the body of a rabbit an hour after birth contains more than four times as much iron as that of a rabbit two and a half months old. It thus appears probable that at the period of puberty, and later, there is a storage of iron in the system preparatory to the exercise of the maternal runctions. It is precisely between the ages of fifteen and twenty-three, as Stockman found by an analysis of his own cases (*British Medical Journal*, December 14, 1895), that the majority of cases occur; there was, indeed, he found, no case in which the first onset was later than the age of twenty-three. A similar result is revealed by the charts of Lloyd Jones, which cover a vastly greater number of cases.

We owe to Lloyd Jones an important contribution to the knowledge of chlorosis in its physiological or normal relationships. He has shown that chlorosis is but the exaggeration of a condition that is normal at puberty (and, in many women, at each menstrual period), and which, there is good reason to believe, even has a favorable influence on fertility. He found that light-complexioned persons are more fertile than the dark-complexioned, and that at the same time the blood of the latter is of less specific gravity, containing less hæmoglobin. Lloyd Jones also reached the generalization that girls who have had chlorosis are often remarkably pretty, so that the tendency to chlorosis is associated with all the sexual and reproductive aptitudes that make a woman attractive to a man. His conclusion is that the normal condition of which chlorosis is the extreme and pathological condition. is a preparation for motherhood (E. Lloyd Jones, "Chlorosis: The Special Anæmia of Young Women," 1897; also numerous reports to the British Medical Association, published in the *British Medical Journal*. There was an interesting discussion of the theories of chlorosis at the Moscow International Medical Congress, in 1898; see proceedings of the congress, volume iii, section v, pp. 224 *et seq.*).

We may thus, perhaps, understand why it is that hysteria and anæmia are often combined, and why they are both most frequently found in adolescent young women who have yet had no sexual experiences. Chlorosis is a physical phenomenon; hysteria, largely a psychic phenomenon; yet, both alike may, to some extent at least, be regarded as sexual aptitude showing itself in extreme and pathological forms.

III.

The Prevalence of Masturbation—Its Occurrence in Infancy and Childhood—Is it More Frequent in Males or Females?—After Adolescence Apparently more Frequent in Women—Reasons for the Sexual Distribution of Masturbation—The Alleged Evils of Masturbation—Historical Sketch of the Views Held on This Point—The Symptoms and Results of Masturbation—Its Alleged Influence in Causing Eye Disorders—Its Relation to Insanity and Nervous Disorders—The Evil Effects of Masturbation Usually Occur on the Basis of a Congenitally Morbid Nervous System—Neurasthenia Probably the Commonest Accompaniment of Excessive Masturbation—Precocious Masturbation Tends to Produce Aversion to Coitus—Psychic Results of Habitual Masturbation—Masturbation in Men of Genius—Masturbation as a Nervous Sedative—Typical Cases—The Greek Attitude toward Masturbation—Attitude of the Catholic Theologians—The Mohammedan Attitude—The Modern Scientific Attitude—In What Sense is Masturbation Normal?—The Immense Part in Life Played by Transmuted Auto-erotic Phenomena.

THE foregoing sketch will serve to show how vast is the field of life—of normal and not merely abnormal life—more or less infused by auto-erotic phenomena. If, however, we proceed to investigate precisely the exact extent, degree, and significance of such phenomena, we are met by many difficulties. We find, indeed, that no attempts have been made to study auto-erotic phenomena, except as regards the group—a somewhat artificial group, as I have already tried to show—collected under the term "masturbation," while even here such attempts have only been made among abnormal classes of people, or have been conducted in a manner scarcely likely to yield reliable results.[1] Still there is a certain significance in the more careful investigations which have been made to ascertain the precise frequency of masturbation.

Berger, an experienced specialist in nervous diseases, concluded, in his *Vorlesungen,* that 99 per cent. of young men and

---

[1] For a bibliography of masturbation, see Rohleder, *Die Masturbation,* pp. 11-18; also, Arthur MacDonald, *Le Criminel Type,* pp. 227 *et seq.; cf.* G. Stanley Hall, *Adolescence,* vol. i, pp. 432 *et seq.*

women masturbate occasionally, while the hundredth conceals
the truth;[1] and Hermann Cohn appears to accept this statement
as generally true in Germany. So high an estimate has, of
course, been called in question, and, since it appears to rest on no
basis of careful investigation, we need not seriously consider it.
It is useless to argue on suppositions; we must cling to our
definite evidence, even though it yields figures which are probably
below the mark. Rohleder considers that during adolescence at
least 95 per cent. of both sexes masturbate, but his figures are
not founded on precise investigation.[2] Julian Marcuse, on the
basis of his own statistics, concludes that 92 per cent. male
individuals have to some extent masturbated in youth. Perhaps,
also, weight attaches to the opinion of Dukes, physician to Rugby
School, who states that from 90 to 95 per cent. of all boys at
boarding school masturbate.[3] Seerley, of Springfield, Mass.,
found that of 125 academic students only 8 assured him they had
never masturbated; while of 347, who answered his questions, 71
denied that they practiced masturbation, which seems to imply
that 79 per cent. admitted that they practiced it.[4] Brockman,
also in America, among 232 theological students, of the average
age of 23½ years and coming from various parts of the United
States, found that 132 spontaneously admitted that masturbation
was their most serious temptation and all but one of these
admitted that he yielded, 69 of them to a considerable extent.
This is a proportion of at least 56 per cent., the real proportion
being doubtless larger, since no question had been asked as to
sexual offenses; 75 practiced masturbation after conversion, and
24 after they had decided to become ministers; only 66 mentioned sexual intercourse as their chief temptation; but altogether
sexual temptations outnumbered all others together.[5] Moraglia,
who made inquiry of 200 women of the lower class in Italy,

[1] Oskar Berger, *Archiv für Psychiatrie*, Bd. 6, 1876.

[2] *Die Masturbation*, p. 41.

[3] Dukes, *Preservation of Health*, 1884, p. 150.

[4] G. Stanley Hall, *Adolescence*, vol. i, p. 434.

[5] F. S. Broekman, "A Study of the Moral and Religious Life of
Students in the United States," *Pedagogical Seminary*, September, 1902.
Many pitiful narratives are reproduced.

found that 120 acknowledged either that they still masturbate or that they had done so during a long period.[1] Gualino found that 23 per cent. men of the professional classes in North Italy masturbate about puberty; no account was taken of those who began later. "Here in Switzerland," a correspondent writes, "I have had occasion to learn from adult men, whom I can trust, that they have reached the age of twenty-five, or over, without sexual congress. 'Wir haben nicht dieses Bedürfniss,' is what they say. But I believe that, in the case of the Swiss mountaineers, moderate onanism is practiced, as a rule." In hot countries the same habits are found at a more precocious age. In Venezuela, for instance, among the Spanish creoles, Ernst found that in all classes boys and girls are infested with the vice of onanism. They learn it early, in the very beginning of life, from their wet-nurses, generally low Mulatto women, and many reasons help to foster the habit; the young men are often dissipated and the young women often remain single.[2] Niceforo, who shows a special knowledge of the working-girl class at Rome, states that in many milliners' and dressmakers' workrooms, where young girls are employed, it frequently happens that during the hottest hours of the day, between twelve and two, when the mistress or forewoman is asleep, all the girls without exception give themselves up to masturbation.[3] In France a country cure assured Debreyne that among the little girls who come up for their first communion, 11 out of 12 were given to masturbation.[4] The medical officer of a Prussian reformatory told Rohleder that nearly all the inmates over the age of puberty masturbated. Stanley Hall knew a reform school in America where masturbation was practiced without exception, and he who could

---

[1] Moraglia, "Die Onanie beim normalen Weibe und bei den Prostituten," Zeitschrift für Criminal-Anthropologie, 1897, p. 489. It should be added that Moraglia is not a very critical investigator. It is probable, however, that on this point his results are an approximation to the truth.

[2] Ernst, "Anthropological Researches on the Population of Venezuela, Memoirs of the Anthropological Society, vol. iii, 1870, p. 277.

[3] Niceforo, Il Gergo nei Normali, etc., 1897, cap. V.

[4] Debreyne, Mœchialogie, p. 64. Yet theologians and casuists, Debreyne remarks, frequently never refer to masturbation in women.

practice it oftenest was regarded with hero-worship.[1] Ferriani,
who has made an elaborate study of youthful criminality in Italy,
states that even if all boys and girls among the general population do not masturbate, it is certainly so among those who have
a tendency to crime. Among 458 adult male criminals, Marro
(as he states in his *Caratteri dei Delinquenti*) found that only
72 denied masturbation, while 386 had practiced it from an early
age, 140 of them before the age of thirteen. Among 30 criminal
women Moraglia found that 24 acknowledged the practice, at all
events in early youth (8 of them before the age of 10, a precocity
accompanied by average precocity in menstruation), while he sus-
pected that most of the remainder were not unfamiliar with the
practice. Among prostitutes of whatever class or position Moraglia found masturbation (though it must be pointed out that he
does not appear to distinguish masturbation very clearly from
homosexual practices) to be universal; in one group of 50 prostitutes everyone had practiced masturbation at some period; 28
began between the ages of 6 and 11; 19, between 12 and 14, the
most usual period—a precocious one—of commencing puberty;
the remaining 3 at 15 and 16; the average age of commencing
masturbation, it may be added, was 11, while that of the first
sexual intercourse was 15.[2] In a larger group of 180 prostitutes,
belonging to Genoa, Turin, Venice, etc., and among 23 "elegant
cocottes," of Italian and foreign origin, Moraglia obtained the
same results; everyone admitted masturbation, and not less than
113 preferred masturbation, either solitary or mutual, to normal
coitus. Among the insane, as among idiots, masturbation is
somewhat more common among males, according to Blandford,
in England, as also it is in Germany, according to Näcke,[3] while
Venturi, in Italy, has found it more common among females.[4]

There appears to be no limit to the age at which spontaneous
masturbation may begin to appear. I have already referred to

---

[1] Stanley Hall, *op. cit.*, vol. i, p. 34. Hall mentions, also, that
masturbation is specially common among the blind.

[2] Moraglia, *Archivio di Psichiatria*, vol. xvi, fasc. 4 and 5, p. 313.

[3] See his careful study, "Die Sexuellen Perversitäten in der Irrenanstalt," *Psychiatrische Bladen*, No. 2, 1899.

[4] Venturi, *Degenerazioni Psico-sessuali*, pp. 105, 133, 148, 152.

the practice of thigh-rubbing in infants under one year of age. J. P. West has reported in detail 3 cases of masturbation in very early childhood—2 in girls, 1 in a boy—in which the practice had been acquired spontaneously, and could only be traced to some source of irritation in pressure from clothing, etc.[1] Probably there is often in such cases some hereditary lack of nervous stability. Block has recorded the case of a girl—very bright for her age, though excessively shy and taciturn—who began masturbating spontaneously at the age of two; in this case the mother had masturbated all her life, even continuing the practice after marriage, and, though she succeeded in refraining during pregnancy, her thoughts still dwelt upon it, while the maternal grandmother had died in an asylum from "masturbatory insanity."

Freud considers that auto-erotic manifestations are common in infancy, and that the rhythmic function of any sensitive spot, primarily the lips, may easily pass into masturbation. He regards the infantile manifestations of which thumb-sucking is the most familiar example (Lüdeln or Lutschen in German) as auto-erotic, the germ arising in sucking the breasts since the lips are an erogenous zone which may easily be excited by the warm stream of milk. But this only occurs, he points out, in subjects in whom the sensitivity of the lip zone is heightened and especially in those who at a later age are liable to become hysterical.[2] Shuttleworth also points out that the mere fidgetiness of a neurotic infant, even when only a few months old, sometimes leads to the spontaneous and accidental discovery of pleasurable sexual sensations, which for a time appease the restlessness of nervous instability, though a vicious circle is thus established. He has found that, especially among quite young girls of neurotic heredity, self-induced excitement, often in the form of thigh-friction, is more common than is usually supposed.[3]

Normally there appears to be a varying aptitude to experi-

---

[1] J. P. West, *Transactions of the Ohio Pediatric Society*, 1895, *Abstract in Medical Standard*, November, 1895; cases are also recorded by J. T. Winter, "Self-abuse in Infancy and Childhood," *American Journal Obstetrics*, June, 1902.

[2] Freud, *Abhandlungen zur Sexualtheorie*, pp. 36 *et seq.*

[3] G. E. Shuttleworth, *British Medical Journal*, October 3, 1903.

ence the sexual organism, or any voluptuous sensations before puberty. I find, on eliciting the recollections of normal persons, that in some cases there have been voluptuous sensations from casual contact with the sexual organs at a very early age; in other cases there has been occasional slight excitement from early years; in yet other cases complete sexual anæsthesia until the age of puberty. That the latter condition is not due to mere absence of peripheral irritation is shown by a case I am acquainted with, in which a boy of 7, incited by a companion, innocently attempted, at intervals during several weeks, to produce erection by friction of the penis; no result of any kind followed, although erections occurred spontaneously at puberty, with normal sexual feelings.[1]

I am indebted to a correspondent for the following notes:—

"From my observation during five years at a boarding-school, it *seems* that eight out of ten boys were more or less addicted to the practice. But I would not state *positively* that such was the proportion of masturbators among an average of thirty pupils, though the habit was very common. I know that in one bedroom, sleeping seven boys, the whole number masturbated frequently. The act was performed in bed, in the closets, and sometimes in the classrooms during lessons. Inquiry among my friends as to onanism in the boarding-schools to which they were sent, elicited somewhat contradictory answers concerning the frequency of the habit. Dr. —— who went to a French school, told me that *all* the older boys had younger accomplices in mutual masturbation. He also spoke with experience of the prevalence of the practice in a well-known public school in the west of England. B. said *all* the boys at his school masturbated; G. stated that *most* of his schoolmates were onanists; L. said 'more than half' was the proportion.

"At my school, manual masturbation was both solitary and mutual; and sometimes younger boys, who had not acquired the habit, were induced to manipulate bigger boys. One very precocious boy of fifteen always chose a companion of ten 'because his hand was like a woman's.' Sometimes boys entered their friend's bed for mutual excitement. In after-life they showed no signs of inversion. Another boy, aged about fourteen, who had been seduced by a servant-girl, embraced the bolster; the pleasurable sensations, according to his statement, were heightened by imagining that the bolster was a woman. He said that the enjoyment

---

[1] See for a detailed study of sexuality in childhood, Moll's valuable book, *Das Sexualleben des Kindes; cf.* vol. vi of these *Studies*, Ch. II.

of the act was greatly increased during the holidays, when he was able to spread a pair of his sister's drawers upon the pillow, and so intensify the illusion.

"Before puberty the boys appeared to be more continent than afterward. A few of the older and more intelligent masturbators regulated the habit, as some married men regulate intercourse. The big boy referred to, who chose always the same manipulator, professed to indulge only once in twenty days, his reason being that more frequent repetition of the act would injure his health. About twice a week for boys who had reached puberty, and once a week for younger boys, was, I think, about the average indulgence. I have never met with a parallel of one of those cases of excessive masturbation recorded by many doctors. There may have been such cases at this school; but, if so, the boys concealed the frequency of their gratifications.

"My experience proved that many of the lads regarded masturbation as reprehensible; but their plea was 'everyone does it.' Some, often those who indulged inordinately and more secretly than their companions, gravely condemned the practice as sinful. A few seemed to think there was 'no harm in it,' but that the habit might stunt the growth and weaken the body if practiced very frequently. The greater number made no attempt to conceal the habit, they enlarged upon the pleasure of it: it was 'ever so much nicer than eating tarts,' etc.

"The chief cause I believe to be initiation by an older schoolmate. But I have known accidental causes, such as the discovery that swarming up a pole pleasurably excited the organ, rubbing to allay irritation, and simple, curious handling of the erect penis in the early morning before rising from bed."

I quote the foregoing communication as perhaps a fairly typical experience in a British school, though I am myself inclined to think that the prevalence of masturbation in schools is often much overrated, for, while in some schools the practice is doubtless rampant, in others it is practically unknown, or, at all events, only practiced by a few individuals in secret. My own early recollections of (private) school-life fail to yield any reminiscences of any kind connected with either masturbation or homosexuality; and, while such happy ignorance may be the exception rather than the rule, I am certainly inclined to believe that—owing to race and climate, and healthier conditions of life—the sexual impulse is less precocious and less prominently developed during the school-age in England than in some Continental countries. It is probably to this delayed development that we should attribute the contrast that Ferrero finds (*L'Europa Giovane*, pp. 151-56), and certainly states too absolutely, between the sexual reserve of young Englishmen and the sexual immodesty of his own countrymen.

In Germany, Näcke has also stated ("Kritisches zum Kapitel der

16

Sexualität," *Archiv für Psychiatrie*, pp. 354-56, 1899) that he heard nothing at school either of masturbation or homosexuality, and he records the experience of medical friends who stated that such phenomena were only rare exceptions, and regarded by the majority of the boys as exhibitions of "*Schweinerei.*" At other German schools, as Hoche has shown, sexual practices are very prevalent. It is evident that at different schools, and even at the same school at different times, these manifestations vary in frequency within wide limits.

Such variations, it seems to me, are due to two causes. In the first place, they largely depend upon the character of the more influential elder boys. In the second place, they depend upon the attitude of the head-master. With reference to this point I may quote from a letter written by an experienced master in one of the most famous English public schools: "When I first came to ——, a quarter of a century ago, Dr. —— was making a crusade against this failing; boys were sent away wholesale; the school was summoned and lectured solemnly; and the more the severities, the more rampant the disease. I thought to myself that the remedy was creating the malady, and I heard afterward, from an old boy, that in those days they used to talk things over by the fireside, and think there must be something very choice in a sin that braved so much. Dr. —— went, and, under ——, we never spoke of such things. Curiosity died down, and the thing itself, I believe, was lessened. We were told to warn new boys of the dangers to health and morals of such offences, lest the innocent should be caught in ignorance. I have only spoken to a few; I think the great thing is not to put it in boys' heads. I have noticed solitary faults most commonly, and then I tell the boy how he is physically weakening himself. If you notice, it is puppies that seem to go against Nature, but grown dogs, never. So, if two small boys acted thus, I should think it merely an instinctive feeling after Nature, which would amend itself. Many here would consider it a heinous sin, but those who think such things sins make them sins. I have seen, in the old days, most delightful little children sent away, branded with infamy, and scarce knowing why—you might as well expel a boy for scratching his head when it itched. I am sure the soundest way is to treat it as a doctor would, and explain to the boy the physical effects of over-indulgence of any sort. When it is combated from the monkish standpoint, the evil becomes an epidemic." I am, however, far from anxious to indorse the policy of ignoring the sexual phenomena of youth. It is not the speaking about such things that should be called in question, but the wisdom and good sense of the speaker. We ought to expect a head-master to possess both an adequate acquaintance with the nature of the phenomena of auto-erotism and homosexuality, and a reasonable amount of tact in dealing with boys; he may then fairly be trusted to exercise his own judgment.

It may be doubted whether boys should be made too alive to the existence of sexual phenomena; there can be no doubt about their teachers. The same is, of course, true as regards girls, among whom the same phenomena, though less obtrusive, are not less liable to occur.

As to whether masturbation is more common in one sex than the other, there have been considerable differences of opinion. Tissot considered it more prevalent among women; Christian believed it commoner among men; Deslandes and Iwan Bloch hold that there are no sexual differences, and Garnier was doubtful. Lawson Tait, in his *Diseases of Women,* stated his opinion that in England, while very common among boys, it is relatively rare among women, and then usually taught. Spitzka, in America, also found it relatively rare among women, and Dana considers it commoner in boys than in girls or adults.[1] Moll is inclined to think that masturbation is less common in women and girls than in the male sex. Rohleder believes that after puberty, when it is equally common in both sexes, it is more frequently found in men, but that women masturbate with more passion and imaginative fervor.[2] Kellogg, in America, says it is equally prevalent in both sexes, but that women are more secretive. Morris, also in America, considers, on the other hand, that persistent masturbation is commoner in women, and accounts for this by the healthier life and traditions of boys. Pouillet, who studied the matter with considerable thoroughness in France, came to the conclusion that masturbation is commoner among

[1] This is, no doubt, the most common opinion, and it is frequently repeated in text-books. It is scarcely necessary, however, to point out that only the opinions of those who have given special attention to the matter can carry any weight. R. W. Shufeldt ("On a Case of Female Impotency," pp. 5-7) quotes the opinions of various cautious observers as to the difficulty of detecting masturbation in women.

[2] This latter opinion is confirmed by Näcke so far as the insane are concerned. In a careful study of sexual perversity in a large asylum, Näcke found that, while moderate masturbation could be more easily traced among men than among women, excessive masturbation was more common among women. And, while among the men masturbation was most frequent in the lowest grades of mental development (idiocy and imbecility), and least frequent in the highest grades (general paralysis), in the women it was the reverse. (P. Näcke, "Die Sexuellen Perversitäten in der Irrenanstalt," *Psychiatrische en Neurologische Bladen,* No. 2, 1899.)

women, among whom he found it to be equally prevalent in
rich and poor, and especially so in the great centres of civilization.
In Russia, Guttceit states in his *Dreissig Jahre Praxis*, that
from the ages of 10 to 16 boys masturbate more than girls, who
know less about the practice which has not for them the charm
of the forbidden, but after 16 he finds the practice more frequent
in girls and women than in youths and men. Näcke, in Germany, believes that there is much evidence pointing in the same
direction, and Adler considers masturbation very common in
women. Moraglia is decidedly of the opinion, on the ground of
his own observations already alluded to, that masturbation is
more frequent among women; he refers to the fact—a very
significant fact, as I shall elsewhere have to point out—that,
while in man there is only one sexual centre, the penis, in woman
there are several centres,—the clitoris, the vagina, the uterus, the
breasts,[1]—and he mentions that he knew a prostitute, a well-
developed brunette of somewhat nervous temperament, who
boasted that she knew fourteen ways of masturbating herself.

My own opinion is that the question of the sexual distribution of masturbation has been somewhat obscured by that harmful tendency, to which I have already alluded, to concentrate
attention on a particular set of auto-erotic phenomena. We must
group and divide our facts rationally if we wish to command
them. If we confine our attention to very young children, the
available evidence shows that the practice is much more common
in females,[2] and such a result is in harmony with the fact that
precocious puberty is most often found in female children.[3] At

---

[1] Mammary masturbation sometimes occurs; see, *e.g.*, Rohleder,
Die Masturbation (pp. 32-33); it is, however, rare.

[2] Hirschsprung pointed out this, indeed, many years ago, on the
ground of his own experience. And see Rohleder, *op. cit.*, pp. 44-47.

[3] In many cases, of course, the physical precocity is associated with
precocity in sexual habits. An instructive case is reported (*Alienist and
Neurologist*, October, 1895) of a girl of 7, a beautiful child, of healthy
family, and very intelligent, who, from the age of three, was perpetually
masturbating, when not watched. The clitoris and mons veneris were
those of a fully-grown woman, and the child was as well informed upon
most subjects as an average woman. She was cured by care and hygienic
attention, and when seen last was in excellent condition. A medical
friend tells me of a little girl of two, whose external genital organs are
greatly developed, and who is always rubbing herself.

puberty and adolescence occasional or frequent masturbation is common in both boys and girls, though, I believe, less common than is sometimes supposed; it is difficult to say whether it is more prevalent among boys or girls; one is inclined to conclude that it prevails more widely among boys. The sexual impulse, and consequently the tendency to masturbation, tend to be aroused later, and less easily in girls than in youths, though it must also be remembered that boys' traditions and their more active life keep the tendency in abeyance, while in girls there is much less frequently any restraining influence of corresponding character.[1] In my study of inversion I have found that ignorance and the same absence of tradition are probably factors in the prevalence of homosexual tendencies among women.[2] After adolescence I think there can be no doubt that masturbation is more common in women than in men. Men have, by this time, mostly adopted some method of sexual gratification with the opposite sex; women are to a much larger extent shut out from such gratification; moreover, while in rare cases women are sexually precocious, it more often happens that their sexual impulses only gain strength and self-consciousness after adolescence has passed. I have been much impressed by the frequency with which masturbation is occasionally (especially about the period of menstruation) practiced by active, intelligent, and

---

[1] R. T. Morris, of New York, has also pointed out the influence of traditions in this respect. "Among boys," he remarks, "there are traditions to the effect that self-abuse is harmful. Among girls, however, there are no such saving traditions." Dr. Kiernan writes in a private letter: "It has been by experience, that from ignorance or otherwise, there are young women who do not look upon sexual manipulation with the same fear that men do." Guttceit, similarly, remarks that men have been warned of masturbation, and fear its evil results, while girls, even if warned, attach little importance to the warning; he adds that in healthy women, masturbation, even in excess, has little bad results. The attitude of many women in this matter may be illustrated by the following passage from a letter written by a medical friend in India: "The other day one of my English women patients gave me the following reason for having taught the 17-year-old daughter of a retired Colonel to masturbate: 'Poor girl, she was troubled with dreams of men, and in case she should be tempted with one, and become pregnant, I taught her to bring the feeling on herself—as it is safer, and, after all, nearly as nice as with a man.'"

[2] H. Ellis, *Studies in the Psychology of Sex*, volume ii, "Sexual Inversion," Chapter IV.

healthy women who otherwise lead a chaste life. This experience is confirmed by others who are in a position to ascertain the facts among normal people; thus a lady, who has received the confidence of many women, told me that she believes that all women who remain unmarried masturbate, as she found so much evidence pointing in this direction.[1] This statement certainly needs some qualification, though I believe it is not far from the truth as regards young and healthy women who, after having normal sexual relationships, have been compelled for some reason or other to break them off and lead a lonely life.[2] But we have to remember that there are some women, evidently with a considerable degree of congenital sexual anæsthesia (no doubt, in some respect or another below the standard of normal health), in whom the sexual instinct has never been aroused, and who not only do not masturbate, but do not show any desire for normal gratification; while in a large proportion of other cases the impulse is gratified passively in ways I have already referred to. The auto-erotic phenomena which take place in this way, spontaneously, by yielding to revery, with little or no active interference, certainly occur much more frequently in women than in men. On the other hand, contrary to what one might be led to expect, the closely-related auto-erotic phenomena during sleep seem to take place more frequently in men, although in women, as we have found ground for concluding, they reverberate much more widely and impressively on the waking psychical life.

We owe to Restif de la Bretonne what is perhaps the earliest precise description of a woman masturbating. In 1755 he knew a dark young woman, plain but well-made, and of warm temperament, educated in a convent. She was observed one day, when gazing from her window at a young man in whom she was tenderly interested, to become much excited. "Her movements became agitated; I approached her, and really believe that she was uttering affectionate expressions; she had become red. Then she sighed deeply, and became motionless,

---

[1] See, also, the Appendix to the third volume of these *Studies*, in which I have brought forward sexual histories of normal persons.

[2] E. H. Smith, also, states that from 25 to 35 is the age when most women come under the physician's eye with manifest and pronounced habits of masturbation.

stretching out her legs, which she stiffened, as if she felt pain." It is further hinted that her hands took part in this manœuvre (*Monsieur Nicolas*, vol. vi, p. 143).

Pictorial representations of a woman masturbating also occur in eighteenth century engravings. Thus, in France, Baudouin's "Le Midi" (reproduced in Fuchs's *Das Erotische Element in der Karikatur*, Fig. 92), represents an elegant young lady in a rococo garden-bower; she has been reading a book she has now just dropped, together with her sunshade; she leans languorously back, and her hand begins to find its way through her placket-hole.

Adler, who has studied masturbation in women with more care than any previous writer, has recorded in detail the auto-erotic manifestations involved in the case of an intelligent and unprejudiced woman, aged 30, who had begun masturbating when twenty, and practiced it at intervals of a few weeks. She experienced the desire for sexual gratification under the following circumstances: (1) spontaneously, directly before or after menstruation; (2) as a method to cure sleeplessness; (3) after washing the parts with warm (but not cold) water; (4) after erotic dreams; (5) quite suddenly, without definite cause. The phenomena of the masturbatory process fell into two stages: (1) incomplete excitement, (2) the highest pleasurable gratification. It only took place in the evening, or at night, and a special position was necessary, with the right knee bent, and the right foot against the knee of the extended left leg. The bent index and middle fingers of the right hand were then applied firmly to the lower third of the left labium minus, which was rubbed against the underlying parts. At this stage, the manifestations sometimes stopped, either from an effort of self-control or from fatigue of the arm. There was no emission of mucus, or general perspiration, but some degree of satisfaction and of fatigue, followed by sleep. If, however, the manipulation was continued, the second stage was reached, and the middle finger sank into the vagina, while the index finger remained on the labium, the rest of the hand holding and compressing the whole of the vulva, from pubes to anus, against the symphysis, with a backwards and forwards movement, the left hand also being frequently used to support and assist the right. The parts now gave a mushroom-like feeling to the touch, and in a few seconds, or after a longer interval, the complete feeling of pleasurable satisfaction was attained. At the same moment there was (but only after she had had experience of coitus) an involuntary elevation of the pelvis, together with emission of mucus, making the hand wet, this mucus having an odor, and being quite distinct from the ordinary odorless mucus of the vagina; at the same time, the finger in the vagina felt slight contractions of the whole vaginal wall. The climax of sexual pleasure lasted a few seconds, with its concomitant vaginal contractions, then slowly subsided with a feeling of general well-being, the finger at the same time slipping out of the vagina, and she was left in a state of general perspiration, and sleep would immediately follow; when this was not the case, she was frequently conscious of some degree of sensibility in the sacrum, lasting for several hours, and especially felt when sitting. When masturbation was the result of an erotic dream (which occurred but seldom), the first stage was already reached in sleep, and the second was more quickly obtained. During the act it was only occasionally that any thoughts of men or of coitus were present, the attention being fixed on the coming climax. The psychic state afterwards was usually one of self-reproach. (O. Adler, *Die Mangelhafte Geschlechtsempfindung des Weibes*, 1904, pp. 26-29.) The phenomena in this case may be regarded as fairly typical, but there are many individual variations; mucus emissions and vaginal contractions frequently occur before actual orgasm, and there is not usually any insertion of the finger into the vagina in women who have never experienced coitus, or, indeed, even in those who have.

We must now turn to that aspect of our subject which in the past has always seemed the only aspect of auto-erotic phenomena meriting attention: the symptoms and results of chronic masturbation. It appears to have been an Englishman who, at the beginning of the eighteenth century, first called popular attention to the supposed evils of masturbation. His book was published in London, and entitled: *Onania, or the Heinous Sin of Self-pollution, and all its Frightful Consequences in both Sexes, Considered, with Spiritual and Physical Advice*, etc. It is not a serious medical treatise, but an early and certainly superior example of a kind of literature which we have since become familiar with through the daily newspapers. A large part of the book, which is cleverly written, is devoted in the later editions to the letters of nervous and hypochondriacal young men and women, who are too shy to visit the author, but request him to send a bottle of his "Strengthening Tincture," and mention that they are inclosing half a guinea, a guinea, or still larger sum. Concerning the composition of the "Strengthening Tincture" we are not informed.[1] This work, which was subsequently attrib-

---

[1] It may, however, be instructive to observe that at the end of the volume we find an advertisement of "Dr. Robinson's Treatise on the Virtues and Efficacy of a Crust of Bread, Eat Early in the Morning Fasting."

uted to a writer named Bekkers, is said to have passed through no less than eighty editions, and it was translated into German. Tissot, a physician of Lausanne, followed with his *Traité de l'Onanisme: Dissertation sur les Maladies produites par la Masturbation,* first published in Latin (1760), then in French (1764), and afterward in nearly all European languages. He regarded masturbation as a crime, and as "an act of suicide." His book is a production of amusing exaggeration and rhetoric, zealously setting forth the prodigious evils of masturbation in a style which combines, as Christian remarks, the strains of Rousseau with a vein of religious piety. Tissot included only manual self-abuse under the term "onanism;" shortly afterward, Voltaire, in his *Dictionnaire Philosophique,* took up the subject, giving it a wider meaning and still further popularizing it. Finally Lallemand, at a somewhat later period (1836), wrote a book which was, indeed, more scientific in character, but which still sought to represent masturbation as the source of all evils. These four writers—the author of *Onania,* Tissot, Voltaire, Lallemand—are certainly responsible for much. The mistaken notions of many medical authorities, carried on by tradition, even down to our own time; the powerful lever which has been put into the hand of unscrupulous quacks; the suffering, dread, and remorse experienced in silence by many thousands of ignorant and often innocent young people may all be traced in large measure back to these four well-meaning, but (on this question) misguided, authors.

There is really no end to the list of real or supposed symptoms and results of masturbation, as given by various medical writers during the last century. Insanity, epilepsy, numerous forms of eye disease, supra-orbital headache, occipital headache (Spitzka), strange sensations at the top of the head (Savage), various forms of neuralgia (Anstie, J. Chapman), tenderness of the skin in the lower dorsal region (Chapman), mammary tenderness in young girls (Lacassagne), mammary hypertrophy (Ossendovsky), asthma (Peyer), cardiac murmurs (Seerley), the appearance of vesicles on wounds (Baraduc), acne and other forms of cutaneous eruptions (the author of *Onania,* Clipson),

dilated pupils (Skene, Lewis, Moraglia), eyes directed upward
and sideways (Pouillet), dark rings around the eyes, intermittent
functional deafness (Bonnier), painful menstruation (J. Chapman), catarrh of uterus and vagina (Winckel, Pouillet), ovarian
disease (Jessett), pale and discolored skin (Lewis, Moraglia),
redness of nose (Gruner), epistaxis (Joal, J. N. Mackenzie),
morbid changes in nose (Fliess), convulsive cough of puberty
(Gowers), acidity of vagina (R. W. Shufeldt), incontinence of
urine in young women (Girandeau), warts on the hands in women
(Durr, Kriechmar, von Oye), hallucinations of smell and hearing,
(Griesinger, Lewis), intermittent functional deafness (Bonnier),
indican in the urine (Herter), an indescribable odor of the skin
in women (Skene), these are but a few of the signs and consequences of masturbation given by various prominent authorities.[1]

That many of these manifestations do occur in connection
with masturbation is unquestionable; there is also good reason
to believe that some of them may be the results of masturbation acting on an imperfectly healthy organism. But in all
such cases we must speak with great caution, for there appears
to be little reliable evidence to show that simple masturbation,
in a well-born and healthy individual, can produce any evil results beyond slight functional disturbances, and these only when
it is practiced in excess. To illustrate the real pathological relationships of masturbation, a few typical and important disorders
may be briefly considered.

The delicate mechanism of the eye is one of the first portions
of the nervous apparatus to be disturbed by any undue strain
on the system; it is not surprising that masturbation should be
widely incriminated as a cause of eye troubles. If, however, we
inquire into the results obtained by the most cautious and experienced ophthalmological observers, it grows evident that masturbation, as a cause of disease of the eye, becomes merged into
wider causes. In Germany, Hermann Cohn, the distinguished
ophthalmic surgeon of Breslau, has dealt fully with the ques-

---

[1] Pouillet alone enumerates and apparently accepts considerably
over one hundred different morbid conditions as signs and results of
masturbation.

tion.[1] Cohn, who believes that all young men and women masturbate to some extent, finds that masturbation must be excessive for eye trouble to become apparent. In most of his cases there was masturbation several times daily during from five to seven years, in many during ten years, and in one during twenty-three years. In such cases we are obviously dealing with abnormal persons, and no one will dispute the possibility of harmful results; in some of the cases, when masturbation was stopped, the eye trouble improved. Even in these cases, however, the troubles were but slight, the chief being, apparently, photopsia (a subjective sensation of light) with otherwise normal conditions of pupil, vision, color-sense, and retina. In some cases there was photophobia, and he has also found paralysis of accommodation and conjunctivitis. At a later date Salmo Cohn, in his comprehensive monograph on the relationship between the eye and the sexual organs in women, brought together numerous cases of eye troubles in young women associated with masturbation, but in most of these cases masturbation had been practiced with great frequency for a long period and the ocular affections were usually not serious.[2] In England, Power has investigated the relations of the sexual system to eye disease. He is inclined to think that the effects of masturbation have been exaggerated, but he believes that it may produce such for the most part trivial complaints as photopsiæ, muscæ, muscular asthenopia, possibly blepharospasm, and perhaps conjunctivitis. He goes on, however, to point out that more serious complaints of the eye are caused by excess in normal coitus, by sexual abstinence, and especially by disordered menstruation. Thus we see that even when we are considering a mechanism so delicately poised and one so easily disturbed by any jar of the system as vision, masturbation produces no effect except when carried to an extent which argues a hereditarily imperfect organism, while even in these cases the effects are usually but slight, moreover, in no respect specific, but

---

1 "Augenkrankheiten bei Masturbanten," Knapp-Schweigger's *Archiv für Augenheilkunde*, Bd. II, 1882, p. 198.

2 Salmo Cohn, *Uterus und Auge*, 1890, pp. 63-66.

are paralleled and even exceeded by the results of other disturbances of the sexual system.

Let us turn to the supposed influence of masturbation in causing insanity and nervous diseases. Here we may chiefly realize the immense influence exerted on medical science by Tissot and his followers during a hundred years. Mental weakness is the cause and not the result of excessive masturbation, Gall declared,[1] but he was a man of genius, in isolation. Sir William Ellis, an alienist of considerable reputation at the beginning of the last century, could write with scientific equanimity: "I have no hesitation in saying that, in a very large number of patients in all public asylums, the disease may be attributed to that cause." He does, indeed, admit that it may be only a symptom sometimes, but goes on to assert that masturbation "has not hitherto been exhibited in the awful light in which it deserves to be shown," and that "in by far the greater number of cases" it is the true cause of dementia.[2] Esquirol lent his name and influence to a similar view of the pernicious influence of masturbation. Throughout the century, even down to the present day, this point of view has been traditionally preserved in a modified form. In apparent ignorance of the enormous prevalence of masturbation, and without, so far as can be seen, any attempt to distinguish between cause and effect or to eliminate the hereditary neuropathic element, many alienists have set down a large proportion of cases of insanity, idiocy, epilepsy, and disease of the spinal cord to uncomplicated masturbation. Thus, at the Mattcawan State Hospital (New York) for criminal lunatics and insane prisoners, from 1875 to 1907, masturbation was the sole assigned cause of insanity in 160 men (out of 2,595); while, according to Dr. Clara Barrus, among 121 cases of insanity in young women, masturbation is the cause in ten cases.[3] It is unnecessary to multiply examples, for this traditional tendency is familiar to all.

---

[1] *Fonctions du Cerveau*, 1825, vol. iii, p. 337.

[2] W. Ellis, *Treatise on Insanity*, 1838, pp. 335, 340.

[3] Clara Barrus, "Insanity in Young Women," *Journal of Nervous and Mental Disease*, June, 1896.

It appears to have been largely due to Griesinger, in the middle of the last century, that we owe the first authoritative appearance of a saner, more discriminating view regarding the results of masturbation. Although still to some extent fettered by the traditions prevalent in his day, Griesinger saw that it was not so much masturbation itself as the feelings aroused in sensitive minds by the social attitude toward masturbation which produced evil effects. "That constant struggle," he wrote, "against a desire which is even overpowering, and to which the individual always in the end succumbs, that hidden strife between shame, repentance, good intentions, and the irritation which impels to the act, this, after not a little acquaintance with onanists, we consider to be far more important than the primary direct physical effect." He added that there are no specific signs of masturbation, and concluded that it is oftener a symptom than a cause. The general progress of educated opinions since that date has, in the main, confirmed and carried forward the results cautiously stated by Griesinger. This distinguished alienist thought that, when practiced in childhood, masturbation might lead to insanity. Berkhan, in his investigation of the psychoses of childhood, found that in no single case was masturbation a cause. Vogel, Uffelmann, and Emminghaus, in the course of similar studies, have all come to almost similar conclusions.[1] It is only on a congenitally morbid nervous system, Emminghaus insists, that masturbation can produce any serious results. "Most of the cases charged to masturbation," writes Kiernan (in a private letter), basing his opinion on wide clinical experience, "are either hebephrenia or hysteria in which an effect is taken for the cause." Christian, during twenty years' experience in hospitals, asylums, and private practice in town and country, has not found any seriously evil effects from masturbation.[2] He thinks, indeed, that it may be a more serious evil in women than in men. But Yellowlees considers that in women

---

[1] See, for instance, H. Emminghaus, "Die Psychosen des Kindesalters," Gerlandt's *Handbuch der Kinder-Krankheiten*, Nachtrag II, pp. 61-63.

[2] Christian, article "Onanisme," *Dictionnaire encyclopédique des sciences médicales*."

"it is possibly less exhausting and injurious than in the other sex," which was also the opinion of Hammond, as well as of Guttceit, though he found that women pushed the practice much further than men, and Näcke, who has given special attention to this point, could not find that masturbation is a definite cause of insanity in women in a single case.[1] Koch also reaches a similar conclusion, as regards both sexes, though he admits that masturbation may cause some degree of psychopathic deterioration. Even in this respect, however, he points out that "when practiced in moderation it is not injurious in the certain and exceptionless way in which it is believed to be in many circles. It is the people whose nervous systems are already injured who masturbate most easily and practice it more immoderately than others"; the chief source of its evil is self-reproach and the struggle with the impulse.[2] Kahlbaum, it is true, under the influence of the older tradition, when he erected katatonia into a separate disorder (not always accepted in later times), regarded prolonged and excessive masturbation as a chief cause, but I am not aware that he ever asserted that it was a sole and sufficient cause in a healthy organism. Kiernan, one of the earliest writers on katatonia, was careful to point out that masturbation was probably as much effect as cause of the morbid nervous condition.[3] Maudsley (in *Body and Mind*) recognized masturbation as a special exciting cause of a characteristic form of insanity; but he cautiously added: "Nevertheless, I think that self-abuse seldom, if ever, produces it without the co-operation of the insane neurosis."[4] Schüle also recognized a specific masturbatory insanity, but the general tendency to reject any such nosological form is becoming marked; Krafft-Ebing long since rejected it and Näcke decidedly opposes it. Kraepelin states that excessive masturbation can only occur in a dangerous degree in predis-

1 Näcke, *Verbrechen und Wahnsinn beim Weibe*, 1894, p. 57.
2 J. L. A. Koch, *Die Psychopathischen Minderwertigkeiten*, 1892, p. 273 *et seq.*
3 J. G. Kiernan, *American Journal of Insanity*, July, 1877.
4 Maudsley dealt, in his vigorous, picturesque manner, with the more extreme morbid mental conditions sometimes found associated with masturbation, in "Illustrations of a Variety of Insanity," *Journal of Mental Science*, July, 1868.

posed subjects; so, also, Forel and Löwenfeld, as at an earlier period, Trousseau.[1] It is true that Marro, in his admirable and detailed study of the normal and abnormal aspects of puberty, accepts a form of masturbatory insanity; but the only illustrative case he brings forward is a young man possessing various stigmata of degeneracy and the son of an alcoholic father; such a case tells us nothing regarding the results of simple masturbation.[2] Even Spitzka, who maintained several years ago the traditional views as to the terrible results of masturbation, and recognized a special "insanity of masturbation," stated his conclusions with a caution that undermined his position: "Self-abuse," he concluded, "to become a sole cause of insanity, must be begun early and carried very far. In persons of sound antecedents it rarely, under these circumstances, suffices to produce an actual vesania."[3] When we remember that there is no convincing evidence to show that masturbation is "begun early and carried very far" by "persons of sound antecedents," the significance of Spitzka's "typical psychosis of masturbation" is somewhat annulled. It is evident that these distinguished investigators, Marro and Spitzka, have been induced by tradition to take up a position which their own scientific consciences have compelled them practically to evacuate.

Recent authorities are almost unanimous in rejecting masturbation as a cause of insanity. Thus, Rohleder, in his comprehensive monograph (*Die Masturbation*, 1899, pp. 185-92), although taking a very serious view of the evil results of masturbation, points out the unanimity which is now tending to prevail on this point, and lays it down that "masturbation is never the direct cause of insanity." Sexual excesses of any kind, he adds (following Curschmann), can, at the most, merely give an impetus to a latent form of insanity. On the whole, he concludes, the best authorities are unanimous in agreeing that masturbation may certainly injure mental capacity, by weakening memory and depressing intellectual energy; that, further, in hereditarily neurotic subjects, it may produce slight psychoses like *folie du doute*, hypo-

---

[1] See, *e.g.*, Löwenfeld, *Sexualleben und Nervenleiden*, 2d. ed., Ch. VIII.

[2] Marro, *La Pubertà*, Turin, 1898, p. 174.

[3] E. C. Spitzka, "Cases of Masturbation," *Journal of Mental Science*, July, 1888.

chondria, hysteria; that, finally, under no circumstances can it produce severe psychoses like paranoia or general paralysis. "If it caused insanity, as often as some claim," as Kellogg remarks, "the whole race would long since have passed into masturbatic degeneracy of mind. . . . It is especially injurious in the very young, and in all who have weak nervous systems," but "the physical traits attributed to the habit are common to thousands of neurasthenic and neurotic individuals." (Kellogg, *A Text-book of Mental Diseases*, 1897, pp. 94-95.) Again, at the outset of the article on "Masturbation," in Tuke's *Dictionary of Psychological Medicine*, Yellowlees states that, on account of the mischief formerly done by reckless statements, it is necessary to state plainly that "unless the practice has been long and greatly indulged, no permanent evil effects may be observed to follow." Näcke, again, has declared ("Kritisches zum Kapitel der Sexualität," *Archiv für Psychiatrie*, 1899): "There are neither somatic nor psychic symptoms peculiar on onanism. Nor is there any specific onanistic psychosis. I am prepared to deny that onanism ever produces any psychoses in those who are not already predisposed." That such a view is now becoming widely prevalent is illustrated by the cautious and temperate discussion of masturbation in a recent work by a non-medical writer, Geoffrey Mortimer (*Chapters on Human Love*, pp. 199-205).

The testimony of expert witnesses with regard to the influence of masturbation in producing other forms of psychoses and neuroses is becoming equally decisive; and here, also, the traditions of Tissot are being slowly effaced. "I have not, in the whole of my practice," wrote West, forty years ago, "out of a large experience among children and women, seen convulsions, epilepsy, or idiocy *induced* by masturbation in any child of either sex. Neither have I seen any instance in which hysteria, epilepsy, or insanity in women after puberty was *due* to masturbation, as its efficient cause."[1] Gowers speaks somewhat less positively, but regards masturbation as not so much a cause of true epilepsy as of atypical attacks, sometimes of a character intermediate between the hysteroid and the epileptoid form; this relationship he has frequently seen in boys.[2] Leyden, among the causes of diseases of the spinal cord, does not include any form

---

[1] Charles West, *Lancet*, November 17, 1866.

[2] Gowers, *Epilepsy*, 1881, p. 31. Löwenfeld believes that epileptic attacks are certainly caused by masturbation. Féré thought that both epilepsy and hysteria may be caused by masturbation.

of sexual excess. "In moderation," Erb remarks, "masturbation is not more dangerous to the spinal cord than natural coitus, and has no bad effects";[1] it makes no difference, Erb considers, whether the orgasm is effected normally or in solitude. This is also the opinion of Toulouse, of Fürbringer, and of Curschmann, as at an earlier period it was of Roubaud.

While these authorities are doubtless justified in refusing to ascribe to masturbation any part in the production of psychic or nervous diseases, it seems to me that they are going somewhat beyond their province when they assert that masturbation has no more injurious effect than coitus. If sexual coitus were a purely physiological phenomenon, this position would be sound. But the sexual orgasm is normally bound up with a mass of powerful emotions aroused by a person of the opposite sex. It is in the joy caused by the play of these emotions, as well as in the discharge of the sexual orgasm, that the satisfaction of coitus resides. In the absence of the desired partner the orgasm, whatever relief it may give, must be followed by a sense of dissatisfaction, perhaps of depression, even of exhaustion, often of shame and remorse. The same remark has since been made by Stanley Hall.[2] Practically, also, as John Hunter pointed out, there is more probability of excess in masturbation than in coitus. Whether, as some have asserted, masturbation involves a greater nervous effort than coitus is more doubtful.[3] It thus seems somewhat misleading to assert that masturbation has no more injurious effect than coitus.[4]

Reviewing the general question of the supposed grave symp-

---

[1] Ziemssen's *Handbuch*, Bd. XI.

[2] *Adolescence*, vol. i, p. 441.

[3] See a discussion of these points by Rohleder, *Die Masturbation*, pp. 168-175.

[4] The surgeons, it may be remarked, have especially stated the harmlessness of masturbation in too absolute a manner. Thus, John Hunter (*Treatise on the Venereal Disease*, 1786, p. 200), after pointing out that "the books on this subject have done more harm than good," adds, "I think I may affirm that this act does less harm to the constitution in general than the natural." And Sir James Paget, in his lecture on "Sexual Hypochondriasis," said: "Masturbation does neither more nor less harm than sexual intercourse practiced with the same frequency, in the same conditions of general health and age and circumstances."

toms and signs of masturbation, and its pernicious results, we may reach the conclusion that in the case of moderate masturbation in healthy, well-born individuals, no seriously pernicious results necessarily follow.[1] With regard to the general signs, we may accept, as concerns both sexes, what the Obstetrical and Gynecological Society of Berlin decided in 1861, in a discussion of it in women, that there are none which can be regarded as reliable.[2]

We may conclude finally, with Clouston, that the opposing views on the subject may be simply explained by the fact that the writers on both sides have ignored or insufficiently recognized the influence of heredity and temperament. They have done precisely what so many unscientific writers on inebriety have continued to do unto the present day, when describing the terrible results of alcohol without pointing out that the chief factor in such cases has not been the alcohol, but the organization on which the alcohol acted. Excess may act, according to the familiar old-fashioned adage, like the lighted match. But we must always remember the obvious truth, that it makes a con-

---

[1] It is interesting to note that an analogous result seems to hold with animals. Among highly-bred horses excessive masturbation is liable to occur with injurious results. It is scarcely necessary to point out that highly-bred horses are apt to be abnormal.

[2] With regard to the physical signs, the same conclusion is reached by Legludic (in opposition to Martineau) on the basis of a large experience. He has repeatedly found, in young girls who acknowledged frequent masturbation, that the organs were perfectly healthy and normal, and his convictions are the more noteworthy, since he speaks as a pupil of Tardieu, who attached very grave significance to the local signs of sexual perversity and excess. (Legludic, *Notes et Observations de Médecine Légale*, 1896, p. 95.) Matthews Duncan (*Goulstonian Lectures on Sterility in Women*, 1884, p. 97) was often struck by the smallness, and even imperfect development, of the external genitals of women who masturbate. Clara Barrus considers that there is no necessary connection between hypertrophy of the external female genital organs and masturbation, though in six cases of prolonged masturbation she found such a condition in three (*American Journal of Insanity*, April, 1895, p. 479). Bechterew denies that masturbation produces enlargement of the penis, and Hammond considers there is no evidence to show that it enlarges the clitoris, while Guttceit states that it does not enlarge the nymphæ; this, however, is doubtful. It would not suffice in many cases to show that large sexual organs are correlated with masturbation; it would still be necessary to show whether the size of the organs stood to masturbation in the relation of effect or of cause.

siderable difference whether you threw your lighted match into a powder magazine or into the sea.

While we may thus dismiss the extravagant views widely held during the past century, concerning the awful results of masturbation, as due to ignorance and false tradition, it must be pointed out that, even in healthy or moderately healthy individuals, any excess in solitary self-excitement may still produce results which, though slight, are yet harmful. The skin, digestion, and circulation may all be disordered; headache and neuralgia may occur; and, as in normal sexual excess or in undue frequency of sexual excitement during sleep, there is a certain general lowering of nervous tone. Probably the most important of the comparatively frequent results—though this also arises usually on a somewhat morbid soil—is neurasthenia with its manifold symptoms. There can be little doubt that the ancient belief, dating from the time of Hippocrates, that sexual excesses produce spinal disease, as well as the belief that masturbation causes insanity, are largely due to the failure to diagnose neurasthenia.

The following case of neurasthenia, recorded by Eulenburg, may be given as a classical picture of the nervous disturbances which may be associated with masturbation, and are frequently regarded as solely caused by habits of masturbation: Miss H. H., 28 years of age, a robust brunette, with fully developed figure, without any trace of anæmia or chlorosis, but with an apathetic expression, bluish rings around the eyes, with hypochondriacal and melancholy feelings. She complains of pressure on the head ("as if head would burst"), giddiness, ringing in the ears, photopsia, hemicrania, pains in the back and at sacrum, and symptoms of spinal adynamia, with a sense of fatigue on the least exertion in walking or standing; she sways when standing with closed eyes, tendon-reflexes exaggerated; there is a sense of oppression, intercostal neuralgia, and all the signs of neurasthenic dyspepsia; and cardialgia, nausea, flatulence, meteorism, and alternate constipation and diarrhœa. She chiefly complains of a feeling of weight and pain in the abdomen, caused by the slightest movement, and of a form of pollution (with clitoridian spasms), especially near menstruation, with copious flow of mucus, characteristic pains, and hyperexcitability. Menstruation was irregular and profuse. Examination showed tumid and elongated nymphæ, with brown pigmentation; rather large vagina, with rudi-

mentary hymen; and retroflexion of uterus. After much persuasion the
patient confessed that, when a girl of 12, and as the result of repeated
attempts at coitus by a boy of 16, she had been impelled to frequent masturbation. This had caused great shame and remorse, which, however,
had not sufficed to restrain the habit. Her mother having died, she
lived alone with her invalid father, and had no one in whom to confide.
Regarding herself as no longer a virgin, she had refused several offers
of marriage, and thus still further aggravated her mental condition.
(Eulenburg, *Sexuale Neuropathie*, p. 31.)

Since Beard first described neurasthenia, many diverse opinions
have been expressed concerning the relationships of sexual irregularities
to neurasthenia. Gilles de la Tourette, in his little monograph on neurasthenia, following the traditions of Charcot's school, dismisses the
question of any sexual causation without discussion. Binswanger (*Die
Pathologie und Therapie der Neurasthenie*), while admitting that nearly
all neurasthenic persons acknowledge masturbation at some period, considers it is not an important cause of neurasthenia, only differing
from coitus by the fact that the opportunities for it are more frequent,
and that the sexual disturbances of neurasthenia are, in the majority
of cases, secondary. Rohleder, on the other hand, who takes a very
grave view of the importance of masturbation, considers that its most
serious results are a question of neurasthenia. Krafft-Ebing has declared
his opinion that masturbation is a cause of neurasthenia. Christian,
Leyden, Erb, Rosenthal, Beard, Hummel, Hammond, Hermann Cohn,
Curschmann, Savill, Herman, Fürbringer, all attach chief importance to
neurasthenia as a result of masturbation. Collins and Phillip (*Medical
Record*, March 25, 1899), in an analysis of 333 cases of neurasthenia,
found that 123 cases were apparently due to overwork or masturbation.
Freud concludes that neurasthenia proper can nearly always be traced to
excessive masturbation, or to spontaneous pollutions. (*E.g., Sammlung
Kleiner Schriften zur Neurosenlehre*, first series, p. 187.) This view is
confirmed by Gattel's careful study (*Ueber die Sexuellen Ursachen der
Neurasthenie und Angstneurose*, 1898). Gattel investigated 100 consecutive cases of severe functional nervous disorder in Krafft-Ebing's clinic
at Vienna, and found that in every case of neurasthenia in a male
(28 in all) there was masturbation, while of the 15 women with neurasthenia, only one is recorded as not masturbating, and she practiced
coitus reservatus. Irrespective of the particular form of the nervous
disorder, Gattel found that 18 women out of 42, and 36 men out of 58,
acknowledged masturbation. (This shows a slightly larger proportion
among the men, but the men were mostly young, while the women were
mostly of more mature age.) It must, however, always be remembered
that we have no equally careful statistics of masturbation in perfectly
healthy persons. We must also remember that we have to distinguish

between the *post* and the *propter*, and that it is quite possible that neurasthenic persons are specially predisposed to masturbation. Bloch is of this opinion, and remarks that a vicious circle may thus be formed.

On the whole, there can be little doubt that neurasthenia is liable to be associated with masturbation carried to an excessive extent. But, while neurasthenia is probably the severest affection that is liable to result from, or accompany, masturbation, we are scarcely yet entitled to accept the conclusion of Gattel that in such cases there is no hereditary neurotic predisposition. We must steer clearly between the opposite errors of those, on the one hand, who assert that heredity is the sole cause of functional nervous disorders, and those, on the other hand, who consider that the incident that may call out the disorder is itself a sole sufficient cause.

In many cases it has seemed to me that masturbation, when practiced in excess, especially if begun before the age of puberty, leads to inaptitude for coitus, as well as to indifference to it, and sometimes to undue sexual irritability, involving premature emission and practical impotence. This is, however, the exception, especially if the practice has not been begun until after puberty. In women I attach considerable importance, as a result of masturbation, to an aversion for normal coitus in later life. In such cases some peripheral irritation or abnormal mental stimulus trains the physical sexual orgasm to respond to an appeal which has nothing whatever to do with the fascination normally exerted by the opposite sex. At puberty, however, the claim of passion and the real charm of sex begin to make themselves felt, but, owing to the physical sexual feelings having been trained into a foreign channel, these new and more normal sex associations remain of a purely ideal and emotional character, without the strong sensual impulses with which under healthy conditions they tend to be more and more associated as puberty passes on into adolescence or mature adult life. I am fairly certain that in many women, often highly intellectual women, the precocious excess in masturbation has been a main cause, not necessarily the sole efficient cause, in producing a divorce in later life between the physical sensuous impulses and the ideal emotions. The sensuous impulse having been evolved and perverted before the manifestation of the higher emotion, the two groups of feelings have become divorced for the whole of life. This is a common source of much personal misery and family unhappiness, though at the same time the clash of contending impulses may lead to a high development of moral character. When early masturbation is a factor in producing sexual inversion it usually operates in the manner I have here indicated, the repulsion for normal coitus helping to furnish a soil on which the inverted impulse may develop unimpeded.

This point has not wholly escaped previous observers, though they do not seem to have noted its psychological mechanism. Tissot stated that masturbation causes an aversion to marriage. More recently, Loiman ("Ueber Onanismus beim Weibe," *Therapeutische Monatshefte*, April, 1890) considered that masturbation in women, leading to a perversion of sexual feeling, including inability to find satisfaction in coitus, affects the associated centres. Smith Baker, again ("The Neuropsychical Element in Conjugal Aversion," *Journal of Nervous and Mental Disease*, September, 1892), finds that a "source of marital aversion seems to lie in the fact that substitution of mechanical and iniquitous excitations affords more thorough satisfaction than the mutual legitimate ones do," and gives cases in point. Savill, also, who believes that masturbation is more common in women than is usually supposed, regards dyspareunia, or pain in coition, as one of the signs of the habit.

Masturbation in women thus becomes, as Raymond and Janet point out (*Les Obsessions*, vol. ii, p. 307) a frequent cause of sexual frigidity in marriage. These authors illustrate the train of evils which may thus be set up, by the case of a lady, 26 years of age, a normal woman, of healthy family, who, at the age of 15, was taught by a servant to masturbate. At the age of 18 she married. She loved her husband, but she had no sexual feelings in coitus, and she continued to masturbate, sometimes several times a day, without evil consequences. At 24 she had to go into a hospital for floating kidney, and was so obliged to stop masturbating. She here accidentally learnt of the evil results attributed to the habit. She resolved not to do it again, and she kept her resolution. But while still in hospital she fell wildly in love with a man. To escape from the constant thought of this man, she sought relations with her husband, and at times masturbated, but now it no longer gave her pleasure. She wished to give up sexual things altogether. But that was easier said than done. She became subject to nervous crises, often brought on by the sight of a man, and accompanied by sexual excitement. They disappeared under treatment, and she thereupon became entirely frigid sexually. But, far from being happy, she has lost all energy and interest in life, and it is her sole desire to attain the sexual feelings she has lost. Adler considers that even when masturbation in women becomes an overmastering passion, so far as organic effects are concerned it is usually harmless, its effects being primarily psychic, and he attaches especial significance to it as a cause of sexual anæsthesia in normal coitus, being, perhaps, the most frequent cause of such anæsthesia. He devotes an important chapter to this matter, and brings forward numerous cases in illustration (Adler, *Die Mangelhafte Geschlechtsempfindung des Weibes*, pp. 93-119, also 21-23). Adler considers that the frequency of masturbation in women is largely due to the fact that women experience greater difficulties than men in obtaining sexual satisfaction, and so are impelled by unsatisfying coitus to continue masturbation after marriage. He adds that partly from natural shyness, partly from shame of acknowledging what is commonly accounted a sin, and partly from the fear of seeming disgusting or unworthy of sympathy in the doctor's eyes, women are usually silent on this matter, and very great tact and patience may be necessary before a confession is obtained.

On the psychic side, no doubt, the most frequent and the most characteristic result of persistent and excessive masturbation is a morbid heightening of self-consciousness without any co-ordinated heightening of self-esteem.[1] The man or woman who is kissed by a desirable and desired person of the opposite sex feels a satisfying sense of pride and elation, which must always be absent from the manifestations of auto-erotic activity.[2] This must be so, even apart from the masturbator's consciousness of the general social attitude toward his practices and his dread

---

[1] Thus, Bechterew ("La Phobie du Regard," *Archives de Neurologie*, July, 1905) considers that masturbation plays a large part in producing the morbid fear of the eyes of others.

[2] It is especially an undesirable tendency of masturbation, that it deadens the need for affection, and merely eludes, instead of satisfying, the sexual impulse. "Masturbation," as Godfrey well says (*The Science of Sex*, p. 178), "though a manifestation of sexual activity, is not a sexual act in the higher, or even in the real fundamental sense. For sex implies duality, a characteristic to which masturbation can plainly lay no claim. The physical, moral, and mental reciprocity which gives stability and beauty to a normal sexual intimacy, are as foreign to the masturbator as to the celibate. In a sense, therefore, masturbation is as complete a negative of the sexual life as chastity itself. It is, therefore, an evasion of, not an answer to, the sexual problem; and it will ever remain so, no matter how surely we may be convinced of its physical harmlessness."

of detection, for that may also exist as regards normal coitus without any corresponding psychic effects. The masturbator, if his practice is habitual, is thus compelled to cultivate an artificial consciousness of self-esteem, and may show a tendency to mental arrogance. Self-righteousness and religiosity constitute, as it were, a protection against the tendency to remorse. A morbid mental soil is, of course, required for the full development of these characteristics. The habitual male masturbator, it must be remembered, is often a shy and solitary person; individuals of this temperament are especially predisposed to excesses in all the manifestations of auto-erotism, while the yielding to such tendencies increases the reserve and the horror of society, at the same time producing a certain suspicion of others. In some extreme cases there is, no doubt, as Kraepelin believes, some decrease of psychic capacity, an inability to grasp and co-ordinate external impressions, weakness of memory, deadening of emotions, or else the general phenomena of increased irritability, leading on to neurasthenia.

I find good reason to believe that in many cases the psychic influence of masturbation on women is different from its effect on men. As Spitzka observed, although it may sometimes render women self-reproachful and hesitant, it often seems to make them bold. Boys, as we have seen, early assimilate the tradition that self-abuse is "unmanly" and injurious, but girls have seldom any corresponding tradition that it is "unwomanly," and thus, whether or not they are reticent on the matter, before the forum of their own conscience they are often less ashamed of it than men are and less troubled by remorse.

Eulenburg considers that the comparative absence of bad effects from masturbation in girls is largely due to the fact that, unlike boys, they are not terrorized by exaggerated warnings and quack literature concerning the awful results of the practice. Forel, who has also remarked that women are often comparatively little troubled by qualms of conscience after masturbation, denies that this is due to a lower moral tone than men possess (Forel, *Die Sexuelle Frage*, p. 247). In this connection, I may refer to History IV, recorded in the Appendix to the fifth volume of these *Studies*, in which it is stated that of 55 prostitutes of various nationalities, with whom the subject had had relations,

18 spontaneously told him that they were habitual masturbators, while
of 26 normal women, 13 made the same confession, unasked. Guttceit,
in Russia, after stating that women of good constitution had told him
that they masturbated as much as six or ten times a day or night
(until they fell asleep, tired), without bad results, adds that, according to his observations, "masturbation, when not excessive, is, on the
whole, a quite innocent matter, which exerts little or no permanent
effect," and adds that it never, in any case, leads to *hypochondria
onanica* in women, because they have not been taught to expect bad
results (*Dreissig Jahre Praxis*, p. 306). There is, I think, some truth
—though the exceptions are doubtless many—in the distinction drawn
by .W. C. Krauss ("Masturbational Neuroses," *Medical News*, July 13,
1901): "From my experience it [masturbation] seems to have an opposite effect upon the two sexes, dulling the mental and making clumsy
the physical exertions of the male, while in the female it quickens and
excites the physical and psychical movements. The man is rendered
hypoesthetic, the woman hyperesthetic."

In either sex auto-erotic excesses during adolescence in young
men and women of intelligence—whatever absence of gross injury
there may be—still often produce a certain degree of psychic
perversion, and tend to foster false and high-strung ideals of
life. Kraepelin refers to the frequency of exalted enthusiasms in
masturbators, and I have already quoted Anstie's remarks on the
connection between masturbation and premature false work in
literature and art. It may be added that excess in masturbation
has often occurred in men and women whose work in literature
and art cannot be described as premature and false. K. P.
Moritz, in early adult life, gave himself up to excess in masturbation, and up to the age of thirty had no relations with women.
Lenau is said—though the statement is sometimes denied—to
have been a masturbator from early life, the habit profoundly
effecting his life and work. Rousseau, in his *Confessions,* admirably describes how his own solitary, timid, and imaginative
life found its chief sexual satisfaction in masturbation.[1] Gogol,

---

[1] "I learnt that dangerous supplement," Rousseau tells us (Part I.
Bk. III), "which deceives Nature. This vice, which bashfulness and
timidity find so convenient, has, moreover, a great attraction for lively
imaginations, for it enables them to do what they will, so to speak, with
the whole fair sex, and to enjoy at pleasure the beauty who attracts
them, without having obtained her consent."

the great Russian novelist, masturbated to excess, and it has been
suggested that the dreamy melancholy thus induced was a factor
in his success as a novelist. Goethe, it has been asserted, at one
time masturbated to excess; I am not certain on what authority
the statement is made, probably on a passage in the seventh book
of *Dichtung und Wahrheit,* in which, describing his student-life
at Leipzig, and his loss of Aennchen owing to his neglect of
her, he tells how he revenged that neglect on his own physical
nature by foolish practices from which he thinks he suffered for
a considerable period.[1] The great Scandinavian philosopher,
Sören Kierkegaard, suffered severely, according to Rasmussen,
from excessive masturbation. That, at the present day, eminence
in art, literature, and other fields may be combined with the
excessive practice of masturbation is a fact of which I have unquestionable evidence.

I have the detailed history of a man of 30, of high ability in
a scientific direction, who, except during periods of mental strain, has
practiced masturbation nightly (though seldom more than once a night)
from early childhood, without any traceable evil results, so far as his
general health and energy are concerned. In another case, a school-
teacher, age 30, a hard worker and accomplished musician, has masturbated every night, sometimes more than once a night, ever since he
was at school, without, so far as he knows, any bad results; he has
never had connection with a woman, and seldom touches wine or
tobacco. Curschmann knew a young and able author who, from the
age of 11 had masturbated excessively, but who retained physical and
mental freshness. It would be very easy to refer to other examples, and
I may remark that, as regards the histories recorded in various volumes of these *Studies,* a notable proportion of those in which excessive masturbation is admitted, are of persons of eminent and recognized
ability.

---

[1] "Ich hatte sie wirklich verloren, und die Tollheit, mit der ich
meinen Fehler an mir selbst rächte, indem ich auf mancherlei unsinnige
Weise in meine physische Natur stürmte, um der sittlichen etwas zu
Leide zu thun, hat sehr viel zu den körperlichen Uebeln beigetragen,
unter denen ich einige der besten Jahre meines Lebens verlor; ja ich
wäre vielleicht an diesem Verlust völlig zu Grunde gegangen, hätte sich
hier nicht das poetische Talent mit seinen Heilkraften besonders hülf-
reich erwiesen." This is scarcely conclusive, and it may be added that
there were many reasons why Goethe should have suffered physically at
this time, quite apart from masturbation. See, *e.g.,* Bielschowsky, *Life
of Goethe,* vol. i, p. 88.

It is often possible to trace the precise mechanism of the relationship between auto-erotic excitement and intellectual activity. Brown-Séquard, in old age, considered that to induce a certain amount of sexual excitement, not proceeding to emission, was an aid to mental work. Raymond and Janet knew a man considering himself a poet, who, in order to attain the excitation necessary to compose his ideal verses, would write with one hand while with the other he caressed his penis, though not to the extent of producing ejaculation.[1] We must not believe, however, that this is by any means the method of workers who deserve to be accepted seriously; it would be felt, to say the least, as unworthy. It is indeed a method that would only appeal to a person of feeble or failing mental power. What more usually happens is that the auto-erotic excitement develops, *pari passu* and spontaneously, with the mental activity and at the climax of the latter the auto-erotic excitement also culminates, almost or even quite spontaneously, in an explosion of detumescence which relieves the mental tension. I am acquainted with such cases in both young men and women of intellectual ability, and they probably occur much more frequently than we usually suspect.

In illustration of the foregoing observations, I may quote the following narrative, written by a man of letters: "From puberty to the age of 30 (when I married), I lived in virgin continence, in accord with my principle. During these years I worked exceedingly hard—chiefly at art (music and poetry). My days being spent earning my livelihood, these art studies fell into my evening time. I noticed that productive power came in periods—periods of irregular length, and which certainly, to a partial extent, could be controlled by the will. Such a period of vital power began usually with a sensation of melancholy, and it quickened my normal revolt against the narrowness of conventional life into a red-hot detestation of the paltriness and pettiness with which so many mortals seem to content themselves. As the mood grew in intensity, this scorn of the lower things mixed with and gave place to a vivid insight into higher truths. The oppression began to give place to a realization of the eternity of the heroic things; the fatuities were seen as mere fashions; love was seen as the true lord of life; the eternal romance was evident in its glory; the naked strength and beauty

---

[1] *Les Obsessions*, vol. ii, p. 136.

of men were known despite their clothes.   In such mood my work was produced; bitter protest and keen-sighted passion mingled in its building.   The arising vitality had certainly deep relation to the periodicity of the sex-force of manhood.   At the height of the power of the art-creative mood would come those natural emissions with which Nature calmly disposes of the unused force of the male.   Such emissions were natural and healthy, and not exhaustive or hysterical.   The process is undoubtedly sane and protective, unless the subject be unhealthy. The period of creative art power extended a little beyond the end of the period of natural seed emission—the art work of this last stage being less vibrant, and of a gentler force.   Then followed a time of calm natural rest, which gradually led up to the next sequence of melancholy and power.   The periods certainly varied in length of time, controlled somewhat by the force of the mind and the mental will to create; that is to say, I could somewhat delay the natural emission, by which I gained an extension of the period of power."

How far masturbation in moderately healthy persons living without normal sexual relationships may be considered normal is a difficult question only to be decided with reference to individual cases.   As a general rule, when only practiced at rare intervals, and *faute de mieux,* in order to obtain relief for physical oppression and mental obsession, it may be regarded as the often inevitable result of the unnatural circumstances of our civilized social life.   When, as often happens in mental degeneracy,—and as in shy and imaginative persons, perhaps of neurotic temperament, may also sometimes become the case,—it is practiced in preference to sexual relationships, it at once becomes abnormal and may possibly lead to a variety of harmful results, mental and physical.[1]

It must always be remembered, however, that, while the practice of masturbation may be harmful in its consequences, it is also, in the absence of normal sexual relationships, frequently not without good results.   In the medical literature of the last hundred years a number of cases have been incidentally recorded

---

[1] A somewhat similar classification has already been made by Max Dessoir, who points out that we must distinguish between onanists *aus Noth,* and onanists *aus Leidenschaft,* the latter group alone being of really serious importance.   The classification of Dallemagne is also somewhat similar; he distinguishes *onanie par impulsion,* occurring in mental degeneration and in persons of inferior intelligence, from *onanie par evocation ou obsession.*

in which the patients found masturbation beneficial, and such cases might certainly have been enormously increased if there had been any open-eyed desire to discover them. My own observations agree with those of Sudduth, who asserts that "masturbation is, in the main, practiced for its sedative effect on the nervous system. The relaxation that follows the act constitutes its real attraction. . . . Both masturbation and sexual intercourse should be classed as typical sedatives."[1]

Gall (*Fonctions du Cerveau*, 1825, vol. iii, p. 235) mentioned a woman who was tormented by strong sexual desire, which she satisfied by masturbation ten or twelve times a day; this caused no bad results, and led to the immediate disappearance of a severe pain in the back of the neck, from which she often suffered. Clouston (*Mental Diseases*, 1887, p. 496) quotes as follows from a letter written by a youth of 22: "I am sure I cannot explain myself, nor give account of such conduct. Sometimes I felt so uneasy at my work that I would go to the water-closet to do it, and it seemed to give me ease, and then I would work like a hatter for a whole week, till the sensation overpowered me again. I have been the most filthy scoundrel in existence," etc. Garnier presents the case of a monk, aged 33, living a chaste life, who wrote the following account of his experiences: "For the past three years, at least, I have felt, every two or three weeks, a kind of fatigue in the penis, or, rather, slight shooting pains, increasing during several days, and then I feel a strong desire to expel the semen. When no nocturnal pollution follows, the retention of the semen causes general disturbance, headache, and sleeplessness. I must confess that, occasionally, to free myself from the general and local oppression, I lie on my stomach and obtain ejaculation. I am at once relieved; a weight seems to be lifted from my chest, and sleep returns." This patient consulted Garnier as to whether this artificial relief was not more dangerous than the sufferings it relieved. Garnier advised that if the ordinary *régime* of a well-ordered monastry, together with anaphrodisiac sedatives, proved ineffica-

---

[1] W. Xavier Sudduth, "A Study in the Psycho-physics of Masturbation," *Chicago Medical Recorder*, March, 1898. Haig, who reaches a similar conclusion, has sought to find its precise mechanism in the blood-pressure. "As the sexual act produces lower and falling blood-pressure," he remarks, "it will of necessity relieve conditions which are due to high and rising blood-pressure, such, for instance, as mental depression and bad temper; and, unless my observation deceives me, we have here a connection between conditions of high blood-pressure with mental and bodily depression and acts of masturbation, for this act will relieve these conditions and tend to be practiced for this purpose." (*Uric Acid*, 6th edition, p. 154.)

cious, the manœuvre might be continued when necessary (P. Garnier, *Célibut et Célibataires*, 1887, p. 320). H. C. Coe (*American Journal of Obstetrics*, p. 766, July, 1889) gives the case of a married lady who was deeply sensitive of the wrong nature of masturbation, but found in it the only means of relieving the severe ovarian pain, associated with intense sexual excitement, which attended menstruation. During the intermenstrual period the temptation was absent. Turnbull knew a youth who found that masturbation gave great relief to feelings of heaviness and confusion which came on him periodically; and Wigglesworth has frequently seen masturbation after epileptic fits in patients who never masturbated at other times. Moll (*Libido Sexualis*, Bd. I, p. 13) refers to a woman of 28, an artist of nervous and excitable temperament, who could not find sexual satisfaction with her lover, but only when masturbating, which she did once or twice a day, or oftener; without masturbation, she said, she would be in a much more nervous state. A friend tells me of a married lady of 40, separated from her husband on account of incompatibility, who suffered from irregular menstruation; she tried masturbation, and, in her own words, "became normal again;" she had never masturbated previously. I have also been informed of the case of a young unmarried woman, intellectual, athletic, and well developed, who, from the age of seven or eight, has masturbated nearly every night before going to sleep, and would be restless and unable to sleep if she did not.

Judging from my own observations among both sexes, I should say that in normal persons, well past the age of puberty, and otherwise leading a chaste life, masturbation would be little practiced except for the physical and mental relief it brings. Many vigorous and healthy unmarried women or married women apart from their husbands, living a life of sexual abstinence, have asserted emphatically that only by sexually exciting themselves, at intervals, could they escape from a condition of nervous oppression and sexual obsession which they felt to be a state of hysteria. In most cases this happens about the menstrual period, and, whether accomplished as a purely physical act—in the same way as they would soothe a baby to sleep by rocking it or patting it—or by the co-operation of voluptuous mental imagery, the practice is not cultivated for its own sake during the rest of the month.

In illustration of the foregoing statements I will here record a few typical observations of experiences with regard to masturbation. The cases selected are all women, and are all in a fairly normal, and, for the most part, excellent, state of health; some of them, however, belong to somewhat neurotic families, and these are persons of unusual mental ability and intelligence.

OBSERVATION I.—Unmarried, aged 38. She is very vigorous and healthy, of a strongly passionate nature, but never masturbated until a few years ago, when she was made love to by a man who used to kiss her, etc. Although she did not respond to these advances, she was thrown into a state of restless sexual excitement; on one occasion, when in bed in this restless state, she accidentally found, on passing her hand over her body, that, by playing with "a round thing" [clitoris] a pleasurable feeling was produced. She found herself greatly relieved and quieted by these manipulations, though there remained a feeling of tiredness afterward. She has sometimes masturbated six times in a night, especially before and after the menstrual period, until she was unable to produce the orgasm or any feeling of pleasure.

OBSERVATION II.—Unmarried, aged 45, of rather nervous temperament. She has for many years been accustomed, usually about a week before the appearance of the menses, to obtain sexual relief by kicking out her legs when lying down. In this way, she says, she obtains complete satisfaction. She never touches herself. On the following day she frequently has pains over the lower part of the abdomen, such pains being apparently muscular and due to the exertion.

OBSERVATION III.—Aged 29, recently married, belonging to a neurotic and morbid family, herself healthy, and living usually in the country; vivacious, passionate, enthusiastic, intellectual, and taking a prominent part in philanthropic schemes and municipal affairs; at the same time, fond of society, and very attractive to men. For many years she had been accustomed to excite herself, though she felt it was not good for her. The habit was merely practiced *faute de mieux*. "I used to sit on the edge of the bed sometimes," she said, "and it came over me so strongly that I simply couldn't resist it. I felt that I should go mad, and I thought it was better to touch myself than be insane. . . . I used to press my clitoris in. . . . It made me very tired afterward—not like being with my husband." The confession was made from a conviction of the importance of the subject, and with the hope that some way might be found out of the difficulties which so often beset women.

OBSERVATION IV.—Unmarried, aged 27; possesses much force of character and high intelligence; is actively engaged in a professional career. As a child of seven or eight she began to experience what she describes as lightning-like sensations, "mere, vague, uneasy feelings or momentary twitches, which took place alike in the vulva or the vagina or the uterus, not amounting to an orgasm and nothing like it." These sensations, it should be added, have continued into adult life. "I always experience them just before menstruation, and afterward for a few days, and, occasionally, though it seems to me not so often, during the period itself. I may have the sensation four or five times during the day; it is not dependent at all upon external impressions, or my own thoughts, and is sometimes absent for days together. It is just one flash, as if you would snap your fingers, and it is over."

As a child, she was, of course, quite unconscious that there was anything sexual in these sensations. They were then usually associated with various imaginary scenes. The one usually indulged in was that a black bear was waiting for her up in a tree, and that she was slowly raised up toward the bear by means of ropes and then lowered again, and raised, feeling afraid of being caught by the bear, and yet having a morbid desire to be caught. In after years she realized that there was a physical sexual cause underlying these imaginations, and that what she liked was a feeling of resistance to the bear giving rise to the physical sensation.

At a somewhat later age, though while still a child, she cherished an ideal passion for a person very much older than herself, this passion absorbing her thoughts for a period of two years, during which, however, there was no progress made in physical sensation. It was when she was nearly thirteen years of age, soon after the appearance of menstruation, and under the influence of this ideal passion, that she first learned to experience conscious orgasm, which was not associated with the thought of any person. "I did not associate it with anything high or beautiful, owing to the fact that I had imbibed our current ideas in regard to sexual feelings, and viewed them in a very poor light indeed." She considers that her sexual feelings were stronger at this period than at any other time in her life. She could, however, often deny herself physical satisfaction for weeks at a time, in order that she might not feel unworthy of the object of her ideal passion. "As for the sexual satisfaction," she writes, "it was experimental. I had heard older girls speak of the pleasure of such feelings, but I was not taught anything by example, or otherwise. I merely rubbed myself with the wash-rag while bathing, waiting for a result, and having the same peculiar feeling I had so often experienced. I am not aware of any ill effects having resulted, but I felt degraded, and tried hard to overcome the habit. No one had spoken to me of the habit, but from the secrecy of grown people, and passages I had heard from the Bible, I conceived the idea that it was a reprehensible practice. And, while this did not curb my desire, it taught me self-control, and I vowed that each time should be the last. I was often able to keep the resolution for two or three weeks." Some four years later she gradually succeeded in breaking herself of the practice in so far as it had become a habit; she has, however, acquired a fuller knowledge of sexual matters, and, though she has still a great dread of masturbation as a vice, she does not hesitate to relieve her physical feelings when it seems best to her to do so. "I am usually able to direct my thoughts from these sensations," she writes, "but if they seem to make me irritable or wakeful, I relieve myself. It is a physical act, unassociated with deep feeling of any kind. I have always felt that it was a rather unpleasant compromise with my physical nature, but certainly necessary in my case. Yet, I have abstained from gratification for very long periods. If the feeling is not strong at the menstrual period, I go on very well without either the sensation or the gratification until the next period. And, strange as it may seem, the best antidote I have found and the best preventive is to think about spiritual things or someone whom I love. It is simply a matter of training, I suppose,—a sort of mental gymnastics,—which draws the attention away from the physical feelings." This lady has never had any sexual relationships, and, since she is ambitious, and believes that the sexual emotions may be transformed so as to become a source of motive power throughout the whole of life, she wishes to avoid such relationships.

OBSERVATION V.—Unmarried, aged 31, in good health, with, however, a somewhat hysterical excess of energy. "When I was about 26 years of age," she writes, "a friend came to me with the confession that for several years she had masturbated, and had become such a slave to the habit that she severely suffered from its ill effects. At that time I had never heard of self-abuse by women. I listened to her story with much sympathy and interest, but some skepticism, and determined to try experiments upon myself, with the idea of getting to understand the matter in order to assist my friend. After some manipulation, I succeeded in awakening what had before been unconscious and unknown. I purposely allowed the habit to grow upon me, and one night—for I always operated upon myself before going to sleep, never in the morning—I obtained considerable pleasurable satisfaction, but the following day my conscience awoke; I also felt pain located at the back of my head and down the spinal column. I ceased my operations for a time, and then began again somewhat regularly, once a month, a few days after menstruation. During those months in which I exercised moderation, I think I obtained much local relief with comparatively little injury, but, later on, finding myself in robust health, I increased my experiments, the habit grew upon me, and it was only with an almost superhuman effort that I broke myself free. Needless to say that I gave no assistance to my suffering friend, nor did I ever refer to the subject after her confession to me.

"Some two years later I heard of sexual practices between women as a frequent habit in certain quarters. I again interested myself in masturbation, for I had been told something that led me to believe that there was much more for me to discover. Not knowing the most elementary physiology, I questioned some of my friends, and then commenced again. I restricted myself to relief from local congestion and irritation by calling forth the emission of mucus, rather than by seeking pleasure. At the same time, I sought to discover what manipulation of the clitoris would lead to. The habit grew upon me with startling rapidity, and I became more or less its slave, but I suffered from no very great ill effects until I started in search of more discoveries. I found that I was a complete ignoramus as to the formation of a woman's body, and by experiments upon myself sought to discover the vagina. I continued my operations until I obtained an entrance. I think the rough handling of myself during this final stage disturbed my nervous system, and caused me considerable pain and exhaustion at the back of my head, the spinal column, the back of my eyes, and a general feeling of languor, etc.

"I could not bear to be the slave of a habit, and after much suffering and efforts, which only led to falls to lower depths of conscious failure, my better self rebelled, until, by a great effort and much prayer, I kept myself pure for a whole week. This partial recovery gave me hope, but then I again fell a victim to the habit, much to my chagrin, and became hopeless of ever retracing my steps toward my ideal of virtue. For some days I lost energy, spirit, and hope; my nervous system appeared to be ruined, but I did not really despair of victory in the end. I thought of all the drunkards chained by their intemperate habits, of inveterate smokers who could not exist without tobacco, and of all the various methods by which men were slaves, and the longing to be freed of what had, in my case, proved to be a painful and unnecessary habit, increased daily until, after one night when I struggled with myself for hours, I believed I had finally succeeded.

"At times, when I reached a high degree of sexual excitement, I felt that I was at least one step removed from those of morbid and repressed sex, who had not the slightest suspicion of the latent joys of womanhood within them. For a little while the habit took the shape of an exalted passion, but I rapidly tired it out by rough, thoughtless, and too impatient handling. Revulsion set in with the pain of an exhausted and badly used nervous system, and finding myself the slave of a passion, I determined to endeavor to be its master.

"In conclusion, I should say that masturbation has proved itself to be to me one of the blind turnings of my life's history, from which I have gained much valuable experience."

The practice was, however, by no means thus dismissed. Some time later the subject writes: "I have again restarted masturbation for the relief of localized feelings. One morning I was engaged in reading a very heavy volume which, for convenience sake, I held in my lap, leaning back on my chair. I had become deep in my study for an hour or so when I became aware of certain feelings roused by the weight of the book. Being tempted to see what would happen by such conduct, I shifted so that the edge of the volume came in closer contact. The pleasurable feelings increased, so I gave myself up to my emotions for some thirty minutes.

"Notwithstanding the intense pleasure I enjoyed for so long a period, I maintain that it is wiser to refrain, and, although I admit in the same breath that, by gentle treatment, such pleasure may be harmless to the general health, it does lead to a desire for solitude, which is not conducive to a happy frame of mind. There is an accompanying reticence of speech concerning the pleasure, which, therefore, appears to be unnatural, like the eating of stolen fruit. After such an event, one seems to require to fly to the woods, and to listen to the song of the birds, so as to shake off after-effects."

In a letter dated some months later, she writes: "I think I have risen above the masturbation habit." In the same letter the writer remarks: "If I had consciously abnormal or unsatisfied appetites I would satisfy them in the easiest and least harmful way."

Again, eighteen months later, she writes: "It is curious to note that for months this habit is forgotten, but awakens sometimes to self-assertion. If a feeling of pressure is felt in the head, and a slight irritation elsewhere, and experience shows that the time has come for pacification, exquisite pleasure can be enjoyed, never more than twice a month, and sometimes less often."

OBSERVATION VI.—Unmarried, actively engaged in the practice of her profession. Well-developed, feminine in contour, but boyish in manner and movements; strong, though muscles small, and healthy, with sound nervous system; never had anæmia. Thick brown hair; pubic hair thick, and hair on toes and legs up to umbilicus; it began to appear at the age of 10 (before pubic hair) and continued until 18. A few stray hairs round nipples, and much dark down on upper lip, as well as light down on arms and hands. Hips, normal; nates, small; labia minora, large; and clitoris, deeply hooded. Hymen thick, vagina, probably small. Considerable pigmentation of parts. Menstruation began at 15, but not regular till 17; is painless and scanty; the better the state of health, the less it is. No change of sexual or other feelings connected with it; it lasts one to three days.

"I believe," she writes, "my first experience of physical sex sensations was when I was about 16, and in sleep. But I did not then recognize it, and seldom, indeed, gave the subject of sex a thought. I was a child far beyond the age of childhood. The accompanying dreams were disagreeable, but I cannot remember what they were about. It was not until I was nearly 19 that I knew the sexual orgasm in my

waking state. It surprised me completely, but I knew that I had known
it before in my sleep.

"The knowledge came one summer when I was leading a rather
isolated life, and my mind was far from sex subjects, being deep in
books, Carlyle, Ruskin, Huxley, Darwin, Scott, etc. I noticed that when
I got up in the morning I felt very hot and uncomfortable. The clitoris
and the parts around were swollen and erect, and often tender and
painful. I had no idea what it was, but found I was unable to pass
my water for an hour or two. One day, when I was straining a little
to pass water, the full orgasm occurred. The next time it happened,
I tried to check it by holding myself firmly, of course, with the opposite
result. I do not know that I found it highly pleasurable, but it was
a very great relief. I allowed myself a good many experiments, to
come to a conclusion in the matter, and I thought about it. I was
much too shy to speak to any one, and thought it was probably a sin.
I tried not to do it, and not to think about it, saying to myself that
surely I was lord of my body. But I found that the matter was not
entirely under my control. However unwilling or passive I might be,
there were times when the involuntary discomfort was not in my keep-
ing. My touching myself or not did not save me from it. Because
it sometimes gave me pleasure, I thought it might be a form of self-
indulgence, and did not do it until it could scarcely be helped. Soon
the orgasm began to occur fairly frequently in my sleep, perhaps once
or twice a week. I had no erotic dreams, then or at any other time,
but I had nights of restless sleep, and woke as it occurred, dreaming
that it was happening, as, in fact, it was. At times I hardly awoke,
but went to sleep again in a moment. I continued for two or three
years to be sorely tried by day at frequent intervals. I acquired a
remarkable degree of control, so that, though one touch or steadily directed thought would have caused the orgasm, I could keep it off, and
go to sleep without 'wrong doing.' Of course, when I fell asleep, my
control ended. All this gave me a good deal of physical worry, and kept
my attention unwillingly fixed upon the matter. I do not think my body
was readily irritable, but I had unquestionably very strong sexual
impulses.

"After a year or two, when I was working hard, I could not
afford the attention the control cost me, or the prolonged mitigated sexual
excitement it caused. I took drugs for a time, but they lost effect,
produced lassitude, and agreed with me badly. I therefore put away
my scruples and determined to try the effect of giving myself an instant and business-like relief. Instead of allowing my feelings to
gather strength, I satisfied them out of hand. Instead of five hours
of heat and discomfort, I did not allow myself five minutes, if I could
help it.

"The effect was marvelous. I practically had no more trouble. The thing rarely came to me at all by day, and though it continued at times by night, it became less frequent and less strong; often it did not wake me. The erotic images and speculations that had begun to come to me died down. I left off being afraid of my feelings, or, indeed, thinking about them. I may say that I had decided that I should be obliged to lead a single life, and that the less I thought about matters of sex, the more easy I should find life. Later on I had religious ideas which helped me considerably in my ideals of a decent, orderly, self-contained life. I do not lay stress on these; they were not at all emotional, and my physical and psychical development do not appear to have run much on parallel lines. I had a strong moral sense before I had a religious one, and a 'common-sense' which I perhaps trusted more than either.

"When I was about 28 I thought I might perhaps leave off the habit of regular relief I had got into. (It was not regular as regards time, being anything from one day to six weeks.) The change was probably made easier by a severe illness I had had. I gave this abstinence a fair trial for several years (until I was about 34), but my nocturnal manifestations certainly gathered strength, especially when I got much better in health, and, finally, as at puberty, began to worry my waking life. I reasoned that by my attempt at abstinence I had only exchanged control for uncontrol, and reverted to my old habits of relief, with the same good results as before. The whole trouble subsided and I got better at once. (The orgasm during sleep continued, and occurs about once a fortnight; it is increased by change of air, especially at the seaside, when it may occur on two or three nights running.) I decided that, for the proper control of my single life, relief was normal and right. It would be very difficult for anyone to demonstrate the contrary to me. My aim has always been to keep myself in the best condition of physical and mental balance that a single person is capable of."

There is some interest in briefly reviewing the remarkable transformations in the attitude toward masturbation from Greek times down to our own day. The Greeks treated masturbation with little opprobrium. At the worst they regarded it as unmanly, and Aristophanes, in various passages, connects the practice with women, children, slaves, and feeble old men. Æschines seems to have publicly brought it as a charge against Demosthenes that he had practiced masturbation, though, on the other hand, Plutarch tells us that Diogenes—described by Zeller, the

historian of Greek philosophy, as "the most typical figure of
ancient Greece"—was praised by Chrysippus, the famous philosopher, for masturbating in the market-place. The more strenuous Romans, at all events as exemplified by Juvenal and Martial,
condemned masturbation more vigorously.[1] Aretæus, without
alluding to masturbation, dwells on the tonic effects of retaining
the semen; but, on the other hand, Galen regarded the retention
of semen as injurious, and advocated its frequent expulsion, a
point of view which tended to justify masturbation. In classical
days, doubtless, masturbation and all other forms of the auto-
erotic impulse were comparatively rare. So much scope was
allowed in early adult age for homosexual and later for hetero-
sexual relationships that any excessive or morbid development of
solitary self-indulgence could seldom occur. The case was
altered when Christian ideals became prominent. Christian
morality strongly proscribed sexual relationships except under certain specified conditions. It is true that Christianity discouraged
all sexual manifestations, and that therefore its ban fell equally on
masturbation, but, obviously, masturbation lay at the weakest line
of defence against the assaults of the flesh; it was there that
resistance would most readily yield. Christianity thus probably
led to a considerable increase of masturbation. The attention
which the theologians devoted to its manifestations clearly bears
witness to their magnitude. It is noteworthy that Mohammedan
theologians regarded masturbation as a Christian vice. In Islam
both doctrine and practice tended to encourage sexual relationships, and not much attention was paid to masturbation, nor even
any severe reprobation directed against it. Omer Haleby remarks that certain theologians of Islam are inclined to consider
the practice of masturbation in vogue among Christians as allowable to devout Mussulmans when alone on a journey; he himself
regards this as a practice good neither for soul nor body (seminal
emissions during sleep providing all necessary relief); should,
however, a Mussulman fall into this error, God is merciful![2]

[1] Northcote discusses the classic attitude towards masturbation,
Christianity and Sex Problems, p. 233.
[2] *El Ktab*, traduction de Paul de Régla, Paris, 1893.

In Theodore's Penitential of the seventh century, forty days' penance is prescribed for masturbation. Aquinas condemned masturbation as worse than fornication, though less heinous than other sexual offences against Nature; in opposition, also, to those who believed that *distillatio* usually takes place without pleasure, he observed that it was often caused by sexual emotion, and should, therefore, always be mentioned to the confessor. Liguori also regarded masturbation as a graver sin than fornication, and even said that *distillatio*, if voluntary and with notable physical commotion, is without doubt a mortal sin, for in such a case it is the beginning of a pollution. On the other hand, some theologians have thought that *distillatio* may be permitted, even if there is some commotion, so long as it has not been voluntarily procured, and Caramuel, who has been described as a theological *enfant terrible*, declared that "natural law does not forbid masturbation," but that proposition was condemned by Innocent XI. The most enlightened modern Catholic view is probably represented by Debreyne, who, after remarking that he has known pious and intelligent persons who had an irresistible impulse to masturbate, continues: "Must we excuse, or condemn, these people? Neither the one nor the other. If you condemn and repulse absolutely these persons as altogether guilty, against their own convictions, you will perhaps throw them into despair; if, on the contrary, you completely excuse them, you maintain them in a disorder from which they may, perhaps, never emerge. Adopt a wise middle course, and, perhaps, with God's aid, you may often cure them."

Under certain circumstances some Catholic theologians have permitted a married woman to masturbate. Thus, the Jesuit theologian, Gury, asserts that the wife does not sin "*quæ se ipsam tactibus excitat ad seminationem statim post copulam in quâ vir solus seminavit.*" This teaching seems to have been misunderstood, since ethical and even medical writers have expended a certain amount of moral indignation on the Church whose theologians committed themselves to this statement. As a matter of fact, this qualified permission to masturbate merely rests on a false theory of procreation, which is clearly expressed in the word *seminatio*. It was believed that ejaculation in the woman is as necessary to fecundation as ejaculation in the man. Galen, Avicenna, and Aquinas recognized, indeed, that such feminine semination was not necessary; Sanchez, however, was doubtful, while Suarez and Zacchia, following Hippocrates, regarded it as necessary. As sexual intercourse without fecundation is not approved by the Catholic Church, it thus became logically necessary to permit women to masturbate whenever the ejaculation of mucus had not occurred at or before coitus.

The belief that the emission of vaginal mucus, under the influence of sexual excitement in women, corresponded to spermatic emission, has led to the practice of masturbation on hygienic grounds. Garnier

(*Célibat*, p. 255) mentions that Mesué, in the eighteenth century, invented a special pessary to take the place of the penis, and, as he stated, effect the due expulsion of the feminine sperm.

Protestantism, no doubt, in the main accepted the general Catholic tradition, but the tendency of Protestantism, in reaction against the minute inquisition of the earlier theologians, has always been to exercise a certain degree of what it regarded as wholesome indifference toward the less obvious manifestations of the flesh. Thus in Protestant countries masturbation seems to have been almost ignored until Tissot, combining with his reputation as a physician the fanaticism of a devout believer, raised masturbation to the position of a colossal bogy which during a hundred years has not only had an unfortunate influence on medical opinion in these matters, but has been productive of incalculable harm to ignorant youth and tender consciences. During the past forty years the efforts of many distinguished physicians—a few of whose opinions I have already quoted—have gradually dragged the bogy down from its pedestal, and now, as I have ventured to suggest, there is a tendency for the reaction to be excessive. There is even a tendency to-day to regard masturbation, with various qualifications, as normal. Remy de Gourmont, for instance, considers that masturbation is natural because it is the method by which fishes procreate: "All things considered, it must be accepted that masturbation is part of the doings of Nature. A different conclusion might be agreeable, but in every ocean and under the reeds of every river, myriads of beings would protest."[1] Tillier remarks that since masturbation appears to be universal among the higher animals we are not entitled to regard it as a vice; it has only been so considered because studied exclusively by physicians under abnormal conditions.[2] Hirth, while asserting that masturbation must be strongly repressed in the young, regards it as a desirable method of relief for adults, and especially, under some circumstances, for women.[3] Venturi, a well-known Italian alienist, on the other

[1] Remy de Gourmont, *Physique de l'Amour*, p. 133.
[2] Tillier, *L'Instinct Sexuel*, Paris, 1889, p. 270.
[3] G. Hirth, *Wege zur Heimat*, p. 648.

hand, regards masturbation as strictly physiological in youth; it is the normal and natural passage toward the generous and healthy passion of early manhood; it only becomes abnormal and vicious, he holds, when continued into adult life.

The appearance of masturbation at puberty, Venturi considers, "is a moment in the course of the development of the function of that organ which is the necessary instrument of sexuality." It finds its motive in the satisfaction of an organic need having much analogy with that which arises from the tickling of a very sensitive cutaneous surface. In this masturbation of early adolescence lies, according to Venturi, the germ of what will later be love: a pleasure of the body and of the spirit, following the relief of a satisfied need. "As the youth develops, onanism becomes a sexual act comparable to coitus as a dream is comparable to reality, imagery forming in correspondence with the desires. In its fully developed form in adolescence," Venturi continues, "masturbation has an almost hallucinatory character; onanism at this period psychically approximates to the true sexual act, and passes insensibly into it. If, however, continued on into adult age, it becomes morbid, passing into erotic fetichism; what in the inexperienced youth is the natural auxiliary and stimulus to imagination, in the degenerate onanist of adult age is a sign of arrested development. Thus, onanism," the author concludes, "is not always a vice such as is fiercely combated by educators and moralists. It is the natural transition by which we reach the warm and generous love of youth, and, in natural succession to this, the tranquil, positive, matrimonial love of the mature man." (Silvio Venturi, *Le Degenerazioni Psico-sessuale*, 1892, pp. 6-9.)

It may be questioned whether this view is acceptable even for the warm climate of the south of Europe, where the impulses of sexuality are undoubtedly precocious. It is certainly not in harmony with general experience and opinion in the north; this is well expressed in the following passage by Edward Carpenter (*International Journal of Ethics*, July, 1899): "After all, purity (in the sense of continence) *is* of the first importance to boyhood. To prolong the period of continence in a boy's life is to prolong the period of *growth*. This is a simple physiological law, and a very obvious one; and, whatever other things may be said in favor of purity, it remains, perhaps, the most weighty. To introduce sensual and sexual habits—and one of the worst of them is self-abuse—at an early age, is to arrest growth, both physical and mental. And what is even more, it means to arrest the capacity for affection. All experience shows that the early outlet toward sex cheapens and weakens affectional capacity."

I do not consider that we can decide the precise degree in which masturbation may fairly be called normal so long as we take masturbation by itself. We are thus, in conclusion, brought back to the point which I sought to emphasize at the outset: masturbation belongs to a group of auto-erotic phenomena. From one point of view it may be said that all auto-erotic phenomena are unnatural, since the natural aim of the sexual impulse is sexual conjunction, and all exercise of that impulse outside such conjunction is away from the end of Nature. But we do not live in a state of Nature which answers to such demands; all our life is "unnatural." And as soon as we begin to restrain the free play of sexual impulse toward sexual ends, at once auto-erotic phenomena inevitably spring up on every side. There is no end to them; it is impossible to say what finest elements in art, in morals, in civilization generally, may not really be rooted in an auto-erotic impulse. "Without a certain overheating of the sexual system," said Nietzsche, "we could not have a Raphael." Auto-erotic phenomena are inevitable. It is our wisest course to recognize this inevitableness of sexual and transmuted sexual manifestations under the perpetual restraints of civilized life, and, while avoiding any attitude of excessive indulgence or indifference,[1] to avoid also any attitude of excessive horror, for our horror not only leads to the facts being effectually veiled from our sight, but itself serves to manufacture artificially a greater evil than that which we seek to combat.

The sexual impulse is not, as some have imagined, the sole root of the most massive human emotions, the most brilliant human aptitudes,—of sympathy, of art, of religion. In the complex human organism, where all the parts are so many-fibred and so closely interwoven, no great manifestation can be reduced to one single source. But it largely enters into and molds all of these emotions and aptitudes, and that by virtue of its two most peculiar characteristics: it is, in the first place, the deepest and

---

[1] Féré, in the course of his valuable work, *L'Instinct Sexuel*, stated that my conclusion is that masturbation is normal, and that *"l'indulgence s'impose."* I had, however, already guarded myself against this misinterpretation.

most volcanic of human impulses, and, in the second place,—unlike the only other human impulse with which it can be compared, the nutritive impulse,—it can, to a large extent, be transmuted into a new force capable of the strangest and most various uses. So that in the presence of all these manifestations we may assert that in a real sense, though subtly mingled with very diverse elements, auto-erotism everywhere plays its part. In the phenomena of auto-erotism, when we take a broad view of those phenomena, we are concerned, not with a form of insanity, not necessarily with a form of depravity, but with the inevitable by-products of that mighty process on which the animal creation rests.

APPENDIX A.

The Influence of Menstruation on the Position of Women.

A question of historical psychology which, so far as I know, has never been fully investigated is the influence of menstruation in constituting the emotional atmosphere through which men habitually view women.[1] I do not purpose to deal fully with this question, because it is one which may be more properly dealt with at length by the student of culture and by the historian, rather than from the standpoint of empirical psychology. It is, moreover, a question full of complexities in regard to which it is impossible to speak with certainty. But we here strike on a factor of such importance, such neglected importance, for the proper understanding of the sexual relations of men and women, that it cannot be wholly ignored.

Among the negroes of Surinam a woman must live in solitude during the time of her period; it is dangerous for any man or woman to approach her, and when she sees a person coming near she cries out anxiously: *"Mi kay! Mi kay!"*—I am unclean! I am unclean! Throughout the world we find traces of the custom of which this is a typical example, but we must not too hastily assume that this custom is evidence of the inferior position occupied by semi-civilized women. It is necessary to take a broad view, not only of the beliefs of semi-civilized man regarding menstruation, but of his general beliefs regarding the supernatural forces of the world.

There is no fragment of folk-lore so familiar to the European world as that which connects woman with the serpent. It is,

---

[1] Several recent works, however, notably Frazer's *Golden Bough* and Crawley's *Mystic Rose*, throw light directly or indirectly on this question.

indeed, one of the foundation stones of Christian theology.[1] Yet there is no fragment of folk-lore which remains more obscure. How has it happened that in all parts of the world the snake or his congeners, the lizard and the crocodile, have been credited with some design, sinister or erotic, on women?

Of the wide prevalence of the belief there can be no doubt. Among the Port Lincoln tribe of South Australia a lizard is said to have divided man from woman.[2] Among the Chiriguanos of Bolivia, on the appearance of menstruation, old women ran about with sticks to hunt the snake that had wounded the girl. Frazer, who quotes this example from the *"Lettres édifiantes et curieuses,"* also refers to a modern Greek folk-tale, according to which a princess at puberty must not let the sun shine upon her, or she would be turned into a lizard.[3] The lizard was a sexual symbol among the Mexicans. In some parts of Brazil at the onset of puberty a girl must not go into the woods for fear of the amorous attacks of snakes, and so it is also among the Macusi Indians of British Guiana, according to Schomburgk. Among the Basutos of South Africa the young girls must dance around the clay image of a snake. In Polynesian mythology the lizard is a very sacred animal, and legends represent women as often giving birth to lizards.[4] At a widely remote spot, in Bengal, if you

---

[1] Robertson Smith points out that since snakes are the last noxious animals which man is able to exterminate, they are the last to be associated with demons. They were ultimately the only animals directly and constantly associated with the Arabian *jinn*, or demon, and the serpent of Eden was a demon, and not a temporary disguise of Satan (*Religion of Semites*, pp. 129 and 442). Perhaps it was, in part, because the snake was thus the last embodiment of demonic power that women were associated with it, women being always connected with the most ancient religious beliefs.

[2] In the northern territory of the same colony menstruation is said to be due to a bandicoot scratching the vagina and causing blood to flow (*Journal of the Anthropological Institute*, p. 177, November, 1894). At Glenelg, and near Portland, in Victoria, the head of a snake was inserted into a virgin's vagina, when not considered large enough for intercourse (Brough Smyth, *Aborigines of Victoria*, vol. ii, p. 319).

[3] Frazer, *Golden Bough*, vol. ii, p. 231. Crawley (*The Mystic Rose*, p. 192) also brings together various cases of primitive peoples who believe the bite of a snake to be the cause of menstruation.

[4] Meyners d'Estrez, "Etude ethnographique sur le lézard chez les peuples malais et polynésiens." *L'Anthropologie*, 1892; see also, as regards the lizard in Samoan folk-lore, *Globus*, vol. lxxiv, No. 16.

dream of a snake a child will be born to you, reports Sarat Chandra Mitra.[1]   In the Berlin Museum für Volkerkunde there is a carved wooden figure from New Guinea of a woman into whose vulva a crocodile is inserting its snout, while the same museum contains another figure of a snake-like crocodile crawling out of a woman's vulva, and a third figure shows a small round snake with a small head, and closely resembling a penis, at the mouth of the vagina.   All these figures are reproduced by Ploss and Bartels.   Even in modern Europe the same ideas prevail.   In Portugal, according to Reys, it is believed that during menstruation women are liable to be bitten by lizards, and to guard against this risk they wear drawers during the period.   In Germany, again, it was believed, up to the eighteenth century at least, that the hair of a menstruating woman, if buried, would turn into a snake. It may be added that in various parts of the world virgin priestesses are dedicated to a snake-god and are married to the god.[2] At Rome, it is interesting to note, the serpent was the symbol of fecundation, and as such often figures at Pompeii as the *genius patrisfamilias*, the generative power of the family.[3]   In Rabbinical tradition, also, the serpent is the symbol of sexual desire.

There can be no doubt that—as Ploss and Bartels, from whom some of these examples have been taken, point out—in widely different parts of the world menstruation is believed to have been originally caused by a snake, and that this conception is frequently associated with an erotic and mystic idea.[4] How the connection arose Ploss and Bartels are unable to say.   It can

[1] *Journal Anthropological Society of Bombay*, 1890, p. 589.

[2] Boudin (*Etude Anthropologique: Culte du Serpent*, Paris, 1864, pp. 66-70) brings forward examples of this aspect of snake-worship.

[3] Attilio de Marchi, *Il Culto privato di Roma*, p. 74. The association of the power of generation with a god in the form of a serpent is, indeed, common; see, *e.g.* Sir W. M. Ramsay, *Cities of Phrygia*, vol. i, p. 94.

[4] It is noteworthy that one of the names for the penis used by the Swahili women of German East Africa, in a kind of private language of their own, is "the snake" (Zache, *Zeitschrift für Ethnologie*, p. 73, 1899). It may be added that Maeder ("Interprétation de Quelques Rêves," *Archives de Psychologie*, April, 1907) brings forward various items of folk-lore showing the phallic significance of the serpent, as well as evidence indicating that, in the dreams of women of to-day, the snake sometimes has a sexual significance.

only be suggested that its shape and appearance, as well as its venomous nature, may have contributed to the mystery everywhere associated with the snake—a mystery itself fortified by the association with women—to build up this world-wide belief regarding the origin of menstruation.

This primitive theory of the origin of menstruation probably brings before us in its earliest shape the special and intimate bond which has ever been held to connect women, by virtue of the menstrual process, with the natural or supernatural powers of the world. Everywhere menstruating women are supposed to be possessed by spirits and charged with mysterious forces. It is at this point that a serious misconception, due to ignorance of primitive religious ideas, has constantly intruded. It is stated that the menstruating woman is "unclean" and possessed by an evil spirit. As a matter of fact, however, the savage rarely discriminates between bad and good spirits. Every spirit may have either a beneficial or malignant influence. An interesting instance of this is given in Colenso's *Maori Lexicon* as illustrated by the meaning of the Maori word *atua*.

The importance of recognizing the special sense in which the word "unclean" is used in this connection was clearly pointed out by Robertson Smith in the case of the Semites. "The Hebrew word *tame* (unclean)," he remarked, "is not the ordinary word for things physically foul; it is a ritual term, and corresponds exactly to the idea of *taboo*. The ideas 'unclean' and 'holy' seem to us to stand in polar opposition to one another, but it was not so with the Semites. Among the later Jews the Holy Books 'defiled the hands' of the reader as contact with an impure thing did; among Lucian's Syrians the dove was so holy that he who touched it was unclean for a day; and the *taboo* attaching to the swine was explained by some, and beyond question correctly explained, in the same way. Among the heathen Semites,[1] therefore, unclean animals, which it was pollution to eat, were simply

---

[1] W. R. Smith, *Kinship and Marriage in Early Arabia*, 1885, p. 307. The point is elaborated in the same author's *Religion of Semites*, second edition, Appendix on "Holiness, Uncleanness, and Taboo," pp. 446-54. See also Wellhausen, *Reste Arabischen Heidentums*, second edition, pp. 167-77. Even to the early Arabians, Wellhausen remarks (p. 168),

holy animals." Robertson Smith here made no reference to menstruation, but he exactly described the primitive attitude toward menstruation. Wellhausen, however, dealing with the early Arabians, expressly mentions that in pre-Islamic days, "clean" and "unclean" were used solely with reference to women in and out of the menstrual state. At a later date Frazer developed this aspect of the conception of taboo, and showed how it occurs among savage races generally. He pointed out that the conceptions of holiness and pollution not having yet been differentiated, women at childbirth and during menstruation are on the same level as divine kings, chiefs, and priests, and must observe the same rules of ceremonial purity. To seclude such persons from the rest of the world, so that the dreaded spiritual danger shall not spread, is the object of the taboo, which Frazer compares to "an electrical insulator to preserve the spiritual force with which these persons are charged from suffering or inflicting harm by contact with the outer world." After describing the phenomena (especially the prohibition to touch the ground or see the sun) found among various races, Frazer concludes: "The object of secluding women at menstruation is to neutralize the dangerous influences which are supposed to emanate from them at such times. The general effect of these rules is to keep the girl suspended, so to say, between heaven and earth. Whether enveloped in her hammock and slung up to the roof, as in South America, or elevated above the ground in a dark and narrow cage, as in New Zealand, she may be considered to be out of the way of doing mischief, since, being shut off both from the earth and from the sun, she can poison neither of these great sources of life by her deadly contagion. The precautions thus taken to isolate or insulate the girl are dictated by regard for her own safety as well as for the safety of others. . . . In short, the girl is viewed as charged with a powerful force which, if not kept within bounds, may prove the destruction both of the girl herself and of all with whom she comes in contact. To

"clean" meant "profane and allowed," while "unclean" meant "sacred and forbidden." It was the same, as Jastrow remarks (*Religion of Babylonia*, p. 662), among the Babylonian Semites.

repress this force within the limits necessary for the safety of all concerned is the object of the taboos in question. The same explanation applies to the observance of the same rules by divine kings and priests. The uncleanliness, as it is called, of girls at puberty and the sanctity of holy men do not, to the primitive mind, differ from each other. They are only different manifestations of the same supernatural energy, which, like energy in general, is in itself neither good nor bad, but becomes beneficent or malignant according to its application."[1]

More recently this view of the matter has been further extended by the distinguished French sociologist, Durkheim. Investigating the origins of the prohibition of incest, and arguing that it proceeds from the custom of exogamy (or marriage outside the clan), and that this rests on certain ideas about blood, which, again, are traceable to totemism,—a theory which we need not here discuss,—Durkheim is brought face to face with the group of conceptions that now concern us. He insists on the extreme ambiguity found in primitive culture concerning the notion of the divine, and the close connection between aversion and veneration, and points out that it is not only at puberty and each recurrence of the menstrual epoch that women have aroused these emotions, but also at childbirth. "A sentiment of religious horror," he continues, "which can reach such a degree of intensity, which can be called forth by so many circumstances, and reappears regularly every month to last for a week at least, cannot fail to extend its influence beyond the periods to which it was originally confined, and to affect the whole course of life. A being who must be secluded or avoided for weeks, months, or years preserves something of the characteristics to which the isolation was due, even outside those special periods. And, in fact, in these communities, the separation of the sexes is not merely intermittent; it has become chronic. The two elements of the population live separately." Durkheim proceeds to argue that the origin of the occult powers attributed to the feminine organism is to be found in primitive ideas concerning blood. Not only menstrual blood but any kind of blood is the object of

[1] J. G. Frazer, *The Golden Bough*, Chapter IV.

such feelings among savage and barbarous peoples. All sorts of precautions must be observed with regard to blood; in it resides a divine principle, or as Romans, Jews, and Arabs believed, life itself. The prohibition to drink wine, the blood of the grape, found among some peoples, is traced to its resemblance to blood, and to its sacrificial employment (as among the ancient Arabians and still in the Christian sacrament) as a substitute for drinking blood. Throughout, blood is generally taboo, and it taboos everything that comes in contact with it. Now woman is chronically "the theatre of bloody manifestations," and therefore she tends to become chronically taboo for the other members of the community. "A more or less conscious anxiety, a certain religious fear, cannot fail to enter into all the relations of her companions with her, and that is why all such relations are reduced to a minimum. Relations of a sexual character are specially excluded. In the first place, such relations are so intimate that they are incompatible with the sort of repulsion which the sexes must experience for each other; the barrier between them does not permit of such a close union. In the second place, the organs of the body here specially concerned are precisely the source of the dreaded manifestations. Thus it is natural that the feelings of aversion inspired by women attain their greatest intensity at this point. Thus it is, also, that of all parts of the feminine organization it is this region which is most severely shut out from commerce." So that, while the primitive emotion is mainly one of veneration, and is allied to that experienced for kings and priests, there is an element of fear in such veneration, and what men fear is to some extent odious to them.[1]

These conceptions necessarily mingled at a very early period with men's ideas of sexual intercourse with women and especially with menstruating women. Contact with women, as Crawley shows by abundant illustration, is dangerous. In any case, indeed, the same ideas being transferred to women also,

---

[1] E. Durkheim, "La Prohibition de l'Inceste et ses Origines," *L'Année Sociologique*, Première Année, 1898, esp. pp. 44, 46-47, 48, 50-57. Crawley (*Mystic Rose*, p. 212) opposes Durkheim's view as to the significance of blood in relation to the attitude towards women.

coitus produces weakness, and it prevents the acquisition of supernatural powers. Thus, among the western tribes of Canada, Boas states: "Only a youth who has never touched a woman, or a virgin, both being called *tc 'e 'its*, can become shamans. After having had sexual intercourse men as well as women become *t 'k-e 'el*, *i.e.*, weak, incapable of gaining supernatural powers. The faculty cannot be regained by subsequent fasting and abstinence."[1] The mysterious effects of sexual intercourse in general are intensified in the case of intercourse with a menstruating woman. Thus the ancient Indian legislator declares that "the wisdom, the energy, the strength, the sight, and the vitality of a man who approaches a woman covered with menstrual excretions utterly perish."[2] It will be seen that these ideas are impartially spread over the most widely separated parts of the globe. They equally affected the Christian Church, and the Penitentials ordained forty or fifty days penance for sexual intercourse during menstruation.

Yet the twofold influence of the menstruating woman remains clear when we review the whole group of influences which in this state she is supposed to exert. She by no means acts only by paralyzing social activities and destroying the powers of life, by causing flowers to fade, fruit to fall from the trees, grains to lose their germinative power, and grafts to die. She is not accurately summed up in the old lines:—

> "Oh! menstruating woman, thou'rt a fiend
> From whom all nature should be closely screened."

Her powers are also beneficial. A woman at this time, as Ælian expressed it, is in regular communication with the starry bodies. Even at other times a woman when led naked around the orchard protected it from caterpillars, said Pliny, and this belief is acted upon (according to Bastanzi) even in the Italy of to-day.[3] A garment stained with a virgin's menstrual blood, it

---

[1] *British Association Report on North Western Tribes of Canada*, 1890, p. 581.

[2] *Laws of Manu*, iv, 41.

[3] Pliny, who, in Book VII, Chapter XIII, and Book XXVIII, Chapter XXIII, of his *Natural History*, gives long lists of the various good and evil influences attributed to menstruation, writes in the latter

is said in Bavaria, is a certain safeguard against cuts and stabs. It will also extinguish fire. It was valuable as a love-philter; as a medicine its uses have been endless.[1] A sect of Valentinians even attributed sacramental virtues to menstrual blood, and partook of it as the blood of Christ. The Church soon, however, acquired a horror of menstruating women; they were frequently not allowed to take the sacrament or to enter sacred places, and it was sometimes thought best to prohibit the presence of women altogether.[2] The Anglo-Saxon Penitentials declared that menstruating women must not enter a church. It appears to have been Gregory II who overturned this doctrine.

In our own time the slow disintegration of primitive animistic conceptions, aided certainly by the degraded conception of sexual phenomena taught by mediæval monks—for whom woman was *"templum ædificatum super cloacam"*—has led to a disbelief in the more salutary influences of the menstruating woman. A fairly widespread faith in her pernicious influence alone survives. It may be traced even in practical and commercial—one might add, medical—quarters. In the great sugar-refineries in the North of France the regulations strictly forbid a woman to enter the factory while the sugar is boiling or cooling, the reason given being that, if a woman were to enter during her period, the sugar would blacken. For the same reason—to turn to the East—no woman is employed in the opium manufactory at Saigon, it being said that the opium would turn and

place: "Hailstorms, they say, whirlwinds, and lightnings, even, will be scared away by a woman uncovering her body while her monthly courses are upon her. The same, too, with all other kinds of tempestuous weather; and out at sea, a storm may be stilled by a woman uncovering her body merely, even though not menstruating at the time. At any other time, also, if a woman strips herself naked while she is menstruating, and walks round a field of wheat, the caterpillars, worms, beetles, and other vermin will fall from off the ears of corn."

[1] See Bourke, *Scatologic Rites of all Nations*, 1891, pp. 217-219, 250 and 254; Ploss and Max Bartels, *Das Weib*, vol. i; H. L. Strack, *Der Blutaberglaube in der Menschheit*, fourth edition, 1892, pp. 14-18. The last mentioned refers to the efficacy frequently attributed to menstrual blood in the Middle Ages in curing leprosy, and gives instances, occurring even in Germany to-day, of girls who have administered drops of menstrual blood in coffee to their sweethearts, to make sure of retaining their affections.

[2] See, *e.g.*, Dufour, *Histoire de la Prostitution*, vol. iii, p. 115.

become bitter, while Annamite women say that it is very difficult for them to prepare opium-pipes during the catamenial period.[1] In India, again, when a native in charge of a limekiln which had gone wrong, declared that one of the women workers must be menstruating, all the women—Hindus, Mahometans, aboriginal Gonds, etc.,—showed by their energetic denials that they understood this superstition.[2]

In 1878 a member of the British Medical Association wrote to the *British Medical Journal*, asking whether it was true that if a woman cured hams while menstruating the hams would be spoiled. He had known this to happen twice. Another medical man wrote that if so, what would happen to the patients of menstruating lady doctors? A third wrote (in the *Journal* for April 27, 1878): "I thought the fact was so generally known to every housewife and cook that meat would spoil if salted at the menstrual period, that I am surprised to see so many letters on the subject in the *Journal*. If I am not mistaken, the question was mooted many years ago in the periodicals. It is undoubtedly the fact that meat will be tainted if cured by women at the catamenial period. Whatever the rationale may be, I can speak positively as to the fact."

It is probably the influence of these primitive ideas which has caused surgeons and gynæcologists to dread operations during the catamenial period. Such, at all events, is the opinion of a distinguished authority, Dr. William Goodell, who wrote in 1891[3]: "I have learned to unlearn the teaching that women must not be subjected to a surgical operation during the monthly flux. Our forefathers, from time immemorial, have thought and taught that the presence of a menstruating woman would pollute solemn religious rites, would sour milk, spoil the fermentation in wine-vats, and much other mischief in a general way. Influenced

---

[1] Dr. L. Laurent gives these instances, "De Quelques Phénomènes Mécaniques produits au moment de la Menstruation," *Annales des Sciences Psychiques*, September and October, 1897.

[2] *Journal Anthropological Society of Bombay*, 1890, p. 403. Even the glance of a menstruating woman is widely believed to have serious results. See Tuchmann, "La Fascination," *Mélasine*, 1888, pp. 347 *et seq.*

[3] As quoted in the *Provincial Medical Journal*, April, 1891.

by hoary tradition, modern physicians very generally postpone all operative treatment until the flow has ceased. But why this delay, if time is precious, and it enters as an important factor in the case? I have found menstruation to be the very best time to curette away fungous vegetations of the endometrium, for, being swollen then by the afflux of blood, they are larger than at any other time, and can the more readily be removed. There is, indeed, no surer way of checking or of stopping a metrorrhagia than by curetting the womb during the very flow. While I do not select this period for the removal of ovarian cysts, or for other abdominal work, such as the extirpation of the ovaries, or a kidney, or breaking up intestinal adhesions, etc., yet I have not hesitated to perform these operations at such a time, and have never had reason to regret the course. The only operations that I should dislike to perform during menstruation would be those involving the womb itself."

It must be added to this that we still have to take into consideration not merely the surviving influence of ancient primitive beliefs, but the possible existence of actual nervous conditions during the menstrual period, producing what may be described as an abnormal nervous tension. In this way, we are doubtless concerned with a tissue of phenomena, inextricably woven of folk-lore, autosuggestion, false observation, and real mental and nervous abnormality. Laurent (*loc. cit.*) has brought forward several cases which may illustrate this point. Thus, he speaks of two young girls of about 16 and 17, slightly neuropathic, but without definite hysterical symptoms, who, during the menstrual period, feel themselves in a sort of electrical state, "with tingling and prickling sensations and feelings of attraction or repulsion at the contact of various objects." These girls believe their garments stick to their skin during the periods; it was only with difficulty that they could remove their slippers, though fitting easily; stockings had to be drawn off violently by another person, and they had given up changing their chemises during the period because the linen became so glued to the skin. An orchestral performer on the double-bass informed Laurent that whenever he left a tuned double-bass in his lodgings during his wife's period a string snapped; consequently he always removed his instrument at this time to a friend's house. He added that the same thing happened two years earlier with a mistress, a *café-concert* singer, who had, indeed, warned him beforehand. A harpist also informed Laurent that she had been obliged to give up her profession because during her periods several strings of her harp, always the same strings, broke, especially when she was playing. A friend of Laurent's, an official in Cochin China, also told him that the strings of his violin often snapped during the menstrual periods of his Annamite mistress, who informed him that Annamite women are familiar with the phenomenon, and are careful not to play on their instruments at this time. Two young ladies, both good violinists, also affirmed that ever since their first menstruation they had noted a tendency for the strings to snap at this period; one, a genuine artist, who often performed at charity concerts, systematically refused to play at these times, and was often embarrassed to find a pretext; the other, who admitted that she was nervous and irritable at such times, had given up playing on account of the trouble of changing the strings so frequently. Laurent also refers to the frequency with which women break things during the menstrual periods, and considers that this is not simply due to the awkwardness caused by nervous exhaustion or hysterical tremors, but that there is spontaneous breakage. Most usually it happens that a glass breaks when it is being dried with a cloth; needles also break with unusual facility at this time; clocks are stopped by merely placing the hand upon them.

I do not here attempt to estimate critically the validity of these alleged manifestations (some of which may certainly be explained by the unconscious muscular action which forms the basis of the phenomena of table-turning and thought-reading); such a task may best be undertaken through the minute study of isolated cases, and in this place I am merely concerned with the general influence of the menstrual state in affecting the social position of women, without reference to the anaylsis of the elements that go to make up that influence.

There is only one further point to which attention may be

called. I allude to the way in which the more favorable side of the primitive conception of the menstruating woman—as priestess, sibyl, prophetess, an almost miraculous agent for good, an angel, the peculiar home of the divine element—was slowly and continuously carried on side by side with the less favorable view, through the beginnings of European civilization until our own times. The actual physical phenomena of menstruation, with the ideas of taboo associated with that state, sank into the background as culture evolved; but, on the other hand, the ideas of the angelic position and spiritual mission of women, based on the primitive conception of the mystery associated with menstruation, still in some degree persisted.

It is evident, however, that, while, in one form or another, the more favorable aspect of the primitive view of women's magic function has never quite died out, the gradual decay and degradation of the primitive view has, on the whole, involved a lower estimate of women's nature and position. Woman has always been the witch; she was so even in ancient Babylonia; but she has ceased to be the priestess. The early Teutons saw *"sanctum aliquid et providum"* in women who, for the mediæval German preacher, were only *"bestiæ bipedales"*; and Schopenhauer and even Nietzsche have been more inclined to side with the preacher than with the half-naked philosophers of Tacitus's day. But both views alike are but the extremes of the same primitive conception; and the gradual evolution from one extreme of the magical doctrine to the other was inevitable.

In an advanced civilization, as we see, these ideas having their ultimate basis on the old story of the serpent, and on a special and mysterious connection between the menstruating woman and the occult forces of magic, tend to die out. The separation of the sexes they involve becomes unnecessary. Living in greater community with men, women are seen to possess something, it may well be, but less than before, of the angel-devil of early theories. Menstruation is no longer a monstrific state requiring spiritual taboo, but a normal physiological process, not without its psychic influences on the woman herself and on those who live with her.

APPENDIX B.

Sexual Periodicity in Men.

By F. H. Perry-Coste, B.Sc. (Lond.).

In a recent *brochure* on the "Rhythm of the Pulse"[1] I showed *inter alia* that the readings of the pulse, in both man and woman, if arranged in lunar monthly periods, and averaged over several years, displayed a clear, and sometimes very strongly marked and symmetrical, rhythm.[2] After pointing out that, in at any rate some cases, the male and female pulse-curves, both monthly and annual, seemed to be converse to one another, I added: "It is difficult to ignore the suggestion that in this tracing of the monthly rhythm of the pulse we have a history of the monthly function in women; and that, if so, the tracing of the male pulse may eventually afford us some help in discovering a corresponding monthly period in men: the existence of which has been suggested by Mr. Havelock Ellis and Professor Stanley Hall, among other writers. Certainly the mere fact that we can trace a clear monthly rhythm in man's pulse seems to point strongly to the existence of a monthly physiological period in him also."

Obviously, however, it is only indirectly and by inference that we can argue from a monthly rhythm of the pulse in men to a male sexual periodicity; but I am now able to adduce more direct evidence that will fairly demonstrate the existence of a sexual periodicity in men.

---

[1] First published in the *University Magazine and Free Review* of February, 1898, and since reprinted as a pamphlet. A preliminary communication appeared in *Nature*, May 14, 1891.

[2 Later study (1906) has convinced me that my attempt to find a lunar-monthly period in the female pulse was vitiated by a hopeless error: for any monthly rhythm in a woman must be sought by arranging her records according to her own menstrual month; and this menstrual month may vary in different women, from considerably less than a lunar month to thirty days or more.]

We will start from the fact that celibacy is profoundly un-natural, and is, therefore, a physical—as well as an emotional and intellectual—abnormality. This being so, it is entirely in accord with all that we know of physiology that, when relief to the sex-ual secretory system by Nature's means is denied, and when, in consequence, a certain degree of tension or pressure has been attained, the system should relieve itself by a spontaneous dis-charge—such discharge being, of course, in the strict sense of the term, pathological, since it would never occur in any animal that followed the strict law of its physical being without any re-gard to other and higher laws of concern for its fellows.

Notoriously, that which we should have anticipated *a priori* actually occurs; for any unmarried man, who lives in strict chastity, periodically experiences, while sleeping, a loss of semi-nal fluid—such phenomena being popularly referred to as *wet dreams.*[1]

During some eight or ten years I have carefully recorded the occurrence of such discharges as I have experienced myself, and I have now accumulated sufficient data to justify an attempt to formulate some provisional conclusions.[2]

In order to render these observations as serviceable as may be to students of periodicity, I here repeat (at the request of Mr. Havelock Ellis) the statement which was subjoined, for the same reasons, to my "Rhythm of the Pulse." These observations upon myself were made between the ages of 20 and 33. I am about 5 feet, 9 inches tall, broad-shouldered, and weigh about 10 stone 3 lbs. *net*—this weight being, I believe, about 7 lbs. below the normal for my height. Also I have green-brown eyes, very dark-brown hair, and a complexion that leads strangers frequently to

---

[1] I may add, however, that in my own case these discharges are—so far as I can trust my waking consciousness—frequently, if not usually, dreamless; and that strictly sexual dreams are extremely rare, notwith-standing the possession of a strongly emotional temperament.

[2] If I can trust my memory, I first experienced this discharge when a few months under fifteen years of age, and, if so, within a few weeks of the time when I was, in an instant, suddenly struck with the thought that possibly the religion in which I had been educated might be false. It is curiously interesting that the advent of puberty should have been heralded by this intellectual crisis.

mistake me for a foreigner—this complexion being, perhaps, attributable to some Huguenot blood, although on the maternal side I am, so far as all information goes, pure English. I can stand a good deal of heat, enjoy relaxing climates, am at once upset by "bracing" sea-air, hate the cold, and sweat profusely after exercise. To this it will suffice to add that my temperament is of a decidedly nervous and emotional type.

Before proceeding to remark upon the various rhythms that I have discovered, I will tabulate the data on which my conclusions are founded. The numbers of discharges recorded in the years in question are as follows:—

In 1886, 30.   (Records commenced in April.)
In 1887, 40.
In 1888, 37.
In 1889, 18.   (Pretty certainly not fully recorded.)
In 1890, 0   (No records kept this year.[1])
In 1891, 19.   (Records recommenced in June.)
In 1892, 35.
In 1893, 40.
In 1894, 38.
In 1895, 36.
In 1896, 36.
In 1897, 35.
Average, 37.   (Omitting 1886, 1889, and 1891.)

Thus I have complete records for eight years, and incomplete records for three more; and the remarkable concord between the respective annual numbers of observations in these eight years not only affords us intrinsic evidence of the accuracy of my records, but, also, at once proves that there is an undeniable regularity in the occurrence of these sexual discharges, and, therefore, gives us reason for expecting to find this regularity

[1] This unfortunate breach in the records was due to the fact that, failing to discover any regularity in, or law of, the occurrences of the discharges, I hecame discouraged and abandoned my records. In June, 1891, a re-examination of my pulse-records having led to my discovery of a lunar-monthly rhythm of the pulse, my interest in other physiological periodicities was reawakened, and I recommenced my records of these discharges.

rhythmical. Moreover, since it seemed reasonable to expect that there might be more than one rhythm, I have examined my data with a view to discovering (1) an annual, (2) a lunar-monthly, and (3) a weekly rhythm, and I now proceed to show that all three such rhythms exist.

The Annual Rhythm.

It is obvious that, in searching for an annual rhythm, we must ignore the records of the three incomplete years; but those of the remaining eight are graphically depicted upon Chart 8. The curves speak so plainly for themselves that any comment were almost superfluous, and the concord between the various curves, although, of course, not perfect, is far greater than the scantiness of the data would have justified us in expecting. The curves all agree in pointing to the existence of three well-defined maxima,—viz., in March, June, and September,—these being, therefore, the months in which the sexual instinct is most active; and the later curves show that there is also often a fourth maximum in January. In the earlier years the March and June maxima are more strikingly marked than the September one; but the uppermost curve shows that on the average of all eight years the September maximum is the highest, the June and January maxima occupying the second place, and the March maximum being the least strongly marked of all.

Now, remembering that, in calculating the curves of the annual rhythm of the pulse, I had found it necessary to average two months' records together, in order to bring out the full significance of the rhythm, I thought it well to try the effect upon these curves also of similarly averaging two months together. At first my results were fairly satisfactory; but, as my data increased year by year, I found that these curves were contradicting one another, and therefore concluded that I had selected unnatural periods for my averaging. My first attempted remedy was to arrange the months in the pairs December-January, February-March, etc., instead of in January-February, March-April, etc.; but with these pairs I fared no better than with the former. I then arranged the months in the triplets,

January-February-March, etc.; and the results are graphically recorded on Chart 7. Here, again, comment would be quite futile, but I need only point out that, *on the whole,* the sexual activity rises steadily during the first nine months in the year to its maximum in September, and then sinks rapidly and abruptly during the next three to its minimum in December.

The study of these curves suggests two interesting questions, to neither of which, however, do the data afford us an answer.

In the first place, are the alterations, in my case, of the maximum of the discharges from March and June in the earlier years to September in the later, and the interpolation of a new secondary maximum in January, correlated with the increase in age; or is the discrepancy due simply to a temporary irregularity that would have been equally averaged out had I recorded the discharges of 1881-89 instead of those from 1887 to 1897?

The second question is one of very great importance—socially, ethically, and physically. How often, in this climate, should a man have sexual connection with his wife in order to maintain himself in perfect physiological equilibrium? My results enable us to state definitely the minimum limits, and to reply that 37 embraces annually would be too few; but, unfortunately, they give us no clue to the maximum limit. It is obvious that the necessary frequency should be greater than 37 times annually,—possibly very considerably in excess thereof,—seeing that the spontaneous discharges, with which we are dealing, are due to over-pressure, and occur only when the system, being denied natural relief, can no longer retain its secretions; and, therefore, it seems very reasonable to suggest that the frequency of natural relief should be some multiple of 37. I do not perceive, however, that the data in hand afford us any clue to this multiple, or enable us to suggest either 2, 3, 4, or 5 as the required multiple of 37. It is true that other observations upon myself have afforded me what I believe to be a fairly satisfactory and reliable answer so far as concerns myself; but these observations are of such a nature that they cannot be discussed here, and I have no inclination to offer as a counsel to others an opinion which I am unable to justify by the citation of facts and statistics. Moreover, I am quite unable to opine whether, given 37 as the annual frequency of spontaneous discharges in a number of men, the multiple required for the frequency of natural relief should be the same in every case. For aught I know to the contrary, the physiological idiosyncrasies of men may be so varied that, given two men with an annual frequency of 37 spontaneous discharges, the desired multiple may be in one case X and in the other 2X.[1] Our data, however, do clearly denote that the frequency in the six or eight summer months should bear to the frequency of the six or four winter months the proportion of three or four to two.[2] It should never be forgotten, however, that, under all conditions, both man and wife should exercise prudence, both *selfward* and *otherward,* and that each should utterly refuse to gratify self by accepting a sacrifice, however willingly offered, that may be gravely prejudicial to the health of the other; for only experience can show whether, in any

---

[1] As a matter of fact, I take it that we may safely assert that no man who is content to be guided by his own instinctive cravings, and who neither suppresses these, on the one hand, nor endeavors to force himself, on the other hand, will be in any danger of erring by either excess or the contrary.

[2 It is obvious that the opportunity of continuing such an inquiry as that described in this Appendix, ceases with marriage; but I may add (1906) that certain notes that I have kept with scrupulous exactness during eight years of married life, lend almost no support to the suggestion made in the text—*i.e.*, that sexual desire is greater at one season of the year than at another. The nature of these notes I cannot discuss; but, they clearly indicate that, although there is a slight degree more of sexual desire in the second and third quarters of the year, than in the first and fourth, yet, this difference is so slight as to be almost negligible. Even if the months be rearranged in the triplets—November-December-January, etc.,—so as to bring the maximum months of May, June, and July together, the difference between the highest quarter and the lowest amounts to an increase of only ten per cent. upon the latter—after allowing, of course, for the abnormal shortness of February; and, neglecting February, the increase in the maximum months (June and July) over the minimum (November) is equal to an increase of under 14 per cent. upon the latter. These differences are so vastly less than those shown on Chart 7 that they possess almost no significance: but, lest too much stress be laid upon the apparently *equalizing* influence of married life, it must be added that the records discussed in the text were obtained during residence in London, whereas, since my marriage, I have lived in South Cornwall, where the climate is both milder and more equable.]

union, the receptivity of the woman be greater or less than, or equal to, the *physical* desire of the man. To those, of course, who regard marriage from the old-fashioned and grossly immoral standpoint of Melancthon and other theologians, and who consider a wife as the divinely ordained vehicle for the chartered intemperance of her husband, it will seem grotesque in the highest degree that a physiological inquirer should attempt to advise them how often to seek the embraces of their wives; but those who regard woman from the standpoint of a higher ethics, who abhor the notion that she should be only the vehicle for her husband's passions, and who demand that she shall be mistress of her own body, will not be ungrateful for any guidance that physiology can afford them. It will be seen presently, moreover, that the study of the weekly rhythm does afford us some less inexact clue to the desired solution.

One curious fact may be mentioned before we quit this interesting question. It is stated that "Solon required [of the husband] three *payments* per month. By the Misna a daily debt was imposed upon an idle vigorous young husband; *twice a week* on a citizen; once in thirty days on a camel-driver; once in six months on a seaman."[1] Now it is certainly striking that Solon's "three payments per month" exactly correspond with my records of 37 discharges annually. Had Solon similarly recorded a series of observations upon himself?

THE LUNAR-MONTHLY RHYTHM.

We now come to that division of the inquiry which is of the greatest physiological interest, although of little social import. Is there a monthly period in man as well as in woman? My records indicate clearly that there is.

In searching for this monthly rhythm I have utilized not only the data of the eight completely-recorded years, but also those of the three years of 1886, 1889, and 1891, for, although it would obviously have been inaccurate to utilize these incom-

---

[1] Selden's *Uxor Hebraica* as quoted in Gibbon's *Decline and Fall*, vol. **v**, p. 52, of Bohn's edition.

plete records when calculating the yearly rhythm, there seems
no objection to making use of them in the present section of
the inquiry. It is hardly necessary to remark that the terms
"first day of the month," "second day," "third day," etc., are to
be understood as denoting "new-moon day," "day after new
moon," "third lunar day," and so on; but it should be explained
that, since these discharges occur at night, I have adopted the
astronomical, instead of the civil, day; so that a new moon occurring between noon yesterday and noon to-day is reckoned as
occurring yesterday, and yesterday is regarded as the first lunar
day: thus, a discharge occurring in the night between December
31st and January 1st is tabulated as occurring on December 31st,
and, in the present discussion, is assigned to the lunar day com-
prised between noon of December 31st and noon of January 1st.

Since it is obvious that the number of discharges in any
one year—averaging, as they do, only 1.25 per day—are far too
few to yield a curve of any value, I have combined my data in
two series. The dotted curve on Chart 9 is obtained by combining the results of the years 1886-92: two of these years are
incompletely recorded, and there are no records for 1890; the
total number of observations was 179. The broken curve is
obtained by combining those of the years 1893-97, the total number of observations being 185. Even so, the data are far too
scanty to yield a really characteristic curve; but the *continuous*
curve, which sums up the results of the eleven years, is more
reliable, and obviously more satisfactory.

If the two former curves be compared, it will be seen that,
on the whole, they display a general concordance, such differences as exist being attributable chiefly to two facts: (1) that
the second curve is more even throughout, neither maximum nor
minimum being so strongly marked as in the first; and (2) that
the main maximum occurs in the middle of the month instead
of on the second lunar day, and the absence of the marked
initial maximum alters the character of the first week or so of
this curve. It is, however, scarcely fair to lay any great stress
on the characters of curves obtained from such scanty data, and

we will, therefore, pass to the continuous curve, the study of which will prove more valuable.[1]

Now, even a cursory examination of this continuous curve will yield the following results:—

1. The discharges occur most frequently on the second lunar day.

2. The days of the next most frequent discharges are the 22d; the 13th; the 7th, 20th, and 26th; the 11th and 16th; so that, if we regard only the first six of these, we find that the discharges occur most frequently on the 2d, 7th, 13th, 20th, 22d, and 26th lunar days—*i.e.*, the discharges occur most frequently on days separated, on the average, by four-day intervals; but actually the period between the 20th and 22d days is that characterized by the most frequent discharges.

3. The days of minimum of discharge are the 1st, 5th, 15th, 18th, and 21st.

4. The curve is characterized by a continual see-sawing; so that every notable maximum is immediately followed by a notable minimum. Thus, the curve is of an entirely different character from that representing the monthly rhythm of the pulse,[2] and this is only what one might have expected; for, whereas the *mean* pulsations vary only very slightly from day to day,—thus giving rise to a gradually rising or sinking curve, —a discharge from the sexual system relieves the tension by exhausting the stored-up secretion, and is necessarily followed by some days of rest and inactivity. In the very nature of the case, therefore, a curve of this kind could not possibly be otherwise than most irregular if the discharges tended to occur most frequently upon definite days of the month; and thus the very irregularity of the curve affords us proof that there is a regular male periodicity, such that on certain days of the month there is greater probability of a spontaneous discharge than on any other days.

---

[1] I may add that the curve yielded by 1896-97 is remarkably parallel with that yielded by the preceding nine years, but I have not thought it worth while to chart these two additional curves.

[2] See "Rhythm of the Pulse," Chart 4.

5. Gratifying, however, though this irregularity of the curve may be, yet it entails a corresponding disadvantage, for we are precluded thereby from readily perceiving the characteristics of the monthly rhythm as a whole. I thought that perhaps this aspect of the rhythm might be rendered plainer if I calculated the data into two-day averages; and the result, as shown in Chart 10, is extremely satisfactory. Here we can at once perceive the wonderful and almost geometric symmetry of the monthly rhythm; indeed, if the third maximum were one unit higher, if the first minimum were one unit lower, and if the lines joining the second minimum and third maximum, and the fourth maximum and fourth minimum, were straight instead of being slightly broken, then the curve would, in its chief features, be geometrically symmetrical; and this symmetry appears to me to afford a convincing proof of the representative accuracy of the curve. We see that the month is divided into five periods; that the maxima occur on the following pairs of days: the 19th-20th, 13th-14th, 25th-26th, 1st-2d, 7th-8th; and that the minima occur at the beginning, end, and exact middle of the month. There have been many idle superstitions as to the influence of the moon upon the earth and its inhabitants, and some beliefs that—once deemed equally idle—have now been re-instated in the regard of science; but it would certainly seem to be a very fascinating and very curious fact if the influence of the moon upon men should be such as to regulate the spontaneous discharges of their sexual system. Certainly the lovers of all ages would then have "builded better than they knew," when they reared altars of devotional verse to that chaste goddess Artemis.

The Weekly Rhythm.

We now come to the third branch of our inquiry, and have to ask whether there be any weekly rhythm of the sexual activity. A priori it might be answered that to expect any such weekly rhythm were absurd, seeing that our week—unlike the lunar month of the year—is a purely artificial and conventional period; while, on the other hand, it might be retorted that the existence of an induced weekly periodicity is quite conceivable, such periodicity being induced by the habitual difference between our occupation, or mode of life, on one or two days of the week and that on the remaining days. In such an inquiry, however, *a priori* argument is futile, as the question can be answered only by an induction from observations, and the curves on Chart 11 (*A* and *B*) prove conclusively that there is a notable weekly rhythm. The existence of this weekly rhythm being granted, it would naturally be assumed that either the maximum or the minimum would regularly occur on Saturday or Sunday; but an examination of the curves discloses the unexpected result that the day of maximum discharge varies from year to year. Thus it is[1]

Sunday in   1888, 1892, 1896.
Tuesday in   1894.
Thursday in   1886, 1897.
Friday in   1887.
Saturday in   1893 and 1895.

Since, in Chart 11, the curves are drawn from Sunday to Sunday, it is obvious that the real symmetry of the curve is brought out in those years only which are characterized by a Sunday maximum; and, accordingly, in Chart 12 I have depicted the curves in a more suitable form.

Chart 12 *A* is obtained by combining the data of 1888, 1892, and 1896: the years of a Sunday maximum. Curve 12 *B* represents the results of 1894, the year of a Tuesday maximum — multiplied throughout by three in order to render the curve strictly comparable with the former. Curve 12 *C* represents 1886 and 1897 — the years of a Thursday maximum — similarly multiplied by 1.5. In Curve 12 *D* we have the results of 1887 — the year of a Friday maximum — again multiplied by three; and in Curve 12 *E* those of 1893 and 1895 — the years of a Saturday maximum — multiplied by 1.5. Finally, Curve 12 *F* represents the combined results of all nine years plus (the latter half of)

---

[1] As will be observed, I have omitted the results of the incompletely recorded years of 1889 and 1891. The apparent explanation of this curious oscillation will be given directly.

1891; and this curve shows that, on the whole period, there is a very strongly marked Sunday maximum.

I hardly think that these curves call for much comment. In their general character they display a notable concord among themselves; and it is significant that the most regular of the five curves are *A* and *E*, representing the combinations of three years and of two years, respectively, while the least regular is *B*, which is based upon the records of one year only. In every case we find that the maximum which opens the week is rapidly succeeded by a minimum, which is itself succeeded by a secondary maximum,—usually very secondary, although in 1894 it nearly equals the primary maximum,—followed again by a second minimum—usually nearly identical with the first minimum,—after which there is a rapid rise to the original maximum. The study of these curves fortunately amplifies the conclusion drawn from our study of the annual rhythm, and suggests that, in at least part of the year, the physiological condition of man requires sexual union at least twice a week.

As to Curve 12 *F,* its remarkable symmetry speaks for itself. The existence of two secondary maxima, however, has not the same significance as had that of our secondary maximum in the preceding curves; for one of these secondary maxima is due to the influence of the 1894 curve with its primary Tuesday maximum, and the other to the similar influence of Curve *C* with its primary Thursday maximum. Similarly, the veiled third secondary maximum is due to the influence of Curve *E.* Probably, any student of curves will concede that, on a still larger average, the two secondary maxima of Curve *F* would be replaced by a single one on Wednesday or Thursday.

One more question remains for consideration in connection with this weekly rhythm. Is it possible to trace any connection between the weekly and yearly rhythms of such a character that the weekly day of maximum discharge should vary from month to month in the year; in other words, does the greater frequency of a Sunday discharge characterize one part of the year, that of a Tuesday another, and so on? In order to answer this question I have re-calculated all my data, with results that are graphically represented in Chart 13. These curves prove that the Sunday maxima discharges occur in March and September, and the minima in June; that the Monday maxima discharges occur in September, Friday in July, and so on. Thus, there is a regular rhythm, according to which the days of maximum discharge vary from one month of the year to another; and the existence of this final rhythm appears to me very remarkable. I would especially direct attention to the almost geometric symmetry of the Sunday curve, and to the only less complete symmetry of the Thursday and Friday curves. Certainly in these rhythms we have an ample field for farther study and speculation.

I have now concluded my study of this fascinating inquiry; a study that is necessarily incomplete, since it is based upon records furnished by one individual only. The fact, however, that, even with so few observations, and notwithstanding the consequently exaggerated disturbing influence of minor irregularities, such remarkable and unexpected symmetry is evidenced by these curves, only increases one's desire to have the opportunity of handling a series of observations sufficiently numerous to render the generalizations induced from them absolutely conclusive. I would again appeal[1] to heads of colleges to assist this inquiry by enlisting in its aid a band of students. If only one hundred students, living under similar conditions, could be induced to keep such records with scrupulous regularity for only twelve months, the results induced from such a series of observations would be more than ten times as valuable as those which have only been reached after ten years' observations on my part; and, if other centuries of students in foreign and colonial colleges—*e.g.,* in Italy, India, Australia, and America—could be similarly enlisted in this work, we should quickly obtain a series of results exhibiting the sexual needs and sexual peculiarities of the male human animal in various climates. Obviously, however, the records of any such students would be worse than useless unless their care and accuracy, on the one hand, and their habitual chastity, on the other, could be implicitly guaranteed.

---

1 See "Rhythm of the Pulse," p. 21.

APPENDIX C.

The Auto-erotic Factor in Religion.

The intimate association between the emotions of love and religion is well known to all those who are habitually brought into close contact with the phenomena of the religious life. Love and religion are the two most volcanic emotions to which the human organism is liable, and it is not surprising that, when there is a disturbance in one of these spheres, the vibrations should readily extend to the other. Nor is it surprising that the two emotions should have a dynamic relation to each other, and that the auto-erotic impulse, being the more primitive and fundamental of the two impulses, should be able to pass its unexpended energy over to the religious emotion, there to find the expansion hitherto denied it, the love of the human becoming the love of the divine.

> "I was not good enough for man,
> And so am given to God."

Even when there is absolute physical suppression on the sexual side, it seems probable that thereby a greater intensity of spiritual fervor is caused. Many eminent thinkers seem to have been without sexual desire.

It is a noteworthy and significant fact that the age of love is also the age of conversion. Starbuck, for instance, in his very elaborate study of the psychology of conversion shows that the majority of conversions take place during the period of adolescence; that is, from the age of puberty to about 24 or 25.[1]

It would be easy to bring forward a long series of observations, from the most various points of view, to show the wide

-----

[1] Starbuck, *The Psychology of Religion*, 1899. Also, A. H. Daniels, "The New Life," *American Journal of Psychology*, vol. vi, 1893. *Cf.* William James, *The Varieties of Religious Experience*.

(310)

recognition of this close affinity between the sexual and the religious emotions. It is probable, as Hahn points out, that the connection between sexual suppression and religious rites, which we may trace at the very beginning of culture, was due to an instinctive impulse to heighten rather than abolish the sexual element. Early religious rites were largely sexual and orgiastic because they were largely an appeal to the generative forces of Nature to exhibit a beneficial productiveness. Among happily married people, as Hahn remarks, the sexual emotions rapidly give place to the cares and anxieties involved in supporting children; but when the exercise of the sexual function is prevented by celibacy, or even by castration, the most complete form of celibacy, the sexual emotions may pass into the psychical sphere to take on a more pronounced shape.[1] The early Christians adopted the traditional Eastern association between religion and celibacy, and, as the writings of the Fathers amply show, they expended on sexual matters a concentrated fervor of thought rarely known to the Greek and Roman writers of the best period.[2] As Christian theology developed, the minute inquisition into sexual things sometimes became almost an obsession. So far as I am aware, however (I cannot profess to have made any special investigation), it was not until the late Middle Ages that there is any clear recognition of the fact that, between the religious emotions and the sexual emotions, there is not only a superficial antagonism, but an underlying relationship. At this time so great a theologian and philosopher as Aquinas said that it is especially on the days when a man is seeking to make himself pleasing to God that the Devil troubles him by polluting him with seminal emissions. With somewhat more psychological insight, the wise old Knight of the Tower, Landry, in the fourteenth century, tells his daughters that "no young woman, in

---

1 Ed. Hahn, *Demeter und Baubo*, 1896, pp. 50-51. Hahn is arguing for the religious origin of the plough, as a generative implement, drawn by a sacred and castrated animal, the ox. G. Herman, in his *Genesis*, develops the idea that modern religious rites have arisen out of sexual feasts and mysteries.

2 Bloch (*Beiträge zur Ætiologie der Psychopathia Sexualis*, Bd. I, p. 98) points out the great interest taken by the saints and ascetics in sex matters.

love, can ever serve her God with that unfeignedness which she
did aforetime.   For I have heard it argued by many who, in
their young days, had been in love that, when they were in the
church, the condition and the pleasing melancholy in which they
found themselves would infallibly set them brooding over all
their tender love-sick longings and all their amorous passages,
when they should have been attending to the service which was
going on at the time.   And such is the property of this mystery
of love that it is ever at the moment when the priest is holding
our Saviour upon the altar that the most enticing emotions come."
After narrating the history of two queens beyond the seas
who indulged in amours even on Holy Thursday and Good Friday, at midnight in their oratories, when the lights were put out,
he concludes: "Every woman in love is more liable to fall in
church or at her devotion than at any other time."

The connection between religious emotion and sexual emotion was very clearly set forth by Swift about the end of the
seventeenth century, in a passage which it may be worth while to
quote from his "Discourse Concerning the Mechanical Operation
of the Spirit."   After mentioning that he was informed by a very
eminent physician that when the Quakers first appeared he was
seldom without female Quaker patients affected with nymphomania, Swift continues: "Persons of a visionary devotion,
either men or women, are, in their complexion, of all others the
most amorous.   For zeal is frequently kindled from the same
spark with other fires, and from inflaming brotherly love will
proceed to raise that of a gallant.   If we inspect into the usual
process of modern courtship, we shall find it to consist in a devout
turn of the eyes, called *ogling;* an artificial form of canting and
whining, by rôte, every interval, for want of other matter, made
up with a shrug, or a hum; a sigh or a groan; the style compact
of insignificant words, incoherences, and repetitions.   These I
take to be the most accomplished rules of address to a mistress;
and where are these performed with more dexterity than by the
saints?   Nay, to bring this argument yet closer, I have been
informed by certain sanguine brethren of the first class, that in
the height and *orgasmus* of their spiritual exercise, it has been

frequent with them[1] . . .; immediately after which, they found the *spirit* to relax and flag of a sudden with the nerves, and they were forced to hasten to a conclusion. This may be farther strengthened by observing with wonder how unaccountably all females are attracted by visionary or enthusiastic preachers, though never so contemptible in their *outward mien;* which is usually supposed to be done upon considerations purely spiritual, without any carnal regards at all. But I have reason to think, the sex hath certain characteristics, by which they form a truer judgment of human abilities and performings than we ourselves can possibly do of each other. Let that be as it will, thus much is certain, that however spiritual intrigues begin, they generally conclude like all others; they may branch upwards toward heaven, but the root is in the earth. Too intense a contemplation is not the business of flesh and blood; it must, by the necessary course of things, in a little time let go its hold, and fall into *matter.* Lovers for the sake of celestial converse, are but another sort of Platonics, who pretend to see stars and heaven in ladies' eyes, and to look or think no lower; but the same *pit* is provided for both."

To come down to recent times, in the last century the head-master of Clifton College, when discussing the sexual vices of boyhood, remarked that the boys whose temperament exposes them to these faults are usually far from destitute of religious feelings; that there is, and always has been, an undoubted co-existence of religion and animalism; that emotional appeals and revivals are far from rooting out carnal sin; and that in some places, as is well known, they seem actually to stimulate, even at the present day, to increased licentiousness.[2]

---

[1] This omission was made by the original publisher of the "Discourse;" several of the most important passages throughout have been similarly cut out.

[2] Rev. J. M. Wilson, *Journal of Education,* 1881. At about the same period (1882) Spurgeon pointed out in one of his sermons that by a strange, yet natural law, excess of spirituality is next door to sensuality. Theodore Schroeder has recently brought together a number of opinions of religious teachers, from Henry More the Platonist to Baring Gould, concerning the close relationship between sexual passion and religious passion, *American Journal of Religious Psychology,* 1908.

It is not difficult to see how, even in technique, the method of the revivalist is a quasi-sexual method, and resembles the attempt of the male to overcome the sexual shyness of the female. "In each case," as W. Thomas remarks, "the will has to be set aside, and strong suggestive means are used; and in both cases the appeal is not of the conflict type, but of an intimate, sympathetic and pleading kind. In the effort to make a moral adjustment it consequently turns out that a technique is used which was derived originally from sexual life, and the use, so to speak, of the sexual machinery for a moral adjustment involves, in some cases, the carrying over into the general process of some sexual manifestations."[1]

The relationship of the sexual and the religious emotions— like so many other of the essential characters of human nature— is seen in its nakedest shape by the alienist. Esquirol referred to this relationship, and, many years ago, J. B. Friedreich, a German alienist of wide outlook and considerable insight, emphasized the connection between the sexual and the religious emotions, and brought forward illustrative cases.[2] Schröder Van der Kolk also remarked: "I venture to express my conviction that we should rarely err if, in a case of religious melancholy, we assumed the sexual apparatus to be implicated."[3] Régis, in France, lays it down that "there exists a close connection between mystic ideas and erotic ideas, and most often these two orders of conception are associated in insanity."[4] Berthier considered that erotic forms of insanity are those most frequently found in convents. Bevan-Lewis points out how frequently religious exaltation occurs at puberty in women, and religious depression at the climacteric, the period of sexual decline.[5] "Religion is very closely allied to love," remarks Savage, "and the

---

[1] W. Thomas, "The Sexual Element in Sensibility," *Psychological Review*, Jan., 1904.

[2] *System der gerichtlichen Psychologie*, second edition, 1842, pp. 266-68; and more at length in his *Allgemeine Diagnostik der psychischen Krankheiten*, second edition, 1832, pp. 247-51.

[3] *Handboek van de Pathologie en Therapie der Krankzinnigheid*, 1863, p. 139 of English edition.

[4] *Manuel pratique de Médecine mentale*, 1892, p. 31.

[5] *Text-book of Mental Diseases*, p. 393.

love of woman and the worship of God are constantly sources of trouble in unstable youth; it is very interesting to note the frequency with which these two deep feelings are associated."[1] "Closely connected with salacity, particularly in women," remarks Conolly Norman, when discussing mania (Tuke's *Dictionary of Psychological Medicine*), "is religious excitement. . . . Ecstasy, as we see in cases of acute mental disease, is probably always connected with sexual excitement, if not with sexual depravity. The same association is constantly seen in less extreme cases, and one of the commonest features in the conversation of an acutely maniacal woman is the intermingling of erotic and religious ideas." "Patients who believe," remarks Clara Barrus, "that they are the Virgin Mary, the bride of Christ, the Church, 'God's wife,' and 'Raphael's consort,' are sure, sooner or later, to disclose symptoms which show that they are some way or other sexually depraved."[2] Forel, who devotes a chapter of his book *Die Sexuelle Frage*, to the subject, argues that the strongest feelings of religious emotion are often unconsciously rooted in erotic emotion or represent a transformation of such emotion; and, in an interesting discussion (Ch. VI) of this question in his *Sexualleben unserer Zeit*, Bloch states that "in a certain sense we may describe the history of religions as the history of a special manifestation of the human sexual instinct." Ball, Brouardel, Morselli, Vallon and Marie,[3] C. H. Hughes,[4] to mention but a few names among many, have emphasized the same point.[5] Krafft-Ebing deals briefly with the connection between holiness and the sexual emotion, and the special liability of the saints to sexual temptations; he thus states his own conclusions: "Religious and sexual emotional states at the height of their development exhibit a harmony in quantity and quality of excitement, and can thus in certain circumstances act vicariously.

[1] G. H. Savage, *Insanity*, 1886.
[2] *American Journal of Insanity*, April, 1895.
[3] "Des Psychoses Religieuses," *Archives de Neurologie*, 1897.
[4] "Erotopathia," *Alienist and Neurologist*, October, 1893.
[5] Reference may be specially made to the interesting chapter on "Délire Religieux" in Icard's *La Femme pendant la Période Menstruelle*, pp. 211-234.

Both," he adds, "can be converted into cruelty under pathological conditions."[1]

After quoting these opinions it is, perhaps, not unnecessary to point out that, while sexual emotion constitutes the main reservoir of energy on which religion can draw, it is far from constituting either the whole content of religion or its root. Murisier, in an able study of the psychology of religious ecstasy, justly protests against too crude an explanation of its nature, though at the same time he admits that "the passion of the religious ecstatic lacks nothing of what goes to make up sexual love, not even jealousy."[2]

Sérieux, in his little work, *Recherches Cliniques sur les Anomalies de l'Instinct Sexuel,* valuable on account of its instructive cases, records in detail a case which so admirably illustrates this phase of auto-erotism on the borderland between ordinary erotic day-dreaming and religious mysticism, the phenomena for a time reaching an insane degree of intensity, that I summarize it. "Thérèse M., aged 24, shows physical stigmata of degeneration. The heredity is also bad; the father is a man of reckless and irregular conduct; the mother was at one time in a lunatic asylum. The patient was brought up in an orphanage, and was a troublesome, volatile child; she treated household occupations with contempt, but was fond of study. Even at an early age her lively imagination attracted attention, and the pleasure which she took in building castles in the air. From the age of seven to ten she masturbated. At her first communion she felt that Jesus would for ever be the one master of her heart. At thirteen, after the death of her mother, she seemed to see her, and to hear her say that she was watching over her child. Shortly

[1] *Psychopathia Sexualis,* eighth edition, pp. 8 and 11. Gannouchkine ("La Volupté, la Cruanté et la Religion," *Annales Medico-Psychologique,* 1901, No. 3) has further emphasized this convertibility.

[2] E. Murisier, "Le Sentiment Religieux dans l'Extase," *Revue Philosophique,* November, 1898. Starbuck, again (*Psychology of Religion,* Chapter XXX), in a brief discussion of this point, concludes that "the sexual life, although it has left its impress on fully developed religion, seems to have originally given the psychic impulse which called out the latent possibilities of developments, rather than to have furnished the raw material out of which religion was constructed."

afterward she was overwhelmed by a new grief, the death of a teacher for whom she cherished great affection on account of her pure character. On the following day she seemed to see and hear this teacher, and would not leave the house where the body lay. Tendencies to melancholy appeared. Saddened by the funeral ceremonies, exhorted by nuns, fed on mystic revery, she passed from the orphanage to a convent. She devoted herself solely to the worship of Jesus; to be like Jesus, to be near Jesus, became her constant pre-occupations. The Virgin's name was rarely seen in her writings, God's name never. 'I wanted,' she said, 'to love Jesus more than any of the nuns I saw, and I even thought that he had a partiality for me.' She was also haunted by the idea of preserving her purity. She avoided frivolous conversation, and left the room when marriage was discussed, such a union being incompatible with a pure life; 'it was my fixed idea for two years to make my soul ever more pure in order to be agreeable to Him; the Beloved is well pleased among the lilies.'

"Already, however, in a rudimentary form appeared contrary tendencies [strictly speaking they were not contrary, but related, tendencies]. Beneath the mystic passion which concealed it sexual desire was sometimes felt. At sixteen she experienced emotions which she could not master, when thinking of a priest who, she said, loved her. In spite of all remorse she would have been willing to have relations with him. Notwithstanding these passing weaknesses, the idea of purity always possessed her. The nuns, however, were concerned about her exaltation. She was sent away from the convent, became discouraged, and took a place as a servant, but her fervor continued. Her confessor inspired her with great affection; she sends him tender letters. She would be willing to have relations with him, even though she considers the desire a temptation of the devil. The ground was now prepared for the manifestation of hallucinations. 'One evening in May,' she writes, 'after being absorbed in thoughts of my confessor, and feeling discouraged, as I thought that Jesus, whom I loved so much, would have nothing to do with me, "Mother," I cried out, "what must I do to win your son?" My eyes were fixed on the sky, and I remained in a state of mad expectation. It was absurd. I to become the mother of the World! My heart went on repeating: "Yes, he is coming; Jesus is coming!" ' The psychic erethism, reverberating on the sensorial and sensory centres, led to genital, auditory, and visual hallucinations, which produced the sensation of sexual connection. 'For the first time I went to bed and was not alone. As soon as I felt that touch, I heard the words: "Fear not, it is I." I was lost in Him whom I loved. For many days I was cradled in a world of pleasure; I saw Him everywhere, overwhelming me with His chaste caresses.' On the following day at mass she seemed to see Calvary before her. 'Jesus was naked and surrounded by a thousand voluptuous imaginations; His arms were loosened from the cross, and he said to me: "Come!" I longed to fly to Him with my body, but could not make up my mind to show myself naked. However, I was carried away by a force I could not control, I threw myself on my Saviour's neck, and felt that all was over between the world and me.' From that day, 'by sheer reasoning,' she has understood everything. Previously she thought that the religious life was a renunciation of the joys of marriage and enjoyment generally; now she understands its object. Jesus Christ desires that she should have relations with a priest; he is himself incarnated in priests; just as St. Joseph was the guardian of the Virgin, so are priests the guardians of nuns. She has been impregnated by Jesus, and this imaginary pregnancy pre-occupies her in the highest degree. From this time she masturbated daily. She cannot even go to communion without experiencing voluptuous sensations. Her delusions having thus become systematized, nothing shakes her tenacity in seeking to carry them out; she attempts at all costs to have relations with her confessor, embraces him, throws herself at his knees, pursues him, and so becomes a cause of scandal. When brought to the asylum, there is intense sexual excitement, and she masturbates a dozen times a day, even when talking to the doctor. The sexual organs are normal, the vulva moist and red, the vagina is painful to touch; the contact of the finger causes erectile turgescence. She has had no rest, she says, since she has learned to love her Jesus. He desires her to have sexual relations with someone, and she cannot succeed; 'all my soul's strength is arrested by this constant endeavor.' Her new surroundings modify her behavior, and now it is the doctor whom she pursues with her obsessions. 'I expected everything from the charity of the priests I have known; I have not deserved what I wanted from them. But is not a doctor free to do everything for the good of the patients intrusted to him by Providence? Cannot a doctor thus devote himself? Since I have tasted the tree of life I am tormented by the desire to share it with a loving friend.' Then she falls in love with an employee, and makes the crudest advances to him, believing that she is thus executing the will of Jesus. 'Necessity makes laws,' she exclaims to him, 'the moments are pressing, I have been waiting too long.' She still speaks of her religious vocation which might be compromised by so long a delay. 'I do not want to get married.' Gradually a transformation took place; the love of God was effaced and earthly love became more intense than ever. 'Quitting the heights in which I wished to soar, I am coming so near to earth that I shall soon fix my desires there.' In a last letter Thérèse recognizes with terror the insanity to which the exaltation of her imagination had led her. 'Now I only believe in God and in suffering; I feel that it is necessary for me to get married.' "

Mariani[1] has very fully described a case of erotico-religious insanity (climacteric paranoia on an hysterical basis) in a married woman of 44. During the early stages of her disorder she inflicted all sorts of penances upon herself (fasting, constant prayer, drinking her own urine, cleaning dirty plates with her tongue, etc.). Finally she felt that by her penances she had obtained forgiveness of her sins, and then began a stage of joy and satisfaction during which she believed that she had entered into a state of the most intimate personal relationship with Jesus. She finally recovered. Mariani shows how closely this history corresponds with the histories of the saints, and that all the acts

---

[1] "Una Santa," *Archivio di Psichiatria*, vol. xix, pp. 438-47, 1898.

and emotions of this woman can be exactly paralleled in the lives of famous saints.[1]

The justice of these comparisons becomes manifest when we turn to the records that have been left by holy persons.   A most instructive record from this point of view is the autobiography of Sœur Jeanne des Anges, superior of the Ursulines of Loudun in the seventeenth century.[2]   She was clever, beautiful, ambitious, fond of pleasure, still more of power.   With this, as sometimes happens, she was highly hysterical, and in the early years of her religious life was possessed by various demons of unchastity and blasphemy with whom for many years she was in constant struggle.   She fell in love with a priest of Loudun, Grandier, a man whom she had never even seen, only knowing of him as a powerful and fascinating personality at whose feet all women fell, and she imagined that she and the other nuns of her convent were possessed through his influence.   She was thus the cause of the trial and execution of Grandier, a famous case in the annals of witchcraft.   In her autobiography Sœur Jeanne describes in detail how the demons assailed her at night, appearing in lascivious attitudes, making indecent proposals, raising the bedclothes, touching all parts of her body, imploring her to yield to them, and she tells how strong her temptation was to yield.   On one night, for instance, she writes: "I seemed to feel someone's breath, and I heard a voice saying: 'The time for resistance has gone by, you must no longer rebel; by putting off your consent to what has been proposed you will be injured; you cannot persist in this resistance; God has subjected you to the demands of a nature which you must satisfy on occasions so urgent.'   Then I felt impure impressions in my imagination and disordered movements in my body.   I persisted in saying at the bottom of my heart that I would do nothing.   I turned to God and asked Him for strength in this extraordinary struggle.   Then there was a loud noise in my room, and I felt as if someone had

---

[1] With regard to the sexual element in the worship of the Virgin, see "Ueber den Mariencultus," L. Feuerbach's *Sammtliche Werke*, Bd. I, 1846.

[2] Published for the first time (with a Preface by Charcot) in a volume of the *Bibliothèque Diabolique*, 1886.

approached me and put his hand into my bed and touched me; and having perceived this I rose, in a state of restlessness, which lasted for a long time afterward. Some days later, at midnight, I began to tremble all over my body as I lay in bed, and to experience much mental aniexty without knowing the cause. After this had lasted for some time I heard noises in various parts of my room; the sheet was twice pulled without entirely uncovering me; the oratory close to my bed was upset. I heard a voice on the left side, toward which I was lying. I was asked if I had thought over the advantageous offer that had been made to me. It was added: 'I have come to know your reply; I will keep my promise if you will give your consent; if, on the contrary, you refuse, you will be the most miserable girl in the world, and all sorts of mischances will happen to you.' I replied: 'If there were no God I would fear those threats; I am consecrated to Him.' It was replied to me: 'You will not get much help from God; He will abandon you.' I replied: 'God is my father; He will take care of me; I have resolved to be faithful to Him.' He said: 'I will give you three days to think over it.' I rose and went to the Holy Sacrament with an anxious mind. Having returned to my room, and being seated on a chair, it was drawn from under me so that I fell on the floor. Then the same things happened again. I heard a man's voice saying lascivious and pleasant things to seduce me; he pressed me to give him room in my bed; he tried to touch me in an indecent way; I resisted and prevented him, calling the nuns who were near my room; the window had been open, it was closed; I felt strong movements of love for a certain person, and improper desire for dishonorable things."

She writes again, at a later period: "These impurities and the fire of concupiscence which the evil spirit caused me to feel, beyond all that I can say, forced me to throw myself on to braziers of hot coal, where I would remain for half an hour at a time, in order to extinguish that other fire, so that half my body was quite burnt. At other times, in the depth of winter, I have sometimes passed part of the night entirely naked in the snow, or in tubs of icy water. I have besides often gone among thorns so that I have been torn by them; at other times I have rolled in nettles, and I have passed whole nights defying my enemies to attack me, and assuring them that I was resolved to defend myself with the grace of God." With her confessor's permission, she also had an iron girdle made, with spikes, and wore this day and night for nearly six months until the spikes so entered her flesh that the girdle could only be removed with difficulty. By means of these austerities she succeeded in almost exorcising the demons of unchastity, and a little later, after a severe illness, of which she believed that she was miraculously cured by St. Joseph, she appeared before the world almost as a saint, herself possessing a miraculous power of healing; she traveled through France, bringing healing wherever she went; the king, the queen, and Cardinal Richelieu were at her feet, and so great became the fame of her holiness that her tomb was a shrine for pilgrims for more than a century after her death. It was not until late in life, and after her autobiography terminates, that sexual desire in Sœur Jeanne (though its sting seems never to have quite disappeared) became transformed into passionate love of Jesus, and it is only in her later letters that we catch glimpses of the complete transmutation. Thus, in one of her later letters we read: "I cried with ardor, 'Lord! join me to Thyself, transform Thyself into me!' It seemed to me that that lovable Spouse was reposing in my heart as on His throne. What makes me almost swoon with love and admiration is a certain pleasure which it seems to me that He takes when all my being flows into His, restoring to Him with respect and love all that He has given to me. Sometimes I have permission to speak to our Lord with more familiarity, calling Him my Love, interesting Him in all that I ask of Him, as well for myself as for others."

The lives of all the great saints and mystics bear witness to operations similar to those so vividly described by Sœur Jeanne des Anges, though it is very rarely that any saint has so frankly presented the dynamic mechanism of the auto-erotic process. The indications they give us, however, are sufficiently clear. It is enough to refer to the special affection which the mystics have ever borne toward the Song of Songs,[1] and to note how the most earthly expressions of love in that poem enter as a perpetual refrain into their writings.[2]

The courage of the early Christian martyrs, it is abundantly evident, was in part supported by an exaltation which they frankly drew from the sexual impulse. Felicula, we are told in the acts of Achilles and Nereus,[3] preferred imprisonment, torture, and death to marriage or pagan sacrifices. When on the rack she was bidden to deny Christianity, she exclaimed: *"Ego non nego amatorem meum!"*—I will not deny my lover who for my sake has eaten gall and drunk vinegar, crowned with thorns.

her dear master; she is betrothed to Him, He is the most passionate of lovers, nothing can be sweeter than His caresses, they are so excessive she is beside herself with the delight of them. The central imagination of the mystic consists essentially, as Ribot remarks, in a love romance.[1]

If we turn to the most popular devotional work that was ever written, *The Imitation of Christ,* we shall find that the "love" there expressed is precisely and exactly the love that finds its motive power in the emotions aroused by a person of the other sex. (A very intellectual woman once remarked to me that the book seemed to her "a sort of religious aphrodisiac.") If we read, for instance, Book III, Chapter V, of this work ("De Mirabili affectu Divini amoris"), we shall find in the eloquence of this solitary monk in the Low Countries neither more nor less than the emotions of every human lover at their highest limit of exaltation. "Nothing is sweeter than love, nothing stronger, nothing higher, nothing broader, nothing pleasanter, nothing fuller nor better in heaven or in earth. He who loves, flies, runs, and rejoices; he is free and cannot be held. He gives all in exchange for all, and possesses all in all. He looks not at gifts, but turns to the giver above all good things. Love knows no measure, but is fervent beyond all measure. Love feels no burden, thinks nothing of labor, strives beyond its force, reckons not of impossibility, for it judges that all things are possible. Therefore it attempts all things, and therefore it effects much when he who is not a lover fails and falls. . . . My Love! thou all mine, and I all thine."

There is a certain natural disinclination in many quarters to recognize any special connection between the sexual emotions and the religious emotions. But this attitude is not reasonable. A man who is swayed by religious emotions cannot be held responsible for the indirect emotional results of his condition; he can be held responsible for their control. Nothing is gained by refusing to face the possibility that such control may be necessary, and much is lost. There is certainly, as I have tried to

---

[1] Ribot, *La Logique des Sentiments*, p. 174.

indicate, good reason to think that the action and interaction between the spheres of sexual and religious emotion are very intimate. The obscure promptings of the organism at puberty frequently assume on the psychic side a wholly religious character; the activity of the religious emotions sometimes tends to pass over into the sexual region; the suppression of the sexual emotions often furnishes a powerful reservoir of energy to the religious emotions; occasionally the suppressed sexual emotions break through all obstacles.

INDEX OF AUTHORS.

(327)

INDEX OF SUBJECTS.

DIAGRAMS.

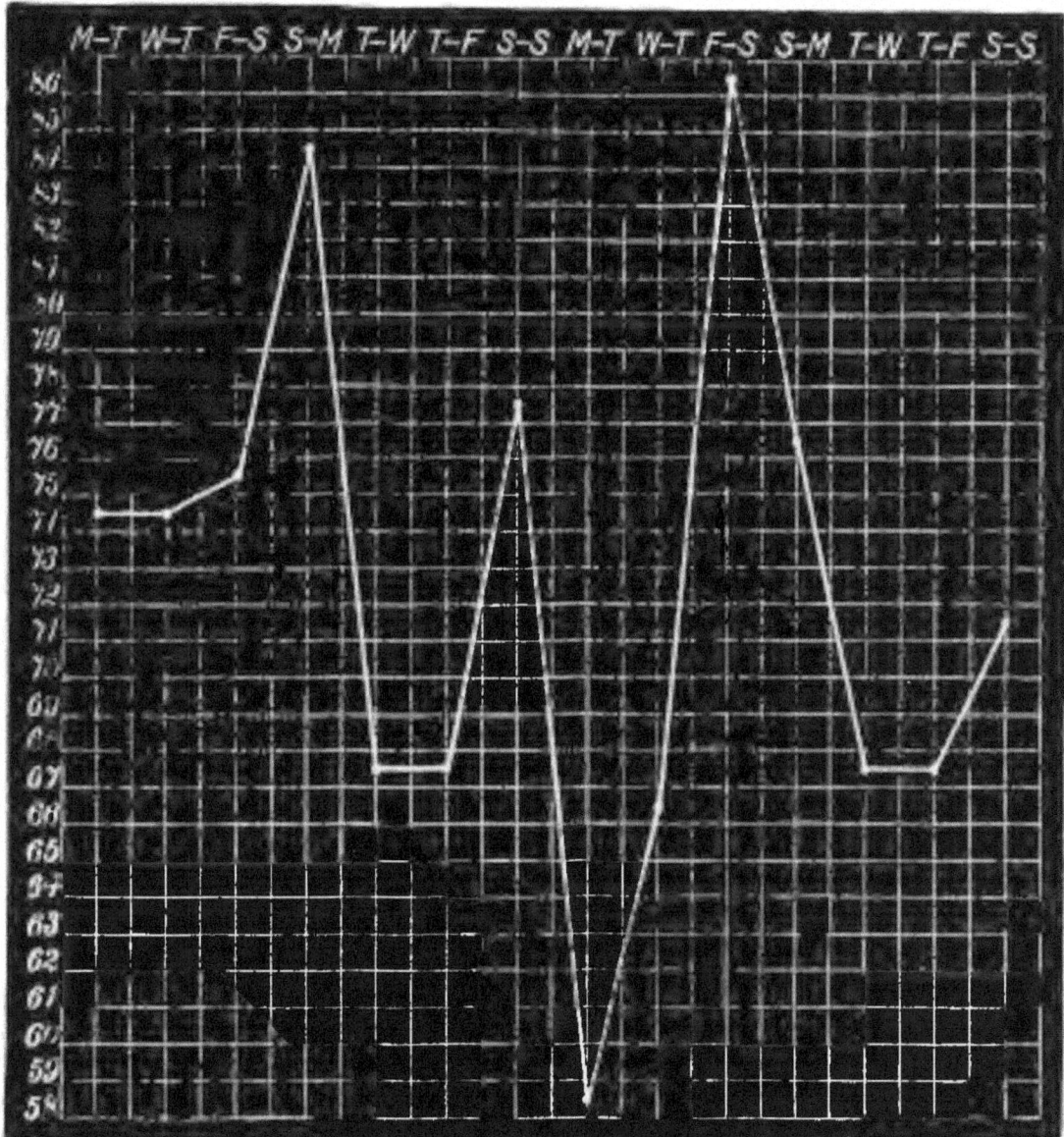

CHART I.—The Monthly Ecbolic Curve.

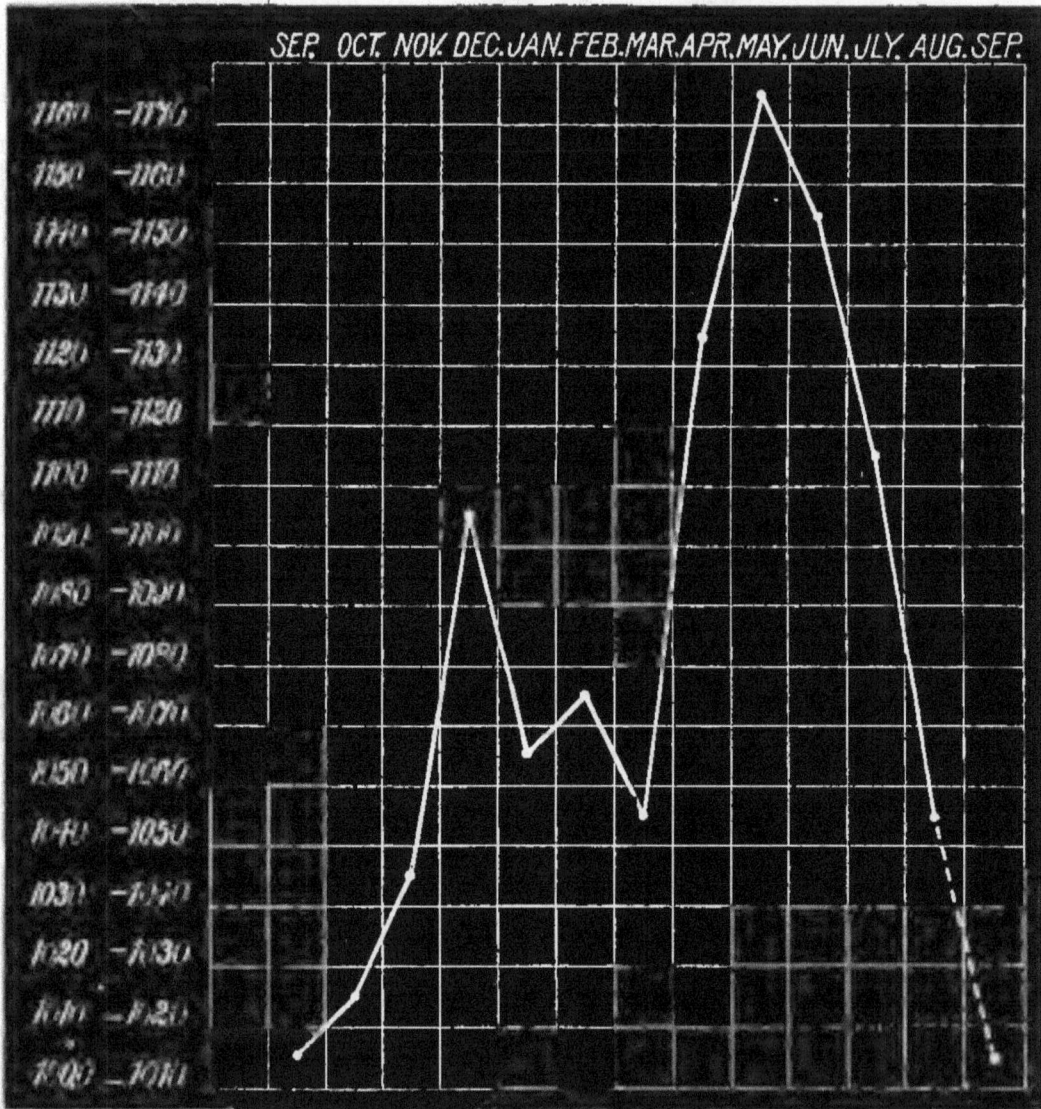

CHART II.—The Annual Curve of the Conception-rate in Europe.

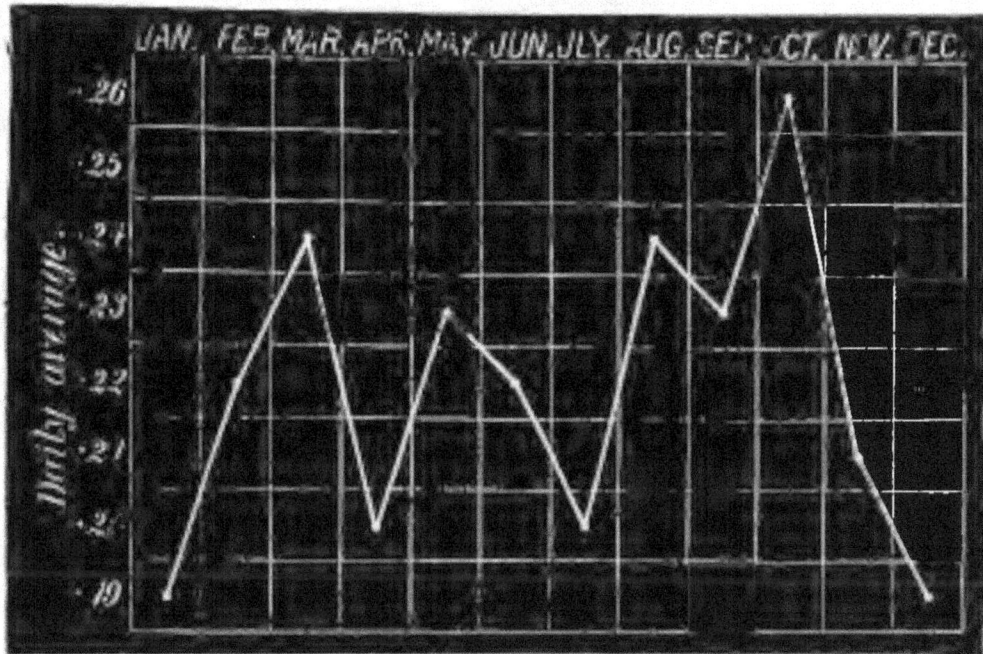

CHART III.—The Annual Ecbolic Curve.

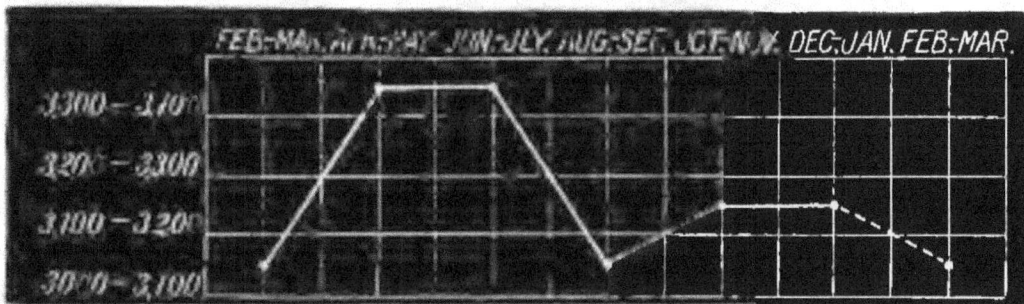

CHART IV.—Curve of the Annual Incidence of Insanity in London.

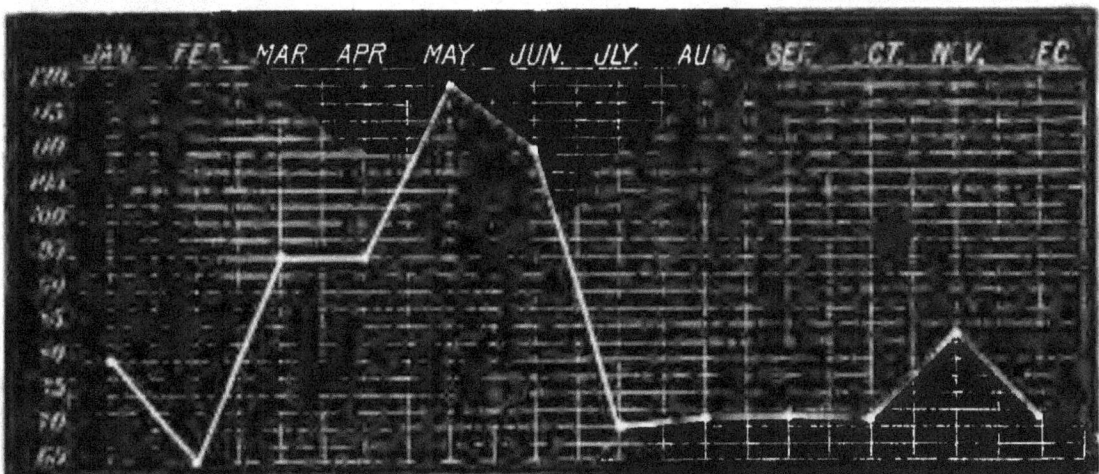

CHART V.—Curve of the Annual Incidence of General Paralysis
in Paris (Garnier).

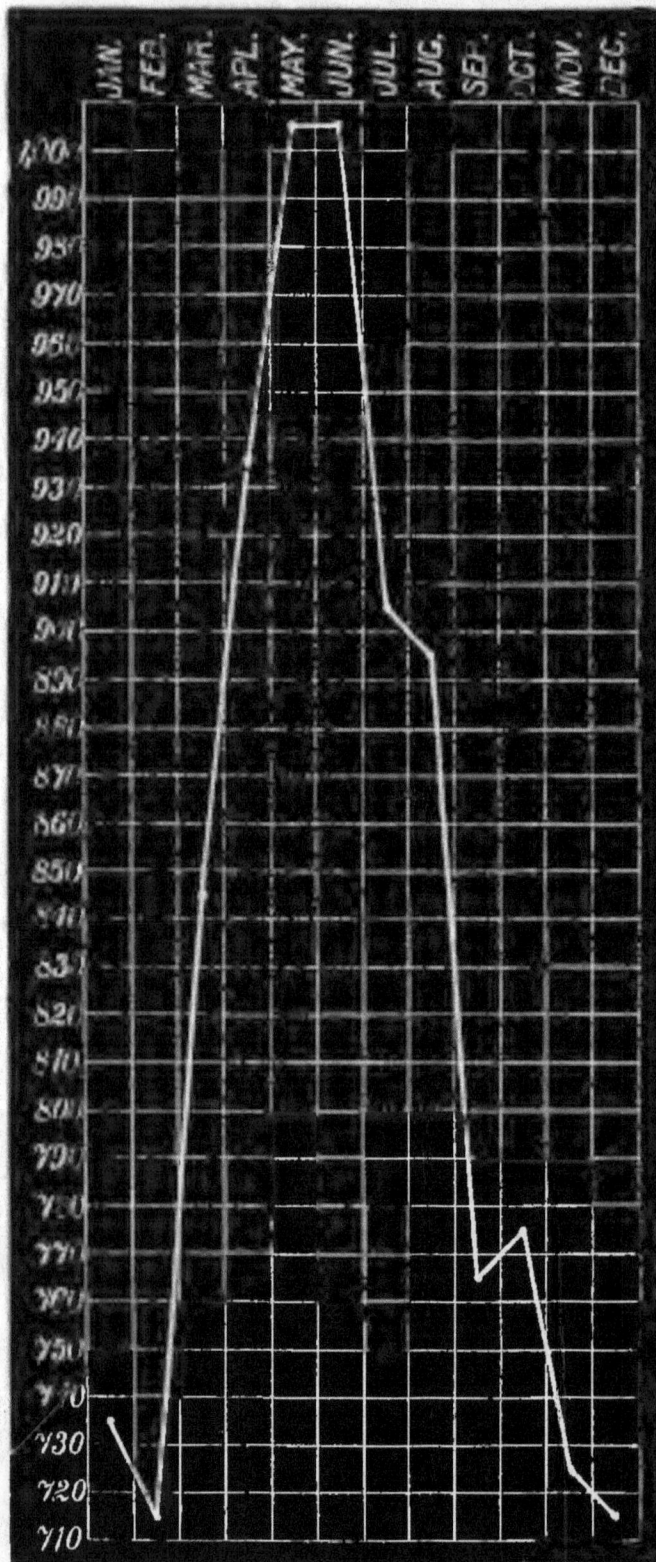

CHART VI.—The Suicide-rate in London.   CHART VII.

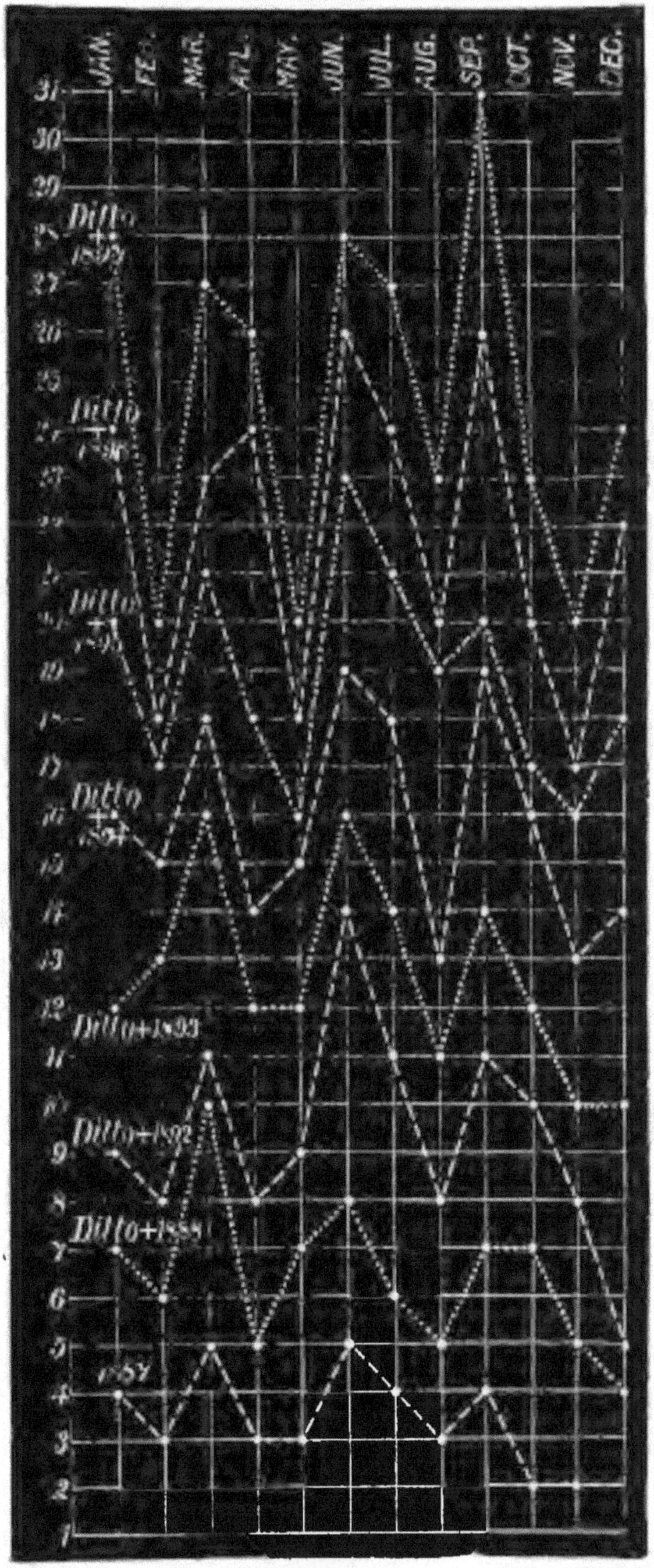
JAN.
MAR.
APL.
MAY.
JUN.
JUL.
AUG.
SEP.
OCT.
NOV.
DEC.
Ditto+1893
Ditto+1892

CHART VIII.

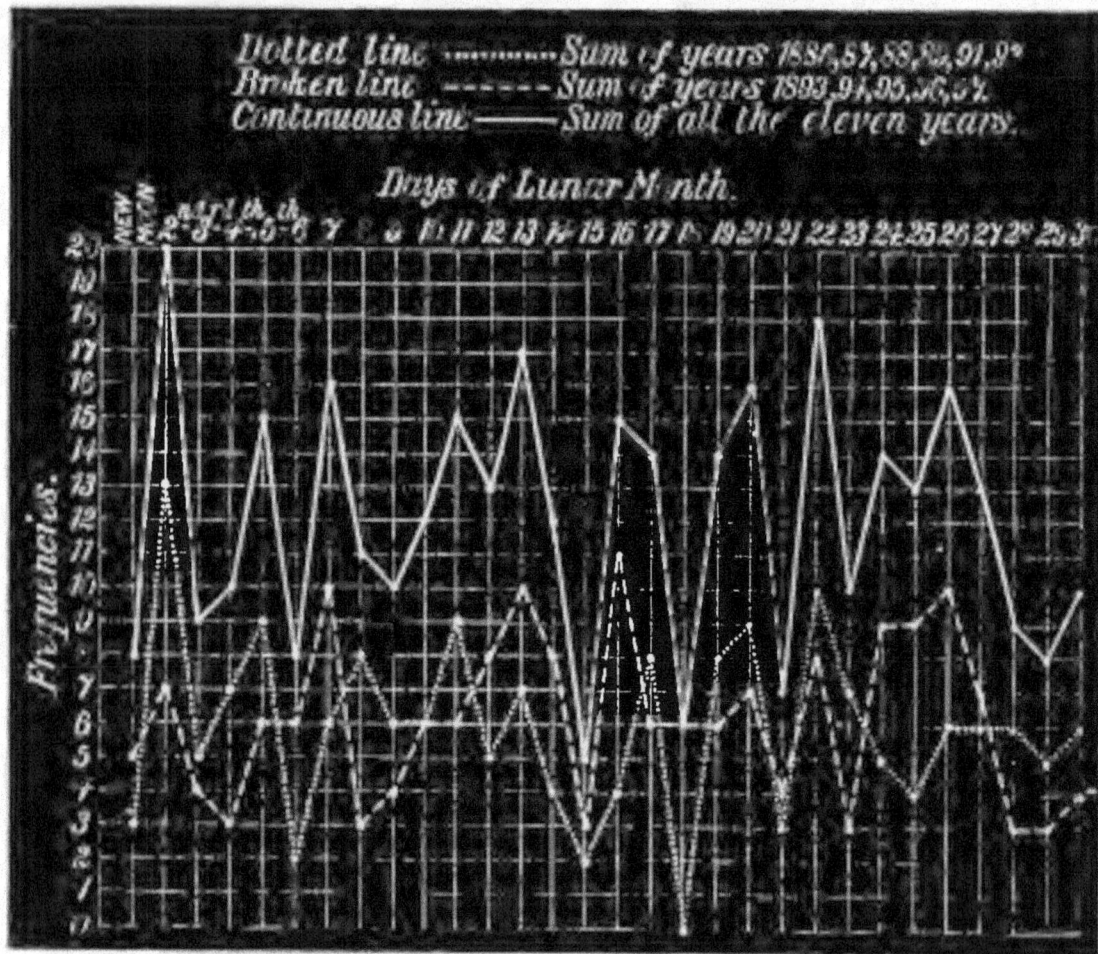

CHART IX.—Lunar-monthly Rhythm of Male Sexual Period.

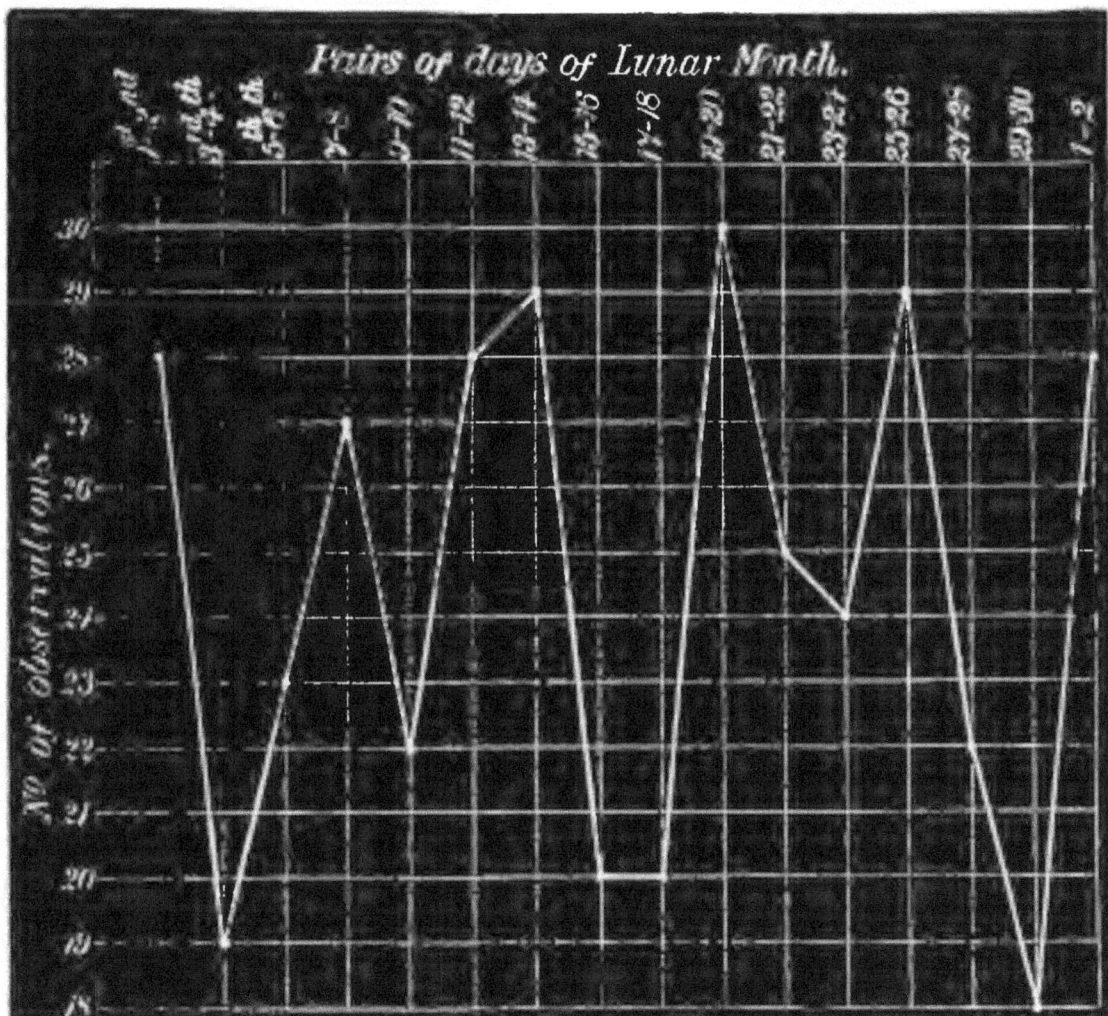

CHART X.—Curves of Lunar-monthly Rhythm as Smoothed by
taking Pairs of Days.

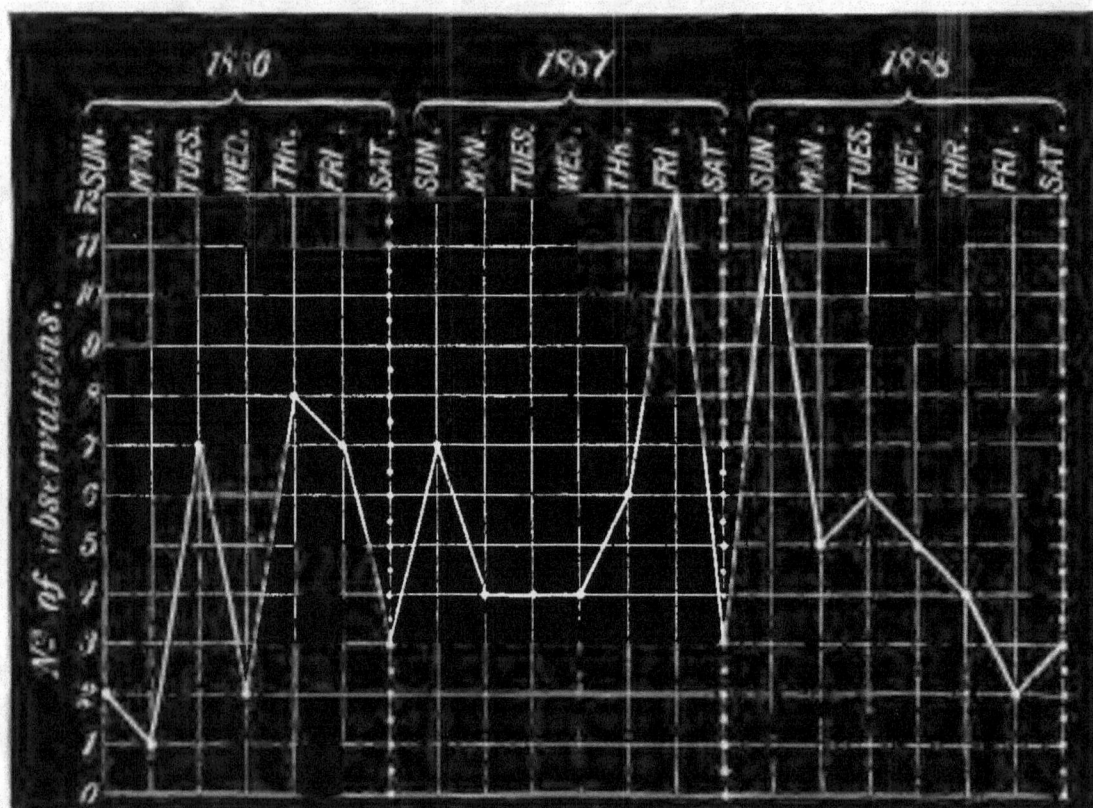

CHART XIA.—Weekly Rhythm of Male Sexual Period.

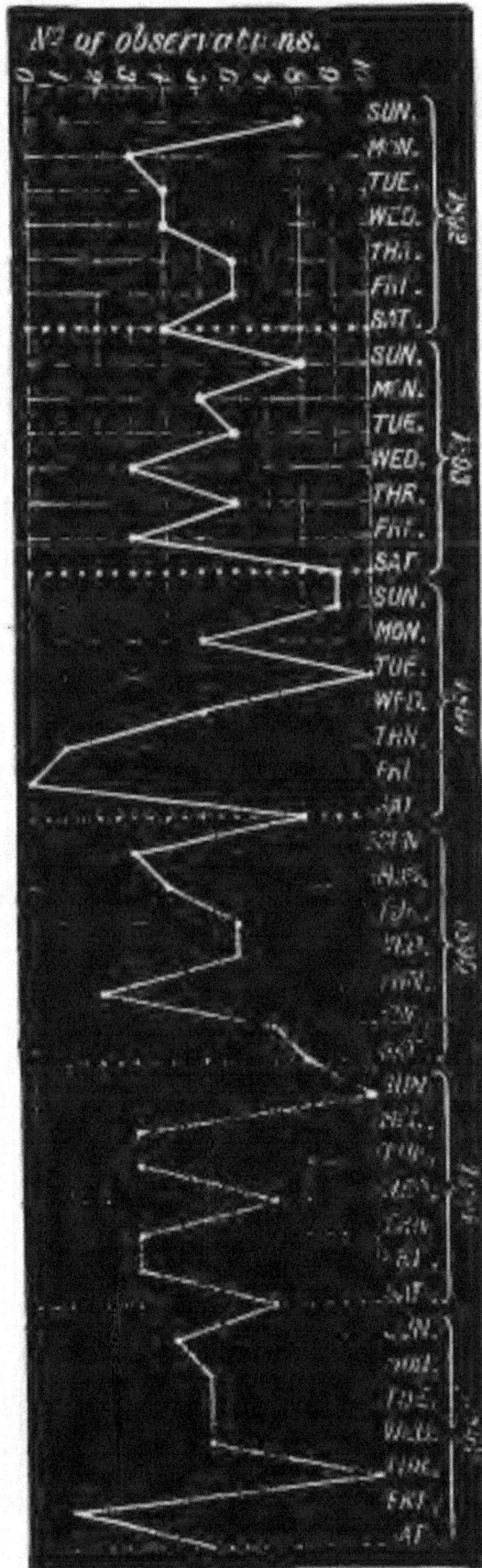

CHART XIB.—Weekly Rhythm of Male Sexual Period,

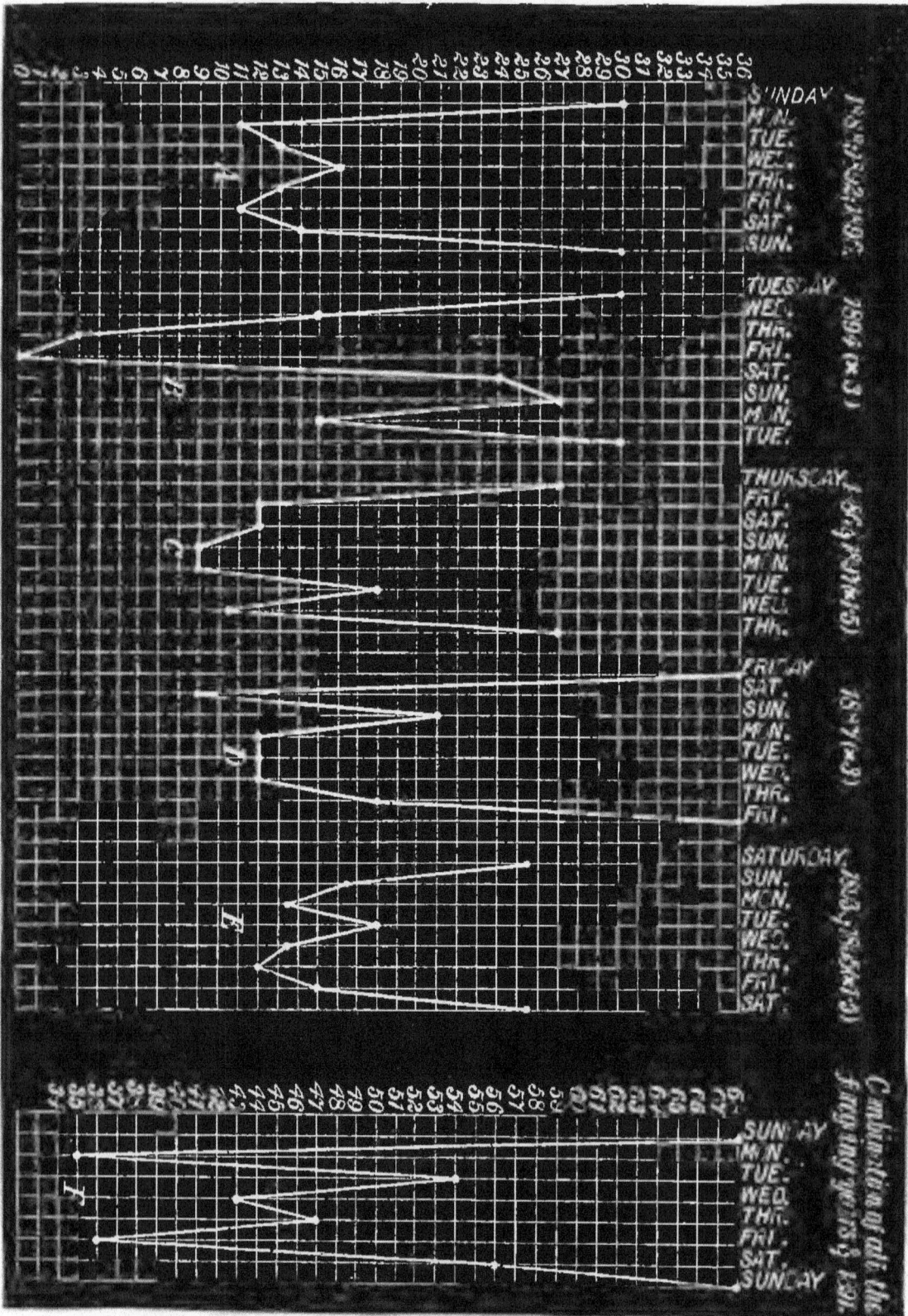

CHART XII.—Weekly Rhythm of Male Sexual Period.

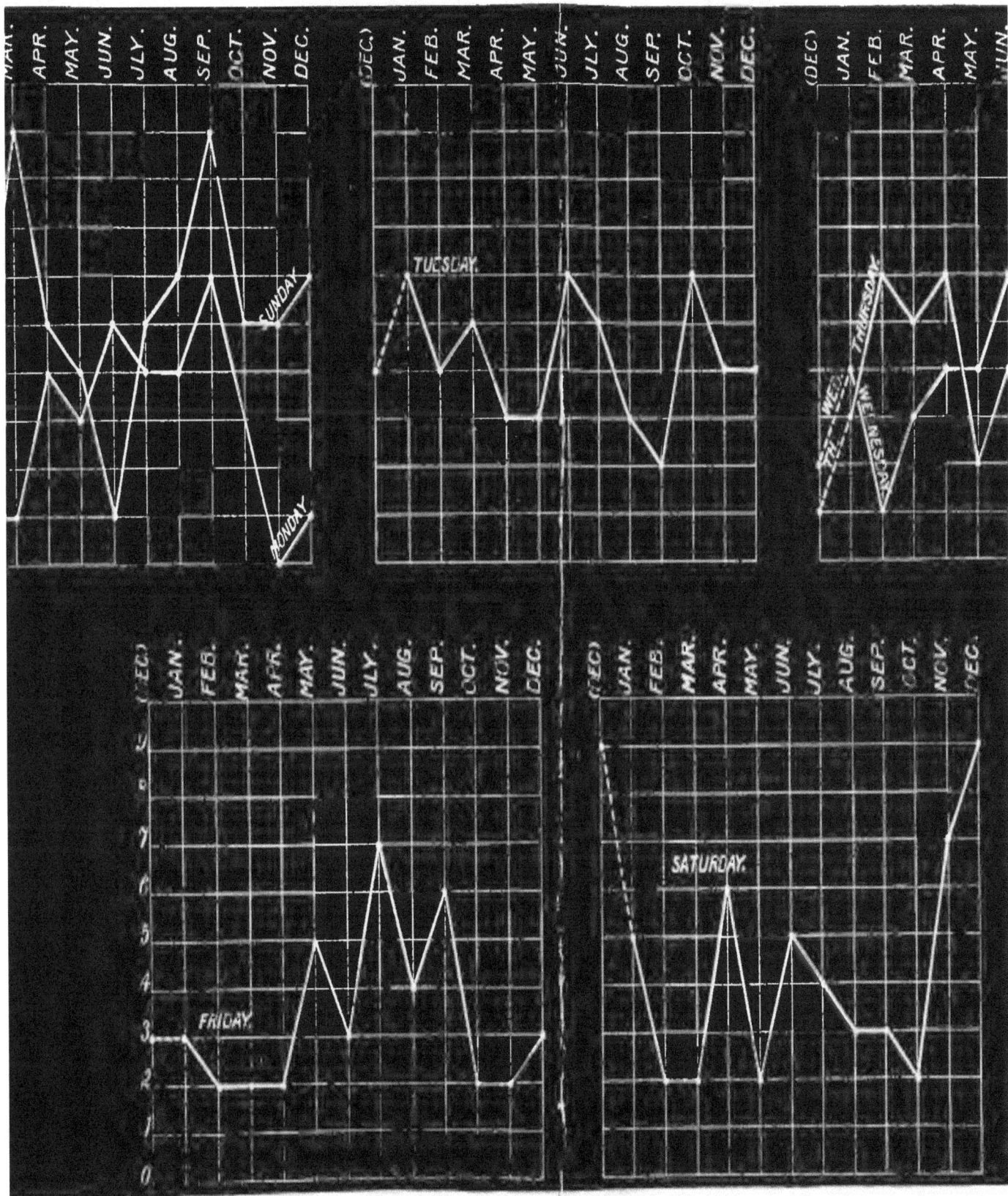

CHART XIII.—Joint Weekly Rhythm of Male Sexual Period, years 1886, 1887, 1888, 1892, 1893, 1894, 1895, 1896, 1897 combine

www.ingramcontent.com/pod-product-compliance
Lightning Source LLC
Chambersburg PA
CBHW080324270326
41927CB00014B/3091